Praise for *Steal This Computer Book*

"If ever a book on cyberculture wore a fedora and trench coat and leaned against a lamp-post on a foggy street, this is the one. It is an unabashed look at the dark side of the Net—the stuff many other books gloss over. It's hard-edged, wisecracking, and often quite cynical as it pours over the reality of online scams, illegal activities, and simple annoyances."
—Amazon.com editorial review

"If this book had a soundtrack, it'd be Lou Reed's 'Walk on the Wild Side.'"
—*InfoWorld*

"A documentary tour into sourcing information, defeating Internet filters, banned books & web pages, hactivism, hate groups, hackers, viruses, con games, and a whole bunch of other things that should make you squirm if you've got a heartbeat and a little paranoia."
—*The Inquirer*

"A provocative look at the ways the Internet can be used, misused, and abused"
—*Security Management Online*

"This book has some of the best information about protecting yourself, your family and your computer from illegal or malicious acts perpetrated electronically . . . it is almost as compelling as a good novel."
—kickstartnews.com

"A technology classic that is as entertaining and irreverent as it is informative"
—*MacDirectory*

"A terrific guide to the world of hacking, cracking and malware"
—*Software Developer (SD) Times*

"I found the book fascinating, at times almost addicting."
—*MacCompanion*

"A quirky, colorful tour of the anti-social side of the Internet"
—*Unix Review*

"A delightfully irresponsible primer"
—*Chicago Tribune*

"This book is not going to make a lot of people very happy—and it's going to make a lot of others very nervous."
—*Houston Chronicle*

"If you're smart, and you work on the Internet, you'll get [*Steal This Computer Book*] before that teen-aged computer geek down the block does."
—*The Sarasota Herald-Tribune*

STEAL THIS COMPUTER BOOK 4.0

What They Won't Tell You About the Internet

WALLACE WANG

NO STARCH PRESS

San Francisco

Publisher: William Pollock
Managing Editor: Elizabeth Campbell
Developmental Editor: Patricia Witkin
Cover and Interior Design: Octopod Studios
Technical Reviewer: Raven Alder
Copyeditor: Publication Services, Inc.
Compositor: Riley Hoffman
Proofreaders: Megan Dunchak; Publication Services, Inc.; Stephanie Provines
Indexer: Publication Services, Inc.

For information on book distributors or translations, please contact No Starch Press, Inc. directly:

No Starch Press, Inc.
555 De Haro Street, Suite 250, San Francisco, CA 94107
phone: 415.863.9900; fax: 415.863.9950; info@nostarch.com; http://www.nostarch.com

The information in this book is distributed on an "As Is" basis, without warranty. While every precaution has been taken in the preparation of this work, neither the author nor No Starch Press, Inc. shall have any liability to any person or entity with respect to any loss or damage caused or alleged to be caused directly or indirectly by the information contained in it.

Library of Congress Cataloging-in-Publication Data

```
Wang, Wally.
  Steal this computer book 4.0 : what they won't tell you about the Internet / Wallace Wang.
      p. cm.
  Includes index.
  ISBN 1-59327-105-0
 1.  Internet.  I. Title.
  TK5105.875.I57W3727 2006
  005.8--dc22
                                              2005037435
```

ACKNOWLEDGMENTS

If it weren't for the wonderful people at No Starch Press, this book would still be just another good idea floating around the publishing industry. The most important person involved in the creation of this book is William Pollock, who provided guidance for the book and gently nursed it from a rough idea to a completed manuscript. Three other extremely important people are Patricia Witkin, Raven Alder, and Elizabeth Campbell, all of whom worked tirelessly to ensure that the manuscript was as complete and error-free as possible. Thanks also to Riley Hoffman, who laid out the pages you see here.

Many hackers deserve credit for their work that directly or indirectly influenced this book. While I have never met many of these people, their books, text files, websites, and software creations have helped influence my thoughts about the "underground" aspect of the computer industry.

Additional thanks go to Steve Schirripa (who appears in HBO's hit show *The Sopranos*) and Don Learned for giving me my break in performing at the Riviera Comedy Club (www.rivierahotel.com) in Las Vegas. Also a big thanks go out to all the stand-up comedians I've had the pleasure of working with over the years, including Dobie Maxwell, Judy Tenuta, Larry Omaha, Darrell Joyce, Kip Addotta, Bob Zany, Gerry Bednob, Patrick DeGuire, and Doug James.

More thanks go to Roger Feeny at the Ann Arbor Comedy Showcase (www.aacomedy.com), Joe Jarred at Funniez Comedy Club, Mark Ridley at the Comedy Castle (www.comedycastle.com), and Russ Rivas at Laffs Comedy Club (www.laffscomedy.com) for running the best comedy clubs in the country.

Final thanks go to stand-up comedians Barry Crimmins, Jimmy Tingle, George Carlin, and Will Durst for their delightfully insightful humor that reveals the truth while making you laugh at the same time. If you want to know what's really happening with our governments, foreign policies, and world leaders, listen to these four comedians. I guarantee you'll learn more about world news, politicians, and international politics from their stand-up comedy acts than you ever could from *Newsweek*, the *New York Times*, the *Wall Street Journal*, the *CBS Evening News*, or CNN.

This book is dedicated to everyone who believes in the true principles of democracy—which pretty much eliminates 90 percent of the people running the government.

People get mad at me for these views [anti–American government opinions]. They say, "If you don't like this country, why don't you get out of it?" And I say, "Because I don't want to be victimized by its foreign policy."

—BARRY CRIMMINS

I predict that with military enrollment down the US military will actively start to seek out gay recruits.

—JIMMY TINGLE

I'm completely in favor of the separation of Church and State. My idea is that these two institutions screw us up enough on their own, so both of them together is certain death.

—GEORGE CARLIN

Q. Why are there no Democrats on Star Trek?

A. Because it's set in the future.

—WILL DURST

BRIEF CONTENTS

CONTENTS IN DETAIL

x

14
FINDING PEOPLE ON THE INTERNET 189

15
PROPAGANDA AS NEWS AND ENTERTAINMENT 201

16
HACKTIVISM: ONLINE ACTIVISM 221

17
HATE GROUPS AND TERRORISTS ON THE INTERNET 239

PART 5: THE FUTURE—HACKING FOR PROFIT

18
IDENTITY THEFT AND SPAM 249

PART 6: PROTECTING YOUR COMPUTER AND YOURSELF

21
COMPUTING ON A SHOESTRING: GETTING STUFF FOR (ALMOST) FREE
303

22
COMPUTER FORENSICS: THE ART OF DELETING AND RETRIEVING DATA
313

INTRODUCTION

This book won't turn you into a hacker any more than reading a military manual will turn you into a soldier. You won't find step-by-step instructions explaining how to break into a computer, nor will you find technical discussions of all the flaws inherent to any particular type of operating system. This isn't a technical book about computer hacking. This is a philosophy book about the implications of hacking. Hacking isn't just about breaking into computers. Hacking is about exploring, extending boundaries, and searching for knowledge for its own sake.

Too many people are thinking of security instead of opportunity. They seem more afraid of life than death.

—JAMES F. BYRNES

So if you're looking for detailed information about writing C code to create buffer overflows in an Apache server, or you want to find out how to configure a SonicWALL firewall to protect a corporate network from attack, look somewhere else. But if you want a book that explores both the technical and social implications of the hidden, darker side of the Internet that most people never see, read about, or hear about, keep reading. The world of hackers, virus writers, political activists, phone phreakers, censorship, and disguised propaganda awaits you.

Not surprisingly, some people will find the information in this book distasteful, disturbing, and downright dangerous. Some will see this same information as an excuse to cause havoc and make trouble for others. Neither of these is correct.

The purpose of this book isn't to teach you how to be a hacker, but rather to teach you to think like one. That means challenging your preconceived notions about right and wrong and looking beyond the limitations of your culture's way of thinking. Computers and the Internet can open your mind to new worlds that you've never dreamed of—or turn off your mind and funnel your thinking down the narrow confines of a fantasy world that only you choose to see. The choice is yours.

If you want to use your computer as a tool to expand your awareness rather than as a substitute for it, this book is for you. We need you in this world more than ever before.

YOUR OWN REVOLUTION

Don't get me wrong. This book isn't advocating the overthrow of your government or the development of a radically different one. Instead, this book advocates a more personal form of revolution—a revolution within your own thinking. Instead of blindly blaming national governments, international corporations, ethnic groups, sexual preferences, multicultural organizations, ideological beliefs, religious institutions, or political parties for all the world's problems, this book suggests that:

- If you change the way you think, you'll change the way you act.

- If you change the way you act, you'll be able to change the way others act and think.

- If you change the way others act and think, you can help change the world—one person at a time.

But it all begins with you.

None of us can be correct 100 percent of the time, and the first step toward true change is admitting that neither you nor I—nor your parents, your boss, your spouse, your family, your government, or your church—know everything.

There's no shame in not knowing everything, but there is shame in pretending we know everything when we don't. We can and must learn from each other, regardless of what we look like, where we live, what we believe in, or which flag we salute. Open, honest communication is the only way we can change this world for the better, and that's where this book and your computer come into play.

Communication's the thing

Although computers are still notoriously difficult, confusing, and downright frustrating to use, they represent a quantum leap in communication similar to the inventions of the alphabet and the printing press. With personal computers and the Internet, people can send and receive email, research information through the World Wide Web, and exchange ideas with people all over the world.

But don't be fooled by the marketing hype designed to suck you into the computer revolution. The world of computers and the Internet is fraught with hidden dangers that the computer marketing departments don't mention, such as Trojan horses, electronic espionage, remote computer monitoring, hate groups, con artists, pedophiles, pornography, and terrorism—all just a mouse click away.

This book not only reveals these dangers, but also helps you understand how people create them in the first place. The more you know about something, the better you can avoid or fight it. Besides exploring the underground nature of the Internet that television and magazine ads conveniently ignore, this book exposes the darker side of the computer industry itself.

Truth is nothing but a point of view

This book doesn't pretend to be a comprehensive resource for every possible legal and illegal activity you might run across on the Internet, but the information it contains can help or hurt others. Fundamentally, the information itself is neutral. Crash your government's computer network and you may be labeled a terrorist. Do the same thing to an enemy's computer network, and your government may proclaim you a hero. Good and evil depend solely on your point of view.

So, welcome to the side of computers that the computer industry doesn't want you to know about, a world where slickly printed tutorials and training classes don't exist.

This is the underground of the real computer revolution, where everyone is encouraged to question, explore, and criticize, but most importantly, to learn how to think for himself or herself.

And to many governments, corporations, and religions, people who know how to think for themselves can be the most dangerous threats in the world.

WHAT'S IN THIS BOOK

Hacking isn't restricted to computers. Hacking, the essence of which is being curious and not letting obstacles get in your way, can encompass activities as diverse as lockpicking and exploring abandoned buildings. What you'll find in this book are discussions of hacking covering a wide range of topics that happen to include computers.

The first part of the book demonstrates how hacking techniques were applied long before the invention of the computer. These early hacking techniques involved the telephone system, and, not surprisingly, these old telephone hacking techniques are gaining new life in the world of VoIP (voice over Internet protocol), which allows people to place calls over the Internet.

Telephone hackers (also known by their more colorful nickname, *phone phreakers*) also pioneered the art of human hacking known as *social engineering*. Social engineering means nothing more than smooth talking a victim into revealing valuable information such as passwords, ID numbers, or even names of certain people. Although it has its roots in phone phreakers trying to glean bits of information about the telephone system from reluctant telephone operators and technicians, social engineering has made a prominent return to the headlines in the form of phishing and identity theft, in which hackers use the Internet to social engineer victims out of their passwords, credit card data, and Social Security numbers. What's old is new again, and by understanding the hacking techniques of the past, you can better predict the hacking threats of the future.

The second part of the book focuses on the early personal computer hackers, who specialized in cracking copy-protection software, writing viruses and Trojan horses, and mingling with like-minded individuals on electronic bulletin boards before eventually migrating to the Internet. Despite their initial battles, the software industry still hasn't found a way to eradicate these early hacker threats, and the problem has only continued to grow.

The third part of the book discusses the shift hackers made to the Internet and traces their history from the early denial of service attacks to the more sophisticated infiltration hacking techniques. You'll see how the Internet has expanded both the reach and the power of hackers.

The fourth part of the book shows how hackers have adapted their techniques for profit with the blessing of some supportive businesspeople who have a financial interest in their success. You'll learn about how businesses can manipulate search engines to promote their websites over their competitors', how programmers have adopted adware and spyware in order to make a profit whether anyone uses their programs or not, and how hackers are inundating the Internet with spam.

The fifth part of the book predicts what the future holds for hacking—money! This section discusses all the latest and upcoming concerns, from adware and spyware to identity theft to banner ads, pop-up ads, and search engine spamming.

The sixth and final part of the book describes how you can protect yourself from the various threats on the Internet, from the oldest hacker tactics, including scams and phone phreaking, to the newest variations, such as phishing and identity theft.

The hacking threat is real. The problem is that the danger from hacking isn't just coming from malicious individuals; it's coming from so-called trusted organizations as well, and that's more frightening than any digital terrorist scenario that anyone can make up.

PART 1

THE EARLY HACKERS

1

THE HACKER MENTALITY

Hackers are no more criminals than lawyers, politicians, or TV evangelists are. (Okay, so maybe that's not the best analogy.) The point is that being a hacker doesn't necessarily make you a criminal. Your attitude makes you a hacker, but if you're not careful, your actions can make you a criminal.

With the news media ready to blame every computer glitch on malicious hackers, too many people get a one-sided point of view that hackers are just completely evil, bent-on-destruction-of-the-civilized-world malcontents who'd love nothing better than to demolish everything good in society and sow terror and chaos in their wake. (Of course, that's the same one-sided view used to slander some people as "terrorists" or "insurgents" while others call those exact same people "freedom fighters" and "patriots," but that's a subject for Chapter 17.)

Whether a hacker fits the stereotypical image of a nerd with pocket protectors, thick glasses, and awkward social skills is irrelevant (and most don't). A hacker is not defined by how he looks or behaves, but rather by how he thinks, and the most crucial aspect in developing a true hacker mentality is learning how to think for yourself.

QUESTIONING AUTHORITY

To truly start thinking for yourself, begin by questioning authority. This doesn't mean rebelling against, overthrowing, or ignoring authority. It means listening to what any authority figure or organization tells you and discerning their motives. As every con artist knows, the first step to getting someone to do what you want is to hide your own motives and pretend that you really want to help them instead. (See Chapter 13 for more information about how con games work over the Internet.) Questioning authority means nothing more than asking how the authority figure or organization will benefit if you do what they tell you to do.

There are three possible reasons an authority figure or organization would tell you something:

- It really is for your own good.

- It's all they know at the moment.

- It's really for their benefit, not yours.

Parents tell children to eat their vegetables not because they want to torture their kids or make them miserable, but because eating a balanced diet is actually good for kids, no matter how distasteful they may find broccoli or spinach to be. Similarly, governments tell their citizens how to survive natural disasters or avoid trouble while traveling in foreign countries because that information really can help people survive. Parents may benefit by having healthier kids and saving money buying carrots and celery instead of hamburgers and french fries, but financial motives are secondary to their children's health. Similarly, governments may benefit from having live taxpayers rather than dead citizens, but that's secondary to the real motive of basic public safety. More often than many people might like to admit, authority figures and organizations do have your best interests at heart, which is why blindly rebelling against all forms of authority is ultimately as counterproductive as ignoring traffic lights to protest government interference and then getting hurt—or hurting someone else—when you crash your car.

Of course, authority figures and organizations don't always have such pure, altruistic motives at heart. That's why it's important to question authority. Many times, the authorities really don't know what they're doing. If you follow their orders without question, you're the one who will suffer any consequences, not them.

When the United States government exposed Army soldiers to atomic bomb blasts in the 1950s, as shown in Figure 1-1, they didn't intend for the soldiers to get hit by radiation so they could later die of leukemia. At the time, the government wanted to study the effects of atomic bomb blasts among conventional military forces, so they took all the precautions they believed necessary to protect the solders' welfare. In this case, the government's actions were born out of ignorance. However, the subsequent decision to hide the problematic test results and avoid responsibility for the soldiers' health falls more under the category of malicious self-interest. Ignorance can be forgiven only when combined with accountability, and that's something few authorities will ever take upon themselves. You should always question not only what anyone in authority wants you to do, but why they should have any authority over you in the first place.

More frightening is when authorities act purely for their own benefit while stealing, injuring, or killing the rest of us. Dictatorships throughout history, in countries such as China, Germany, Afghanistan, North Korea, Iraq, Zimbabwe, Japan, Iran, Cuba, Russia, and Saudi Arabia, have routinely executed or imprisoned anyone who questioned their authority. Under such dictatorships, the citizens are supposed to do all the work while the authorities enjoy all the money (which is something most Americans can empathize with when income tax time rolls around April 15, just before Congress votes itself another pay raise and takes one of its many recesses).

Such blatant abuses of authority are perpetrated by individuals and corporations as well as by governments. For instance, consider Jim Jones, who founded the People's Temple as an urban Christian mission that offered free meals, beds to sleep in, and even jobs, along with a sense of community. In San Francisco, where the group settled, city officials such as Mayor George Moscone, Supervisor Harvey Milk, and Assemblyman Willie Brown supported Jones (in return for the support of the People's Temple at election time). Even newspapers, including the *San Francisco Chronicle*, praised Jones and his People's Temple for setting up drug treatment clinics, child care services, and senior citizen programs.

Such benevolent actions masked the megalomania of Jim Jones, who ultimately led his church to Guyana, where he physically and emotionally abused his followers before ordering them to commit mass suicide by drinking cyanide-laced fruit punch.

Figure 1-1: To avoid looking directly at an atomic bomb blast, US soldiers cover their faces with their hands. This is the same position government authorities will later use to avoid looking directly at these veterans while refusing to grant compensation for illnesses suffered as a result of excessive radiation exposure.

Tobacco companies may be spending money on anti-smoking advertisements, but they're still in the business of making and selling cigarettes. The United States may feel justified in using military force to promote democracy in Iraq, but it has yet to send in the Marines to promote democracy in Saudi Arabia. Islamic radicals may claim they're fighting pro-Western dictatorships in the Middle East, but they're still blowing up innocent Muslim women and children with their car bombs. Mother Teresa may have had her critics, but none of them can deny that she tried to do good. Jim Jones had his supporters, but none of them can deny that he deliberately did something bad.

Too often, good actions can mask bad intentions. That's why you need to question authority. If you don't, you may become part of the problem, or as the American legal system likes to put it, "an accessory to the crime."

QUESTIONING ASSUMPTIONS

As any oppressive authoritarian regime knows, physical restraints are less effective than mental ones. Why build prisons when you can brainwash people into doing what you want? Because your thoughts define your limitations, you must question your own assumptions.

Assumptions aren't necessarily bad. When you send email, you assume it's going to get to the intended recipient. When you save a file, you assume it's going to be on your hard disk the next time you want it. An assumption is basically a mental shortcut that allows you to think about something else. Few people would send email if they had to worry whether it would really arrive at its destination or not, and almost nobody would use a computer if they couldn't assume their files would still be on their hard disk after saving them. Unfortunately, assumptions aren't always right. Email doesn't always reach its intended recipient, and sometimes when you save a file, a virus or computer crash can make it disappear.

Although useful, assumptions can lead to several problems:

– Assumptions may be based on beliefs rather than facts.

– Assumptions may be based on facts taken out of context.

– Assumptions, whether based on facts or beliefs, limit and restrict thinking.

In the world of technology, Bell Telephone created its telephone monopoly and assumed people would use it to make phone calls the way Bell Telephone intended. When phone phreakers defied this assumption and rummaged through the telephone system on their own, the facts proved that phreakers were manipulating the phone system in ways that even the telephone company had never dreamed of. (See Chapter 2 for more on phone phreaking.)

Many of the flaws in computer security stem from assumptions based on beliefs rather than facts. Computer scientists believe that a particular program is secure—until hackers discover that manipulating a program feature in an unintended manner can crack open that computer's defenses.

Sometimes assumptions can be based on facts that hold true in certain circumstances but not in others. When Microsoft created MS-DOS and Windows, it assumed that those operating systems were safe, and they were—until people began connecting computers to local area networks (LANs) and the Internet. In isolation, MS-DOS and Windows were safe platforms. In a network, these same operating systems became breeding grounds for viruses, Trojan horses, and worms (see Chapters 4 and 5).

When computer scientists created standards for sending and receiving email over the Internet, they assumed that people would only send emails to people they knew. Unfortunately, they never foresaw that free message delivery would attract unscrupulous salespeople and create the nuisance known as spam (see Chapter 18).

Even if assumptions are based on facts, they still limit your thinking. When faced with a computer login screen, most people automatically assume that the only way to get past this first line of defense is to type a valid user name and password, either by stealing or guessing it. If you make that assumption, however, you might never come up with alternate approaches, such as flooding the computer with a massive chunk of data that has an executable program tacked on the end. This can overload the computer's memory and allow the executable program to run without the computer recognizing it, essentially bypassing any security measures, including a request for a valid password. (See Chapter 9 for more information about sneaking past a computer's defenses.)

By identifying assumptions, you can better understand how they may have influenced your current thoughts and actions. Then you can deliberately break out of their inherent restrictions by challenging your assumptions. You might discover something new simply by looking at the world from another point of view.

DEVELOPING VALUES

Of course, if you do nothing but question authorities and assumptions, you'll wind up reacting to life rather than pursuing it, much like adolescents who define themselves by rebelling against their parents' wishes and values, rather than choosing the life they want to live on their own.

So in addition to questioning authorities and assumptions, hackers also develop a sense of values to guide their actions. Values, like assumptions, are beliefs, but they are beliefs generated from within and not imposed by others, such as parents or governments. At the simplest level, values help people make choices, such as whether they choose Linux over Windows or learn the Perl programming language rather than C++.

Shared values can forge friendships (for an example of people using technology to promote their ideas, visit Republican Voices at www.republicanvoices.org); conflicting values can tear people apart (see Chapter 17 for more information about hate groups and terrorists).

Anyone can choose values, especially values that will garner favor from others. For example, politicians may endorse the values of religious organizations just to gain their political support, and then promptly ignore those same religious values ("Thou shalt not commit adultery" or "Thou shalt not kill") when they finally get elected to office. What's more important than the values you choose is whether you abide by them all the time or only when it's convenient, which reveals your *true* values.

Hypocrisy is what fuels rebellions in the first place, causing others to question an authority figure's standing as an authority and reject any values that person may want to force on them (see Chapter 16 for more information about political activism on the Internet). When authorities want to mask their own hypocrisy, they often resort to censorship (see Chapter 11) and lies (see Chapter 15 for more information about propaganda).

In the world of computer hacking, people only know who you are by your online actions. Your identity may be anonymous, but your true personality isn't, and that's what makes the world of computers both liberating and terrifying at the same time, depending on who you really are.

THE THREE STAGES OF HACKING

The mentality of a hacker typically goes through three stages, whether the hacker is merely exploring a new operating system or learning social skills for work situations:

- Stage I: Curiosity

- Stage II: Control

- Stage III: Conscious intent

Hackers come from different backgrounds and cultures, but every hacker shares the same sense of curiosity that drew him or her to the technology in the first place. At the initial curiosity stage, hackers simply want to know how things work, whether they're studying the Internet, a copy-protected DVD, or the telephone system. At the outset, hackers want to understand what's possible and why.

Once they learn enough about a particular system, hackers can graduate to the second stage of hacking, in which they gradually learn to control and manipulate the system. Any problems that hackers cause at this point, such as crashing a computer or erasing a hard disk, occur more often out of sheer clumsiness than deliberate intent.

Hackers reach the third and final stage when they put their newfound skills to work for a purpose. At this point, hackers seek a specific result; whether it's good or bad is irrelevant. Hackers want to achieve whatever goal they set for themselves, and they're willing to pursue it with relentless determination until they get there.

No matter what the intention or the result, hacking involves tackling new challenges and stimulating your mind. It sometimes involves breaking the law and trespassing on other people's property, but many times it's just about having fun. Whether hackers are rerouting phone calls, modifying software, or stealing passwords over the Internet, hacking isn't about proving anyone wrong. Hacking is about proving that other ways of doing things can also be right.

2

THE FIRST HACKERS:
THE PHONE PHREAKERS

The first phone phreakers were teenage boys.

That fact alone isn't too surprising, until you realize that those first hackers appeared in 1878, when teenage boys worked as telephone operators for the fledgling Bell Telephone network. Hiring teenage boys seemed logical; telegraph offices often hired them to work similar jobs as telegraph delivery messengers. Putting teenage boys in charge of the telephone network made good sense right up until they started randomly mixing telephone lines to connect total strangers as a prank and started talking back to customers and interfering in their conversations just for laughs.

Bell Telephone quickly replaced its prepubescent male operators with more dependable women. Still, the spirit of playfulness that first surfaced among those teenagers would soon reappear to haunt the telephone networks again.

When the telephone company replaced human operators with automated electronic switching systems (ESSs) in the 1960s, the telephone hackers (also known by their more colorful nickname, *phone phreakers*) found new opportunities to toy with the telephone system.

You couldn't always trick a human operator into granting you free phone calls, but you could trick the telephone network's automated switching systems into doing so. With nothing but primitive computers routing telephone calls around the country, phone phreakers quickly learned that if you knew the right signals, you could get the telephone system to do anything from granting free long-distance telephone calls to letting you connect multiple phone lines to form conference calls—all without the telephone company's knowledge.

We find no real satisfaction or happiness in life without obstacles to conquer and goals to achieve.

—MAXWELL MALTZ, creator of self-improvement program Psycho-Cybernetics

A SHORT HISTORY OF PHONE PHREAKING

Unlike computer hacking, which can often be practiced in isolation on a single personal computer, phone phreaking was pretty complicated and thus required more extensive preparation. You might be reprogramming the phone company's computers one moment, soldering wires together to alter a pay phone the next, and then chatting with a telephone employee to get the passwords for a different part of the phone system. Like computer hacking, phone phreaking is an intellectual game in which players try to learn as much as they can about the system (usually) without getting caught.

Perhaps the most famous phone phreaker is John Draper (www.webcrunchers .com/crunch), nicknamed Captain Crunch because of his accidental discovery of a unique use for a toy whistle found in a box of Cap'n Crunch cereal. He found that blowing this toy whistle into his phone's mouthpiece emitted a 2600Hz tone, the exact frequency used to instruct the telephone company's switching systems to make free telephone calls.

Others soon discovered this secret, and some even developed the ability to whistle a perfect 2600Hz tone. For those unable to obtain the original Cap'n Crunch toy whistle, entrepreneurs began selling devices known as *blue boxes* that emitted the 2600Hz tone and other telephone company signal tones. Steve Wozniak and Steve Jobs, the founders of Apple Computer, even sold blue boxes to college students so they could make free phone calls from their dormitories.

Blue boxes worked as long as the telephone company relied on their old electro-mechanical switching systems. But eventually these were replaced with newer electronic switching systems (ESSs), which rendered blue boxes (and the infamous 2600Hz tone) useless (although blue boxes may still work on older phone systems outside the United States).

Of course, ESSs brought with them a whole new set of problems. With the older electromechanical switching systems, a technician had to physically manipulate switches and wires to modify the switching system. With an ESS, technicians could alter the switching system remotely over the phone lines.

If a technician could perform this magic over the telephone, however, phone phreakers could do the same—if they knew the proper codes and procedures. Obviously, the telephone company wanted to keep this information secret, but the phone phreakers wanted to let everyone know how the telephone system worked (which is partly what the ongoing struggle between the telephone company and phone phreakers is all about).

NOTE: *To learn more about phone phreaking, visit Hack Canada (www.hackcanada .com) or Phone Losers of America (www.phonelosers.org). Or try the alt.phreaking and alt.2600.phreakz newsgroups for messages about phreaking.*

PHONE PHREAKING URBAN LEGENDS

If you have a telephone, anyone in the world, including the legions of phone phreakers just goofing around with the telephone system, can call you. Steve Wozniak reportedly once called the Vatican and pretended to be Henry Kissinger. Other phone phreakers have attempted to call the Kremlin via the White House hotline and have rerouted a prominent TV evangelist's business number to a 1-900 sex line.

Because a large part of phone phreaking lore involves performing progressively more outrageous acts and then boasting about them, the following phone phreaking stories may or may not be true. Nevertheless, they will give you an idea of what phone phreakers can achieve given the right information. (These are "urban myths" circulating on the Internet and are reprinted here with minor editing for the sake of clarity and explanation.)

The toilet paper crisis in Los Angeles

Part of the thrill of phone phreaking is discovering areas of the telephone network that the general public wouldn't normally access. In the early '70s, two phone phreakers discovered an unlisted phone number that only a handful of people had the right to know about. They decided to use it to make the ultimate prank phone call. What follows is an edited version of the firsthand account of one of the phreakers.

[At the time of the prank,] it was really easy for phone phreakers to pop into the phone company's AutoVerify trunks. This procedure is used when someone legitimately needs to break in on a busy phone line. Ordinarily, it goes like this:

The operator selects a special trunk (phone line), class marked (reserved) for this service, and dials either the last five digits of the phone number, or a special Terminating Toll Center (TTC) code like 052, followed by the entire seven-digit number. After that, the operator hears scrambled conversation on the line. The parties talking hear nothing, not even a click.

Next, the operator "flashes forward" by causing the equipment to send a tone burst at 2600Hz, which makes a three-way connection and places a beep tone on the line so that both original parties can hear the click (flash, in this case) followed by a high-pitched beep. At this point, the parties can hear the operator and vice versa. In the case of a legitimate interruption, the operator announces that there is an emergency and the line should be released. This service is available today for a $2 fee ($1 in certain areas).

Earlier, I had mapped every 800 number that terminated in Washington, DC, by scanning the entire 800-424 prefix. That scan found an impressive quantity of juicy numbers that allowed free access to Congressional phone lines, special White House access numbers, and so on.

While scanning 800-424, I got this dude whose bad attitude caught my attention. I was determined to find out who he was. I called back and said, "This is White Plains tandem office for AT&T, which subscriber have we reached?"

This person said, "This is the White House CIA crisis hotline!"

"Oh!" I said, "We're having a problem with crossed lines. Now that I know who this is, I can fix it. Thank you for your time—good-bye!"

I had a very special 800 number.

Eventually my friends and I had one of our info-exchanging binges, and I mentioned this incident to them. One friend wanted to dial it immediately, but I persuaded him to wait. I wanted to pop up on the line, using AutoVerify to hear the conversation.

But first we needed to determine which exchange this number terminated in, because AutoVerify didn't know about 800 numbers.

At the time, all 800 numbers had a one-to-one relation between prefix and area code. For instance, 800-424 = 202-xxx, where *xxx* was the three-digit exchange determined by the last four digits. In this case, 800-424-9337 mapped to 202-227-9337. The 227 (which could be wrong) was a special White House prefix used for faxes, telexes, and, in this case, the CIA crisis line.

Next we got into the class marked trunk (which had a different sounding chirp when seized) and MF'ed KP-054-227-9337-ST into this special class marked trunk. ("MF" stands for multi-frequency, the method by which the phone phreakers sent the specific code into the telephone trunk.) Immediately we heard the connection tone and put it up on the speaker so we would know when a call came in.

Several hours later, a call came in. It appeared to have CIA-related talk, and the code name "Olympus" was used to summon the president. I had been in another part of the building and rushed into the room just in time to hear the tail end of the conversation.

We had the code word that would summon Nixon to the phone. Almost immediately, another friend started to dial the number. I stopped him and recommended that he stack at least four tandems (switches connecting different lines or trunks of the telephone network) before looping the call to the White House. (Stacking tandems means routing a phone call between different switches, making it harder for anyone to trace exactly which phone number you're calling from. After routing a phone call through multiple switches, looping connects the caller to the desired phone number.)

Sure enough, the man at the other end said "9337."

My other friend said, "Olympus, please!"

The man at the other end said, "One moment, sir!" About a minute later, a man that sounded remarkably like Nixon said, "What's going on?"

My friend said, "We have a crisis here in Los Angeles!"

Nixon said, "What's the nature of the crisis?"

My friend said in a serious tone of voice, "We're out of toilet paper, sir!"

Nixon said, "WHO IS THIS?"

My friend then hung up. We never did learn what happened to that tape, but I think this was one of the funniest pranks.

To the best of my recollection, this was about four months before Nixon resigned because of the Watergate crisis.

The Santa Barbara nuclear hoax

Making crank calls can be fun, and it's a bigger rush as you fool more and more people. However, as the two phone phreakers in the following example found out, sometimes a crank call can go a little bit too far . . .

Two Southern Californian phone phreakers once tied up every long-distance line coming into Santa Barbara using two side-by-side phone booths on the beach and some very simple phone phreaking equipment. When people tried to call into Santa Barbara, their calls were rerouted to the two phreakers, who told all callers that a mysterious explosion had wiped out the city.

The first call was from a mother to her son, a student at the University of California, Santa Barbara campus. The two phreakers told the woman that they were with the National Guard Emergency Communications Center and that there was no longer any University of California at Santa Barbara. In breathless tones they said the campus and, in fact, the entire city of Santa Barbara had been wiped out in a freakish nuclear accident; a "nuclear meltdown," they told her. She was politely asked to hang up in order to clear the line for emergency phone calls.

A few minutes later the horrified mother called back, this time with operator assistance. The phone phreakers calmly repeated their story to the operator, asked her not to place calls to Santa Barbara, and told her not to worry.

Within minutes, newspaper and television reporters, FBI agents, and police officers began calling from all over the country. Hundreds of anxious people who had heard about the "meltdown" phoned to check on relatives and friends. The phreakers told the callers that they had reached the National Guard base 50 miles away from the disaster site and that they were tied into emergency circuits. After about an hour the two phreakers became frightened by the chaos they were causing and restored the phone system to normal. They were never caught.

The next day, the *Los Angeles Times* carried a short news article headlined "Nuclear hoax in Santa Barbara." The text explained how authorities were freaked out and how puzzled they were. The phone company commented, "We don't really know how this happened, but it cleared right up!"

The president's secret

Phone phreakers don't necessarily abuse their power over the telephone system; they just want to explore every part of the phone network and understand how it operates. But as this phone phreaker discovered, sometimes certain phone numbers are best left alone.

Some years back, a telephone fanatic in the Northwest made an interesting discovery about the 804 area code (Virginia). He found that the 840 exchange in the 804 area code did something strange. In calling every 804-840-*xxxx* phone number but one, he would get a recording as if the exchange didn't exist. However, if he dialed 804-840 followed by four rather predictable numbers (like 1-2-3-4), he got a ring!

After one or two rings, somebody picked up. Because he was experienced with this kind of thing, he could tell that the call didn't "supe," that is, no charges were being incurred for calling this number. (Calls that get you to an error message or a special operator generally don't "supe," or supervise.) A female voice with a hint of a southern accent said, "Operator, can I help you?"

"Yes," he said, "What number have I reached?"

"What number did you dial, sir?"

He made up a number that was similar.

"I'm sorry. That is not the number you reached." Click.

He was fascinated. What in the world was this? He knew he was going to call back, but before he did, he tried some more experiments. He tried the 840 exchange in several other area codes. In some, it came up as a valid exchange. In others, exactly the same thing happened—the same last four digits, the same southern belle.

He later noticed that the area codes where the number functioned properly formed a beeline from Washington, DC, to Pittsburgh, PA. He called back from a pay phone.

"Operator, can I help you?"

"Yes, this is the phone company. I'm testing this line and we don't seem to have an identification on your circuit. What office is this, please?"

"What number are you trying to reach?"

"I'm not trying to reach any number. I'm trying to identify this circuit."

"I'm sorry, I can't help you."

"Ma'am, if I don't get an ID on this line, I'll have to disconnect it. We show no record of it here."

"Hold on a moment, sir."

After about a minute, she came back. "Sir, I can have someone speak to you. Would you give me your number, please?"

He had anticipated this and had the pay phone number ready. After he gave it, she said, "Mr. XXX will get right back to you."

"Thanks." He hung up the phone. It rang. Instantly. "Oh my God," he thought, "They weren't asking for my number—they were confirming it!"

"Hello," he said, trying to sound authoritative.

"This is Mr. XXX. Did you just make an inquiry to my office concerning a phone number?"

"Yes. I need an identi- . . ."

"What you need is advice. Don't ever call that number again. Forget you ever knew it."

At this point my friend got so nervous, he immediately hung up. He expected to hear the phone ring again, but it didn't.

Over the next few days, he racked his brain trying to figure out what the number was. He knew it was something big—so big that the number was programmed into every central office in the country. He knew this because if he tried to dial any other number in that exchange, he'd get a local error message, as if the exchange didn't exist.

It finally came to him. He had an uncle who worked for a federal agency. If, as he suspected, this was government-related, his uncle could probably find out what it was. He asked the next day and his uncle promised to look into it.

When they met again, his uncle was livid. He was trembling. "Where did you get that number?" he shouted. "Do you know I almost got fired for asking about it? They kept wanting to know where I got it!"

Our friend couldn't contain his excitement. "What is it?" he pleaded. "What's the number?"

"IT'S THE PRESIDENT'S BOMB SHELTER!"

He never called the number again after that. He knew that he could probably cause quite a bit of excitement by calling the number and saying something like, "The weather's not good in Washington. We're coming over for a visit." But my friend was smart. He knew that there were some things that were better left unsaid and undone.

TRUE AND VERIFIED PHONE PHREAKING STORIES

The previous phone phreaking stories may be more fiction than fact. However, the following tales are true, and perhaps more frightening than anything anyone could ever make up.

Making free phone calls, courtesy of the Israeli Army

The Israeli Army is considered the best in the world; even its radio stations enjoy round-the-clock protection provided by armed soldiers patrolling the perimeters. But those radio stations aren't safe from phone phreakers. Armed guards and barbed wire mean nothing to someone who can probe a network through the telephone lines. And as blind phone phreaker Munther "Ramy" Badir explains, an army outpost has phone lines that cannot be tapped by the police, so there is no monitoring. "These are the safest lines on which to do something."

In 1993, Ramy and his two brothers Muzher and Shadde Badir, all completely blind since birth, drew the attention of authorities when they broke into Bezeq International, Israel's largest telecommunications provider. After hacking Bezeq's phone networks and giving themselves calling privileges, the Badir brothers made a deal to direct phone calls to a Dominican Republic phone sex service and get paid for each call. (Visit any hacker website and you'll see it's common to direct visitors to sex services as a money-making scheme.)

To ensure that they would get paid as much as possible, the Badir brothers made phone calls to the Dominican Republican sex service themselves, billing their phone calls to companies such as Nortel and Comverse. When a Bezeq International anti-fraud engineer discovered the lines the Badir brothers were using and blocked them, the brothers simply called Bezeq International, impersonated the anti-fraud engineer's voice, and ordered the lines unblocked.

Next the brothers attacked an Israeli phone sex service and talked the secretary into revealing her boss's computer password. Armed with this information, they hacked into the phone sex service's computers and made off with 20,000 customer credit card numbers. When the sex service's boss confronted them, they retaliated by programming all his telephones to ring continuously, with no one on the line.

According to authorities, the Badir brothers next broke into an Israeli Army radio station's phone system and activated a function called Direct Inward Systems Access (DISA). Not only did this allow multiple people to share a single telephone line, but it also enabled anyone to place long-distance phone calls that would be charged to the Israeli Army radio station.

Next, the brothers sold access to the hacked phone system so that anyone could make free phone calls from their home, cloned cell phones, or phone kiosks set up along the Gaza Strip. As Israeli authorities closed in on them, the brothers fought back by taking down the police phone systems, crashing their computers, and even eavesdropping on their telephone calls.

When Israeli police finally raided the Badir brothers' home, they found nothing more incriminating than an ordinary laptop computer. "It's all in our heads," Ramy said. "The police took my laptop, which contained programs for running through thousands of numbers very quickly, but I had it designed to erase everything on the hard drive if it was opened by somebody other than me. They lost all the material."

Between 1999 and 2004, Ramy ultimately spent a little more than four years in prison and his brothers served community service and a suspended sentence. Like many reformed hackers, Ramy insists that he's now going to work in security. "I am inventing a PBX firewall. I know all the weakest spots of a telephone system. I can protect any system from infiltration. I am going to the other side, coming up with devices that will keep the phreakers out."

Phone phreaking for escorts in Las Vegas

While most phone phreakers use their skills to make free phone calls or to toy around with the telephone system, some have used their skills to help organized crime syndicates reroute phone calls around Las Vegas.

If you've ever walked along the Las Vegas Strip, you've been bombarded by people handing out flyers and brochures for all types of in-room adult entertainment services. Vending machines bolted to the sidewalks also freely dispense similar pornographic "reading" material, showing bodies, names, and telephone numbers. With such an abundance of pornographic material within reach of any passerby, you'd think that these escort services would be inundated with phone calls from lonely visitors holed up in hotel rooms across the city.

In the old days, that was true. Nowadays, though, despite the abundance of advertising, these adult entertainment businesses are lucky to get one or two calls a night, and, inevitably, these calls come from people who are either outside of Las Vegas or calling from a pay phone or cell phone. These phone calls aren't routed through the big casino/hotel switchboards in Las Vegas. If anyone tries to call these services from the telephone in a Las Vegas hotel room, the calls either don't connect or are mysteriously rerouted to a rival adult entertainment service (presumably controlled by organized crime). Naturally, most callers aren't aware that their phone call went to a different service provider than the one they called, since they wind up getting a woman to come to their room anyway.

Sometimes the phone calls aren't rerouted but are traced instead. So when a caller reaches an adult entertainment service, a rival service that's tracing the phone line sends a girl to the customer first. By the time the girl from the intended adult service shows up, the customer is already being serviced by the competition's girl.

The next time you're in Las Vegas, pick up a brochure for an adult entertainment business off the Strip and call using your hotel room telephone. Spend the next 10 or 15 minutes asking questions and then hang up without asking for a girl. If a rival adult service has been tracing your call, a girl should show up at your hotel room within 15 minutes anyway, asking, "Did you call for an entertainer?" Ask the girl what service she came from and she'll likely respond with a noncommittal answer such as, "Which service did you call? I work for several of them."

Then again, you might want to avoid this experiment altogether, since wasting the time (and money) of those in organized crime is rarely a healthy decision.

PHONE PHREAKING TOOLS AND TECHNIQUES

The goal of every phone phreaker is to learn more about the telephone system, preferably without paying for any phone calls in the process. Whether they access the telephone system from an appliance inside their own home, a public pay phone, or someone else's "borrowed" (stolen) phone line, phone phreakers have found a variety of ways to avoid paying for their phone calls.

Shoulder surfing

The crudest level of phreaking is known as shoulder surfing, which is simply looking over another person's shoulder as they punch in their telephone calling card number at a public pay phone.

The prime locations for shoulder surfing are airports, where travelers are more likely to use calling cards than change to make a call. Given the hectic nature of a typical airport, few people take notice of someone peering over their shoulder while they punch in their calling card number, or listening in as they give it to an operator.

Once you have another person's calling card number, you can charge as many calls as you like until the victim receives the next billing statement and notices your mysterious phone calls. Of course, once the victim notifies the phone company, that calling card number is usually canceled. (Since shoulder surfing involves stealing from individuals, true phone phreakers look down on it as an activity unworthy of anyone but common thieves and juvenile delinquents. True phone pheakers only believe in stealing service from the telephone company, and even then they don't feel that they're actually causing any harm or costing the company any money.)

As more people rely on cell phones and fewer on pay phones and calling cards, shoulder surfing is a dying art, but it can still be a handy technique for stealing a password or PIN from someone using a computer or automated teller machine.

Phone phreaking with color boxes

Another way to avoid paying for phone calls is to trick the phone company into thinking either that you already paid for them or that you never made them in the first place. To physically manipulate the phone networks, phone phreakers trick the telephone system through telephone color boxes, which either emit special tones or physically alter the wiring on the phone line.

Although the Internet abounds with instructions and plans for building various telephone color boxes, many of the older ones, such as blue boxes, no longer work with today's phone systems in the United States—although they might still work in other countries, particularly Third World nations where old technology has been redeployed.

Here are some descriptions of various color boxes that others have made and used. But first, a warning from a phone phreaker regarding the legality of building and using such boxes:

> *You have received this information courtesy of neXus. We do not claim to be hackers, phreaks, pirates, traitors, etc. We only believe that an alternative to making certain info/ideas illegal as a means to keep people from doing bad things - is make information free, and educate people how to handle free information responsibly. Please think and act responsibly. Don't get cockey, don't get pushy. There is always gonna be someone out there that can kick your ass. Remember that.*

Blue box

The blue box, the first of the telephone color boxes, reportedly got its name because the first one confiscated by police just happened to be blue. To use a blue box, phone phreakers would dial a phone number to connect to the telephone network and then turn on the box to emit its 2600Hz tone. This tricked the telephone system into thinking that they had hung up. Then the phone phreaker could either whistle different tones or use additional color boxes to emit tones that would dial an actual phone number. Since the blue box had already tricked the telephone system into thinking the caller had hung up, the subsequent calls made would not be charged.

Red box

When you insert a coin into a pay phone, it triggers a relay that emits a tone specific to that coin (a nickel makes a different sound than a dime or a quarter). A *red box* simulates the sound of money dropping into a pay phone. The telephone system listens to all the tones emitted to determine how much money has been deposited. When the total amount deposited equals the amount needed to make a phone call, the telephone system connects the pay phone to the network.

Green box

A *green box* generates three tones that can control a pay phone: coin collect (CC), coin return (CR), and ringback (RB). What happens is that one phone phreaker uses an ordinary pay phone to call a phone phreaker who has a green box attached to his phone. The phone phreaker receiving the call can activate the green box to send the coin collect (CC) tone (to trick the pay phone into thinking the phone phreaker dropped money into the pay phone), the coin return (CR) tone (to force the pay phone to spit coins into its return slot), or the ringback (RB) tone (to cause the green box phone to call the pay phone, allowing the phone phreaker at the pay phone to receive a phone call and talk to the other person free of charge).

Black box

Unlike blue boxes or red boxes, which prevent you from being charged for making calls, a *black box* prevents other people from being charged when they call you.

A black box works by controlling the voltage on your phone line. Before you receive a phone call, the voltage is zero. It jumps to 48V, however, the moment the phone rings. As soon as you pick up the phone, it drops back down to 10V, and the phone company begins billing the calling party.

A black box keeps the voltage on your phone line at a steady 36V so that it never drops low enough to signal the phone company to start billing. As far as the telephone company can tell, your phone keeps ringing because you haven't answered it yet, even while you're chatting happily with your friends. (Black box calls should be kept short, however, because the telephone company may get suspicious if your phone keeps "ringing" for a long period of time without the caller hanging up.)

Silver box

A *silver box* modifies your phone to generate four special tones designated "A"—Flash, "B"—Flash Override Priority, "C"—Priority Communication, and "D"—Priority Overide (Top Military). Although the telephone company has never designated any official use for these extra tones, that hasn't stopped phone phreakers from experimenting with them. For example, phone phreakers discovered that if you generated the "D" tone and pressed 6 or 7, you could reach loop ends, which are two phone numbers that the telephone company uses to test connections. If two phone phreakers accessed these loop ends at the same time, they could make free phone calls to each other.

Phone phreaking with color box programs

Making a telephone color box often involved soldering or connecting wires, resistors, and capacitors together. But with the advent of personal computers, people found they could write programs to mimic different telephone color boxes. By running these programs on a laptop or handheld computer and placing the mouthpiece of the phone over the computer speaker, phone phreakers could manipulate the telephone system without having to build actual boxes.

Although telephone color boxes are largely obsolete, many phone phreakers have created software implementations of their favorite ones, dubbed *tone generators*. For example, Hack Canada (www.hackcanada.com) offers a red box program (called RedPalm) that runs on a Palm handheld computer, and some hacker sites still offer a combination red/blue box program dubbed Switchboard (see Figure 2-1).

Remember, tone generators simply play different tones, just like an MP3 player. Why not simply save those tones as MP3 files for playback on any digital audio device? Why not is right. To download an MP3 tone, visit the Phreaks and Geeks site (www.phreaksandgeeks.com).

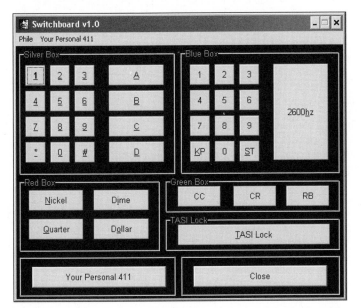

Figure 2-1: The Switchboard program mimics a blue, red, green, and silver box for emitting tones from a computer.

Phreaking with war dialers and prank programs

Besides writing programs to mimic telephone color boxes, phone phreakers have also created programs called *war dialers* or *demon dialers*. War dialers are an old, but still effective, method for breaking into another computer (see Figure 2-2).

War dialers try a range of phone numbers in a hunt for telephone lines connected to a modem and a computer, which makes every person, corporation, and organization a potential target. The war dialers record the phone numbers that respond with the familiar whine of a computer (or fax) modem, and a hacker can then use this list and dial each number individually to determine what type of computer he has reached and how he might be able to break into it.

For example, many businesses have special phone lines that allow traveling employees to control their desktop computers with their laptop computers and remote-control software, such as pcAnywhere or LapLink. If a hacker finds this special phone number and uses a copy of the same software, guess what? With the right password, he can take over the desktop computer too and then erase or copy all of its files.

Since war dialers repetitively dial a range of phone numbers, such as 483-1000, 483-1001, 483-1002, and so on, many companies try to find and stop any such repetitive dialing. To defeat this, war dialers can be reprogrammed to throw off any possible detection attempts by dialing a range of phone numbers in nonsequential order.

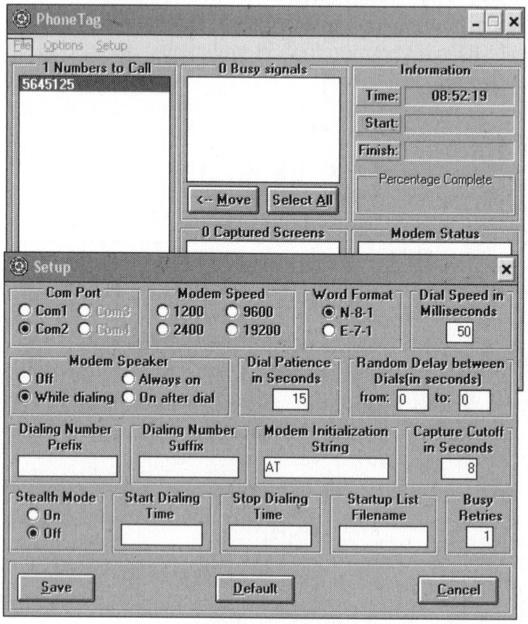

Figure 2-2: A war dialer can scan a range of phone numbers to find one that has a waiting computer and modem on the other end.

NOTE: *To defeat war dialers, many companies use a callback device that's only designed to accept specific numbers. When someone wants to connect to the company computer, they need to call from one of the preapproved numbers stored in the callback device's memory. Once they connect, they send a signal to the callback device to call back to one of the preapproved phone numbers. The caller then hangs up and waits for that call. Since the callback device restricts the phone numbers allowed to connect to the computer, hackers are effectively blocked from breaking into a computer through a modem (hopefully).*

Like any tool, war dialers can be used by hackers to break into a computer or by security professionals to probe a company's vulnerabilities. Since computer security is so lucrative, SandStorm Enterprises (http://sandstorm.net) sells a commercial war dialer called PhoneSweep, which is designed for security professionals to test for any unsecured modems connected to their company's phone system. Unlike most hacker war dialers, PhoneSweep can generate reports and graphs that show the percentage of phone numbers called that had a modem or returned a busy signal.

As a free alternative to PhoneSweep, download a copy of TeleSweep Secure from SecureLogix (www.securelogix.com). SecureLogix originally sold TeleSweep Secure commercially, but now gives it away for free in the hopes that satisfied customers will upgrade to its Voice Firewall product.

Since war dialers can dial a number repeatedly, they can also be used to harass people. Some of the more unusual harassment programs can dial a single number over and over again at random intervals or play a computer-generated voice to insult a caller the moment he or she picks up the phone (have a look at Shit Talker in Figure 2-3). But if you use one, just remember that caller ID is a common feature nowadays, and allows a victim to track your phone number, so beware.

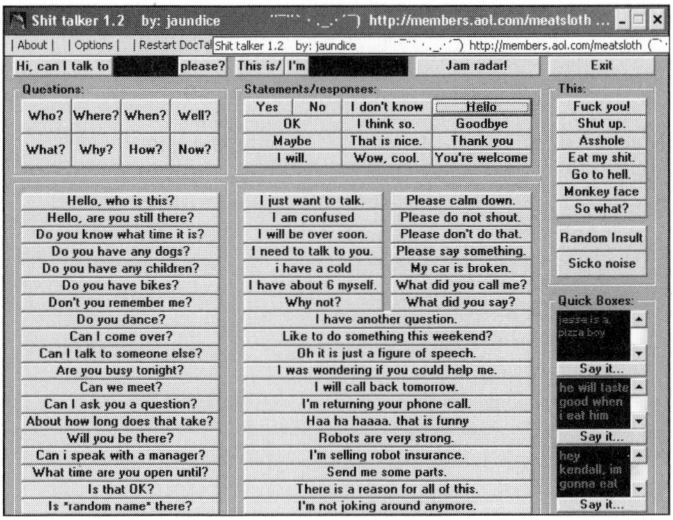

Figure 2-3: Many hacker programs are designed specifically to harass others.

Phreaking cellular phones

The popularity of cellular phones has attracted both outright thieves and phone phreakers. At the simplest level, stealing cell phone service can be as easy as signing up using a fake or stolen identity, although it's even easier just to steal someone's cell phone and use it until the real owner cancels the service.

Of course, both of these methods are fairly crude. For a more sophisticated way to steal cell phone service, thieves have turned to *cloning*.

Every cell phone contains both a unique electronic serial number (ESN) and a mobile identification number (MIN). Every time someone uses a cell phone, he transmits his unique ESN and MIN to the cell phone network, which verifies that the ESN/MIN combination is valid.

The problem is that when older analog cell phones transmitted their ESN/MIN numbers at the start of every call, anyone with a cell phone scanner could intercept those numbers and store them on another cell phone, essentially cloning the ESN/MIN numbers of a valid cell phone. Any calls made through this "cloned" cell phone would show up on the bill of the legitimate cell phone customer.

Since a cloned phone can only be used until the real cell phone owner notices the outrageous number of additional calls showing up on the bill, some thieves resort to a technique known as *tumbling*. Originally, tumbling meant using a random ESN and MIN number to make a free call. Once the cell phone company received these random ESN/MIN numbers, they had to validate these numbers. Since this process could take time, the cell phone companies often let random ESN/MIN numbers get one free phone call without validating the numbers. Eventually, the cell phone companies could validate ESN/MIN numbers almost instantaneously, so tumbling took a new form where a thief steals multiple combinations of valid ESN/MIN numbers and uses a different one each time he makes a phone call. Tumbling spreads out the number of illegal phone calls among a large number of legitimate cell phone owners, who are more likely to accept (or not notice) one or two strange calls rather than dozens each month.

In part to protect users from cloning fraud, cell phone companies have introduced digital transmission and encryption, often advertised with cryptic names such as TDMA (Time Division Multiple Access), CDMA (Code Division Multiple Access), GSM (Global System for Multiple Communication), or Spread Spectrum. (Analog cell phones used FDMA, which stands for Frequency Division Multiple Access.)

In additional to encrypting a cellular phone's ESN/MIN numbers, many cellular phone networks now include voice and radio frequency authentication. Voice authentication can identify unfamiliar calling patterns and radio frequency authentication can identify the unique radio frequency characteristics (known as the *fingerprint*) of each cell phone.

Such defenses are expensive, which means they're more often used in big cities while rural areas are left unprotected. To protect yourself, study your cell phone bills every month to identify strange calls. Also, minimize your cell phone use in areas such as airport terminals or parking lots since cell phone thieves scan the airwaves in crowded places where people are most likely to use cell phones.

To keep up with the latest cell phone hacking news and information, visit Cell Phone Hacks (www.cellphonehacks.com), Collusion Magazine (www.collusion.org), or the Temple of the Screaming Electron (www.totse.com), which is shown in Figure 2-4.

While phone phreakers aren't likely to target your personal cell phone, they are likely to target the cell phones of celebrities like Paris Hilton (if you can legitimately call Paris Hilton a "celebrity"). In 2005, a 17-year-old Massachusetts teenager hacked into Paris Hilton's cell phone and spread her cell phone number, along with the cell phone numbers and email addresses of Ashlee Simpson, Christina Aguilera, Ashley Olsen, Vin Diesel, former O.J. Simpson attorney Robert Shapiro, Anna Kournikova, Eminem, and Lindsay Lohan, across the Internet.

Not surprisingly, this teenager didn't hack into Paris Hilton's cell phone using some undiscovered flaw. Instead, this teenager took advantage of the fact that Paris Hilton's cell phone was protected by a password. If Paris Hilton forgot her password, she could still access her cell phone by answering the default question, "What is your favorite pet's name?"

Since Paris Hilton made no secret of her love and affection for her Chihuahua, named Tinkerbell, it was a simple matter of typing in "Tinkerbell" to gain access to Paris Hilton's cell phone. As this Paris Hilton cell phone hack showed, sometimes the simplest solutions are the best way to sneak past any technical defenses.

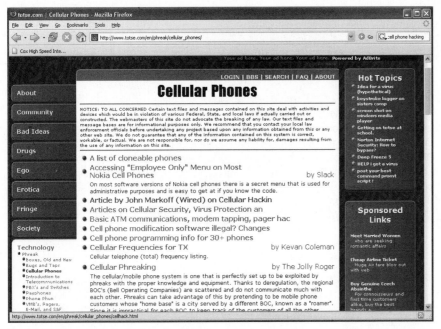

Figure 2-4: Hacker websites and e-zines offer information about cloning cell phones and stealing cell phone service.

Hacking voice mailboxes

Voice mail is the corporate alternative to answering machines. Rather than give each employee a separate answering machine, voice mail provides multiple mailboxes on a single machine. Because a voice mail system is nothing more than a programmable computer, phone phreakers quickly found a way to set up their own private voice mailboxes buried within legitimate voice mailbox systems.

To find a voice mail system, phone phreakers simply use a war dialer to find a corporate voice mail system phone number. (Many even have toll-free numbers for the convenience of corporate executives.) After calling the voice mail system, users often need to press a key, such as * or #, to enter the mailbox. A recording will usually ask for a valid mailbox number, typically three or four digits. Finally, users type a password to access the mailbox, play back messages, or record a new message or greeting.

Most people choose a password that's easy to remember (and easy to guess). Some people base their password on their mailbox number, either the mailbox number itself or the mailbox number backwards (if the mailbox number is 2108, try 8012 as the password). Others might use a password that consists of a repeated number (such as 3333) or a simple series (6789).

Once a phone phreaker finds a voice mail system phone number, the next step is to guess a password for one or more mailboxes, either by typing in a series of passwords or by running a voice mailbox hacking program, like VMB Hacker, that dials a range of three- or four-digit numbers until it finds a combination that works (see Figure 2-5).

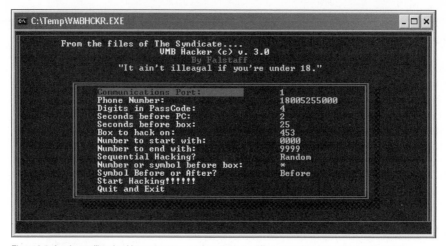

Figure 2-5: A voice mailbox hacking program can exhaustively try different combinations of numbers until it finds one that accesses a voice mailbox.

With access to an existing voice mailbox, a phone phreaker can listen to messages and learn more about a particular person or company in order to gather information that may be useful later for prying deeper into a particular company's computer systems.

In addition, most voice mail systems have several empty mailboxes at any given time, either leftovers from previous employees or extra capacity for anticipated newcomers, and phone phreakers can take over these empty mailboxes and set up a virtual presence for themselves within an unsuspecting corporation. And, if the voice mail system provides a toll-free number, the phone phreaker can receive free phone messages from anywhere.

NOTE: *Even if the voice mail system doesn't offer a toll-free number, phone phreakers can often reprogram the voice mail system to forward their calls anywhere in the world, essentially getting long-distance phone service at the hacked company's expense.*

The simplest way to defeat voice mailbox hacking is to turn off call forwarding, which will make the system a less inviting target for phone phreakers. Next, make sure that unused mailboxes are really empty, and have no outgoing message.

Despite these precautions, voice mailbox hacking is relatively straightforward, and even changing passwords frequently will do nothing more than delay a hacker by forcing him or her to find a new mailbox to attack and take over. As a result, many companies simply ignore or tolerate this minor transgression. As long as the hackers don't mess up the voice mail system for legitimate users, it's often cheaper to simply pretend they don't exist on the system at all.

Hacking VoIP

Although the early tactics of phone phreakers no longer work on today's telephone systems, phone phreaking may soon regain popularity as telephone networks switch to VoIP (voice over Internet protocol), which transfers voice calls partially or entirely over the Internet. Whereas early phone phreakers could redirect phone calls through the telephone company's switches, VoIP phone phreakers will be able to access, intercept, and manipulate the actual voices, which are stored in data packets when they are transferred on phone calls across the Internet.

For example, programs like Vomit (http://vomit.xtdnet.nl), which stands for Voice Over Misconfigured Internet Telephones, or Cain & Abel (www.oxid.it) can snare data packets from a VoIP conversation and convert them to audio files so you can eavesdrop on VoIP phone calls, just like in the early days of the telephone system when teenage boys listened in on supposedly private phone calls. Of course, VoIP phone phreakers will likely follow the same path as their predecessors and end up not only listening to other people's phone calls, but disrupting them as well.

By accessing individual voice data packets, VoIP phone phreakers can inject their own data packets into a VoIP phone call, including profanity or other words that will change the nature of the call. For example, the speaker might say something as simple as "How are Madge and the kids?" but the person on the other end would hear the original sentence plus any profanity or other comments that the VoIP phone phreaker added. You can imagine the possibilities.

Inserting individual VoIP voice data packets into a conversation may be annoying, but more serious is that phone phreakers could block a valid phone call and replace it with a completely different one. The speaker thinks he's saying one thing but the listener hears something else. Since every VoIP call gets routed across the Internet through multiple computers, it's possible for hackers to break into a computer, intercept all VoIP phone calls, and modify the voice messages as they pass by.

By capturing voice data packets and editing them within an audio editing program, phone phreakers can fabricate entire messages and leave them on an unsuspecting victim's voice mail. The victim will hear what seems to be the voice of a trusted person, but the message may be something that the caller never said.

Caller ID spoofing, whereby VoIP phreakers can mask their true phone number and impersonate another phone number, is even simpler. Spoofing caller ID can trick people into answering telemarketer phone calls, or can make the phone line of identity thieves appear to come from a credible business or organization like eBay or the Red Cross.

By following the trail of data packets, VoIP phone phreakers could even trace a phone call from one person to another, which could come in handy for finding someone else's phone number. For example, if you were to tap into the VoIP phone of a known drug dealer, you could trace his calls to find the phone numbers of his suppliers (or contacts with corrupt police officers), or tap into a movie star agent's VoIP network to find the phone numbers of his clients (then eavesdrop on his phone calls and sell any juicy gossip to the entertainment tabloids, much like the reporter who recorded cell phone conversations between Tom Cruise and Nicole Kidman).

Just as email has allowed people to send spam for free, so will VoIP allow phone phreakers to hijack a VoIP network and flood it with *spam over Internet telephony (SPIT)*. So not only will people receive spam in their email accounts, but with VoIP, they'll also risk getting telemarketing calls to their voice mailboxes too.

Or, if phone phreakers simply want to annoy people, they can flood a network with bogus data, creating a *clipping* attack, which can disrupt or "clip" your phone calls so people can only hear every second or third word spoken. A more malicious phone phreaker might opt for *V-bombing*, which floods a voice mailbox to prevent someone from receiving valid messages.

In the old days, shutting down the entire telephone network of a major corporation, like Monsanto or Halliburton, used to require understanding of how the phone network worked. But with more corporations relying on VoIP phone networks, shutting down a phone system requires little more than a simple *denial of service (DoS)* attack that floods the network with more data than it can handle, effectively blocking all phone service along with other Internet transmissions. For a more subtle approach, phone phreakers could selectively block the ports used to make VoIP phone calls so that, while the rest of the phone system appears to work properly, certain people wouldn't be able to make calls or receive them.

Of course, phone phreakers aren't the only threat. Vonage, an early VoIP provider, has had its service disrupted by two broadband providers, Madison River and Clearwire, that saw its service as a potential competitor. Madison River blocked all Vonage VoIP calls until the Federal Communications Commission fined it $15,000. Clearwire also blocked Vonage VoIP calls, but Vonage simply developed technical workarounds to avoid the digital blockade.

This Vonage vs. Madison River/Clearwire battle isn't likely the only fight occurring between VoIP providers and Internet service providers. If phone phreakers want to get paid to hack the phone system, they might find the greatest demand for their services coming from broadband providers who want to "discourage" customers from switching to VoIP services in lieu of the broadband provider's own telephone services. VoIP has come under attack from governments that want to protect their monopolies over state-run telephone service, too. For example, Costa Rica's Instituto Costarricense de Electricidad (ICE) tried to regulate VoIP as part of its national telephone service, and other nations are likely to do the same.

Even the FBI sees VoIP as a threat. The agency claims, ironically, that it will be much harder to wiretap VoIP calls than traditional phone calls, and so VoIP could become a "haven for criminals, terrorists, and spies." (While computer security experts warn that VoIP is *more* prone to eavesdropping, the FBI claims just the opposite. Go figure.)

NOTE: *For more on VoIP security, visit Voice over IP Security Alliance at www .voipsa.org.*

As VoIP phone networks become more popular, their simplicity reduces our dependence on traditional landlines and cellular phone networks as well. After all, why pay for minutes on a cell phone calling plan when you can make that same phone call over a VoIP phone for a fixed monthly rate? Perhaps all the phone phreaking tricks previously done on cell phones will trickle down to mobile VoIP phones too.

Like cell phones, you can't trust VoIP to keep your conversation private or even connect you to the phone number you dialed. But at least your long-distance phone charges should decrease, which makes avoiding long-distance phone calling charges one of the few phone phreaking techniques that VoIP probably won't revitalize.

Perhaps the biggest threat to VoIP isn't protecting your privacy but in providing you with service in the first place. Unlike landline phone service that runs on a separate power grid, VoIP phone service depends on the Internet and computers to remain running. If a power outage occurs, through natural disasters or deliberate sabotage, guess what? A landline phone system may still work, but a VoIP phone system will be dead. With VoIP, the simplest denial of service attack you can do is simply finding a way to pull the plug.

3

HACKING PEOPLE, PLACES, AND THINGS

Hacking is more than just manipulating computers. As phone phreakers discovered in their quest to control the telephone system, hacking can be performed on anything, and as you'll soon see, people have been hacking in a variety of ways for years. Hacking involves studying a system to see how it works, playing with the system to see how to control it, and then manipulating the system to put it under your control.

Trust that little voice
in your head that says
"Wouldn't it be interesting
if. . . ." And then do it.

—DUANE MICHALS, artist

SOCIAL ENGINEERING: THE ART OF HACKING PEOPLE

Perhaps the oldest form of hacking is *social engineering*, which involves using people to get what you want. Unlike con games that steal money, social engineering steals information. But since social engineering victims are unaware that they have been tricked, they're often willing to help the same person who fooled them again and again. (Politicians are probably the ultimate social engineers.)

Say, for example, a hacker wants someone's password at a particular company. Rather than ask that person directly (which would probably fail), he might try a more easily manipulated source, such as a secretary. The hacker could deliberately foul up a computer at that company, then call the secretary (while masquerading as a technician), and ask if she has noticed any problems with the computer. When the secretary says yes, the "technician" claims that fixing the problem requires the (desired) password. More often than not, the secretary will give out this password and the "technician" will fix the very problem that he created in the first place. The computer problem "mysteriously" disappears and the secretary thinks that everything is now okay, not realizing that she has just given her boss's password to a hacker. The secretary suffers no loss, and the password's owner is unaware that it's been stolen.

Rather than go through another person, hackers might social engineer a target directly. For example, a hacker might discover the phone number to a corporate technical support line, then reroute those calls to herself. When the target finds that his computer is suddenly not working, he calls technical support. The hacker answers the line and asks for the target's password. Since the target initiated the call, he will likely supply any information requested just to get his computer working again. Once the target gives the hacker the password, the hacker "fixes" the computer, and the problem once again "mysteriously" disappears. The hacker has succeeded in obtaining the password, and the target never realizes that he gave it away.

Studying a target

Social engineering can be particularly effective for gathering bits of information a little at a time. While hackers could social engineer people without knowing anything about them, the company they work for, or the type of job they do, studying a target before trying to social engineer anyone will likely gather much more useful information.

One favorite tactic for researching a target is *dumpster diving*. As the name implies, this activity involves digging through a company's trash bins for valuable tidbits of information, such as out-of-date phone directories (which can provide names, phone numbers, and department names), business cards (which can match names with titles and departments), and handwritten notes (which can reveal passwords or current project names).

Dumpster diving helps a hacker plan the best way to launch an attack without the target ever being aware of the hacker's existence. However, in some cases, dumpster diving may not yield enough information. In those cases, hackers might take the riskier path of dressing up as janitors, temporary workers, or new employees and physically wandering around the premises, noting what they see and where equipment is located. If this surveillance takes place after hours or during lunch, hackers can even peek inside workers' desks and examine computers. With physical access, hackers can try to access a network from a trusted computer, or install a keystroke logging program to snare the users' passwords as they type them in (see Chapter 9 for more about these techniques).

Since visiting a targeted company in person may be too risky or impractical for some hackers (a 13-year-old is likely to have trouble masquerading as a temporary employee), hackers might call certain people either to get information from them or to discover the names of others who can provide the information.

When talking on the phone, hackers often disguise their voices and play different characters. Thus, a hacker might use multiple voices to call the same worker so the victim thinks she's providing information to a different person each time. (Few workers will be suspicious of ten different people calling for information, but the same person calling repeatedly would definitely arouse suspicion.)

Armed with one bit of personal information about a target, a hacker can often prowl the Internet and pick up additional bits of information about people, from their personal web pages, to their posted resumes on job-hunting sites like Monster.com, to their biography listed under a corporate web page. The more information a hacker gathers about a target, the more likely he'll appear "credible" and successfully social engineer the target out of valuable information.

Gaining familiarity

The key to social engineering is to gain the trust of others. This is often accomplished by acknowledging, rather than questioning, the target's position or authority and developing a rapport with the target. For example, hassled secretaries are unlikely to answer questions from a total stranger, but once the hacker develops a rapport with him or her (perhaps by making fun of his own boss in a way that the secretary might relate to), the hacker can erase any suspicions. This works especially well if the hacker can toss out the names of important people, projects, or procedures with the familiarity of someone who has worked at or with the company for several years.

Having established a rapport, the social engineer next asks the victim for help. Since helping others—especially someone perceived as trustworthy—can make people feel important, most victims of social engineering will willingly give the hacker the requested information. The victim doesn't feel like he or she is really losing anything; the hacker has only asked for information after all, not something tangible like money.

Hackers rarely ask for information point blank. Instead, they obfuscate their true purpose with casual requests for assistance and friendly small talk. For example, a hacker might complain to a secretary about the company's working conditions, casually mention that he's in building F (which anyone at the company would know is isolated from the rest of the company's buildings), then suddenly remark that he forgot his password back at his desk, which is way across the parking lot in another building. He may ask the victim if she knows another password that he could borrow for the moment. The victim will volunteer someone else's password or, more likely, just give her own. Either way, the hacker now has what he wanted.

At this point, the hacker could just hang up and yell, "SUCKER!!!!" However, he doesn't want to arouse suspicion, so he might chat a little more about the company and the people involved, and then complete whatever task he needed the password for in the first place.

Social engineering victims rarely learn that they've been victimized. Even if people later learn that someone broke into the computer network using a stolen password, the social engineering victim usually believes that he or she gave the password to help an employee rather than a hacker. As a result, the hacker can often victimize the same target repeatedly.

If you can be fooled by a magician's sleight of hand, you can be fooled by social engineering. In fact, chances are good that you have already fallen victim to social engineering and don't even know it.

The keys to social engineering

Social engineering works because it's a low-risk activity. If the hacker asks for a password and someone refuses or even gets suspicious, the hacker can just hang up and ask somebody else. No matter how suspicious targets may get, they'll never be able to find the hacker. Even if they go to the trouble of tracing the hacker's phone number, authorities can't arrest him or her because no crime has been committed. Even with the longest odds, given enough time, the hacker will always succeed.

Another reason that social engineering works so well is that it involves an indirect attack, which allows the hacker to avoid raising suspicion and cover his or her tracks. No one is likely to connect a computer break-in with three different phone calls made to three different people on three different days. You can't stop social engineering with a firewall, and given the large number of people in any company, it's not just possible that one person will fall victim to social engineering aren't just good; it's guaranteed.

Many large corporations now offer ongoing educational programs warning workers of common social engineering tactics. Still, no matter how many employees resist a social engineer, it only takes one to fall victim for the hacker to succeed.

PICKING LOCKS

Show a hacker a locked door and the first thing he wants to do is find out what's on the other side. Whether the door is hiding a janitor's closet, a half-constructed restroom, or a vault containing gold and jewelry is irrelevant. Hackers want to get to the other side, and a locked door just gets in their way. And, not surprisingly, many hackers are equally proficient at breaking into computers and picking physical locks.

Most physical locks succeed in preventing entry not because they're mechanically complicated, but because people don't know how they work. A locked screen door can stop a two-year-old baby just as effectively as a locked car door can defeat most adults, although a knowledgeable locksmith or car thief can unlock most car doors with a metal Slim Jim within seconds. Given their mindset, it shouldn't come as a surprise that hackers also enjoy picking locks.

The theory of lockpicking

There are several ways to pick a lock. At the crudest level, you could use brute-force and just keep smashing it with a hammer until it breaks open. At the other extreme, you could find an unexpected trick to open the lock, the way people discovered they could pick the Kryptonite Evolution 2000 U-Lock (www.kryptonitelock.com) by jamming the top of an ordinary ballpoint pen into its keyhole. (The company later corrected this glaring flaw, but not before considerable embarrassment; you can see a how-to video here: http://media .weblogsinc.com/common/videos/pt/lock.wmv.)

Of course, rather than attack a lock directly, it's often easier to attack the much weaker area around it. For example, while you could pick the lock on the anti–car theft device the Club, it's simpler to break the steering wheel, slide the Club off, and then drive the car away with a broken steering wheel, bypassing the security of the Club altogether.

Similarly, spring locks (such as those typically found guarding office doors) can often be picked by sliding a credit card or other thin tool to push the latch open without bothering to pick the lock open at all.

To pick a lock, you must first understand how that particular lock works. Although there are many different types of lock designs, the most common is a pin-and-tumbler design, as shown in Figure 3-1.

This design holds a lock shut using five or six pins, with each pin split into two halves. Springs push both halves of the pins downward to prevent the plug from turning. When you insert a key into the plug, the jagged ridges of the key push up each pin so that the breaks in each pin lie flush with the top of the plug. Once all of the pin halves are aligned, you can turn the plug to open the lock. So to pick a pin-and-tumbler lock you push up all the pins, and hold them in place until you can turn the plug.

The tools and techniques

Two common lockpicking tools are the *pick* and the *tension wrench*. The pick (shown in Figure 3-2) looks like a dentist's tool. The tension wrench can be as simple as a flathead screwdriver and is used to turn the plug once all the pin breaks are aligned with the plug.

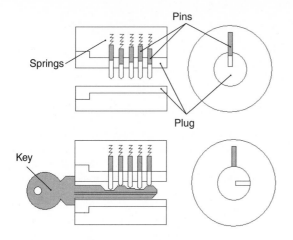

Figure 3-1: A pin-and-tumbler design uses pins that drop down to hold
a lock in place.

To pick a lock, you use the pick to push up each pin until the break between its
two halves is flush with the plug. If a pin isn't held in place, it will fall back down, so
lockpickers twist the plug slightly to one side to create a ridge. Once the lockpicker has
pushed the halves of a single pin flush with the plug, a slight twist pushes the pin side-
ways so that, instead of falling back in place (and locking), the tip of the pin half rests on
the ridge of the twisted plug as shown in Figure 3-2.

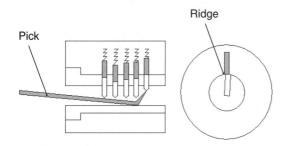

Figure 3-2: A pick pushes up each pin so that it rests on the edge (or ridge)
of the plug.

The lockpicker repeats this step for each pin until one half of each pin lies on the
slight ridge created by twisting the plug to one side. Once this is achieved, the lockpicker
twists the tension wrench to mimic a key and opens the lock.

While simple in concept, it takes practice to pick a lock, and it's tricky to feel (or
hear) when each pin is properly positioned. Lockpickers sometimes use a faster technique called *raking*, in which they twist the plug while they brush or rake a pick under the
pins to push them all up in one quick motion. This usually results in pushing one or more
pin halves up to rest on the ridge of the plug, at which point the lockpicker needs to push
up only the remaining pins individually to open the lock.

Experienced lockpickers often carry a variety of different size picks for different types of locks. Some use an electric pick gun, which vibrates to push up the pins as the plug is twisted.

You can buy lockpicking books and tools from a variety of websites, one of which is shown in Figure 3-3. As with computer hacking, picking locks isn't a crime, but you should use your skills wisely.

Figure 3-3: You can buy lockpicking tools and instruction books online.

For more information about lockpicking, read the alt.locksmithing FAQ at www .indra.com/archives/alt-locksmithing. To learn about other ways to pick locks, such as lock bumping, read the Bumping Locks file at www.toool.nl/bumping.pdf.

EXPLORING URBAN AREAS

Rather than pay to visit an amusement park and absorb its sanitized experiences, many hackers prefer the excitement and unpredictability of exploring the buildings around them for free. Urban explorers often tour abandoned buildings for their historical value (shut-down subway tunnels, empty factories, boarded-up hotels, or abandoned missile silos). They also enjoy prowling around buildings currently in use, such as utility tunnels beneath a convention center, the roofs of warehouses, or construction sites. If the general public would normally never see it, the urban explorer wants to be there.

Although the idea of crawling through an old sewage pipe or wading through stag-nant water in the bottom of an abandoned mine shaft might not sound appealing, it's no more uncomfortable than camping in a forest and enduring mosquito bites, bird drop-pings, and primitive toilet facilities (or spending five days a week in a sterile office cubicle, locked in a business suit, with eye-irritating fluorescent lighting, while counting the hours until your escape).

The urban explorer's goal is to wander and explore as a modern-day archaeologist, admiring the wonders around us. To learn more about the fine art of urban exploring, visit Infiltration Magazine (www.infiltration.org), as shown in Figure 3-4. This magazine provides urban exploring tips that range from the plainly practical (wear comfortable clothes and thick-soled shoes, and bring a flashlight) to the more obscure (grappling hooks can be handy for scaling buildings but impractical to hide if confronted by a security guard).

Figure 3-4: Infiltration Magazine offers plenty of stories and pictures to encourage you on the proper techniques for infiltrating urban areas.

The goal of urban exploration isn't to steal or deface anything, but simply to look around, even if that involves a little bit of trespassing. Sometimes this might require social engineering (to get past a security guard or to avoid arrest when confronted by one), a little bit of stamina (to climb stairs or crawl through holes in walls), and a lot of problem solving (to figure out how to cross an I-beam three stories up without falling so that you can escape from aggressive guard dogs).

Urban exploring can prove embarrassing (and useful) to governments. For example, the Russian urban exploring group Diggers of the Underground Planet once found a secret subway system under Moscow that Stalin reportedly had built to allow government authorities a quick escape from the city in an emergency. The acquired knowledge of these same urban explorers came in handy in October 2002, when Chechen rebels took over a Moscow theater and held more than 900 people hostage. Vadim Mikhailov of the Diggers of the Underground Planet led Russian authorities to the theater through a little-known underground route, of which neither the rebels nor the authorities were even aware.

Whether urban explorers want to see the employee lounge in the basement of a five-star hotel or map out the steam tunnels beneath a college campus, the goal is to have fun, see something cool that can be talked about later, and get back in one piece to do it again.

HACKING THE AIRWAVES

In the United States, the Federal Communications Commission (FCC)—www.fcc.gov—is a government agency that regulates interstate and international communications by radio, television, wire, satellite, and cable. You aren't allowed to broadcast anything unless you get FCC approval for a given frequency. Regulation can prevent equipment and radio signals from interfering with each other, but critics claim it also gives the FCC the power to deny ordinary people permission to broadcast information while granting the same right to corporations. Regulation of the airwaves can effectively translate into censorship, as demonstrated in countries such as China and Cuba.

To fight back against blatant censorship or corporate-regulated radio broadcasting, some people have created *pirate radio stations* to broadcast music, news, and information without their government's approval. Pirate radio stations often operate secretly (until the authorities shut them down) or semi-legally. A handful of British pirate radio stations once broadcasted from ships anchored just outside British territorial waters, thereby skirting British laws regulating broadcasting. (Of course, British law made it illegal for people to *listen* to these same pirate broadcasts, but at least the stations could operate with impunity.)

Radio stations along the borders of countries that regulate radio broadcasts often skirt the laws of the countries that receive their broadcasts. For example, Mexican radio stations routinely broadcast English-language programs at 250,000 watts, far in excess of the 50,000 watts allowed by FCC regulations. Then again, the United States has no qualms about breaking other countries' laws by broadcasting its Voice of America radio programs into Cuba, Vietnam, and China. As always, the legality of anything depends solely on what's being done and who's doing it, regardless of their reasons why.

Rather than hassle with bulky transmitters and run the risk of upsetting the authorities, many people are turning to their personal computers and audio files (typically MP3 files) to broadcast information they want to share. By sending streaming audio across the Internet, wannabe radio broadcasters can broadcast anything to the world without breaking any laws. (Of course, they may still be breaking the free speech laws of their government, but that's another story.) Figure 3-5 shows an advertisement for a program called Pirate Radio (www.pirateradio.com) that can broadcast your audio files around the world to anyone who cares to listen.

In fact, you can even turn an ordinary iPod into a pirate radio transmitter. iPod pirate radio broadcasters simply load up their iPod with audio files, attach a transmitter, and drive around with a bumper sticker advertising the frequency on which they're transmitting. Anyone can tune their car radios to this frequency and hear the iPod pirate radio broadcast—until the driver pulls too far away and the signal disappears.

Some popular iPod FM transmitters include iTrip (www.griffintechnology.com), TuneFM (www.belkin.com), and iRadio (www.ipodworld.co.uk).

Rather than broadcast on an unused frequency, some iPod pirate radio stations prefer to hijack a currently used frequency, such as that used by a local rap music station. When a car stops at an intersection with its windows rolled down and rap music blaring from its speakers, the nearby iPod pirate radio broadcaster simply fires up the music and hijacks the rap music station's frequency. Instead of hearing rap, the offending driver may now hear Barry Manilow, John Tesh, Yanni, or whatever other music the iPod owner decides to transmit blaring from his or her car speakers, instead.

Figure 3-5: With a personal computer and a program like Pirate Radio, anyone can broadcast audio information over the Internet.

Even simpler are *podcasts*, prerecorded MP3 audio files stored on a website that anyone can download and listen to at their convenience. Podcasts avoid government airwave regulations altogether (although they may also skirt government regulations about *content*). Podcast.net (www.podcast.net) organizes thousands of different audio programs by category and content.

Some popular commercial Windows programs for creating podcasts include ePodCastProducer (www.industrialaudiosoftware.com), RecorderPro (www.soniclear .com), and WebPodStudio (www.lionhardt.ca).

For the Macintosh, podcasting programs include CastEasy (www.casteasy.com) and RapidWeaver (www.realmacsoftware.com).

HACKING HISTORY (OR, HEMP FOR VICTORY)

Hacking is about discovering the truth, and nothing has distorted, warped, and twisted the truth so much as history, or rather the official and generally accepted version of history. There's a big difference between what really happened in the past and what authorities think or say (or wish) really happened. As a result, history, seemingly built on a rock-solid foundation of facts, actually consists of nothing more than selective facts mixed in with educated and not-so-educated guesses.

History is malleable and can be changed to suit a government's needs. If you're going to start thinking like a hacker, begin by questioning the biggest assumptions of all: what your schools, culture, teachers, parents, churches, and history books may tell you about the past.

The Japanese textbook controversy

The Japanese government has a problem. On one hand, they want to teach history to Japanese students, but on the other hand, they are less than enthusiastic about reporting what the Japanese government did to China, Korea, the United States, the Philippines, Thailand, and practically every other country they fought or conquered during World War II. After all, why would the Japanese government want to tell its schoolchildren that the Japanese imprisoned armies of Korean women to serve as sex slaves for Japanese soldiers? Or that its military beheaded, raped, and massacred thousands of Chinese civilians in the city of Nanking, to the point where a Nazi Party representative even appealed to Adolf Hitler to stop the atrocities?

NOTE: *To this day, the Japanese government refuses to acknowledge the atrocities in Nanking. Without knowing this little bit of trivia, you couldn't fully understand the nature of current Japanese and Chinese relations, which would probably place you at the same level of ignorance regarding Asian foreign affairs as the average American member of Congress.*

If a nation's citizens learn potentially troubling facts about previous administrations, could that undermine their confidence and faith in the current government? Perhaps, and that's what makes history textbooks so important in shaping the thinking of future generations. Richard H. Minear, a professor of Japanese history at the University of Massachusetts and the author of the books *Victor's Justice: The Tokyo War Crimes* and *Dr. Seuss Goes to War*, answers the question this way: "As a practicing historian, I encounter at every turn the power textbooks exercise over my students' minds . . . our students believe absolutely what they read in textbooks."

Fujioka Nobukatsu, a professor of education at Tokyo University, decided to "correct history" by emphasizing a "positive view" of Japan's past and removing any textbook references to what he calls "dark history." Fujioka formed the Japanese Society for History Textbook Reform (www.tsukurukai.com), which published *The New History Textbook*. This textbook ignited controversy in China, North and South Korea, and even in Japan itself with claims that the Japanese military tried to liberate Asia from Western colonization during World War II, as the following excerpt shows:

> When Japanese troops occupied in 1942, having defeated Dutch forces, Indonesians lined the roads and cheered. Japanese forces were a liberating army to rid them of the Dutch. During the occupation, which lasted three and a half years, the Japanese trained PETA, a military force, opened middle schools, and established a common language. The many reforms implemented served as a foundation for future independence. But when war neared its end and food was scarce, Japanese military police sometimes forced locals to do harsh labor, and were cruel to the local people in other ways as well.

Hiding history to protect the present

Rewritten history can not only reinterpret the past, but also erase it altogether. For example, in the March 2, 1998 issue of *Time*, then-President George Bush, Sr. and his National

Security Advisor Brent Scowcroft published an essay entitled "Why We Didn't Remove Saddam," which offered the President's justification for leaving Saddam Hussein in power after the first war in Iraq:

> *While we hoped that popular revolt or coup would topple Saddam, neither the U.S. nor the countries of the region wished to see the breakup of the Iraqi state. We were concerned about the long-term balance of power at the head of the Gulf. Trying to eliminate Saddam . . .would have incurred incalculable human and political costs. . . . We would have been forced to occupy Baghdad and, in effect, rule Iraq. The coalition would instantly have collapsed, the Arabs deserting it in anger and other allies pulling out as well. . . .Going in and occupying Iraq, thus unilaterally exceeding the U.N.'s mandate, would have destroyed the precedent of international response to aggression we hoped to establish. Had we gone the invasion route, the U.S. could conceivably still be an occupying power in a bitterly hostile land.*

However, as The Memory Hole (www.thememoryhole.org) reports, this essay has strangely disappeared from the magazine's own website. You can read the entire essay at The Memory Hole (www.thememoryhole.org/mil/bushsr-iraq.htm).

Why would *Time* completely erase all evidence of an essay that appeared within its own pages? Governments may be embarrassed by their past, but should a supposedly objective news magazine feel the same way too?

Watching movies for fun and propaganda

History often embarrasses people in the present, so it's only natural that authorities, like the fictional Oceania government depicted in George Orwell's novel *1984*, routinely rewrite history if it contradicts the current line of thinking. Fortunately, sites like the Prelinger Archives, located at the Internet Archive site (www.archive.org), preserve history as seen through films produced by various corporations and government agencies over the years.

These 1950s-era films are interesting, amusing, and often unintentionally hilarious, such as *Are You Popular?*, which teaches adolescents proper etiquette; *Duck and Cover*, which teaches children how to survive a nuclear war; and *Boys Beware*, which teaches teenage boys how to avoid potential sexual molesters. By watching these films, you can get an idea of how people used to live and think.

But perhaps more stunning are the various propaganda films that the American government produced against the Japanese (during World War II when the Chinese were our friends) and against the Chinese (during the Korean War when the Japanese were our friends). Paramount Pictures even created a Superman cartoon called *Eleventh Hour*, in which Superman sneaks into a Japanese World War II shipyard and sabotages the Japanese war effort. Government propaganda films will show you how the government demonized past enemies, just as they demonize today's enemies.

One of the oddest films was produced by the United States Department of Agriculture and was called *Hemp for Victory*. This movie extols the many benefits of hemp farming and claims that growing hemp will aid the war effort. Figure 3-6 shows images from the movie, including a government-issued tax stamp that proudly identifies certain farmers as patriotic hemp growers.

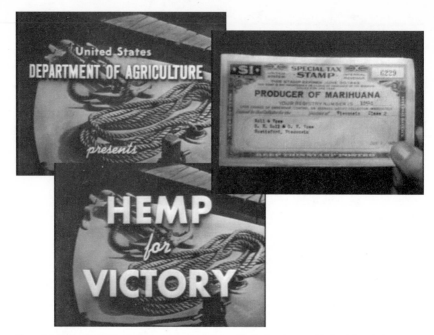

Figure 3-6: During World War II, the government encouraged hemp farming as patriotic, while today's government declares hemp farming illegal and immoral. Which government should you believe?

Watching old movies like *Hemp for Victory* makes you realize how any government's definition of "legality" can change over time. If yesterday's patriots would be today's criminals, might not today's patriots become tomorrow's criminals, as well? Just because something's legal today doesn't necessarily make it right.

Hackers always question authority and the rules (and laws) it creates. But questioning doesn't always mean rebelling or rejecting. Sometimes questioning can mean just reaching back through time and learning how certain laws originated in the first place. If you don't want to question the present by researching the past, you don't have to. Just keep following orders, and within the framework of today's laws, you'll be the upstanding citizen that your government always wanted you to be.

PART 2

THE PC PIONEERS

4

ANSI BOMBS AND VIRUSES

In the beginning, personal computers were physically isolated from one another. To share files, people had to copy data onto a floppy disk and then carry that floppy disk over to another computer. This method of sharing files, dubbed the *sneakernet* (since the data travels via foot power), made sharing information slow and tedious, but it also reduced the threat that malicious software, known as *malware*, could spread quickly, if at all.

Before the Internet, there were electronic bulletin board systems, also known as BBSs. A BBS consists of a single computer connected to one or more phone lines that allowed callers to connect, read and write messages, play games, or copy files. The number of users that could be on a BBS at any given time was limited by the number of phone lines physically connected to the BBS host computer. On some BBSs, only one user could be on at a time, while on others, dozens or even hundreds of users could be logged on simultaneously.

A BBS allowed people to share messages with each other, but the most popular BBS activity was sharing the latest freeware and shareware files. To encourage people to upload their own files, many BBSs enforced a strict upload-to-download ratio. For every two or three files you uploaded, you'd be entitled to download one in return. In this way, a BBS could constantly expand its file library.

Of course, with so many people sharing files, the inevitable happened: Malicious hackers abused the community honor system. Rather than uploading files that were exactly what they purported to be, they started planting malicious payloads that would catch other users unprepared and wipe out their data. Two of the earliest of these malware threats were ANSI bombs and computer viruses.

> I think computer viruses should count as life. I think it says something about human nature that the only form of life we have created so far is purely destructive. We've created life in our own image.
>
> –STEPHEN HAWKING

THE MAKING OF AN ANSI BOMB

Back in the heyday of the now-outmoded MS-DOS operating system, computers often booted up by loading a program called ANSI.SYS. This ANSI.SYS program was a special program called a device driver, which allowed a computer to display colors and fancy (for its time) graphics.

One function provided by the ANSI.SYS driver, which had unintended consequences, was to remap the keys on the keyboard. In its intended practical use, this allowed you to create keyboard macros, or shortcuts, such as launching a specific program whenever you pressed a function key. However, this also allowed malicious hackers to reprogram your computer to erase a file every time you pressed the E key.

How an ANSI bomb works

ANSI.SYS key-remapping commands consist of cryptic-looking text that specifies, using ANSI numeric codes, which keys to redefine. In the following two examples, the ANSI codes of 99 and 66 represent the letters *C* and *c* respectively:

```
ESC[99;"format c:";13p
```

```
ESC[66;"format c:";13p
```

In the above two commands, the keys for letters *C* and *c* are redefined to run the "`format c:`" command followed by the ENTER key (ANSI code number 13) when they are pressed. Naturally, the moment the computer tries to run the "`format c:`" command to reformat the hard disk, a message will appear and ask, "Do you really want to reformat drive C: (Y/N)?"

Most users would likely answer "No" by pressing either the n or N key. So the ANSI bomb also includes driver commands to redefine both the N (ANSI code 110) and the n keys (ANSI code 78) to represent the Y (ANSI code 121) and y keys (ANSI code 89):

```
ESC[110;121;13p
```

```
ESC[78;89;13p
```

Now when the user presses either the n or N key, the ANSI bomb actually gives the computer the y or Y response instead, which tells it to go ahead and format the entire hard disk.

Planting an ANSI bomb

To trick people into running an ANSI bomb, malicious hackers would often disguise them in innocent-looking batch files. Batch files are nothing more than text files containing one or more MS-DOS commands to run. With a batch file, the user needs only to type the batch file name to run a group of commands, rather than entering them in one by one at the MS-DOS command line.

Malicious hackers on a BBS would create an ANSI bomb using either an ordinary text editor or a specialized ANSI bomb–making program, as shown in Figure 4-1. They would either save the malicious code in a text file with a generic name, such as install.bat (commonly used for the batch files that install freeware or shareware) or insert it into the batch file used by some other popular shareware program. Then they would upload the rigged file to the BBS and its unsuspecting users. Unfortunately for these good citizens, they would thus run the ANSI bomb, which would redefine the keyboard and cause havoc on their machines.

More insidious ANSI bombs would copy themselves into the autoexec.bat batch file, which is the first batch file the computer runs when it boots up. The ANSI bomb would then load every time the user turned on the computer, and so cause problems over and over again.

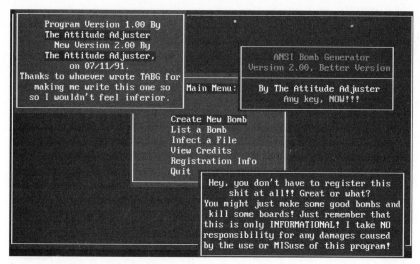

Figure 4-1: An ANSI bomb–making program can simplify the process of creating and planting an ANSI bomb.

Since few BBS users knew what ANSI bomb commands looked like, they often had no idea how to identify rigged batch files. Although ANSI bombs themselves are now largely obsolete since the introduction of Microsoft Windows, they do demonstrate a timeless and universal strategy used by malicious people: exploiting a victim's trust (the user's willingness to run programs downloaded from the BBS) and ignorance (disguising the ANSI bomb as a legitimate program).

THE SPREAD OF COMPUTER VIRUSES

The most common victims of ANSI bombs were the BBS operators themselves, who would eagerly run each new shareware program someone uploaded to their BBS just to test it out. However, after an ANSI bomb wiped out the files on the BBS host computer, it could at least be counted on not to spread to anyone else.

What malicious hackers needed was a program carrying a malicious payload that could hide within a trusted program and spread without relying on the victim running the rigged program. These hackers found their solution in *computer viruses*.

Like their biological counterparts, computer viruses survive by "infecting" a carrier, such as a file or a floppy disk. Once a virus infects a host, it relies on that host to spread it around. The three most common infection methods are:

- Infecting program files

- Infecting the boot sectors of floppy disks

- Infecting documents using the macro capabilities of a word processor or spreadsheet (a method that's still practical today)

Spreading a file-infecting virus

In the old days, programs used to fit on a single floppy disk. If you wanted to play a video game or run an application like WordPerfect or Microsoft Excel, you could ask a friend to copy the program to a floppy disk and hand it to you. As a result, one of the earliest forms of virus infection involved programs shared via floppy disk.

File-infecting viruses still exist, but they can only spread if someone transfers an infected program file over the Internet or via an infected CD/DVD. However, most programs nowadays consist of several files, so rather than copy individual program files off a hard disk, most people just copy the program's original installation CD/DVD. Unless a virus can infect this original installation CD/DVD, it won't be able to spread this way, and as a result, this method of infection poses little threat in today's computing environment.

Parasitic program infectors

When a virus infects a file, it has three choices: It can insert itself at the front, the back, or in the middle of the file. A virus that plants itself in the middle of a file by deleting part of the file it's infecting is known as an *overwriting virus*.

When a virus attaches itself to the front or back of a file, it changes the file's size and usually doesn't harm the infected file. Such parasitic viruses don't alter the infected program, so a user can run programs plagued with such viruses without even noticing the infection. The vulnerability of this mode of infection is that a parasitic virus can easily be spotted by the change it causes in the infected program's file size.

Overwriting file infectors

Overwriting viruses attempt to mask their presence by physically replacing some of the infected program file's code with the virus code. The infected program's file size won't change (which would be a dead giveaway that the file may be infected), but the host program won't work while the virus runs and tries to infect other program files. Since overwriting viruses destroy the host program, few victims are likely to share the infected host program with other users. So, while overwriting viruses harm the victim's computer more seriously than parasitic viruses do, they're also less likely to spread to other machines.

Spreading a boot-sector virus

Boot-sector viruses infect the boot sector of a disk, which tells the computer how to use that particular disk. A boot-sector virus spreads whenever you boot from or access an infected hard drive or removable disk (such as a floppy or CD).

At one time, boot-sector viruses were the most common type of infection, but as fewer people share floppy disks nowadays, they have become much more rare. Back when people used floppy disks to transfer files from one computer to another, they would often leave the disk behind in the floppy drive. When someone turned on a computer with an inserted floppy disk, it would first try to boot up from the floppy disk. If the floppy disk was infected with a boot-sector virus, that virus would then infect the hard disk or lurk in memory so it could infect any other floppy disks inserted into the computer. Boot-sector viruses thus typically spread through the sharing of infected floppy disks, although it's still possible nowadays for a boot-sector virus to spread by infecting bootable CDs.

Spreading a multipartite virus

Both file infectors and boot-sector viruses have their strengths and weaknesses. File-infecting viruses can only spread if the user runs the infected program. If the virus happens to infect a seldom-used file, the virus may never spread and do its damage.

Similarly, boot sector viruses spread only when a computer boots up from an infected floppy or hard disk. To increase their chances of spreading, some viruses combine the features of both file infectors and boot-sector viruses. These are called *multipartite viruses* and can infect either (or both) files and boot sectors. Although this increases their chances of spreading themselves, multipartite viruses are also more vulnerable to detection because of their increased size and susceptibility to antivirus programs. They're also more complicated to write, and with fewer people sharing (or even using) floppy disks anymore, file, boot-sector, and multipartite viruses are quickly fading into obscurity. Your computer can still get infected by these nasty viruses, but the odds are getting slimmer every day.

Spreading a macro virus

Macro viruses only infect files created by a specific program, such as documents created in Microsoft Word or spreadsheets created in Microsoft Excel. When you load an infected document, the macro virus tries to spread to any similar documents stored on your computer. Since so many people use Microsoft Word, the most common macro viruses target Word documents, although a handful of macro viruses also target Excel and Microsoft PowerPoint files too.

Unlike other types of viruses that are written using programming languages such as assembly language, C/C++, BASIC, or Pascal, macro viruses are written using the macro programming language specific to its target application. Most macro viruses are written using Microsoft's macro language, called Visual Basic for Applications (VBA), although a few are written in WordBasic, an older macro programming language for Microsoft Word.

Word-processing macro viruses infect the template files that define the margins, font, and general formatting for every document created by a particular word processor. Try to create a new document from a template infected by a macro virus, and the macro virus will then attempt to infect another template.

Because most people share documents rather than templates, macro viruses cleverly convert infected documents into template files, while maintaining the appearance of an ordinary document file. So, you might think you're opening an ordinary document for editing, when you're actually opening a template file instead.

Despite their prevalence in the wild, macro viruses tend to infect only documents created using Microsoft products such as Word, Excel, and PowerPoint. Some people have tried writing macro viruses to infect WordPro or WordPerfect documents, but those documents store their macros in a separate file and thus are less fertile ground for spreading viruses. (Not to mention, far fewer people use WordPro and WordPerfect compared to Microsoft Word.) In contrast, when you copy a Word or Excel document file onto a floppy disk, through a network, or over the Internet, you're automatically copying both your document and any macros it contains in a single file, which gives the macro virus a chance to spread.

To minimize the threat of macro viruses, Microsoft Word 2003 offers a special macro security feature that you can access by choosing Tools ▸ Macro ▸ Security to display a Security dialog box as shown in Figure 4-2. Then click the Very High or High radio buttons to limit the ability for macro viruses to run.

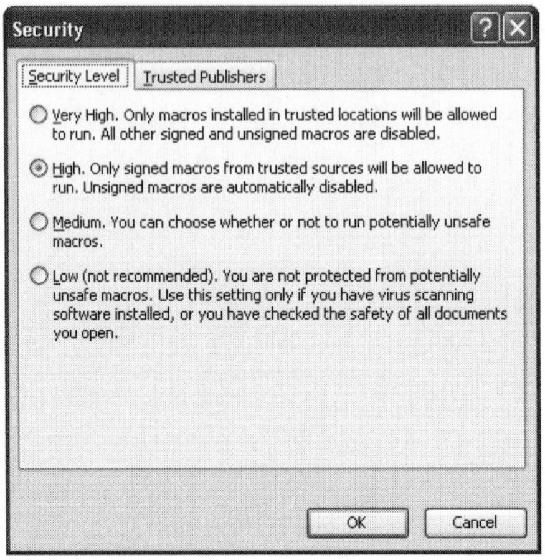

Figure 4-2: Microsoft Word 2003 offers some protection from macro viruses.

Microsoft Office 2007 goes even further in eliminating macro viruses by changing the file format of Office files themselves. While this won't stop someone from writing new macro viruses specifically for Microsoft Office 2007 files, it prevents the majority of existing macro viruses from infecting Office 2007 files.

HOW VIRUSES AVOID DETECTION

Viruses can survive only if they remain undetected long enough to spread to other computers. Virus programmers have used a variety of tactics to increase a virus's longevity.

Infection methods

Antivirus programs can spot a virus in one of two ways. First, an antivirus program may recognize a particular virus's signature, which is nothing more than the specific instructions embedded in the virus program that tell it how to behave and act. A virus's signature is like a criminal's fingerprint—each one is unique and distinct.

A second way an antivirus program can detect a virus is by its behavior. Antivirus programs can often detect the presence of a previously unknown virus by noticing when it tries to infect another file or disk, which is called heuristic analysis or detection.

To sneak past an antivirus program, viruses may employ a variety of proliferation methods:

Direct infection   The virus infects a disk or additional files each time the user runs the infected program or opens the infected document. If the user doesn't do either of those things, the virus can't spread. This is the simplest but also the most noticeable way of infecting a computer and can be detected by antivirus programs fairly easily.

Fast infection   The virus infects any file accessed by an infected program. For example, if a virus infects your antivirus program, watch out! Each time an infected antivirus program examines a file, it can actually infect that file immediately after certifying that it is virus-free.

Slow infection   The virus only infects newly created files or files modified by a legitimate program. By doing this, viruses attempt to mask their presence more thoroughly from antivirus programs. For example, antivirus programs often watch for a program trying to modify a file it typically should not be accessing. If you run Windows Explorer and click a file to rename it, your antivirus program won't raise an alarm, since Windows Explorer is allowed to modify files. But if a virus infects Windows Explorer, renaming a file could cause it to become infected at the same time.

Sparse infection   This type of virus takes its time infecting files and does so arbitrarily. By spreading slowly and unpredictably, these viruses reduce the odds that their activities (but not necessarily their existence) will be detected.

RAM-resident infection   This type of virus buries itself in your computer's working memory (RAM), and each time you run a program or insert a floppy disk, the virus infects that program or disk. RAM-resident infection is the only way that boot-sector viruses can spread, since the victim must physically insert an infected floppy disk into his computer.

Stealth

Viruses normally reveal their presence during infection by changing the size, time, and date stamps of the files that they infect. However, file-infecting viruses that use stealth techniques may accomplish their dirty work without causing any of those modifications, thus remaining hidden and undetected.

Boot-sector viruses always use stealth techniques. When the computer reads a disk's boot sector, the virus quickly loads a copy of the real boot sector (which it has safely stashed away in another location on the disk). This is like using call forwarding to answer the phone from the neighborhood pool hall when your parents call you at home to make sure you're behaving yourself. As far as your parents are concerned, they called your home number and you answered. All's well at home, or so they think. Boot-sector viruses use similar stealth techniques to hide their presence from the computer. But that doesn't always fool good antivirus programs. To slip past them, viruses may use polymorphism.

Polymorphism

If criminals could modify their fingerprints each time they committed a crime, they would be harder to catch. That's the idea behind polymorphism. A *polymorphic virus* changes its signature—the set of instructions that makes up that virus—each time it infects a file. Theoretically, this means that an antivirus program can never find it.

However, because viruses need to make sure they don't infect the same file over and over again, and thus reveal themselves by consuming disk space, a polymorphic virus must still leave a small, stable, and distinct signature that it (or an antivirus program) can find. Of course, once the virus has been caught and examined—by an antivirus software vendor, for example—antivirus programs can find these same signatures. That's why antivirus programs need constant and frequent updates to recognize the latest viruses.

Retaliators

The best defense is a good offense. Rather than passively hiding from antivirus programs, many viruses actively search them out and attack them. These retaliating viruses either modify the antivirus program so that it can't detect the virus, or they infect the antivirus program itself and make it complicit in spreading the virus. In both cases, the attacked antivirus program cheerfully displays a "Your computer is virus-free" message while the virus is happily spreading throughout your computer.

HOW ANTIVIRUS PROGRAMS WORK

An antivirus program serves two purposes: one, to detect and remove any viruses currently on your computer, and two, to prevent any viruses from infecting your computer in the first place. To detect and remove viruses, antivirus programs rely on a database of virus signatures. Your antivirus program scans every file on your hard disk, looking for instances of these virus signatures. For additional protection, many antivirus programs will also scan any email you send or receive.

You have to be diligent about keeping your antivirus program updated with the very latest library of known virus signatures, however, or newly discovered threats may not be detected during the scan. For this reason, antivirus programs can never be 100 percent effective against viruses. To scan for the signature of a virus, the vendor of the antivirus software must first get a copy of the virus and dissect it to figure out how it works. Then the vendor can update the signature database so that its antivirus program will recognize and remove that particular virus.

Since scanning for virus signatures can never protect against unknown viruses, antivirus programs also use something called heuristic analysis, which involves monitoring for suspicious behavior, such as a program suddenly trying to modify another file. The moment heuristic analysis detects suspicious activity, it can warn you to stop the suspicious program from running.

Comparing antivirus programs

Antivirus programs are only as effective as their virus signature databases. Since it's impossible for one company to find and dissect every new virus that appears, antivirus companies cooperate with one another. The moment one antivirus company makes a new discovery, it shares the information with its rivals (although not always as quickly as those rivals might like, thus giving its own product a chance to catch one more virus than a competing product). This arrangement helps all antivirus companies keep their programs up to date.

Even though antivirus companies share information, each must still provide its own customers a way to update their antivirus programs to catch the latest threats. Because companies update their signature databases on differing schedules, even the most recent versions of different antivirus programs can vary in terms of detecting and eliminating viruses from their customers' computers. So, at any given time, one antivirus program will detect more viruses than another, although this usually changes within days. As a result, there isn't a "best" antivirus program that can claim to catch all viruses or that can consistently catch more viruses than any of its competitors. The best antivirus program is simply the one that you like and find most convenient to use. (To learn more about which antivirus programs are good at catching the latest batch of viruses, visit the Virus Bulletin site at www.virusbtn.com.)

Choosing an antivirus program

Since no antivirus program can catch 100 percent of all viruses all the time, it's best to run two at a time. But that can get expensive. Here's a cheaper option.

First, use a free online virus scanner, as shown in Figure 4-3, such as one of the following:

Trend Micro's Housecall	http://housecall.trendmicro.com/housecall
Panda's Active Scan	www.pandasoftware.com/products/activescan.htm
RAV AntiVirus Online Virus Scan	www.ravantivirus.com/scan
BitDefender Online Scanner	www.bitdefender.com/scan8/ie.html

Second, get an antivirus program that can automatically scan your computer for viruses and block any suspicious behavior. While there are plenty of commercial antivirus programs, three free ones (for personal use only) include:

AntiVir	www.free-av.com
AVG Anti-Virus	www.grisoft.com
Avast Antivirus	www.avast.com

For completely free, open-source antivirus programs, visit:

Clam AntiVirus	www.clamav.net
Open AntiVirus Project	www.openantivirus.org

Figure 4-3: Online scanners can detect viruses on your computer, but cannot stop them from infecting your computer.

Combining a free antivirus program with periodic checkups by a free online virus scanner can protect your computer at no extra cost to you. After all, it's not your fault that viruses attack Windows so often, so why should you spend additional money?

If you use a Macintosh or Linux computer, your threat of viruses is both much less and much greater. Currently, there are only a handful of viruses that infect Macintosh and Linux computers, so the number of existing viruses that could attack a Macintosh or Linux computer is relatively small. However, since so few Macintosh and Linux users worry about viruses, few people own, let alone use, Macintosh or Linux antivirus programs. The moment someone invents a new way to infect and spread a virus among Macintosh or Linux users, it will likely spread rapidly among many defenseless computers. The bottom line is that if you don't have an antivirus program, you will get infected eventually, no matter what type of computer and operating system you use.

Technically speaking, the biggest threats no longer come from viruses but from *worms* and *spyware*. Worms are essentially viruses that can spread by themselves, and spyware programs track your Internet behavior or retrieve information from your computer and send it elsewhere without your knowledge. (You'll learn more about worms in Chapter 5 and spyware in Chapter 20.) Because of these new threats, most antivirus programs scan not only for viruses, but for worms and spyware as well.

WHY PEOPLE WRITE VIRUSES

Viruses are just computer programs that someone has taken the time to write and test, so people might wonder—why would anyone do something destructive and harmful to someone they don't know and will likely never see? Basically, some people write viruses for the same reasons that other people spray graffiti on buildings, smash car windows, or throw rocks from overpasses. The reason why people do any of these things is because they can, and because they can often get away with doing it.

For fun

Many people write computer viruses just to see if they can do it.

Virus writing requires detailed knowledge of a specific operating system, so for many programmers, writing a virus was a way to test and prove their knowledge. Many of these early viruses were designed more as proof of concept than as deliberate attempts to sabotage other people's computers.

Reflecting their creators' spirit of curiosity and lack of malice, these early viruses often did nothing more than play a constant beep through the computer's speaker or reprogram the keyboard to generate a question mark or other symbol every time the E key was pressed. Annoying, to be sure, but ultimately harmless.

Some viruses even got playful and displayed a graphic image on the screen, such as an ambulance or a man strolling across the bottom of the screen. One playful virus would randomly display the message, "I want a cookie," on the screen. The only way to make the message go away was to type **cookie**. Other viruses displayed political or humorous messages, as shown in Figure 4-4.

Figure 4-4: The Monopoly virus pokes fun at Bill Gates and his monopoly on the operating system market.

For notoriety

Although people write and release viruses every day, the large majority of viruses fail to spread due to poor programming. Many virus writers want the notoriety of creating viruses that spread faster and cause the greatest amount of damage possible. If a virus writer could panic an entire nation and get his virus reported by name in *USA Today* or on CNN, his reputation would soar in the underground virus community.

So malicious virus writers developed ever trickier tactics for slipping past antivirus programs and spreading as quickly as possible. Their ultimate goal is to create a virus that would become a household name, like the Michelangelo, Melissa, Chernobyl, and I Love You viruses. Although these virus writers could never publicly bask in the notoriety of their creations, they could still gain some measure of fame among their underground hacker friends.

Many virus writers even banded together and formed their own virus-writing groups with names like Amateur Virus Creation & Research Group (AVCR), Corrupted Programming International (CPI), Phalcon/Skism, and Youngsters Against McAfee (YAM). These groups often published their own newsletters, with names like 40Hex, The Crypt Newsletter, and VLAD (Virus Labs and Distribution) Magazine, that explained how their latest virus creations worked. Virus-writing groups typically ran their own BBSs or websites, stocked with live viruses that others could download and run. The more newsletters they published and the more viruses they spread, the greater the notoriety the group could gain.

Fewer virus-writing groups exist today, partly because worms spread more quickly and easily, partly because virus writers never profit from their creations, and partly because government authorities are getting more adept at identifying and tracking down virus writers, such as the 1999 arrest of David L. Smith, accused of writing and spreading the Melissa virus. Instead, many virus programmers today find it's more profitable to work for companies that make spyware.

FINDING VIRUS-WRITING TUTORIALS

Although most virus-writing tutorials are now obsolete, they can still be fascinating to read to get a flavor of how members of the virus-writing underground used to brag and boast about their accomplishments and share new ideas with each other. To find a collection of these historical virus-writing tutorials and newsletters, visit TextFiles (www.textfiles.com) or Sirkus (www.sirkussystem.com).

American Eagle Publications (www.ameaglepubs.com) even offers PDF versions of early virus-writing tutorials it once published, including *The Little Black Book of Computer Viruses* (shown in Figure 4-5), *The Giant Black Book of Computer Viruses*, and *Computer Viruses, Artificial Life and Evolution*. By reading these tutorials, you'll see how virus writers carefully crafted viruses from scratch using assembly language.

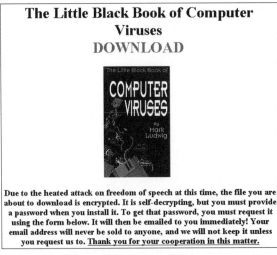

Figure 4-5: *The Little Black Book of Computer Viruses* provides step-by-step instructions for creating different types of viruses in assembly language.

VIRUS-WRITING TOOLKITS

In addition to spreading their notoriety through newsletters and new viruses, a handful of virus groups also created virus-writing toolkits. These toolkits often sported fancy pull-down menus and modern graphical user interfaces to make virus writing as simple as clicking the features you wanted from a menu and then waiting for the toolkit to create your custom virus for you.

One of the earliest virus-writing toolkits was called the Dark Avenger Mutation Engine (MtE). Virus writers could link their creations to MtE, which would mutate the virus's signature, turning an ordinary virus into a polymorphic one. Theoretically, MtE would make functionally identical copies of the same virus appear different from one another, making it impossible for antivirus scanners to detect the virus based on its signature. In practice, however, MtE proved difficult to use and couldn't completely mask a virus's signature, so few virus writers actually created viruses using MtE.

As the first mutation engine, MtE achieved notoriety solely for originating the idea of polymorphic viruses. While MtE never unleashed the flood of undetectable viruses that people originally feared, it did inspire other virus programmers to create toolkits of their own that could be, and were, used to generate viruses easily.

Following the introduction of MtE, other virus writers created similar mutation engines with names like TridenT Polymorphic Engine (TPE) and Dark Angel's Multiple Encryptor (DAME). Like MtE, these other mutation engines had various degrees of success in creating viruses, although none lived up to its original promise of altering a virus completely to avoid detection. Viruses were hard enough to create in the first place, and few virus writers bothered taking the additional time to link their viruses to a buggy, hard-to-use mutation engine.

However, as virus writers studied these later mutation engines, they adopted the ideas and programming techniques for use in their own viruses. So while mutation engines never succeeded in their original goal, they indirectly inspired virus writers to create viruses that were harder for antivirus programs to detect.

The next step in the evolution was the full-fledged virus-creation program. With user-friendly pull-down menus and interfaces, these programs let wannabe virus writers pick and choose the features they wanted, and the virus creation program would create it for them automatically. One of the first virus-creation programs was the Virus Creation Laboratory, shown in Figure 4-6.

Around this time, virus writers focused less attention on devising more dangerous viruses and concentrated more on developing their own virus-writing toolkits, which they eagerly shared with others. Figure 4-7 shows a list of typical virus-writing toolkits that you can still find today being traded on various hacker websites.

Theoretically, virus-creation toolkits would allow anyone to make their own viruses. In reality, they created viruses that either didn't work or were easily detected, so they could not cause much damage. Despite the attempts to automate production, virus-writing toolkits didn't made virus writing easier, nor did they flood the world with undetectable viruses as originally feared. If you want to write a virus, you still have to learn a programming language and understand the weaknesses of a particular operating system, and this effectively limits the art of virus writing to a handful of skilled souls interested in developing something destructive for no other reward than anonymous fame.

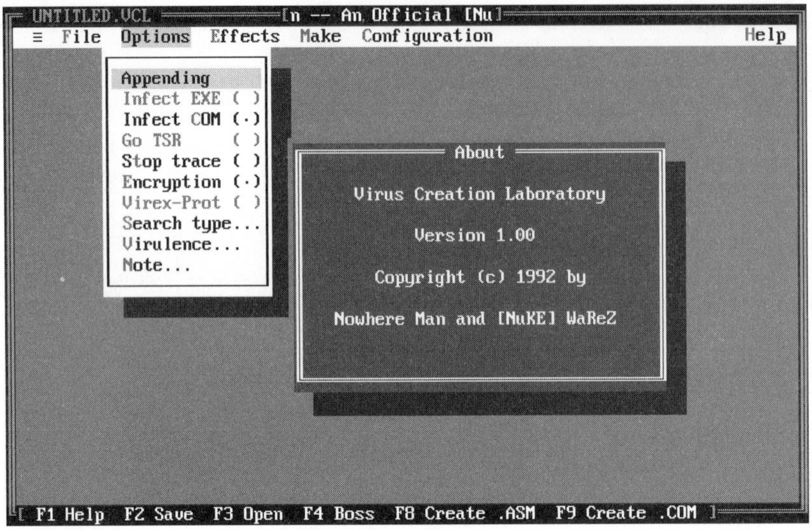

```
┌─ UNTITLED.VCL ══════════════ [n -- An Official [Nu]═══════════════════┐
│  ≡  File  Options  Effects  Make  Configuration              Help     │
│      ┌────────────────┐                                               │
│      │ Appending      │                                               │
│      │ Infect EXE  ( ) │                                              │
│      │ Infect COM  (·) │                                              │
│      │ Go TSR      ( ) │        ┌══════ About ══════┐                 │
│      │ Stop trace  ( ) │        │                   │                 │
│      │ Encryption  (·) │        │ Virus Creation Laboratory          │
│      │ Virex-Prot  ( ) │        │                   │                 │
│      │ Search type... │        │    Version 1.00    │                │
│      │ Virulence...   │        │                   │                 │
│      │ Note...        │        │  Copyright (c) 1992 by             │
│      └────────────────┘        │                   │                 │
│                                │ Nowhere Man and [NuKE] WaReZ        │
│                                └───────────────────┘                 │
│                                                                       │
│ [ F1 Help  F2 Save  F3 Open  F4 Boss  F8 Create .ASM  F9 Create .COM ]│
└───────────────────────────────────────────────────────────────────────┘
```

Figure 4-6: The Virus Creation Laboratory offered pull-down menus to make custom viruses quickly.

VIRUS MYTHS AND HOAXES

Since each new outbreak of a virus causes hysteria and panic among computer users, you can cause nearly as much trouble by inventing a fictional virus as you can by creating a real one. You can learn about the latest virus hoaxes on the Vmyths.com website (www.vmyths.com). The following are examples of typical virus hoaxes. Notice that in each case, the trickster uses potentially confusing technical language and establishes his credibility by associating himself with a trusted and well-known organization.

The mobile phone virus hoax

Among the more disruptive virus hoaxes are those that encourage you to email copies of warnings to your friends. To convince people of their legitimacy, these virus hoaxes often present information that sounds valid and threatening, but is actually useless and completely wrong. Often the hoax is based on a real event, which is a reliable way of inciting panic in an unsuspecting email recipient.

One example is the ICE phone virus hoax, which occurred after a legitimate organization dubbed In Case of Emergency (ICE)—www.icecontact.com—suggested that people make an entry in the directory of their mobile phones containing the name and phone number of someone to be contacted in an emergency, accessed by the letters *ICE*.

Pranksters seized the opportunity. They created and spread the ICE hoax by circulating the following text:

WARNING - ICE IS PHONE BASED VIRUS, SEE BELOW!! Be very careful with this one - although the intention is great it is unfortunately phase one of a phone based virus that is laying a path for propagating very quickly.

Passing it on is part of the virus interestingly, such is the deviousness of the people who write these things. We have already seen the "second phase" where a program is sent as part of a ring-tone download that goes into your address book and looks for something it recognises - you've guessed it, an address book entry marked "ICE or I.C.E." or whatever. It then sends itself to the ICE list, charging you for the privilege.

This hoax takes advantage of the fear of viruses and the introduction of viruses and Trojan horses specifically designed to infect mobile phones, such as RedBrowser, a Trojan horse that sneaks on to mobile phones and then makes calls to Russia, charging the user $5 a call. However, remember that real virus and Trojan horse news appear on legitimate security websites like Symantec or Trend Micro and not through unsolicited email messages. After all, do you rely on email messages from a total stranger for the latest sports scores—let alone for true news?

Virus Creation Programs	
Wave Func's Goofy Batch Virus Generator v1.1c	This program makes batch viruses. Requires MS-DOS to function.
Virus Creation Laboratory v1.0	Belongs to those very popular virus creation programs. Nowhere Man's V.C.L. is a potentially dangerous program, and great care should be using when experimenting with *any* virii, trojans, or logic bombs produced by it.
Nuke GenVirus	Needs MS-DOS to work.
IVP - Instant Virus Production Kit v1.7	Requires MS-DOS v6.0 or higher.
Macro Virus Development Kit v1.0b	Macro Virus Development Kit is a tool which generates macro viruses for Microsoft Winword, according to user specifications.
NRLG - Nuke Randomic Life Generator v0.66b	Generates resident viruses.
Rajaat's Tiny Flexible Mutator v1.1	RTFM is an object module that can be linked to your virus to make it impossible for a scanner to use a simple string. It will encrypt your virus and generates a random decryptor using random registers and random instructions. Therefore, an algorithmic approach will be needed to detect viruses using this object module.
G2 Phalcon/Skism's	Requires MS-DOS v6.0 or higher.
The Super Appending Batch VCK v1.1k	This program generates replicating appending batch virus programs from user-specified parameters. Needs MS-DOS v6.0 or higher.
SkamWerks Labs	This program generates macro viruses for MS Word v6.0.
Trojan Horse Construction Kit v2.0	Simple trojan horse toolkit. Requires MS-DOS v6.0 or higher.
The Simple WinScript Virus Kit v1.1k	VBS WinScript virus construction toolkit.

Figure 4-7: Virus writers soon flooded the hacker underground with virus-writing toolkits with different names and capabilities.

The nuclear war hoax

To give credibility to their hoax, many pranksters often quote trusted authorities, as in the following example, which claims that you can accidentally launch nuclear missiles through an errant email message:

> *Hey. I just got this in the mail, from Symantec, so I thought I'd forward it along. It's a new virus that we should watch out for. PLEASE FORWARD THIS TO EVERYONE YOU KNOW. THIS IS VERY IMPORTANT.*

> *Virus Update, 1/07/02*

> *Symantec Virus Alert Center*

> *Hello Subscriber, As part of our ongoing effort to keep Symantec clients up to date on virus alerts, this e-mail is being sent to all Symantec subscribers. A new, deadly type of virus has been detected in the wild. You should not open any message entitled "LAUNCH NUCLEAR STRIKE NOW," as this message has been programmed to access NORAD computers in Colorado and launch a full-scale nuclear strike on Russia and the former Soviet states. Apparently, a disgruntled ex-Communist hacker has designed a pernicious vb-script that actually bypasses the U.S. arsenal's significant security system and takes command of missiles and bombers directly. By opening the e-mail, you may be causing Armageddon. Needless to say, Armageddon will wipe out your hard drive and damage your computer. Again, we warn you, PLEASE, DO NOT OPEN ANY E-MAIL ENTITLED "LAUNCH NUCLEAR STRIKE NOW." YOU MAY CAUSE A FULL-SCALE NUCLEAR HOLOCAUST. As a precaution, all U.S. nuclear missiles have been set to "Do Not Authorize Launch Via E-mail" to prevent an accidental Armageddon. However, due to a Y2K bug, the possibility still exists that you may end life as we know it on this planet by opening the aforementioned e-mail.*

> *VIRUS NAME: ArmaGeddyLee, HappyOrMaybeNot00, OopsWrongButton00*

> *TRANSMITTAL METHOD: vb-script attached to e-mail*

> *HAZARD: Extremely Super High*

> *AREA OF INFECTION: Detected in wild*

> *CHARACTERISTICS: Destroys life on earth via nuclear Armageddon*

> *Please forward this warning to everyone you can. Thank you for your attention to this matter,*

> *Sincerely,*

> *The Symantec Anti-Virus Team*

As ridiculous as this hoax sounds (would *any* country want to launch nuclear missiles via email?), the use of Symantec's name as a trustworthy source of virus information gives this hoax apparent credibility to the unquestioning. Such hoaxes could be stopped in their tracks if people would only verify the information before forwarding it. All it takes is a quick visit to Symantec's website to determine whether this warning is actually true.

The bait-and-switch virus hoax

Since most people don't understand how viruses work, any seemingly credible virus report will likely grab a lot of attention. To take advantage of this, a porn website once sent out email supposedly coming from "Dave Norton, VirusCenter@CNN.com" that contained the following text:

> CNN Brings you information on the new devistating computer virus known as the 'Lions Den' virus. This virus is reported to be costing internet providers such as AOL, MSN, Yahoo, and Earthlink millions of dollars due to loss of members.

The message then displayed a link that readers could follow to get details about the Lions Den virus and information on protecting their computer from it. Instead of going to the CNN site, however, the link would direct readers directly to the porn site. Once again, this type of hoax could be stopped if people would just verify the information before forwarding it to others.

The publicity-seeking virus hoax

In 2003, a computer security/hacking group named Gobbles Security released a statement claiming that the Recording Industry Association of America (RIAA) had contacted them to develop a computer worm that could spread through security vulnerabilities in several popular filesharing programs. The purported purpose of this worm was to disable the filesharing networks that are typically used to spread illegally copied MP3 music files.

Lending credibility to this hoax was the fact that many people believed that the RIAA actually would stoop to such illegal tactics in order to shut down the filesharing networks. Plus, Gobbles Security had been known to post legitimate security advisories in the past, and had even provided a sample program with their statement that showed how a computer worm could exploit such flaws in filesharing programs.

Ultimately, Gobbles Security admitted that their statement was a fake and that they only did it to generate publicity. This taught everyone that a hoax could catch even seasoned computer professionals unaware. Remember that no matter how trustworthy someone or something may have been in the past, they're always capable of lying to you now in their own interest. Treat all claims with skepticism, including everything you read in this book, and you should be all right.

LEARNING MORE ABOUT VIRUSES

To learn more about viruses (both real ones and hoaxes), visit one of the following websites:

AVP Virus Encyclopedia	www.avp.ch/avpve
F-Secure Security Information Center	www.f-secure.com/virus-info
Sophos	www.sophos.com/virusinfo

Symantec	www.symantec.com/avcenter
McAfee Security	http://us.mcafee.com/virusInfo
Trend Micro	www.trendmicro.com/vinfo

These websites list all known viruses (and virus hoaxes), their characteristics, what damage (if any) they cause, and how to detect them. To exchange messages about computer viruses, visit the comp.virus or alt.comp.virus Usenet newsgroups.

THE FUTURE VIRUS THREAT

As the computing environment changes, today's virus threats die off, only to be replaced by newer types of malware. With few people still using floppy disks, file-infecting and boot-sector viruses can no longer spread as easily. Similarly, as Microsoft changes the file format of its Office suite of products (Word, Excel, PowerPoint, and Access), macro viruses relying on the earlier versions will gradually lose their effectiveness too.

However, despite the decreasing threat from pure viruses, antivirus programs are still important to protect your computer against all types of malware, not just viruses. And to really be safe, you ultimately need to supply your own healthy dose of common sense and practice safe computing habits (such as not indiscriminately copying and running programs from untrusted sources).

5

TROJAN HORSES AND WORMS

Back in the '80s, a programmer named Bob Wallace started a software company based on a unique marketing scheme. Rather than force people to pay for software before using it and risk finding out later that it doesn't quite do what they expected, Wallace gave away his software for free. Under his rules, later dubbed *shareware*, anyone could freely and legally copy and share his program, a word processor called PC-Write. Users who went the extra step and registered the program for $75 not only got a printed manual and technical support, but they also got a $25 commission every time someone else also registered their copy of PC-Write. Naturally, users spread copies of their registered PC-Write program wherever they could, most commonly through BBS systems around the world.

With so many people sharing copies of PC-Write, the inevitable happened. In 1986, a malicious hacker wrote a Trojan horse and disguised it as a legitimate copy of PC-Write. When unsuspecting users tried to run the bogus copy of PC-Write, the Trojan horse would format their hard disk and erase all their files.

I do it for the pleasure of creating something, seeing that it works, and making something that could really survive, spread, and hold its own in the wild. A virus is something that lives. In real life you can't make a kind of animal. You can in the computer. It's like playing God.

—BLUE OWL, member of the Ready Rangers Liberation Front

THE WORLD OF TROJAN HORSES

Although this doctored-up version of PC-Write was one of the most prominent of the early IBM-PC Trojan horses, Trojan horses have been around since the first computers. One of the simplest and oldest types of Trojan horses is a password-stealing program. These are especially common on shared computers used by many different people, such as those in a school computer laboratory. Such computers typically require a user to type in a user name and password, so all a hacker had to do to steal someone's password was create a fake program that looked like the usual login screen. The fake login screen would store the information, return an error message, and then display the real login screen. The unsuspecting user would then retype his user name and password and gain access to the computer, never realizing that he'd actually fed his personal information to a password-stealing Trojan horse during that first login attempt.

Just like the ancient Greek ruse from which it derives its name, Trojan horse programs rely on trickery. Trojan horses usually run only once, but that is enough to wipe out files, steal passwords, or cause other types of damage. After the introduction of the PC-Write Trojan horse, malicious hackers started creating similar Trojan horses masquerading as games or utility programs like those commonly found on BBSs. Most would run once and wipe out all the files stored on a hard disk, thereby removing the Trojan horse itself as well and preventing it from spreading. So while Trojan horses are dangerous, they rely on the gullibility of users in order to propagate themselves.

Because Trojan horses can only work by tricking people into running them, many disguise themselves as enticements, such as naked pictures of the latest celebrities or security updates from trusted companies such as Symantec or Trend Micro. Trojan horse writers are also quick to exploit the latest current events. When someone started spreading the following hoax about a virus named AOL4Free, another individual created a Trojan horse to exploit the rumor:

Subject: E-MAIL VIRUS!!!!! -- THIS IS NOT A JOKE!!!!!!

Anyone who receives this must send it to as many people as you can. It is essential that this problem be reconciled as soon as possible.

A few hours ago, someone opened an E-mail that had the subject heading of "AOL4FREE.COM".

Within seconds of opening it, a window appeared and began to display all his files that were being deleted. He immediately shut down his computer, but it was too late. This virus wiped him out. It ate the Anti-Virus Software that comes with the Windows '95 Program along with F-Prot AVS. Neither was able to detect it.

Please be careful and send this to as many people as possible, so maybe this new virus can be eliminated.

DON'T OPEN E-MAIL NOTING "AOL4FREE"

VIRUS ALERT!!!

Be aware that there are letters going around that you have won free Aol until 1998....or AOL 4 free...... PLEASE DELETE...... contains a virus that will wipe out your harddrive...... after you download and it executes.....

SUBJECT AREA OF EMAIL....... CONGRATULATIONS! You are a WINNER!

SUBJECT AREA OF EMAIL.......AOL 4 Free - Get AOL For Free

SENDERS...............................Matthews27 or VPVVPPVVP

WARN YOUR FRIENDS!!!!!!!!!!!!!!!!!!!!!!!!

The AOL4Free virus didn't actually exist, but soon after this hoax email got into circulation, a malicious hacker went ahead and created one. This Trojan horse claimed it would give users free access to America Online. Since people had already been told that the AOL4Free virus didn't exist, they felt safe running the "new" AOL4Free Trojan horse. This one actually would wipe out all the files on their hard disk.

Taunting the victim

Instead of destroying files, some Trojan horses simply annoy or taunt the user with pranks, such as displaying a fake dialog box that says "Now formatting hard disk" when nothing is actually happening, or playing beeping sounds through the computer's speaker randomly.

An Arabic Trojan horse named Yusufali sneaks into a computer and monitors the title bar of the currently active window, such as a web browser. If it finds words such as *XXX*, *sex*, or *teen*, indicating that the user may be visiting a pornographic website, the Trojan horse displays passages from the Koran, as shown in Figure 5-1.

Figure 5-1: The Yusufali Trojan horse prevents users from looking at pornographic websites.

While Trojan horses like Yusufali don't harm any files, they can prevent you from using your computer, to the point where you may need to reboot to get rid of their annoying distractions.

Attacking the victim's pocketbook

In addition to destroying files, Trojan horses can also cost you money.

In 1989, someone wrote the AIDS Trojan horse, which claimed to offer information about AIDS and HIV. When users ran the program, the Trojan horse would encrypt their hard disk and display a message demanding money in exchange for a password that could be used to decrypt the hard disk and recover their files. If users didn't send any money, the Trojan horse's author asserted, their hard disk would remain encrypted, their data essentially held hostage until the ransom was paid.

In 2005, this type of Trojan horse reappeared when someone spread the PGPcoder Trojan, which would also encrypt files and attempt to extort users for cash in return for a password to unscramble their files. The following year in 2006, another extortion Trojan appeared called Cryzip, starting what security experts say could be the start of a new category of malware tentatively dubbed *ransomware*.

As more people became aware of the dangers of viruses, more computer users started using antivirus programs that could detect both viruses and Trojan horses, so malicious hackers began to search for easier targets. They found their opportunity in the vulnerable world of smart phones, which allow people to play games, retrieve email, and play music. For example, one malicious hacker started circulating a Trojan horse called

Mosquito, which posed as a game that would work on any smart phone running the Symbian operating system. Once someone copied the Mosquito Trojan horse onto his or her smart phone and ran it, the Trojan horse would start sending text messages to phone numbers in the United Kingdom, Germany, the Netherlands, and Switzerland, saddling the victim with huge phone bills.

Besides messing with personal computers and smart phones, malicious hackers have also gone after Sony PlayStation Portable users. Many PlayStation users like to modify their PlayStation units so that they can run other types of programs in addition to official Sony game cartridges, a hobby known as *modding*. Targeting these modders, a malicious hacker wrote the first Trojan horse for Sony PlayStations in 2005, dubbed Trojan.PSPBrick. It would supposedly remove a Sony upgrade that made the device more resistant to modding. When people installed this Trojan horse, however, it would delete key files and turn the PlayStation Portable unit into an unusable piece of hardware.

The coming of the RATs (remote-access Trojans)

Up until the late '90s, hackers wrote more viruses than Trojan horses because viruses could spread more widely and cause greater damage than a Trojan horse ever could. All that changed in 1998 when a hacker group called The Cult of the Dead Cow released Back Orifice, a new type of Trojan horse called a *remote-access Trojan (RAT)*, that took advantage of the Internet. Like other Trojan horses, RATs could only run by tricking users, but once they were launched they could also connect to the Internet and communicate directly with the hacker who created them.

Sneaking a RAT onto a computer

RATs consist of two separate programs: a client file and a server file. The server file infects a computer by deceiving the user into running it. The client file runs on the hacker's computer and controls any computer infected by the RAT's server file.

To trick victims into running the server file, RATs might masquerade as an attached news story (such as a hoax about Osama bin Laden's capture by US military forces), as a file claiming to contain graphic images of celebrities having sex, or as just a simple game, as shown in Figure 5-2.

One problem with RAT server files is that they tend to be fairly large, as big as 1MB. An astute user might wonder why a file containing a purported news story would be so large. To avoid tipping off a potential victim due to the bulky size of a RAT's server file, RAT hackers use two deception strategies: backdoor Trojan horses and binder programs.

Unlike a full-size RAT, a backdoor Trojan horse is usually a small file whose size allows it to masquerade as something else, such as a simple game or a news story. When the victim runs the backdoor Trojan horse, the program does nothing more than open a network port—a "backdoor"—into the infected computer. Now the hacker can send a much larger file, such as a full-featured RAT, through this open port. Once this is installed on the computer, the backdoor Trojan horse has no further use and can be ignored or deleted.

An alternative way to sneak a full-featured RAT onto a computer is to use a binder program, which combines two programs in a single file. When someone runs a "bound" file, both programs run at the same time. Hackers use binder programs to bind RATs to

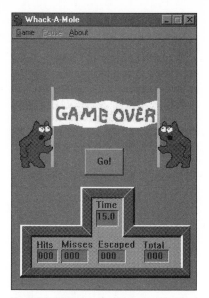

Figure 5-2: RATs often disguise the true identity of a server file by pretending to be a game.

a legitimate program, which can turn any file into a vehicle for installing a Trojan horse. Since most programs, such as game demos or trial versions of utility programs, are already hefty in size, the added bulk of a bound RAT isn't likely to be noticed. When a victim runs a bound file, the RAT secretly installs itself along with the legitimate program.

How RATs work

RATs work by sending information through Internet ports. When computers exchange information over the Internet, they divide their physical Internet connection into virtual ports, with each port handling a specific type of information; for example, email messages are received on one port and web pages are viewed through another. Port numbers identify the type of information received on each port so that the operating system knows where to direct it. For example, by convention, any data arriving at a computer's port 25 should be email, and any data arriving at a computer's port 80 should be a web page.

The first thing a RAT's server program does after infecting a computer is to open one or more ports on its network connection in order to broadcast its presence to the RAT client program. Since a computer can theoretically use thousands of different numbered ports simultaneously, and the gory details are hidden from the casual user by the operating system, most users will never notice if a RAT opens one of the many available ports or if an open port is being used by a RAT rather than a legitimate application.

After opening a port on an infected computer's network connection, the RAT server waits to hear from the RAT client, which runs on the malicious hacker's computer. How does the RAT client locate instances of the RAT server? Hackers simply scan the open ports on every networked computer they can find, searching for the specific port that the RAT server opens after it installs itself. Different RATs use different ports, and a

RAT hacker can thereby tell when its RAT is at work on a machine. For example, a RAT named Backage uses port 411, while another RAT named Ripper Pro uses port 2023, although hackers can configure RATs to connect to any port number.

RAT client files can only control computers infected by the corresponding server file, so a hacker would need to use the Ripper Pro's client file to control computer infected by the Ripper Pro server file, for example. Once a hacker finds an open port used by his particular RAT, he can use the RAT client program to connect to the server and, through it, control the infected computer as if he were physically sitting at the keyboard. Anything typed on the infected computer (passwords, credit card numbers, Social Security numbers, etc.) can be seen by the hacker running the RAT client. This interaction is shown in Figure 5-3.

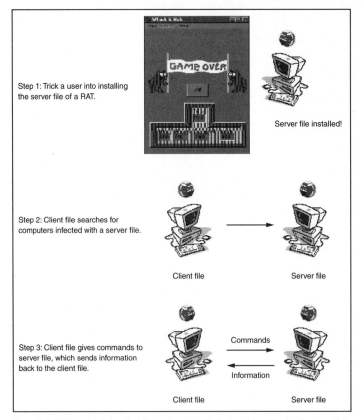

Step 1: Trick a user into installing the server file of a RAT.

Server file installed!

Step 2: Client file searches for computers infected with a server file.

Client file   Server file

Step 3: Client file gives commands to server file, which sends information back to the client file.

Commands

Information

Client file   Server file

Figure 5-3: RATs consist of a client file and a server file that work together to allow a malicious hacker to control a computer remotely over the Internet.

Some RATs can even capture screen images and keystrokes from an infected computer and send them (encoded as plain text) back to the hacker. Figure 5-4 shows the user interface of the Optix Pro RAT client, which provides push-button access to its many features for controlling an infected computer.

Once a RAT's server infects your computer, anyone with the corresponding client program can access and control it. So you then have to worry not only about the hacker

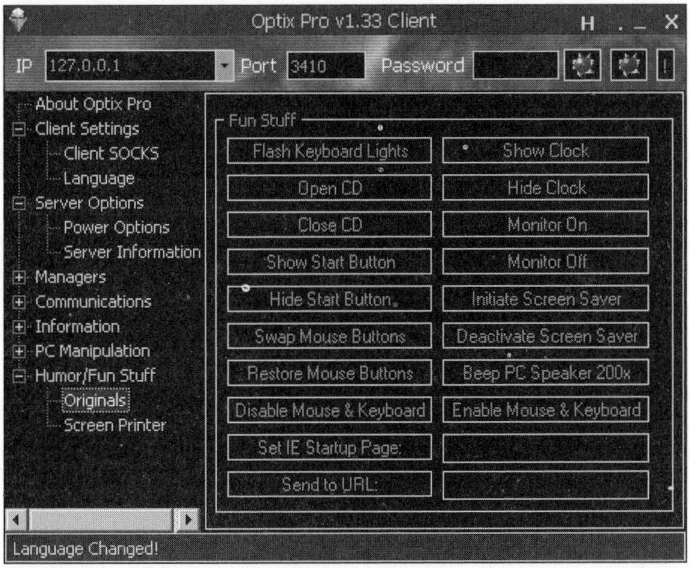

Figure 5-4: A RAT's client file provides a variety of features for controlling a computer infected by that RAT's server file.

who originally created the Trojan horse, you also have to worry about an army of hackers who routinely probe computers on the Internet looking for infected computers with open ports and servers waiting to receive and execute instructions from RAT clients.

WORMS: SELF-REPLICATING VIRUSES

Most "virus outbreaks" these days are actually worms, although the media tends to use the terms "virus" and "worm" interchangeably. Technically, a virus can only spread by infecting something else, such as a program file or a Microsoft Word document, that must then be copied. When someone copies an infected program file or Word document, he or she helps the virus spread.

A worm is more dangerous than a virus because a worm is self-propagating. In its simplest form, a worm program does nothing more than copy and spread itself, but that act alone can often clog network bandwidth and slow down or crash computers, as in the case of the 1988 Morris Internet worm, which reportedly infected up to 6,000 computers. The real danger occurs when the worm delivers a malicious payload as it spreads, such as one that drops a RAT on an infected computer (so that a hacker can spy on it later) or wipes out crucial files.

Worms commonly spread through "always-on" Internet connections, such as cable or DSL modems (used by individuals), or T1 and T3 lines (used by businesses). It's possible to spread a worm through a dial-up connection, but dial-up connections are slow, which also limits the speed that a worm can spread.

Three common ways that worms spread are through email, Internet Relay Chat (IRC) channels or instant messaging services, and Internet ports. Some worms spread themselves exclusively through one method, while others use a combination of methods to ensure they spread as quickly as possible.

Email worms

To spread by email, a worm will search for the address book of an email application such as Microsoft Outlook or Outlook Express. Once the worm finds the address book, it emails copies of itself to some or all of the stored addresses along with a deceptive subject line such as "I Love You" (used by the Love Letter worm in 2000) or "Merry Christmas" (used by the Zafi worm in 2004).

Unlike spam, which comes from an unknown source, a worm's email comes from someone the recipient most likely knows (otherwise the email address wouldn't have been stored in the person's address book in the first place). People are apt to trust email from a familiar source and open the message and its attachments, not suspecting that it includes the worm.

To further entice users to run the malicious attachment, the worm may falsely describe its content as a graphics file (a celebrity having sex), as an electronic greeting card, or as a seemingly harmless text file (a technique used by the MyDoom worm). When the victim opens the attachment, the worm copies email addresses from the new victim's address book and starts emailing itself to a new batch of people all over again.

IRC/Instant messaging worms

IRC networks are groups of chat rooms that anyone can join. To access an IRC network, a user must run an IRC program, called a client, which allows him to connect to an IRC server. After choosing an IRC network to visit, the user then chooses a specific IRC channel in which to chat.

When an IRC worm infects a computer, it starts that computer's IRC client program, usually the popular mIRC program. Once the worm has gotten the IRC client program running on its host computer, it randomly connects to an IRC network and channel and tries to trick the chatters into accepting a file containing a copy of itself, disguising it as an MP3 file from a popular recording artist or a pornographic image of a celebrity.

The moment an unsuspecting IRC user agrees to download the file offered by the IRC worm, the worm infects that person's computer too, and the worm can use the new victim's IRC client to connect to yet another IRC network and start the spread of the worm once more.

Instant messaging (IM) worms work similarly to IRC worms. An IM worm loads an IM program, such as MSN Messenger, and sends out messages to everyone in a chat room offering an enticing file, which, when downloaded, infects the user's computer and continues the cycle.

Internet worms

Both email and IRC worms use Trojan horse strategies to fool victims into infecting their computers. Internet worms can infect a computer without the user even being aware of the attack, infection, and spread. Internet worms scan vulnerable computers for specific open ports and then download themselves onto these machines, often taking advantage of flaws in the target computer's operating system to escape undetected. Once an Internet worm has infected a computer, it then scans the Internet to find other vulnerable computers.

The Santy worm takes a slightly different approach. Instead of directly scanning targeted computers (and thereby risking revealing its presence), the Santy worm uses the Google search engine to find computers running a flawed version of a community forum program known as the PHP Bulletin Board (phpBB). It then targets those specific computers to infect. By taking this approach, the Santy worm doesn't waste time trying to infect computers that won't help it to spread (such as any computer running Mac OS X).

Malicious web pages

The latest technique for installing Trojan horses on unsuspecting computers involves malicious web pages. First, a Trojan horse infects a server that hosts a website. Then, every time someone visits that website, the Trojan horse infects that person's computer.

While the thought of browsing a website that could infect your computer might be scary, the technical details prevent these types of Trojan horses from becoming more widespread. First, the Trojan horse must infect the server hosting a website. So if a hacker wanted to turn Microsoft's website into a malicious web page, he would first have to find the servers that host Microsoft's web pages, and then he would have to get the Trojan horse to infect that computer.

If a hacker is able to successfully infect a server, he then has to infect a user's computer. This relies on ActiveX controls, which are miniature programs that Microsoft uses to update Windows and antivirus vendors use to run online scans of your hard disk. Since ActiveX controls only run under Windows, only Windows computers are vulnerable, and then only those Windows computers that use Internet Explorer. Since neither Firefox nor Opera allow ActiveX controls to run, Trojan horses can't infect computers running those browsers. (ActiveX controls are more often used to install spyware on users' computers than Trojan horses are. See Chapter 20 for more information about spyware.)

Although the threat of malicious web pages is real, the problems involved in infecting the right servers and then infecting users' computers limit malicious web pages as a prominent way to spread Trojan horses and other malicious software.

STOPPING WORMS AND TROJAN HORSES

If you connect to the Internet, chances are good that your computer will eventually be attacked by a Trojan horse or worm. To protect yourself, you need to detect and remove any Trojan horses or worms already on your computer and then prevent them from infecting your computer again.

Step one is to use an antivirus program (see Chapter 4 for a list of antivirus programs), which will look for a Trojan horse or worm's unique fingerprint or signature and remove all traces of it from your computer. For further protection against RATs, you can also buy a dedicated anti–Trojan horse program such as:

Bo Clean	www.nsclean.com
Ewido Security Suite	www.ewido.net
Tauscan	www.agnitum.com
The Cleaner	www.moosoft.com

| Hacker Eliminator | www.lockdowncorp.com |
| TrojanHunter | www.misec.net/trojanhunter |

Since both RATs and worms can sneak in and out of a computer through open network ports, you also need a firewall that blocks these ports. With a firewall in place, even if a RAT or worm *does* infect your computer, it won't be able to communicate and spread to the outside world through its customary ports. Unfortunately, a firewall won't protect against any damage a worm may cause on your machine.

Many worms rely on exploiting flaws in software running on the victim's machine, such as the operating system, so make sure you download every update issued for your operating system and applications. Of course, this won't protect your computer from worms that know how to exploit flaws that haven't yet been reported and patched, but it will at least limit any unnecessary exposure.

To stop the spread and infection of worms, consider using alternatives to popular software. Most RATs and worms target the Windows operating system, so nothing can make your computer more secure than switching to a non-Windows operating system such as Linux or BSD.

If you still insist on using Windows, you can foil email worms by using anything but Microsoft Outlook or Outlook Express. Instead, try Thunderbird (www.mozilla.org), Pegasus Mail (www.pmail.com), or Eudora (www.eudora.com). To stop most IRC worms, switch from mIRC to Visual IRC (www.visualirc.net), XiRCON (www.visualirc.net), or X-Chat (www.xchat.org). For further help in removing worms and Trojan horses from your computer, download a free copy of Microsoft's Malicious Software Removal Tool (www.microsoft.com/security/malwareremove/default.mspx).

The keys to stopping Trojan horses and worms are to prevent their initial access to your computer (by using a firewall to block the ports that they use), to detect and remove any existing Trojan horses and worms (using antivirus and Trojan horse cleaning programs), and to stop using the programs most commonly exploited to spread them (Windows, Outlook, mIRC, etc.). Your computer can still become a target of Trojan horses and worms no matter what defenses you install, but at least there will be less of a chance that your computer will suffer any damage or contribute to the proliferation of these threats.

TRACKING THE THREATS

To stay up to date on the latest security threats, visit CERT (www.cert.org/advisories), Virus List (www.viruslist.com), Security Focus (www.securityfocus.com), SANS (SysAdmin, Audit, Network, Security) Institute (www.sans.org), or Symantec (http://securityresponse.symantec.com).

Ultimately, knowledge and understanding of how Trojan horses and worms spread will be more useful in protecting your computer than all the defensive programs combined. If you don't exercise a little common sense when dealing with suspicious threats, all the firewalls and anti–Trojan horse programs in the world won't be enough to protect your computer.

6

WAREZ (SOFTWARE PIRACY)

When people started selling the first computer programs on paper tape, tape cassettes, floppy disks, and CDs, people discovered that they could easily copy a program and share it with their friends. Such blatant copying prompted the programmer of an Altair computer BASIC interpreter to write an open letter to fellow computer hobbyists, urging them not to copy or pirate software illegally:

AN OPEN LETTER TO HOBBYISTS

By William Henry Gates III

February 3, 1976

To me, the most critical thing in the hobby market right now is the lack of good software courses, books and software itself. Without good software and an owner who understands programming, a hobby computer is wasted. Will quality software be written for the hobby market?

Almost a year ago, Paul Allen and myself, expecting the hobby market to expand, hired Monte Davidoff and developed Altair BASIC. Though the initial work took only two months, the three of us have spent most of the last year documenting, improving and adding features to BASIC. Now we have 4K, 8K, EXTENDED, ROM and DISK BASIC. The value of the computer time we have used exceeds $40,000.

The feedback we have gotten from the hundreds of people who say they are using BASIC has all been positive. Two surprising things are apparent, however, 1) Most of these "users" never bought BASIC (less than 10% of all Altair owners have bought BASIC), and 2) The amount of royalties we have received from sales to hobbyists makes the time spent on Altair BASIC worth less than $2 an hour.

Why is this? As the majority of hobbyists must be aware, most of you steal your software. Hardware must be paid for, but software is something to share. Who cares if the people who worked on it get paid?

Only one thing is impossible for God: To find any sense in any copyright law on the planet.

—MARK TWAIN

Is this fair? One thing you don't do by stealing software is get back at MITS* *for some problem you may have had. MITS doesn't make money selling software. The royalty paid to us, the manual, the tape and the overhead make it a break-even operation. One thing you do do is prevent good software from being written. Who can afford to do professional work for nothing? What hobbyist can put 3-man years into programming, finding all bugs, documenting his product and distribute for free? The fact is, no one besides us has invested a lot of money in hobby software. We have written 6800 BASIC, and are writing 8080 APL and 6800 APL, but there is very little incentive to make this software available to hobbyists. Most directly, the thing you do is theft.*

What about the guys who re-sell Altair BASIC, aren't they making money on hobby software? Yes, but those who have been reported to us may lose in the end. They are the ones who give hobbyists a bad name, and should be kicked out of any club meeting they show up at.

I would appreciate letters from any one who wants to pay up, or has a suggestion or comment. Just write to me at 1180 Alvarado SE, #114, Albuquerque, New Mexico, 87108. Nothing would please me more than being able to hire ten programmers and deluge the hobby market with good software.

Bill Gates

General Partner, Micro-Soft

COPYING COPY-PROTECTED SOFTWARE

Despite Bill Gates's pleas, software piracy not only thrived but also proliferated under the slang name *warez*. In the early days, software publishers tried to protect their products by shipping programs on copy-protected floppy disks, but other companies soon released special programs that could copy a copy-protected floppy disk, ostensibly for backup purposes.

Some software publishers shipped their programs with a hardware device called a dongle, which usually attached to the computer's parallel port. Every time a program would run, it would check to see if this dongle was attached to the computer. If it didn't find the dongle, the program would assume it had been copied illegally and would refuse to run.

Hackers quickly found ways to emulate these dongles using software, essentially tricking a program into thinking a dongle was attached to the computer when it wasn't. Many companies even started selling software dongle emulators, such as Spectrum Software (www.donglefree.com) and SafeKey International (www.safe-key.com).

When fledgling online services such as America Online appeared, software piracy became even more rampant. Hackers formed software cracking groups and gave themselves names like Phrozen Crew, Fantastic Four Cracking Group, and the International

---

* Micro Instrumentation and Telemetry Systems (MITS) was the company that made the first personal computer, the Altair 8800.

Network of Crackers. These cracking groups competed against one another to grab a copy of copy-protected programs (usually games), remove the copy-protection scheme, and distribute the cracked copy of the program on BBSs and online services such as America Online.

To brag about their exploits, cracking groups would insert a screen that appeared whenever someone tried to run a cracked program. These screens, dubbed *crack intros* or simply *cracktros*, often displayed colorful graphics to publicize the name of the cracking group, their BBS number, acknowledgments to their friends, or just a silly message, as shown in Figure 6-1.

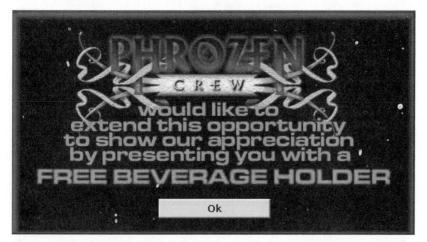

Figure 6-1: Cracktros let everyone know which cracking group had been responsible for cracking a particular program.

To see more examples of cracktros created by various cracking groups, visit Defacto2 (www.defacto2.net), Flashtro (www.flashtro.com), or the World of Cracktros (http://cracktros.planet-d.net).

Among those who didn't partake of cracked programs, copy protection did prevent casual copying, but it also prevented legitimate users from making backup copies of their software. One spilled drink on a copy-protected floppy disk could effectively ruin a $495 program.

To copy-protect their software without inconveniencing legitimate users too much, software publishers have tried a variety of schemes. Some of these methods involved typing in special codes printed in the user manual every time the program started up. Another method involved "locking" a program to a specific hard disk. This required you to "unlock" and delete the program from the first computer before you could use the installation disk on a different computer.

This anecdote may be apocryphal, but it's said that Microsoft even attempted a bizarre form of copy protection on its MS-DOS version of Microsoft Word. Periodically, the program would check to see if it was running off a legitimate copy-protected floppy disk. If it detected a pirated copy, the program would retaliate by trashing any files it could find. Nobody knew about this form of copy protection until Word happened to trash a computer journalist's files. Even worse, the journalist had been running a legitimate copy of Microsoft Word.

Microsoft quickly denied that this form of copy protection existed, then blamed a summer intern for slipping the retaliation feature into Microsoft Word without the company's permission or knowledge.

Although consumers hated it, copy-protection mechanisms remained on most software programs until hard disks became cheaper and more common. Users then needed to copy their software from a floppy disk to their hard disk. Instead of physically blocking their programs from being copied, software publishers resorted to using serial numbers for validation.

DEFEATING SERIAL NUMBERS

To install many programs, you have to type in a serial number, usually found on an enclosed registration card or (if you downloaded the software over the Internet) included in an email message from the software publisher. By typing in a valid serial number, typically an unusual combination of letters and numbers, you "unlock" the software and install it on your computer.

Of course, some people found that serial numbers were easy to defeat. They'd simply copy their valid serial numbers and pass them among their friends. Since they no longer had to use their programming skills to crack any type of copy-protection, warez pirates simply set up websites with huge lists of valid serial numbers for different programs that anyone could use right away, as shown in Figure 6-2.

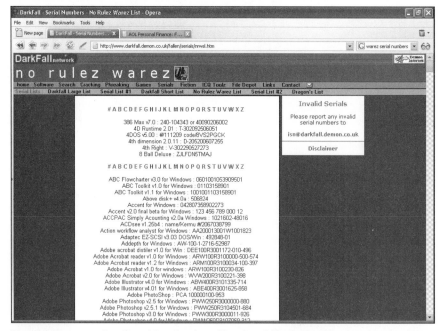

Figure 6-2: Many warez sites offer serial numbers for a wide variety of different programs.

Besides storing serial numbers of different programs on websites, which could get shut down, other hackers have stored serial numbers in databases that you can download, search, and update, as shown in Figure 6-3.

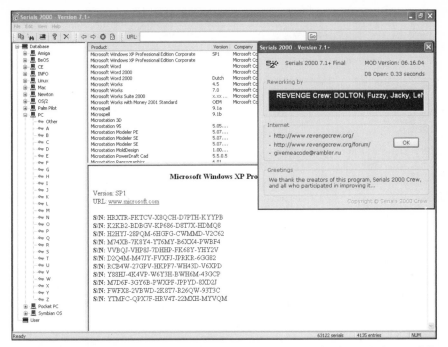

Figure 6-3: You can find a list of serial numbers for different programs stored in the Serials 2000 database, available for download off the Internet.

One problem with this approach is that expanding the database typically requires people to share their valid serial numbers. Since few people are likely to do this, hackers have created special serial number generation programs that use the same algorithms used by the programs themselves.

Although serial numbers appear to be random combinations of numbers and letters, they're actually created by a mathematical formula. So although it's nearly impossible to guess a valid serial number for a program, it's often possible to reverse engineer a program to determine the specific formula it uses during validation.

To reverse engineer a program, hackers use special programs called disassemblers, which can convert a program into assembly language instructions. Once hackers understand the exact verification method, they can create a program to generate random serial numbers that match the target program's serial number verification formula. Most companies use the same serial number verification formula for different products, so hackers develop different serial number generators for different vendors, such as Microsoft and Adobe, as shown in Figure 6-4.

To find websites that list serial numbers or that offer serial number generators, visit CrackHell (www.crackhell.com), KeyGen (www.keygen.us), MegaZip (www.megazip .com), or Serials (www.serials.ws).

NOTE: *Be careful when visiting any hacker sites, as they'll often bombard you with pop-up windows loaded with pornography and try to sneak spyware (see Chapter 20) onto your computer. For safety, browse hacker sites on a non-Windows computer such as one running Linux or Mac OS X.*

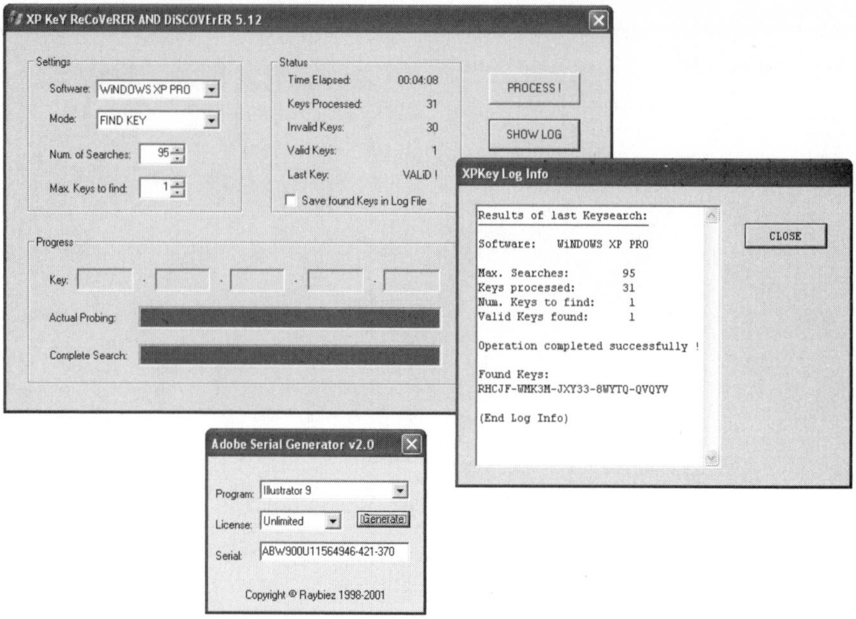

XP KeY ReCoVeRER AND DiSCoVErER 5.12

Settings

Software: WiNDOWS XP PRO

Mode: FIND KEY

Num. of Searches: 95

Max. Keys to find: 1

Status
Time Elapsed: 00:04:08
Keys Processed: 31
Invalid Keys: 30
Valid Keys: 1
Last Key: VALiD !

☐ Save found Keys in Log File

PROCESS !

SHOW LOG

Progress

Key:

Actual Probing:

Complete Search:

XPKey Log Info

Results of last Keysearch:

Software: WiNDOWS XP PRO

Max. Searches: 95
Keys processed: 31
Num. Keys to find: 1
Valid Keys found: 1

Operation completed successfully !

Found Keys:
RHCJF-WMK3M-JXY33-8WYTQ-QVQYV

(End Log Info)

CLOSE

Adobe Serial Generator v2.0

Program: Illustrator 9

License: Unlimited   Generate

Serial: ABW900U11564946-421-370

Copyright © Raybiez 1998-2001

Figure 6-4: Serial key generators can develop "valid" serial numbers for a range of products from companies such as Adobe or Microsoft.

DEFEATING PRODUCT ACTIVATION

The latest attempt to curb software piracy involves product activation. When you install a program that uses product activation, it gathers information about the computer's CPU, hard disk, graphics card, and other hardware to create a unique identifier. Then the program sends this information, along with the serial number entered by the user, to the software publisher. This ties a specific serial number to a particular computer, preventing anyone from reusing that serial number on another computer.

Product activation defeats the rampant sharing of valid serial numbers, but still can't defeat serial number generators since a new serial number can always be generated to be linked to another computer.

More troublesome, from a user's point of view, is that product activation can be a nuisance at best and a major headache at worst. Intuit once sold its popular TurboTax program with product activation that, in many cases, actually prevented people from installing and using the software they legitimately bought. Symantec had similar problems when it started including product activation with its Norton Antivirus program. In Symantec's case, the product activation would ask for a serial number every time the computer booted up. No matter how many times the user typed in his valid serial number, the product activation would eventually shut down after a few days and stop Norton Antivirus from working altogether. In both cases, bugs in the product activation program wound up punishing legitimate users.

Product activation may stop ordinary computer users from pirating software, but it does nothing to stop determined hackers, who are the people most likely to pirate software in the first place. As soon as Microsoft introduced product activation for Windows, hackers developed product activation patches that could modify the operating system and prevent its product activation feature from working, as shown in Figure 6-5.

Figure 6-5: To defeat product activation, many hackers have developed patches that trick a program into thinking it has already been activated.

Like serial numbers and copy protection, product activation discourages casual copying but with added nuisance and expense for the software publisher. No matter what method software publishers use to guard against piracy, they'll only succeed in slowing down software pirates, not eliminating them. Product activation might work in theory, but as every hacker knows, theory means nothing in the real (and virtual) world of computers.

WAREZ WEBSITES

In the old days, people pirated software by copying a program onto a floppy disk and giving the copy to someone else. Later, pirates ran private BBSs and swapped software through the telephone lines.

When pirates discovered the Internet, they set up their own websites for trading illicit software, as shown in Figure 6-6. Some popular lists of hacker sites include Warez List (www.warezlist.com), DirectDL (www.directdl.com), AllSeek (http://top.allseek.info), CrackDB (www.crackdb.com), and Warez Files (www.warez-files.com).

Since websites can easily be tracked by the authorities, pirates soon moved on to swapping programs through filesharing networks (such as FastTrack, Gnutella, and BitTorrent) and Usenet newsgroups.

One problem with filesharing networks is that authorities can track down any user's Internet Protocol (IP) address and then, by linking a computer's IP address to a physical address, could often nab blatant file sharers and punish them.

That's why more pirates have flocked to BitTorrent. Unlike traditional filesharing networks like Gnutella, you don't search anyone else's computer. Instead, you have to visit a website, called an indexing site, that provides a list of files you can download, such as movies, programs, or music. Once you click a file, the indexing site directs you to all the computers that have that file.

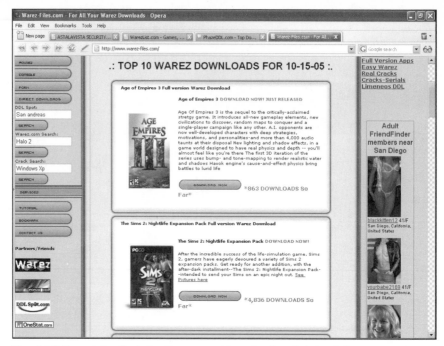

Figure 6-6: Software pirates often trade software amongst themselves through pirate websites.

Even more remarkable is that as soon as you start downloading a file, BitTorrent lets you simultaneously share that file with anyone else. Not only does this speed up file transfers, but it also insures that if your computer loses connection with another computer, you can still download the parts of the file you need from a different computer. Because of its ability to handle large files and its speed in downloading, BitTorrent has quickly become a favorite among pirates of all kinds.

USENET NEWSGROUPS: THE NEW PIRACY BREEDING GROUND

While most pirates use BitTorrent to share files, many pirates also use the seemingly antiquated Usenet newsgroups as well.

On Usenet newsgroups, pirates can upload programs anonymously, and anyone can download them anonymously as well. No matter how hard they might try, the authorities can only identify that software piracy is occurring; they can't trace the offenders.

Initially, Usenet newsgroups were rather cumbersome compared to the point-and-click convenience of web pages. Trying to find a particular program meant scouring through multiple newsgroups. Also, Usenet newsgroups imposed a fixed file size of 10,000 lines per file, which meant that large files, such as pirated programs, had to be broken into parts, which were downloaded individually and then reassembled. If even one part were missing, the program wouldn't work. As a result, Usenet newsgroups often proved too troublesome for less tech-savvy users to handle.

To make searching for files among newsgroups easier, programmers have created a new file format, dubbed NewzBin (NZB), to turn Usenet newsgroups into a fast indexing and downloading resource for warez.

To search a Usenet newsgroup for files, you can visit the more common ones, such as alt.binaries.warez, or you could use a Usenet newsgroup search engine such as alt.binaries.nl (http://alt.binaries.nl), BinCrawler (www.bincrawler.com), Newzbin (www.newzbin.com), or Find Free Files (www.findfreefiles.com), as shown in Figure 6-7.

Figure 6-7: By searching through Usenet newsgroups, you can find a pirated program to download, such as Adobe Illustrator or VMware.

Once you find the pirated program you want, you can use a newsreader program that supports NZB files, such as NewsMan Pro (www.newsmanpro.com), Binary Boy (www.binaryboy.com), NewsBin Pro (www.newsbin.com), or News Rover (www.newsrover.com), as shown in Figure 6-8, to download it without having to search manually.

Combine a NZB-enabled newsreader with a high-speed, dedicated news server such as NewsDemon (www.newsdemon.com), GigaNews (www.giganews.com), or AstraWeb (www.news.astraweb.com), and you can start downloading all the warez you want without anyone knowing who you are.

People have been pirating software ever since computers have been around, and that is not going to change anytime soon. People in developing nations and countries such as China and Russia pirate software because they can't afford it otherwise. That doesn't make piracy right, but given that the cost of a single copy of Adobe Photoshop is more than most people in the world earn in a month, it's safe to say that piracy will always be a more enticing option than buying software honestly, at least for some people.

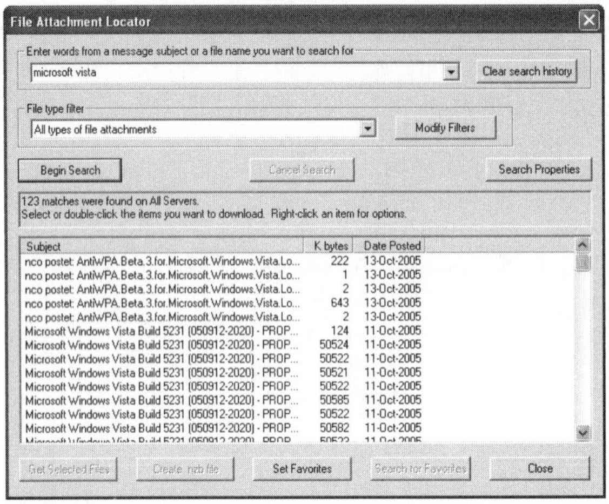

Figure 6-8: A newsreader can help you find warez in a newsgroup, such as a copy of Microsoft Windows Vista along with a patch to disable Windows Vista's product activation feature.

To fight back against piracy, the Motion Picture Association of America (MPAA) and the Recording Industry Association of America (RIAA) have used several techniques with varying degrees of success. Initially, the MPAA/RIAA targeted individuals sharing enormous numbers of files off their computers, such as a thousand or more. By suing these individuals, the MPAA/RIAA hoped to scare away others from sharing files too.

To further discourage piracy, the MPAA/RIAA also "poisoned" the filesharing networks with bogus files. If people kept downloading bogus files, the MPAA/RIAA hoped that they would abandon the filesharing networks and turn to legitimate ones instead.

Next, the MPAA/RIAA started targeting the companies that made the filesharing programs. During 2005, the MPAA/RIAA managed to sue and shut down the publishers of Grokster and WinMX. By taking away the software used to swap files, the MPAA/RIAA hoped to shut down the filesharing networks one by one.

For their latest tactic, the MPAA/RIAA has targeted the search engines that provide access to pirated files, such as BinNews.com, which allowed people to search Usenet newsgroups for warez, or IsoHunt.com, which provided links to BitTorrent files, such as full-length movies or major applications like Adobe Photoshop.

Generally speaking, finding a pirated program can be tedious—and getting that pirated program to work can sometimes be more frustrating than going out and buying it. For hackers, software piracy is a challenge. For the average user, piracy is appealing only when it's convenient. But to dedicated software pirates, piracy can be a way of life, and nothing the software publishers can do will ever stop it.

PART 3

THE INTERNET
HACKERS

7

WHERE THE HACKERS ARE

Hackers are people and, like most people, hackers paradoxically embrace their individuality while immersing themselves in their collective identity as rebels, free thinkers, mischief makers, and technology wizards. Despite appearances to the contrary, people do not become hackers because of how they look, what they wear, or how they speak. People become hackers by virtue of how they think and what they do.

In individuals, insanity is rare; but in groups, parties, nations, and epochs it is the rule.

—FRIEDRICH NIETZSCHE

In the world of hacking, there are "good" hackers (called *white hat hackers*) and there are "bad" hackers (called *black hat hackers*). In between are the so-called *gray hat hackers*, who cross the border between good and bad depending on what's convenient for them at the time (like most people in the world).

Even the definition of *hacker* remains controversial. Some people lump both good and bad hackers together, but others define *hacker* as someone who's simply curious, and use the term *cracker* for someone who's deliberately malicious.

Whatever you call them, hackers are people, and like any group of people (Americans, police officers, teachers, accountants, Christians), some will be good and some will be bad. But unlike most other groups, hackers often rely exclusively on technology, in the form of computers and the Internet, to communicate with each other.

Finding a hacker on the Internet is fairly easy if you know where to look, just as you can find a drug dealer or a policeman if you know where to look in a city (depending on the city, the policeman might *be* the drug dealer).

HACKER WEBSITES

There are two kinds of hacker websites: those run by hackers and those run by reformed hackers who have decided that it's more profitable to become security professionals. Initially, many hackers created websites using free web hosting services such as Tripod (www.tripod.lycos.com), Geocities (http://geocities.yahoo.com), and AngelFire (http://angelfire.lycos.com). Such websites are often short-lived, as hackers grow tired of updating them. Besides, few people are interested in visiting personal websites that bombard visitors with advertisements, as shown in Figure 7-1.

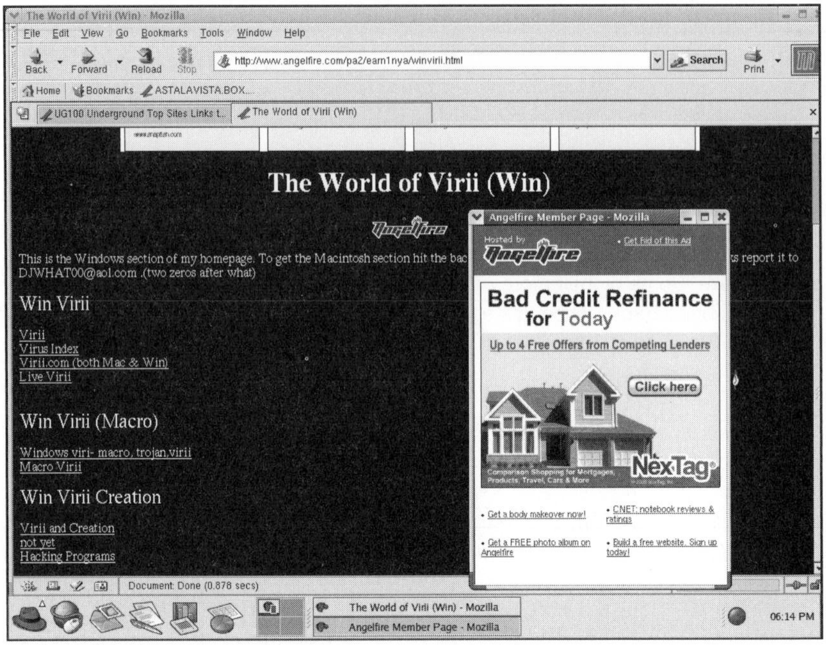

Figure 7-1: Hackers often set up websites on free web hosting services such as Tripod or AngelFire.

On rare occasions, an ambitious hacker may actually spend the time and money to create a website with a descriptive domain address. Like their free web hosting counterparts, these hacker websites rarely last long because anything considered too controversial (such as live computer viruses and software patches designed to circumvent Microsoft Windows' product activation feature) can quickly get the website operator in trouble with the authorities, who will shut it down. It's said that when hackers started distributing a program that disabled Windows XP from running its product activation feature, for example, Microsoft quickly shut down any websites that offered it.

Hacker websites for fun and profit

Although individual hackers rarely set up websites anymore, groups of hackers often do so to provide a platform for their views and a place where they can release their hacker tools or make a profit selling hacker merchandise such as T-shirts or CDs. Some of the more stable hacker group websites are listed in this section.

Attrition.org

This site provides both current and archived news about computer security, including a list of allegedly fraudulent people and organizations in the computer security business (www.attrition.org).

AusPhreak

AusPhreak offers a meeting site for Australian and international hackers to gather and share ideas (www.ausphreak.com).

Chaos Computer Club

One of the oldest hacker groups and one of the largest in Europe, Chaos Computer Club is perhaps best known for its loose affiliation with a West German hacker, Karl Koch, who was accused of breaking into American government computer networks and selling military secrets to the Soviet KGB intelligence agency (www.ccc.de).

Cult of the Dead Cow

The Cult of the Dead Cow (see Figure 7-2) is known for releasing a variety of hacker tools with great fanfare. Some of their more notable hacker tools include the remote-access Trojan horse dubbed Back Orifice, a steganography tool for hiding information in images called Camera/Shy, and an anonymous peer-to-peer tunneling protocol called Six/Four (www.cultdeadcow.com).

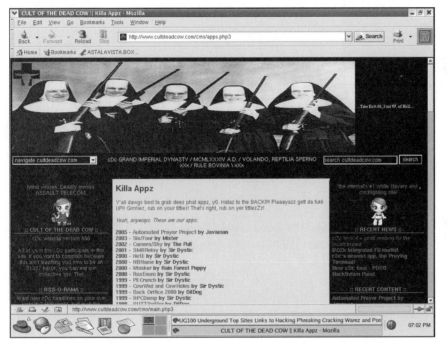

Figure 7-2: Hacker groups such as the Cult of the Dead Cow often run websites for their own amusement and to distribute their own hacking software.

New Order

New Order offers hacker software, security exploits, and lists of interesting projects such as GhostProxy, which is designed to let you browse the Internet anonymously; MD5 Reverse Lookup Database, for helping you crack MD5 encrypted files (also known as *hashes*) used to protect passwords; and Slut-Box, a server specifically set up to allow people to practice breaking into a computer without getting arrested (http://neworder .box.sk).

Nomad Mobile Research Centre

Provides plenty of hacker tools and research papers geared towards finding exploits in popular programs (www.nmrc.org).

The Shmoo Group

Website of security professionals who donate their time to creating useful tools for hacking or for catching hackers (www.shmoo.com).

Underground News

Hacker tools and news are posted on Underground News along with the latest rumors circulating around the computer industry (www.undergroundnews.com).

Computer security "hacking" websites

The main reason most hackers no longer set up their own websites is because there's no money in it. Between the cost of running a website, the time needed to design and maintain it, and the possible legal liabilities of offering programs that encourage piracy, most hackers choose the more lucrative route of calling themselves "security professionals" instead. Rather than risk going to jail for hacking, such reformed hackers/security professionals sell their hacking skills to the highest bidder.

One prominent hacker group, dubbed L0pht Heavy Industries, transformed itself from a hacker group to a computer security firm called @Stake, which in turn was bought out by Symantec. Given the choice between serving prison time or getting paid to hack legally, it's easy to see why hackers would opt to become security professionals.

AntiOnline

This source for hacker news, virus source code, and Trojan horse programs also offers various forums where security professionals can chat and exchange information (www.antionline.com).

DShield

Gathers information from firewalls to track the different types of hacker attacks occurring around the world (www.dshield.org).

Hideaway.net

Hideaway.net provides news, information, and links to different types of security software and anonymous web browsing sites (www.hideaway.net).

Insecure.org

Home of the Nmap security scanner, this site also lists the top security tools to protect your computer and network from attack (www.insecure.org).

PacketStorm

Provides both historical and current information and tools about hackers and the latest exploits (http://packetstormsecurity.org).

Security News Portal

A massive directory of links to various computer security resources, news, companies, and security threats is available at Security News Portal (www.securitynewsportal.com).

SecureRoot

This site organizes links to various hacker and computer security resources in categories for easy browsing (www.secureroot.com), as shown in Figure 7-3.

Figure 7-3: SecureRoot provides a Yahoo!-like portal with links to hacker websites, pages detailing operating system vulnerabilities, and phone phreaking information.

SecurityFocus

Home of the BugTraq mailing list of the latest exploits in different software, SecurityFocus also provides a library of security programs along with a security-related job bank (www .securityfocus.com).

Startplaza.nu

Another huge directory of different computer security companies, hacker groups, and security software tools is available at Startplaza.nu (www.startplaza.nu).

Sys-Security Research

This site provides white papers examining computer security issues with a special emphasis on VoIP (www.sys-security.com).

Talisker's Security Portal

British security website that provides real-time security alerts and updates for government and military organizations (and anyone else who visits their website, too)—www.securitywizardry.com.

WindowsSearch

This site packages coverage of computer security (focusing exclusively on Windows) as well as an online Trojan horse scanner, an email vulnerability scanner, and a network security scanner (www.windowsecurity.com).

Wiretapped

Wiretapped specializes in cryptography and network monitoring with plenty of links to packet capturing, network mapping, and network intrusion detection software (www.wiretapped.net).

Hacker search engines

To find more hacker and security-related websites, you could use an ordinary search engine, such as Google, but you'll wind up sifting through lots of irrelevant links. For a more targeted alternative, use the specialized hacker search engine, AstalaVista (www.astalavista.com). AstalaVista can help you track down everything from the latest source code for the newest worm or virus to the current version of a port scanner designed to probe another computer's defenses.

If AstalaVista can't find a hacker website for you, it also provides a list of additional hacker search engines you can use instead, as shown in Figure 7-4, or you can try http://astalavista.box.sk.

HACKER MAGAZINES

Kids may read *Teen People* magazine, and adults may read *Time* or *Newsweek* (or the *Weekly World News*). Hackers like to read their own magazines, too. Although none of these titles is prominently displayed in the checkout aisles of supermarkets, they can be found in some larger bookstores as well as on the Internet. Hacker magazines tend to have irregular publishing schedules, so don't be surprised if the latest issue is several months old (or if the magazine has stopped publishing altogether).

2600

Published quarterly, *2600* is one of the oldest and most respected hacker magazines. Its website doesn't offer any articles from the magazine, but it does provide the latest hacker news along with lists of hacker conventions (www.2600.com).

Figure 7-4: AstalaVista lists a variety of hacker search engines and even warns you about which ones will try to load spyware or Trojan horses if you visit them.

Blacklisted! 411

Another hacker magazine published sporadically is *Blacklisted! 411* (shown in Figure 7-5). Its website offers articles from back issues along with the latest hacker news (www.blacklisted411.net).

Figure 7-5: Hacker magazines strive for interesting covers that depict some aspect of the hacker culture, such as dumpster diving.

Hacker News Magazine

This interesting French hacker magazine provides hacker tools, news, and articles for browsing (assuming you know how to read French, of course)—www.hackermag.com.

The Hackademy Premium

This French magazine, geared to white hat hackers, provides articles and news in French, Spanish, and English. The staff also offers training classes at their hacking school in Paris (http://premium.thehackademy.net).

Phrack

One of the oldest hacker magazines, in operation since 1985, *Phrack* reported on networking, telephony, phone phreaking, and other computer hacking topics until recently ceasing publication. Maybe by the time you read this another group will have stepped up to keep the magazine going (www.phrack.com).

Private Line

Private Line is an unusual magazine that specializes in all aspects of phone phreaking, including cell phones and VoIP along with ordinary landline telephone systems (www.privateline.com).

HACKER USENET NEWSGROUPS

Hackers often communicate through the anonymity of Usenet newsgroups, sharing information and answering questions between insults, posts of virus source code, ads for get-rich-quick schemes, and links to the latest temporary hacker website that everyone should visit before it gets shut down for one reason or another.

General hacking newsgroups

To start learning about hacking in general, try one of the general-purpose hacking newsgroups listed below. Unlike other types of newsgroups that focus on stamp collecting or photography, hacker newsgroups tend to stray from their topics. For example, the alt.binaries.hacking.beginner newsgroup, which says it is about helping new hackers find and use hacking programs, is often filled with discussions about virus programming and encryption, or vicious insult wars. Other hacking newsgroups include alt.hacker, alt.hacking, alt.binaries.hacking.beginner, alt.binaries.hacking.websites, alt.2600.hackers, and comp.hackers.

Computer virus newsgroups

Computer virus writers often publish their latest creations in newsgroups (or post URLs where you can download them). If you want to find the latest live virus (or virus source code), visit one of the following newsgroups: alt.comp.virus, alt.comp.virus.source, alt.comp.virus.source.code, or comp.virus.

Encryption newsgroups

Because hackers often skirt the legal boundaries of their countries' laws, they wisely hide their identities or messages using encryption, the same technology that government agencies use to protect national secrets. To learn the latest about using and writing encryption to protect your sensitive data (topics you'll read more about in Chapter 22), visit one of the following newsgroups: alt.cypherpunks, alt.security, alt.sources.crypto, misc.security, sci.crypt, or sci.crypt.research.

Cracking newsgroups

Most games and applications are copy-protected to prevent software piracy. Likewise, many shareware programs provide limited functionality until the user pays for a code or key to unlock additional features.

Some hackers try to circumvent, or crack, copy-protected and "locked" shareware programs. Cracking methods include sharing serial numbers, unlocking codes, and using programs designed to unlock or duplicate copy-protected games. To read about these programs and techniques, visit any of the following newsgroups: alt.2600.crack, alt.2600.crackz, alt.binaries.cracked, or alt.cracks.

FINDING HACKERS ON IRC

You can chat with a hacker in real time in one of the many hacker chat rooms that pop up on nearly every Internet Relay Channel (IRC) network. After you install an IRC client program on your computer, such as mIRC (www.mirc.co.uk), you'll need to pick an IRC network to join. Some of the more popular networks are EFnet, DALnet, Undernet, and 2600 net (run by the hacker magazine *2600*).

Once you're connected to an IRC network server, you can create a new chat room or join an existing one. To find a hacker chat room, look for rooms with names like #2600, #phreak, #carding, #cracks, #anarchy, or any other phrase that sounds hackerish.

Using IRC is a special skill in itself, and many hackers may get upset if you intrude on their chat rooms, so use care when exploring the different networks and chat rooms. With enough patience, you can eventually meet and make friends in the various chat rooms and become a regular and experienced IRC user too. For more help in using IRC, pick up Alex Charalabidis' *The Book of IRC*, published by No Starch Press (www.nostarch.com/irc.htm).

HACKER CONVENTIONS

Hacker conventions are great places to meet people you've only interacted with in chat rooms or newsgroups and to listen to speakers from around the world discuss the latest trends in computer security. Since many hacker groups announce their latest hacking tools and techniques at hacker conventions, both the hacker side as well as the law enforcement side of the computer underground, including FBI and Secret Service agents, can be found lurking about at these conferences.

Anyone can attend a hacker convention, including hackers, law enforcement agents, and those who are just curious to see what life looks like in the computer hacking world.

DefCon

DefCon is an annual convention held in Las Vegas, usually attended by hackers, media, and government officials from all over the world. One popular contest is "Spot the Fed," where attendees attempt to locate FBI agents keeping an eye on the conference (www.defcon.org).

HOPE (Hackers on Planet Earth)

Run by the hacker magazine *2600*, this conference focuses on all aspects of hacking, including phone phreaking, virus writing, social engineering, and information warfare (www.2600.com).

Chaos Communication Congress

The largest European hacker conference, Chaos Communication Congress, is run by the German-based Chaos Computer Club (www.ccc.de/congress).

PH-Neutral

German hacker conference for Europeans and anyone else with enough money to fly to Berlin (http://ph-neutral.darklab.org).

RuxCon

Australian security conference dedicated to hacking in the land down under (www.ruxcon .org.au).

ShmooCon

This is an annual east coast hacker conference with plenty of speakers and opportunities to discuss computer security (www.shmoocon.org).

SummerCon

One of the oldest hacker conventions, SummerCon tends to be held in different cities each year so that hackers from different parts of the world can attend (www .summercon.org).

ToorCon

One of the newer computer security conferences, ToorCon, is run by hackers who want to combine their love for hacking with the sunshine of San Diego (www.toorcon.org).

DON'T PANIC: HACKERS ARE PEOPLE, TOO

The more hackers you meet, whether through newsgroups, websites, or in person at hacker conventions, the more likely your perception of hackers will change. Some hackers fit the hacker stereotype, but others deviate dramatically from any preconceived notions.

Of course, as with any group of people, there will always be some whom you would do well to avoid. Some of these malicious hackers may try to snare your credit card number, use your identity online, or just harass you by routing a 1-900 sex hotline to your home phone.

Other hackers may look down on you as a *newbie*, a derogatory term for a newcomer. Ignore these obnoxious people, since even they were newbies at one time too. Just keep learning on your own and from others who are willing to help you, and soon you too will be considered as knowledgeable as the rest of them. When that happens, you'll have to decide how you want the world to see you—as someone who's intelligent and inquisitive, or as someone malicious and destructive. Whatever impression you want people to have about hackers, it's up to you.

8

STALKING A COMPUTER

Like car thieves, hackers usually target the first computer they find with weak defenses. If a computer is too hard to break into, hackers will usually go off in search of easier prey. The reason is simple. Unless hackers have a specific reason for breaking into a particular computer, they can accomplish their goals on any undefended machine and don't need to waste time trying to break into one that's well-protected.

On the other hand, if a hacker really wants to break into your computer because it contains files the hacker wants or because your computer provides the least well-guarded path into a more heavily protected computer network, you can't do anything to stop that hacker from trying. The only safe computer is one that's never turned on.

The streets are safe in Philadelphia. It's only the people who make them unsafe.

—FRANK RIZZO, ex-police chief and mayor of Philadelphia

WHY HACKERS CHOOSE THEIR TARGETS

Sometimes hackers break into computers for fun, just to see if they can do it, or to practice their skills. Hackers often target corporate computers to gain access to their large storage space, which can be perfect for stashing pirated programs or movies. By storing large collections of illegal material on someone else's computer, hackers shift liability from themselves to an unsuspecting stranger.

Sometimes hackers target corporate computers for the information contained in them. In his book *Friendly Spies*, Peter Schweizer claims that Germany financed hackers in an effort called Project Rahab, which mapped out the structure and flaws of computer networks belonging to the governments of France, Japan, England, and the United States. Likewise, China has been accused of using hackers to probe for weaknesses in the computer networks of other countries, and it's likely that the United States and Russia have also developed this capability.

Even if your computer doesn't belong to a top-secret government network or a major corporation, hackers might still target your computer for fun, but increasingly, they're doing it for profit. Few hackers care to see which web pages someone visits, but many would be very interested in seeing the credit card numbers someone types into a particular web page. To snare this type of information, hackers will often install remote-access Trojan horses (see Chapter 5 for more information about RATs) that can capture keystrokes or screen images and send them to the hacker later.

Hackers also break into computers owned by individuals in order to install programs called "bots," which let them control that computer remotely. Unlike RATs, which allow a hacker to gain complete control over an infected computer, bots are much smaller programs that accept and perform a more limited range of commands. By linking bot-infected computers together, a hacker can create an army of "zombies" or "drones." With a single command, they can be instructed to send a flood of data to another computer that will shut it down (a denial of service attack), or send out massive amounts of junk email (spam). (Individual computers connected to high-speed Internet connections, such as DSL or cable modems, are especially prized because they're always available and can blast out information like spam at high speeds.)

There will always be some hacker with a reason to break into any particular system, including yours, whether you're in charge of a corporate computer installation or just your own personal computer.

FINDING A TARGET

When an army needs to find a target, they send out scouts who attempt to infiltrate enemy territory and report back on what they've found. Likewise, when hackers want to break into a computer, they need to scout out possible targets to determine which ones to attack. If hackers don't have a specific computer they want to attack, they'll often scout for targets of opportunity using war dialing, port scanning, and war driving.

War dialing

Before the growth of the Internet, war dialing was the best way to find a computer to attack. Even with today's heavy reliance on the Internet, many companies still use telephone modems to allow salespeople to remotely connect to and control an office computer using programs such as pcAnywhere or LapLink. If a computer happens to be connected to both a network and an outside telephone line, hackers can often sneak in through the telephone line, bypassing defenses deployed on the network. (If a computer is only accessible to the outside through a phone line, war dialing might be the only way to get in at all.) Phone lines typically don't have firewalls or intrusion detection systems.

Many companies get a false sense of security from knowing that a modem's phone number is not listed publicly. But just because a hacker doesn't know the specific phone number to a computer doesn't mean he can't find it. That's what war dialing is all about.

Most company phone numbers all use the same prefix. For example, internal phone lines for a company with the 239 prefix could all have numbers like 239-1029 or 239-8953. A hacker could spend all night dialing different telephone numbers until he reaches one with a modem on the other end, or simply let a computer do this tedious work by running a war dialer (see Chapter 2).

A war dialer can automatically dial a range of phone numbers, such as those from 239-1000 to 239-9999. For each number it tries, it listens for the telltale squeak of an answering modem and, if it hears it, records the telephone number. A hacker can let a war dialer run overnight and wake up the next morning with a list of phone numbers, both listed and unlisted, that are each connected to a modem.

He can then dial each telephone number individually. Before a computer will allow access through a telephone line, it usually asks for a password. All the hacker needs to do is guess the correct password and the computer will throw opens its doors to let the hacker inside.

One of the simplest defenses against war dialing is a callback device. The moment someone (a valid user or an intruder) calls the computer, the callback device hangs up and dials a pre-arranged telephone number that only a valid user would answer. Of course, a really determined hacker could somehow find out the phone number used by the callback device and then use call forwarding on that number to reroute the call to the hacker's phone number.

Port scanning

Port scanning works much like war dialing, but instead of dialing multiple phone numbers to find a way into a computer, scanners probe a range of Internet Protocol (IP) addresses, as shown in Figure 8-1.

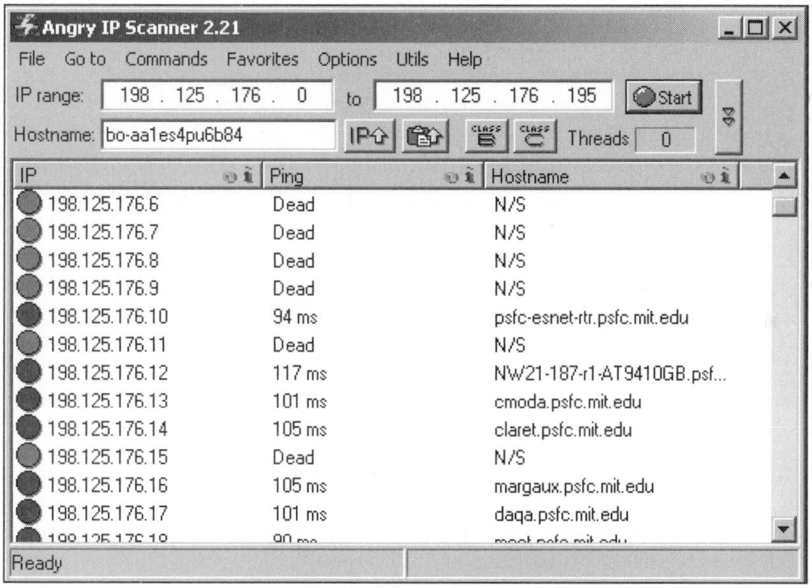

Figure 8-1: A port scanner can scan a range of IP addresses to find a computer to attack.

Every computer connected to the Internet uses ports, opening up countless doors that hackers can use to access a computer. Table 8-1 lists the more common ports, but keep in mind that a computer may have several hundred ports open at any given time.

Computers can communicate over the Internet using two protocols, TCP and UDP. Normally when one computer wants to communicate with another through a port using the TCP protocol, the first computer sends a synchronize (SYN) message to the second computer, which essentially tells it, "I'm ready to connect to your port." The type of communication the first computer wants to initiate determines which port number the computer uses, such as port 110 to send email or port 80 to send a web page. When the target computer receives this message, it sends back a synchronize/acknowledgment (SYN/ACK) message, which says, "Okay, I'm ready too." Now the first computer can send data to this particular open port of the second computer.

Table 8-1: Common types of ports available on servers accessible over the Internet

SERVICE	PORT
File Transfer Protocol (FTP)	21
Telnet	23
Simple Mail Transfer Protocol (SMTP)	25
Gopher	70
Finger	79
Hypertext Transfer Protocol (HTTP)	80
Post Office Protocol, version 3 (POP3)	110

The TCP protocol is often used when reliability is more important than speed, since constantly acknowledging the other computer can slow down communication. That's why sending email or transferring files is usually done using TCP.

The UDP protocol is most often used for streaming video or Internet telephony where speed is more crucial. The UDP protocol saves time because it doesn't go through the "handshaking" process that the TCP protocol requires, but like TCP, UDP can still be exploited.

In legitimate interactions, receiving TCP synchronization messages on a port is no cause for alarm, but receiving them unexpectedly and abundantly can be a telltale sign of an attempt to probe a computer's defenses, like a burglar loudly jiggling the handle of every door on a building, trying to see which ones are locked.

So to mask their probing attempts, port scanners use a variety of evasive techniques. While none of these techniques will work all the time, the combination of these tactics can help identify different ways to get into a computer, such as the following:

TCP connect scanning   Connects to a port by sending a synchronize (SYN) packet, waits for a return acknowledgment packet (SYN/ACK), and then sends another acknowledgment packet to connect (ACK). This type of scanning is what normally happens when two computers communicate through a port. This is easily recognized and often logged by target computers to alert system administrators of a possible hacker attack.

TCP SYN scanning   Connects to a port by sending a SYN packet and waits for a return acknowledgment packet (SYN/ACK), which indicates that the port is listening, but never sends an acknowledging ACK packet back to the target computer. Known as half-scanning, this technique is less likely to be logged and detected than ordinary TCP connect scanning, although now many security programs specifically look for this type of scanning simply because it's more likely to be used by hackers hiding their probing attempts.

TCP FIN scanning   Connects to a port by sending a "No more data from sender" (FIN) packet to a port. A closed port responds with a Reset (RST) message, while an open port simply ignores the FIN packet, thereby revealing its existence as an open port.

Fragmentation scanning   Breaks up the initial SYN packet into smaller pieces to mask its existence from any packet filter or firewall protecting the target computer. Used in conjunction with other scanning techniques such as TCP connect, TCP SYN, or TCP FIN scanning.

FTP bounce attack   Requests a file from an FTP server on the target system using the IP address and port number of another computer, thus masking the source of the attack (the hacker's computer). A successful file transfer indicates an open port on the target computer without revealing the hacker's IP address.

UDP (User Datagram Protocol) scanning   Uses UDP instead of TCP. When a closed UDP port receives a probe, its send an ICMP_PORT_UNREACH error message. Ports that don't send back an ICMP_PORT_UNREACH error message are open.

Once port scanning has determined that a computer on a specific IP address has ports open to attack, the next step is to determine what type of operating system and server software the target computer is using. To make this determination, hackers send data to different ports and analyze the way the computer responds, as shown in the port scanner screenshot in Figure 8-2.

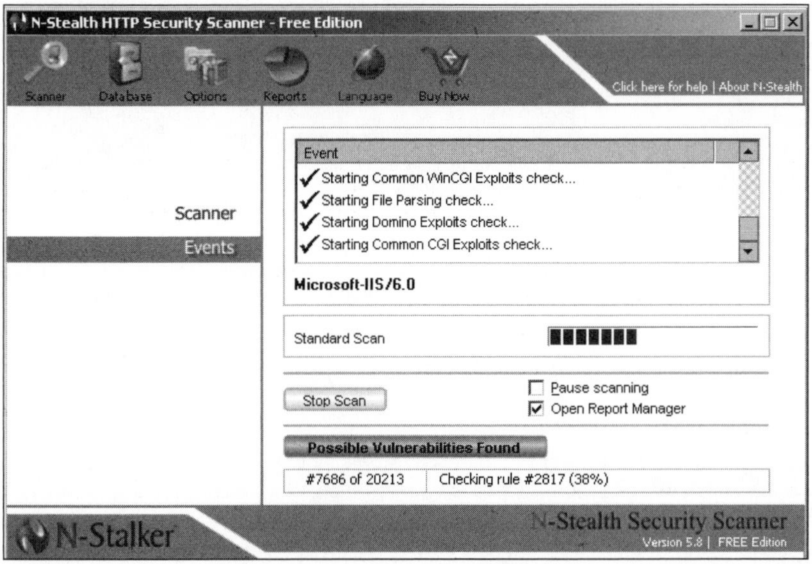

Figure 8-2: The N-Stealth port scanner has identified that this particular target computer is running Microsoft IIS, version 6.0.

Port scanners use a variety of platform-probing techniques, including the following:

FIN probing   Sends a FIN ("No more data from sender") packet to a port and waits for a response. Windows responds to FIN packets with Reset (RST) messages, so if a RST message comes back, the computer is likely running Windows.

FIN/SYN probing   Sends a FIN/SYN packet to a port and waits for a response. Linux systems respond with a FIN/SYN/ACK packet.

TCP initial window checking   Checks the window size on packets returned from the target computer. The window size from the AIX operating system is 0x3F25 and the window size from OpenBSD or FreeBSD is 0x402E.

ICMP message quoting   Sends data to a closed port and waits to receive an error message. All computers should send back the initial IP header of the data with an additional eight bytes tacked on. Solaris and Linux systems, however, return more than eight bytes.

Once a hacker knows the IP address of a target computer, the open ports available on that target computer, and the type of operating system used by the target computer, the hacker can plan his strategy for breaking in, much like a burglar might case a house before trying to break into it in order to determine the best route.

If you want to see how a port scanner works, you can try Angry IP Scanner (www .angryziber.com/ipscan); Nessus (www.nessus.org); iNetTools (www.wildpackets.com); N-Stealth (www.nstalker.com/eng/products/nstealth); Nmap (www.insecure.org/nmap); SAINT (www.saintcorporation.com); or SARA (http://www-arc.com/sara).

Nmap is considered the premier port scanning tool, which offers a variety of scanning and evasion techniques. Since most networks now use firewalls and intrusion detection systems (IDS) to detect port scanners, Nmap breaks its data packets into smaller fragments, which can fool a firewall or IDS from recognizing that a port scan is even taking place.

Nmap also lets you spoof where data is coming from. If a firewall or IDS detects a flood of data coming from one computer, it might rightly conclude a hacker is probing its defenses. But by using Nmap, a hacker can still probe a computer, but each probe appears to come from a different computer (when it's really coming from a single computer). No matter how good a firewall or IDS may be, it can never be 100 percent reliable, and port scanners like Nmap constantly evolve to take advantage of the latest tricks.

War driving

Rather than physically connecting computers with cables to form a network, many companies and individuals are turning to wireless networks instead. The idea is simple. You plug in a device known as a router or access point, which relays signals to and from any computer with a wireless network interface card (NIC). Those computers can then access the resulting wireless network as if they were physically connected to one another through cables.

Any computer with a wireless card within range of the wireless access point can access a wireless network. Unfortunately, it also means that a wireless card plugged into a hacker's laptop across the street could access that same network too. When you set up a wireless network, it's like having a normal wired network with cables sticking out of every window in the building, which anyone can plug into their computer and use to access your network, at any time, without you necessarily knowing about it.

With so many corporations and individuals going wireless these days, hackers can locate wireless networks simply by driving around a neighborhood with a laptop computer, a wireless network interface card, and a scanning program. Sometimes hackers also include a global positioning system (GPS) for mapping out the exact location of the wireless networks they find. The process of driving around and scanning for wireless networks is called *war driving*. (There is also war strolling, war flying, and war boating, but the main idea in each case is the same: cruise a neighborhood and search for wireless networks.)

Once you have a laptop or handheld computer with wireless capability, you can just saunter over near an unguarded wireless "hotspot" (an area where wireless access is available) and use it to connect directly to the Internet.

While coffeehouses and public libraries offer free wireless Internet access as an attractive service to their customers, many individuals and businesses unwittingly offer free wireless Internet access as well. When people set up a wireless network, they usually just plug their wireless router into their Internet connection (such as a cable or DSL modem) and right away, they have wireless access. Unfortunately, these people don't realize that the range of Internet access often extends beyond the physical boundaries of their home or office and spills out into the streets and sidewalks. Anyone can access the Internet through these unintentional wireless hotspots.

As mentioned, to find a wireless (WiFi) hotspot, you can drag your laptop or handheld computer around with you, or you can just use a handy WiFi locator device, such as the ones made by WiFi Seeker (www.wifiseeker.com) or by Intego (www.intego.com/wiFiLocator), shown in Figure 8-3.

Figure 8-3: A WiFi locator device lets you scan for WiFi hotspots without a computer.

In a surprising number of cases, people will set up a wireless network with no thought to security, which means you can access that WiFi network just by turning on your wireless-enabled computer. To prevent this, some people will turn on WiFi encryption, known as Wired Equivalent Privacy (WEP).

WEP encryption scrambles any data sent across a WiFi network, which essentially blocks strangers from accessing a WiFi network. The original WEP encryption standard only used 40-bit encryption keys, but newer, more secure WEP encryption uses 128-bit keys. The longer the keys used to encrypt data, the harder the encryption is to crack. It's a bit like trying to guess a number between 1 and 10 versus guessing a number between 1 and 999,999,999.

To defeat WEP encryption, hackers use special sniffer programs that snare data from the WiFi network for cryptanalysis. The more data the sniffer program grabs, the better its chances of figuring out how the WiFi network is encrypting its data. Given enough time, most sniffer programs will eventually be able to crack WEP encryption, letting the hacker on to the network.

Newer wireless networks now use WiFi Protected Access (WPA), which is a stronger encryption standard. However, even this isn't invulnerable to attack, since hackers have developed a program dubbed coWPAtty, which snares enough data from the wireless network and then uses a dictionary attack (see Chapter 9 for more information about cracking passwords using a dictionary attack) to find the password needed to access the wireless network.

Hackers have developed sniffer programs for all types of computers and operating systems including Windows, Linux, Macintosh, and even Palm and PocketPC handheld computers. To find a sniffer program, visit WarDriving.com (www.wardriving.com). For a specialized operating system designed just to sniff out WiFi networks, download and run a unique Linux distribution dubbed WarLinux (http://sourceforge.net/projects/warlinux).

To defeat sniffers, some corporate networks rely on client-side certificates, which verify that a particular computer is allowed access to a network. If a computer tries to access a network without the proper client-side certificate, the network cuts it off. Client-side certificates make accessing a wireless network harder, but if a hacker hijacks a computer that is allowed to access the network, the hacker can access the network through a "trusted" computer, which proves that there really is no such thing as a "trusted" computer.

The steps to accessing a WiFi network

The first step to accessing a WiFi network is to find a WiFi signal, either by using a WiFi locator device or by letting your WiFi-equipped computer scan the airwaves. Since two WiFi networks may overlap each other, each one identifies itself with a *service set identifier (SSID)*, which is a unique, descriptive name for a network. A computer must know the WiFi network's SSID to connect to it.

There are two ways hackers can retrieve this information. First, they can use a sniffer program to snare data packets out of the air and examine them to piece together the SSID. Second, they can anticipate that the network administrator will have left the WiFi network's default manufacturer settings in place including the default SSID, which is often just the name of the company that makes the WiFi router, such as *LinkSys* or *NetGear*. So when prowling the airwaves, hackers will first try all the various default passwords used by different WiFi manufacturers.

Some WiFi networks may require a user name and a password for access. As with SSID settings, however, nearly all WiFi equipment comes with a default user name and password, and few people bother to change this. So hackers first try feeding a WiFi network a known default password and user name for that particular WiFi manufacturer. If this doesn't work, the hacker can use the sniffer program to study data packets used by the WiFi network and steal a legitimate user's user name and password. In their quest to thwart intruders, some WiFi networks will only grant access to network interfaces with specific (MAC) addresses, which uniquely identify computers on a WiFi network. However, to find a valid MAC address, hackers can do the same basic thing that they do to steal user names and passwords.

If you have a WiFi network, consider it vulnerable to attack. Someone can always attempt to access it from next door, down the street, or from a car parked outside your window. (Quick! Take a look now!)

Finding a WiFi network

If you want to find a WiFi network that openly accepts users (for free or for a fee), visit a WiFi hotspot search engine such as HotSpot Haven (www.hotspothaven.com) or WiFiMaps.com (www.wifimaps.com). By planning ahead, you can always be near a WiFi hotspot, whether you're in Pittsburgh or Pasadena.

However, if you want to find a WiFi network that *isn't* open to the public, you can visit the Wireless Geographic Logging Engine (www.wigle.net), which lists known WiFi hotspots in different parts of the world, as shown in Figure 8-4.

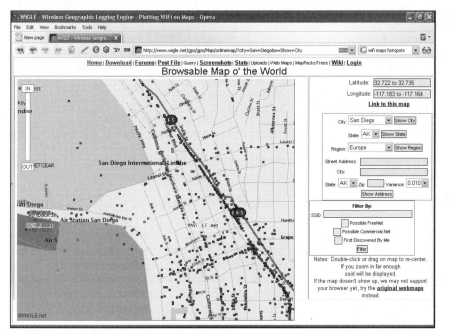

Figure 8-4: A WiFi map can show you possible hotspots near your hometown.

To make finding a WiFi network even easier, hackers have adopted the techniques of late 19th- and early 20th-century hobos who used to carve or draw marks on trees and buildings to warn other hobos of unfriendly towns, sympathetic households, or good places to hop on a passing train. Likewise, war chalking today (visit www.warchalking.org) involves drawing marks around a neighborhood to identify the location and features of a particular wireless network, as shown in Figure 8-5.

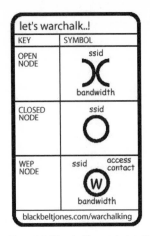

Figure 8-5: War-chalking symbols to identify
the location and status of a wireless network.

Once that first hacker discovers a WiFi network and leaves behind a war-chalking mark, other hackers will likely explore that wireless network. Although many companies make wireless equipment, many wireless hacking tools like Kismet (www.kismetwireless .net), contain a database of default wireless configurations for each manufacturer. Since most people never change these default settings, a hacker using Kismet (or a similar wireless hacking tool) can often access a wireless network right away.

With so many unwanted intruders poking around a network, it's only a matter of time before one of them accidentally or purposely disrupts, deletes, or alters some important files.

Protecting a WiFi network

It's easy to protect a WiFi network from intruders: Just turn it off. Of course, it's not practical to turn it off when you're using it, so here are some simple tips to help protect your WiFi network from an unwanted intruder.

First, try lowering the signal strength from your wireless network's access point. By lowering the signal, you can limit its range from extending beyond the area in which you need it. Next, change all the default settings of your WiFi equipment, such as its SSID identifier and user name and password. Next, turn on MAC address filtering so that your WiFi network only allows computers with network interfaces with specific MAC addresses to access the network. Finally, turn on WEP encryption. While WEP encryption can't protect your network from a determined hacker, it can discourage the opportunistic hacker looking for an easy WiFi network to access. New WiFi equipment supports an improved encryption standard known as WiFi Protected Access (WPA). Given a choice, use WPA instead of WEP encryption.

For those who like to take a proactive stance in defending against hackers, try running a program called Fake AP, created by Black Alchemy (www.blackalchemy.to). The Fake AP program floods the airwaves with phony SSIDs. Now if a hacker tries to find your WiFi network, he'll have to wade through this flood of bogus SSIDs, which decreases the chances that he'll actually find, let alone break into, your WiFi network.

Probing sites by Google hacking

The key to breaking into any computer is to learn what type of software it runs. While it's possible to obtain this information by connecting directly to a target computer and running one of many hacker programs that probe a computer's security perimeter, this is much like a prowler peeking through the windows of a house that he plans to burglarize. It may work, but it risks alerting the target that it's being cased, and also leaves a trail that could potentially lead back to the intruder.

So rather than take this risk, hackers simply let Google find this information for them. Not only does this keep the hacker's identity hidden, but it also prevents the target from knowing it's being probed.

Finding specific webserver software using Google

Hackers often specialize in breaking into specific webserver programs, and they can use Google to help them find more vulnerable computers to attack. To search for websites that run specific webserver programs, just type in the name of the server software you want to find, such as *Microsoft IIS 5.0* or *Red Hat Server 3.0*, using the following query format:

`intitle:index.of "Software name"`

`intitle`	Searches for web pages that contain a particular word or phrase in their titles
`index.of`	Specifies the directory listing of a website, which often has the title "Index of" near the top of the page
`"Software name"`	Specifies a particular webserver program name, such as *Microsoft IIS 6.0* or *Apache 2.2*

This type of Google query examines a website's directory listing to reveal both the way the website organizes its files and the name and version of the webserver software running it, as shown in Figure 8-6.

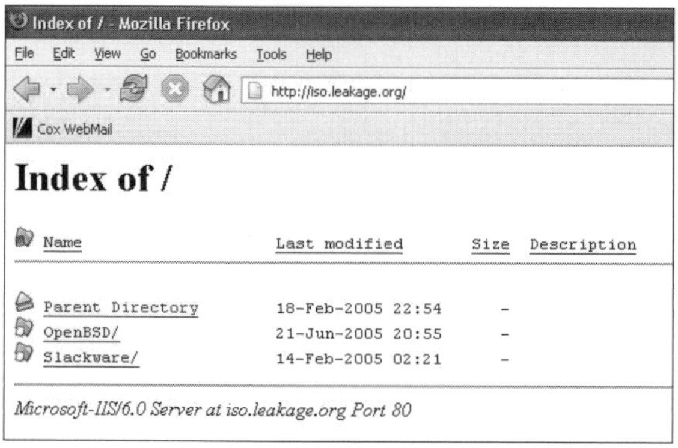

Figure 8-6: A website's directory listing exposes both the directories where crucial files are stored along with the name and version number of the webserver software.

Searching specific websites

Another powerful Google search tool is the `site` operator, which narrows your search to a specific website domain. It has the following format:

`site:"Domain name" "Search term"`

`site`	Searches for web pages stored on sites in a specific domain
`"Domain name"`	Specifies the domain, such as .edu or army.mil
`"Search term"`	Specifies a search word or phrase

While this query can be useful to find specific types of information on specific types of websites, such as looking for information about "terrorism" on all ".gov" website domains, the real power of the `site` operator appears when it is combined with the `intitle` operator. This combination can search websites in specific domains running specific webserver programs.

So if you know how to break into an Apache webserver and you want to know which US Army websites might be running it, you could use the following query, which would display a listing as shown in Figure 8-7:

`site:army.mil intitle:index.of apache`

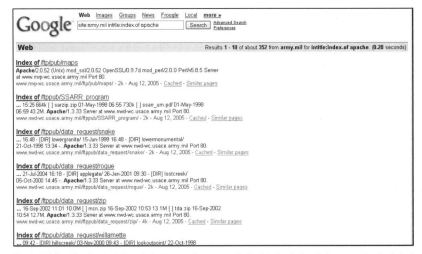

Figure 8-7: By using the `intitle` and `site` keywords, you can find a list of websites that run a particular webserver program.

Once you know which of your targeted websites run specific versions of a webserver program (such as Apache 1.3), you can use Google once more to search for *Apache vulnerabilities* or a similar string to view information about known flaws in that particular webserver program.

NOTE: *Rather than use Google to search for software flaws, you can also browse through computer security sites such as Packetstormsecurity.org and CERT.org that list the latest software vulnerabilities found in webservers.*

Security bulletins are meant to alert system administrators to flaws that they should patch immediately. However, many system administrators either never see these bulletins or don't implement them right away. As a result, hackers can also use security bulletins to find vulnerable websites (and many do).

For example, suppose you find a security bulletin that identifies a flaw in Apache and recommends that users upgrade to Apache version 1.3.27. Armed with this information, you just have to search for any website running an earlier version of Apache, and you'll know that it is likely to be vulnerable to the specific flaw described in the security bulletin. In many cases, security bulletins can be just as helpful to hackers as they are to system administrators.

Probing a website's defenses

Many system administrators run security scanners to probe for holes on their sites. This typically generates a report of its findings for the system administrators to study. Not surprisingly, many system administrators never delete these security scanner reports, and you can use a Google query using the `intitle` operator to look for them once you know the heading the security scanner always stores on its reports.

For example, one popular security scanner is Nessus (www.nessus.org), whose reports you can search for using the following query format:

```
intitle:"Scanner header"
```

To look for Nessus security scanner reports, the scanner header search string is "Nessus Scan Report":

```
intitle:"Nessus Scan Report" "This file was generated by Nessus"
```

This will help you find security scanner reports on other websites, as shown in Figure 8-8.

Even if the vulnerabilities reported by a security scanner report have been closed, a security scanner report can help hackers understand the defenses of a target computer better. Since security scanners can't detect every possible vulnerability, they can give lazy system administrators a false sense of security. If a knowledgeable hacker knows of a security flaw that a scanner doesn't detect, the system administrator may not have detected that flaw either, and there's a good chance that the hacker can exploit the flaw.

Besides security scanners, many system administrators rely on intrusion detection tools, such as the popular open-source Snort (www.snort.org). To create reports, Snort users often run a program called SnorfSnarf. Once again, if system administrators don't delete the SnortSnarf files from their systems, hackers can find them by simply searching with Google for "SnortSnarf alert page." Not only can this alert hackers that a particular website is running the Snort intrusion-detection system, but the retrieved SnortSnarf reports will also show the types of attacks that other hackers have tried (and that have, presumably, failed), as shown in Figure 8-9.

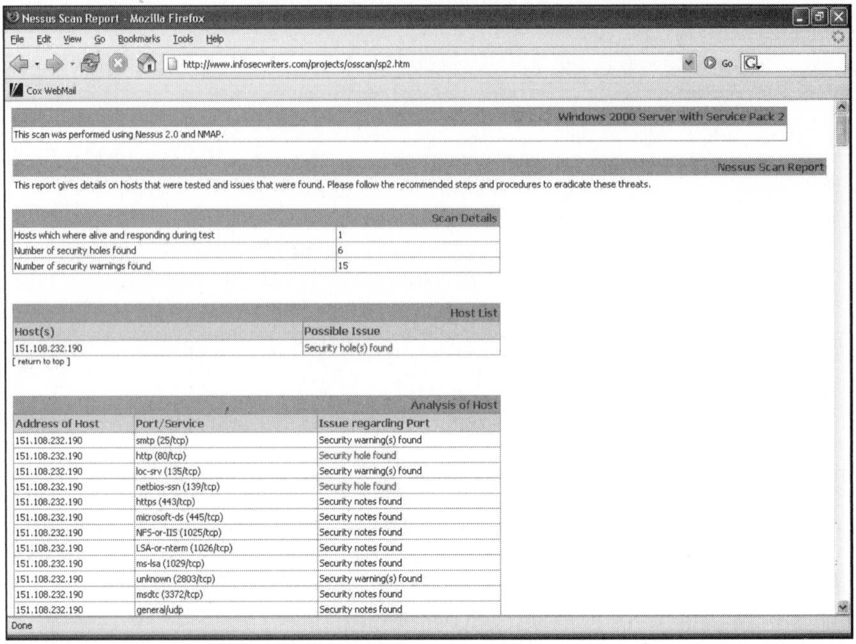

Figure 8-8: By searching for security scanner reports, you can learn what holes might still be open on a system.

Combine the "SnortSnart alert page" query with the `site` operator, and you can find out which websites are running the Snort intrusion-detection program using a query such as this one:

```
site:edu  snortsnarf alert page
```

The above query tells Google to search for all educational websites (.edu) that have used the SnortSnarf program to create a report.

Finding and copying files using Google

Rather than break into a website (and risk getting caught), hackers can often retrieve the site files they want through Google. Many system administrators store user names, addresses, telephone numbers, and even Social Security numbers in a Microsoft Access database file, often called admin.mdb. To search for these types of files, you just need to use the `allinurl` operator. The format of this query is as follows:

```
allinurl:"Filename"
```

allinurl   Searches for web pages that contain "*Filename*" in the web page locator string

"*Filename*"   Specifies the file to find

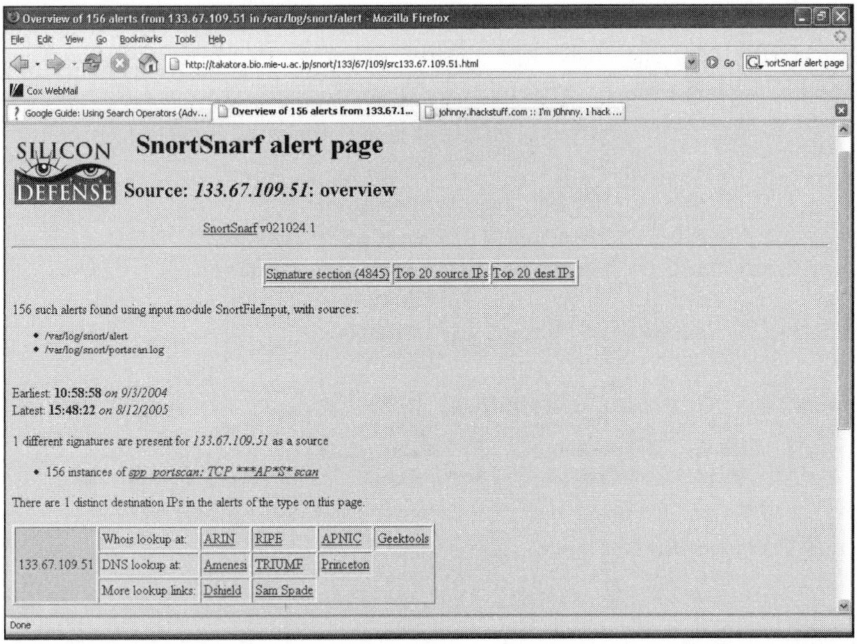

Figure 8-9: Viewing the report files of a website scanner can tell you in advance what types of attacks it is already protected against.

So to find the admin.mbd file, which often contains sensitive information, you would just use this query:

```
allinurl:admin.mdb
```

After finding this file using Google, you can download it through Google and view it, as shown in Figure 8-10, all in the privacy of your own computer.

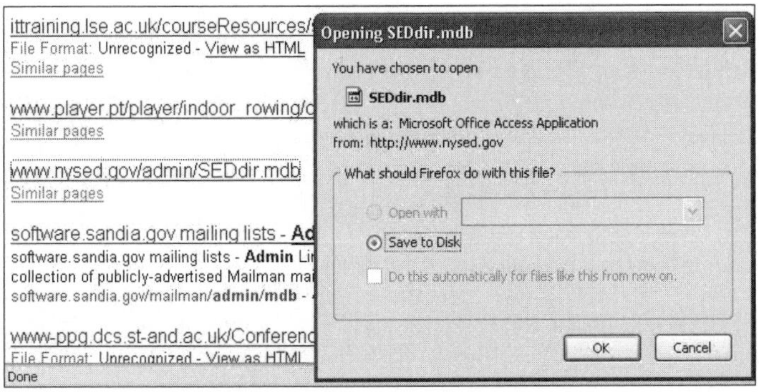

Figure 8-10: After finding a file with a Google query, you can download it from the website.

Another Google search operator that comes in handy for finding specific types of files is the `filetype` operator. Its format is as follows:

```
filetype:"File extension" "Search term"
```

`filetype`	Searches for files having the extension identified by *"File extension"*
"File extension"	Specifies the type of file to search for, such as PDF (Adobe Acrobat files) or DOC (Microsoft Word files)
"Search term"	Specifies a word or phrase to find in these files

So if you wanted to find Microsoft Word documents that contain the phrase *for internal use only*, you could use this query:

```
filetype:doc "for internal use only"
```

Combine the `filetype` operator with the `site` operator and you can search for all Microsoft Word documents that contain *for internal use only* in military websites, as shown below:

```
site:mil filetype:doc "for internal use only"
```

The `filetype` operator isn't likely to uncover any files containing top-secret documents or evidence of conspiracy, but it can be one more way to probe the inner workings of a website. In addition, the `filetype` operator demonstrates just how invasive Google is in indexing information that most website administrators don't even know have thereby been exposed to the world.

Guarding against Google hackers

To defend against Google hackers, keep any sensitive files off your webserver. Just because a file can't be accessed through your web pages doesn't mean that a hacker can't find that file anyway. Even if a sensitive file is only on your website temporarily, you are not safe.

Then try Google hacking your own webserver and see what you find. You may be surprised at how much information Google may already know about your server and how vulnerable your computer might really be.

Search engines like Google constantly troll different websites and store the files they find in a storage area called the cache. Once your website's files have been stored in Google's (or some other search engine's) cache, anyone can view them by using the `cache` operator. For example, if you want to view pages that were previously displayed by a website, you can use the `cache` operator followed by the website address, as shown below:

```
cache:cnn.com
```

This Google query will show you the web pages currently stored on Google for the CNN.com website. These pages will remain in Google's cache until the next time Google refreshes its cache by visiting the CNN.com website, even if CNN.com has removed or altered the pages in the meantime.

Google, like most search engines that regularly "crawl" the Internet to find websites to index, follows certain rules when visiting websites. One of those rules is that website administrators can create a special robots.txt file that specifies which parts of the website the search engine should not explore and store in its cache. So if there are sensitive files that on your computer that you don't want others to see, you can create a robots.txt file to tell Google not to index them. (Of course, it's much safer not to put sensitive files on your webserver computer in the first place.) To learn more about how the robots.txt file works, visit www.robotstxt.org. Just be aware that hackers can also peek at your robots.txt file to see what type of information you want to protect, and then they'll know exactly what type of information to look for in your computer.

Another alternative is to request that search engines (for example, Google) ignore your website altogether. However, while this can prevent hackers from scanning your site using the search engine, it can also keep legitimate users from finding it that way too. To request that Google remove your site from its index, follow the steps listed at www.google.com/remove.html.

Finally, visit the Google Hacking Database (GHDB)—http://johnny.ihackstuff.com— to see how Google has exposed other websites to attack. You can (hopefully) thus learn how not to fall victim to the same tricks.

Every tool on the Internet can be used for good or for bad, and Google is no exception. If you run a website, you must learn about Google hacking in order to lock down your system's defenses. If you're just a curious and non-malicious individual, have fun experimenting with Google. You may find more than you ever imagined.

THE NEXT STEP

With war dialing, port scanning, war driving, and Google hacking, hackers can locate nearly any computer connected to a phone line or the Internet. Unfortunately, once hackers find such a computer, they often can't resist the temptation to break in to it and explore it. And once a hacker has broken into a computer, the results could range from the hacker simply browsing around but altering nothing to his trashing the entire system and wrecking everything in sight. If you're in charge of a system's security, have fun trying to guard against the many ways someone can spy on your system. If you're a hacker, take your pick on which tactics to try first to peek past a computer's security defenses. No matter which method you use, there's a good chance one of them will work and help you circumvent even the most expensive computer security system in the world.

9

CRACKING PASSWORDS

Finding a computer to attack is the first step. Breaking into that computer is the second step. Most hackers succeed not as a result of any innate brilliance on their part, but because of ignorance on the victim's part.

The first line of defense protecting most computers is usually nothing more than a unique combination of letters and numbers known as a password. Passwords are meant to block access to anyone but legitimate users, but they're actually the weakest link in any security system. The most secure passwords are lengthy, consisting of random combinations of numbers, symbols, and both uppercase and lowercase letters. However, most people tend to choose simple, easy-to-remember passwords. They also tend to use the same password for several different systems (for example, their work computer, America Online account, and Windows screensaver). If you discover a person's password, you'll often have the key to a great deal of his or her information, even if it's stored in several different accounts.

When a computer requires a password that you don't know, you have several options:

- Steal a valid password

- Guess the password

- Brute-force the password

The cure for boredom is curiosity. There is no cure for curiosity.

—DOROTHY PARKER

PASSWORD STEALING

If you can get physical access to a computer, the easiest way to steal a password is by shoulder surfing—peeking over someone's shoulder as he or she types. You can also try poking around the person's desk. Most people find passwords hard to remember, so they write them down and store them for easy reference, perhaps on a Post-It stuck to their monitor or inside a desk drawer. That's why hackers often get jobs as janitors. Cleaning offices late at night when no one is around gives them ample opportunity to explore each person's desk and even experiment with the company computers.

If a hacker can't find a password written in plain sight, they may try to social-engineer a password out of a gullible user (see Chapter 3) or try default passwords that come with common types of equipment such as Cisco routers. For a list of default equipment passwords, visit the Default Password List (www.phenoelit.de/dpl/dpl.html), CIRT.net (www.cirt.net/cgi-bin/passwd.pl), or another site called Default Password List (http://defaultpassword.com).

If social engineering or default passwords fail, the next best method is to steal the password using one of the following:

- A keystroke logger

- A desktop monitoring program

- A password recovery program

NOTE: *All of these programs require you to have access to the victim's computer so you can install or run the program without his or her knowledge.*

Using a keystroke logger

A *keystroke recorder* or *logger* records every keystroke a person types and saves this information in a file that a hacker can examine later. By using a keystroke logger, you can retrieve email addresses, email and instant messages, credit card numbers, and (of course) passwords. Some keystroke loggers can even capture screenshot images period-ically so you can see which program someone was using while typing certain keystrokes.

Figure 9-1 shows some of the different options for setting up a keystroke logger, such as where to store captured keystrokes and whether to load automatically when the computer boots up.

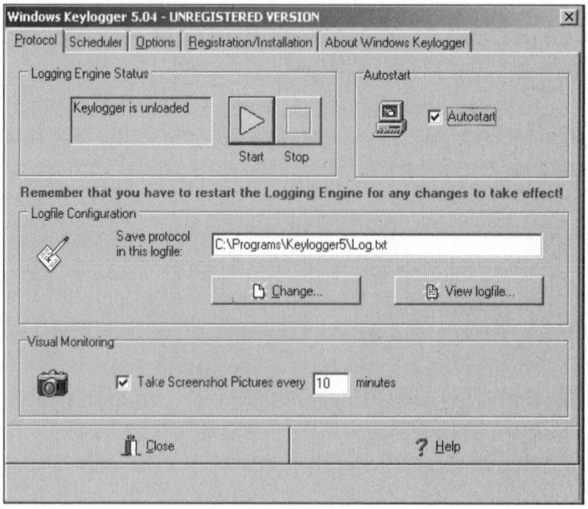

Figure 9-1: A keystroke logger lets you spy on a computer without the user's knowledge.

Unlike most programs, which display their name and accompanying icon in such places as the Windows Start menu and the Windows taskbar, keystroke loggers hide in the background so victims won't even know they're running. Although it's possible to search through a computer's memory, the Windows registry, or the hard disk to find a keystroke logger running, victims won't bother looking if they don't suspect anything is spying on them in the first place.

Since there's always a chance that these software keystroke loggers could be detected, and each program only works with certain operating systems, such as Windows, a second alternative is to use a hardware-based keystroke logger. These types of keystroke loggers plug in between the computer and the keyboard.

Of course, a piece of peripheral hardware can be spotted just by looking at the back of the computer, but it's completely invisible to any software running on that computer. Some people never look at the back of their machine, especially at work. Best of all, hardware keystroke loggers work with any operating system, including FreeBSD, Linux, or Windows XP.

Some popular hardware keystroke loggers include KeyGhost (www.keyghost.com), Hardware Keylogger (www.amecisco.com), Key Phantom (www.keyphantom.com), and KEYKatcher (www.keykatcher.com). To find a software keystroke logger, visit Keylogger.com (www.keylogger.org), which rates the different keystroke loggers by their features and ease of use.

One problem with hardware keystroke loggers is that they can only hold a limited amount of keystrokes, such as 128,000 keystrokes stored in 128MB. While this may sound like a lot of keystrokes, it's possible that the user could type 128,000 keystrokes playing a video game, which fills up the keystroke logger's memory, and then the keystroke logger won't have any more room left to hold the 128,001 through 128,009 keystrokes, which may contain the password you want.

Keystroke loggers cause additional problems from a legal point of view. Some people argue that keystroke logging should be treated as wiretapping and made illegal except for court-authorized use. Others believe it's okay to use a keystroke logger on your own equipment, even if it means spying on other users. Until the courts decide how to categorize keystroke loggers, using one could mean breaking a law that you never even knew existed.

Spying with a desktop monitoring program

Desktop monitoring programs are extra-strength keystroke loggers with added features. Not only can they record keystrokes, but they can also secretly track which programs a person uses, how long the person uses each program, and every website viewed. To identify who has used the computer at any given time, a desktop monitoring program can also secretly turn on a webcam to watch the person sitting in front of the screen, as shown in Figure 9-2.

To find a desktop monitoring program, try these sites: AppsTraka (http://appstraka .hypermart.net), PC Spy (www.softdd.com), Desktop Surveillance (www.omniquad.com), or NetSpy (www.skysof.com).

You can even install some desktop monitoring programs remotely without ever physically accessing a victim's computer. To remotely install a desktop monitoring program, you can send a victim a seemingly harmless email message that contains a link for

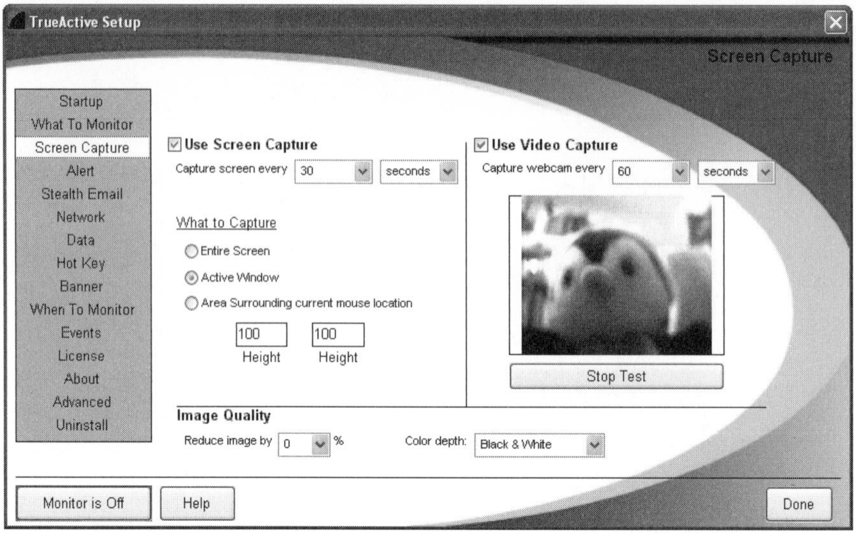

Figure 9-2: A desktop monitoring program can track every program someone uses and take that person's picture too.

them to view a greeting card. However, as soon as they click this link, they'll see the greeting card and install the desktop monitoring program at the same time. Now the desktop monitoring program can spy on a victim from afar much like a RAT (see Chapter 5).

Many corporations now use desktop monitoring programs to protect themselves in case employees start sending inappropriate email messages to others under the company's time. Some corporations have even gone a step further and use desktop monitoring programs to make sure employees are working rather than checking sports scores on the Internet.

Many companies even market desktop monitoring programs as a way to spy on your spouse, kids, or boyfriend/girlfriend to make sure they aren't doing something you don't want them to do. Of course, if you feel the need to monitor (spy on) people close to you, you may have a bigger problem than just knowing what they're doing on a computer.

Using a password recovery program

Because typing a password over and over again to access a program can be a nuisance, many programs let users store passwords. For security, the passwords are hidden behind a string of asterisks on the screen. But people often forget their passwords and then can't access their programs or files. Enter password recovery programs, which can, of course, also be used to retrieve other people's passwords. By running one of these password recovery programs and moving the mouse pointer over an asterisk-hidden password, you can see the plain text underneath, as shown in Figure 9-3.

Some popular password recovery programs include ActMon Password Recovery XP (www.actmon.com/password-recovery), Password Recovery Toolkit (www.lostpassword .com), Peek-a-Boo Password Viewer (www.corteksoft.com), and Revelation (www .snadboy.com).

Besides restricting access to particular programs, passwords can also block access to individual files such as WordPerfect documents or Microsoft Excel spreadsheets.

118

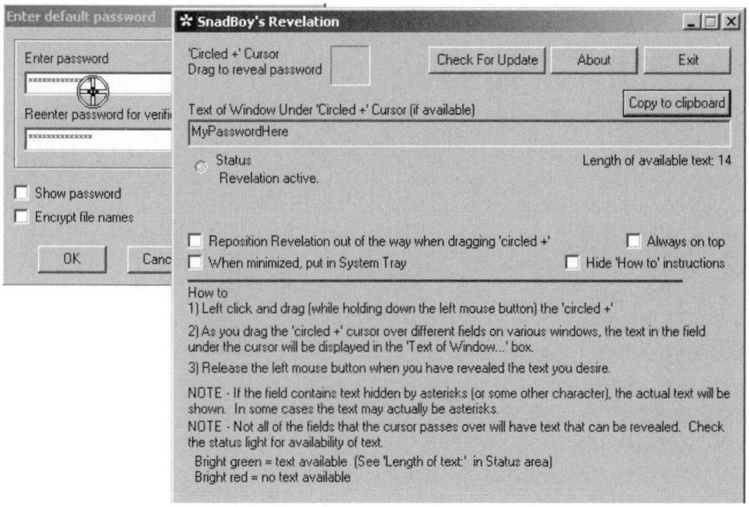

Figure 9-3: The Revelation password recovery program can reveal any password hidden behind a mask of asterisks.

To retrieve or crack password-protected files, get a special program from one of these companies: Access Data (www.accessdata.com), Passware (www.lostpassword.com), ElCom (www.elcomsoft.com), Password Crackers Inc. (www.pwcrack.com), or Alpine Snow (www.alpinesnow.com), which is shown in Figure 9-4.

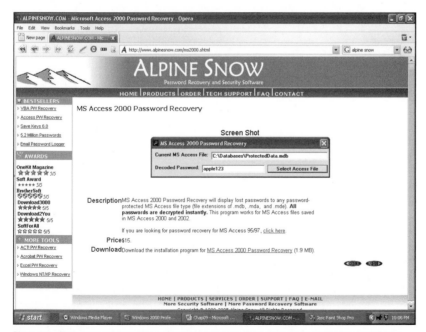

Figure 9-4: You can buy special software to crack the passwords of certain files such as those created by Microsoft Access.

DICTIONARY ATTACKS

Ideally, a password should be a random collection of numbers, symbols, and uppercase and lowercase letters, but few people want to waste time creating a difficult password that they're likely to forget. Instead, most choose easy-to-remember passwords that are ordinary words. To find such simple passwords, hackers have created special password cracking programs that use dictionary files (sometimes called word lists).

Figure 9-5 shows a password-cracking program called Brutus, which tries to break into a website using two files, users.txt and words.txt. The users.txt file contains a list of common user names, and the words.txt file contains common passwords. By mixing and matching different user names and passwords, Brutus can try endless combinations until it finds both a valid user name and the password that works for that user name.

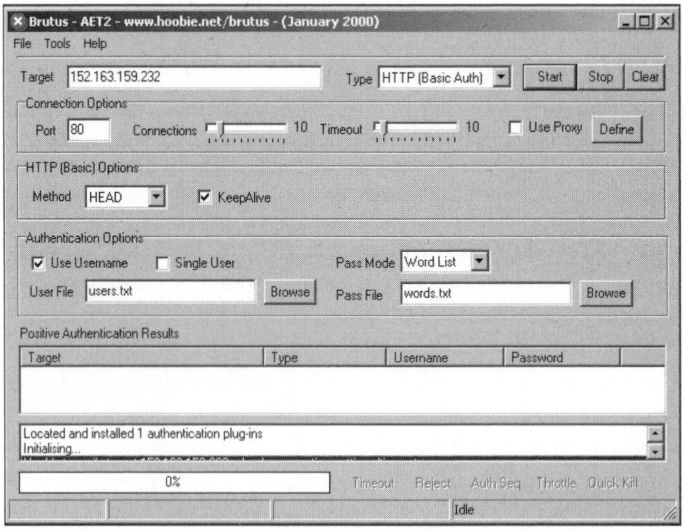

Figure 9-5: The Brutus password cracker can keep mixing various combinations of user names and passwords until it breaks into a website.

A dictionary file simply contains common words that people are likely to use as a memorable password, such as names of actors, popular cartoon characters, and rock bands, *Star Trek* jargon, common male and female names, technology-related words, and other words found in most dictionaries.

The password-cracking program takes a word from the dictionary file and tries this word as a password to access a computer. If the first word isn't right, the program tries another word from its dictionary file until it either finds the correct password or runs out of words. Of course, a hacker can keep trying different dictionary files; if a password is an ordinary word, it's only a matter of time before a dictionary attack will find it.

To increase the odds of uncovering a password, some password-cracking programs will try not only every word in a dictionary file, but also subtle variations on each word such as spelling the word backwards or adding different numbers on the end. So even though a password like *SNOOPY12* won't be found in an ordinary dictionary file, the password-cracking program can still uncover this password by manipulating each word in its dictionary file.

One of the most popular password-cracking tools is John the Ripper (www .openwall.com/john), and one of the largest collections of word lists can be found at the Wordlist Project (www.gattinger.org/wordlists), which offers lists in various languages including English, Spanish, Japanese, and Russian.

To find other password-cracking programs, visit Russian Password Crackers (www.password-crackers.com), AntiOnline (www.antionline.com), and New Order (http://neworder.box.sk).

BRUTE-FORCE PASSWORD ATTACKS

Dictionary attacks can find passwords that are ordinary words or variations of words, but sometimes a password consists of random characters. In these cases, the only solution is to use a brute-force attack.

As the name implies, a *brute-force attack* exhaustively tries every possible combination of numbers, letters, and symbols until it finds the right password. So even if someone's password is as obscure as *NI8$FQ2*, a brute-force attack will eventually find it (and every other password on that computer).

The main drawback of brute-force attacks is time. You can sit in front of a bank's combination lock and try every three-number combination possible, but it may take you a long time to find the one that opens the lock. Similarly, a brute-force attack might take a few thousand years to find a valid password.

For this reason, brute-force attacks are generally useless against individual computers protected by strong passwords (consisting of random letters, numbers, and symbols). However, they are still potentially effective on a network. The more people who use a network, the more likely at least one person will have chosen a simple, easy-to-remember password, such as her dog's name or the first three numbers of her home phone number. A brute-force attack will discover the weakest password into a network, and that's all a hacker needs.

PASSWORDS: THE FIRST LINE OF DEFENSE

Choosing a unique, hard-to-guess password will probably stop all but the most determined hackers. (It can also stop you if you can't remember it.) To foil most hackers, just sprinkle your passwords with some random characters (such as symbols and numbers) or use a special program, such as Quicky Password Generator (www.quickysoftware.com), Masking Password Generator (www.accusolve.biz), or RandPass (www.randpass.com), that can create genuinely random passwords of varying lengths, as shown in Figure 9-6.

Of course, trying to remember a random password can be troublesome, so many people create passwords based on meaningful phrases that they won't forget, such as "IhtP2004," which can stand for "I hate the President," followed by an election year. By taking the first letter of a memorable phrase and sprinkling it with numbers or other characters that make sense only to you, you can create a password that's impossible to guess.

In general, the longer the password, the harder it will be for someone to guess or crack. In Windows NT, passwords are particularly easy to crack since they consist of 14 uppercase characters, divided into two 7-character parts. So rather than force hackers to crack a 14-character password, Windows NT allows hackers to crack a 7-character password twice, which is far simpler to do.

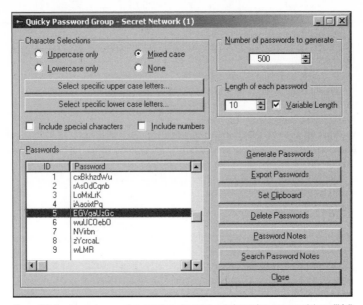

Figure 9-6: A password-generating program can create a truly random password that will foil most hackers.

BLOCKING ACCESS WITH BIOMETRICS

Another way to block access to a computer is through *biometrics*, which identifies authorized users through their unique fingerprints, retina scans, voices, or other physiological or behavioral features. Hackers can always steal or guess obvious passwords like *sex* or *password*, but it's much more difficult to steal—and nearly impossible to guess—someone else's fingerprint pattern.

Biometrics works on the principle that every person has unique characteristics that are impossible to duplicate; even identical twins have different sets of fingerprints. Typically, a biometric security system works by comparing data collected from someone attempting to gain access to the system with a database of authorized data patterns. First, therefore, every authorized user's biometric data must be stored in a database against which the biometric device can check to decide who to accept and who to reject.

Once you've given the biometric device a few samples of each person's data, you need to test the device to ensure that it can accurately identify individuals. The biggest problem with biometric devices is finding the proper balance between false acceptance and false rejection.

As the name implies, *false acceptance* means that the biometric device's criteria accept too much data as valid, so anyone with fingerprints that are somewhat similar to an authorized user's may be granted access. *False rejection* means that the biometric device's criteria are too narrow, which means that even authorized users may have trouble getting it to recognize them and allow them access.

Biometric devices

The most common biometric devices, and the simplest to implement, are fingerprint scanners. To learn more about fingerprint biometric devices, visit DigitalPersona (www.digitalpersona.com), Keytronic (www.keytronic.com), Precise Biometrics (www.precisebiometrics.com), or Ultimaco Safeware (www.ultimaco.com).

Like fingerprints, no two people's signatures are alike, so several companies market signature recognition devices. For more information about these, visit Communication Intelligence Corporation (www.cic.com) or CyberSign (www.cybersign.com).

Hook up a camera to your computer and, with the right software, you can verify authorized users through facial recognition. Users stare into a camera and the computer recognizes them as authorized users. To learn more about facial recognition, visit the Face Recognition Homepage (www.face-rec.org).

For a face detection algorithm demonstration, visit the Pittsburgh Pattern Recognition site (http://demo.pittpatt.com). This demo allows visitors to upload photographs of different people to see how accurately the facial recognition algorithm identifies the same face in different poses and backgrounds.

Voice Security Systems (www.voice-security.com) uses voice prints to deny or allow access. No two people speak exactly alike, so voice recognition systems train computers to listen to each person's unique speaking style. (Unfortunately, if that person has a cold, it's possible that the voice recognition system won't even recognize a valid user's voice.)

Iridian Technologies (www.iridiantech.com) offers an even more exotic biometric device that scans the retina of the eye to identify authorized users. Rather than rely on a single biometric measurement, SAFlink (www.saflink.com) goes further, using voice, face, and fingerprint recognition together to identify authorized users with an ordinary digital camera, microphone, and fingerprint reader. Another company, BioID (www.bioid.com), uses face, voice, and lip movement recognition to identify authorized users. Even if someone fools one biometric device, they probably won't be able to fool the second and third one too.

Defeating biometrics

In theory, no one can duplicate another person's fingerprint, signature, or facial scan, so biometrics should be the ultimate solution for securing access to a computer, right? Wrong.

Biometrics can be fooled surprisingly easily. That's why most biometric devices are used in combination with human security guards or surveillance cameras whose footage can be reviewed later. Besides cruder methods like pulling a gun on an authorized user and forcing him to scan his retina or cutting off a person's finger to get past a fingerprint scanner, there are subtler, less violent ways to trick biometric devices.

When an authorized user puts his fingertip on a fingerprint scanner, the computer verifies his access and he walks away. Of course, an imprint of his valid fingerprint still remains behind on the glass of the fingerprint reader device. Many fingerprint scanners can be fooled by just cupping your hands and breathing over the device, which causes the residue of the authorized user's fingerprint to reappear. The scanner sees the valid fingerprint again and gives you access.

You can capture a valid fingerprint for future use by simply sprinkling graphite powder on the fingerprint scanner and then sticking a piece of ordinary cellophane tape over the surface. The fingerprint is captured on the sticky side of the tape. Now you can stick this piece of tape over the fingerprint scanner, which will recognize it as belonging to a valid user.

Facial recognition devices are even simpler to fool. Just take a picture of an authorized user, hold it up to the scanning camera, and chances are good that the biometric facial recognition device will think it's a valid user. (Newer facial recognition systems ask people to turn their heads slightly to verify that the camera is seeing a real person's face instead of a two-dimensional picture.)

Some retina scanners can be fooled the same way, provided you can get a picture of an authorized user's retina.

Fooling voice recognition devices can be just as easy. Hide a tape recorder and stand near an authorized user speaking into the microphone. Then play back this recording and you've got yourself a valid voice print that the biometric device will recognize. (More advanced voice recognition devices may record dozens of different words and randomly ask the user to repeat one of them. The system might ask the user to say the word *bubbles* one time, and the word *balloon* another time, so a recording of a person's voice won't work most of the time.)

Perhaps the best way to fool any biometric device is to intercept the data going from the biometric reader to the computer. If you can sneak a hardware device, such as USB Agent (www.hitex.com), in between the biometric device and the computer, you'll capture the information entered by a valid user. Now you can feed this biometric data to other computers and trick those computers into thinking you must be someone else, which could be the ultimate identity theft technique.

For another tool to intercept data sent across a USB cable, grab a copy of USB Sniffer for Windows (http://sourceforge.net/projects/usbsnoop) or USB Snoopy (http://mxhaard.free.fr/snoopy.html). Both programs can snare data so you can analyze a valid user's biometric data and then feed it back into the computer later.

No matter how advanced biometric devices may get, there will always be a way to fool them, although it might not be easy. To keep someone from fooling a biometric device, you need a guard to watch over it. Of course, if you can afford to station a guard by your computer, you probably don't need the biometric device in the first place.

GOOD ENOUGH SECURITY

There will never be a foolproof way to keep hackers out of a computer, whether you use passwords, biometric devices, or hardware authentication devices that you plug into a computer to verify your identity. But the more difficult you make it to break into, the more likely most hackers will go off in search of an easier target. Unfortunately, if your computer is connected to a network, the easiest target to break into may be the computer right next to yours. Still, it's important to keep intruders out of your computer because once they get in, finding the hacker and kicking him out is going to take a lot more work.

10

DIGGING INTO A COMPUTER WITH ROOTKITS

Breaking into a computer isn't easy, so once a hacker gets in, his first goal is generally to make sure he can get back into that computer easily at any time. The best way to do this is to control a system administrator account on the computer, otherwise known as a *root account* or just plain *root*.

    To gain and maintain root access, hackers have created special tools called *rootkits*, which are programs, or groups of programs, designed to punch holes through a computer's defenses. That way, if a system administrator finds and blocks the first route the hacker used to access the computer, the rootkit will have created several alternate ways for the hacker to get back inside. Some rootkits, such as Hacker Defender (www.hxdef.org), even have their own websites where you can learn about their latest advances.

    Some of the more common rootkit tools include sniffers and keystroke loggers (for snaring additional passwords), log-cleaning tools (for hiding the hacker's presence on the system), programs for finding common exploitable flaws (for taking advantage of vulnerabilities in the operating system or server software), and Trojan horses (for opening backdoors into the computer and masking the intruder's activities). Once a hacker has installed a rootkit on a computer, he can sneak back in at any time without worrying about being detected.

> The art of war is simple enough. Find out where your enemy is.
>
> —ULYSSES S. GRANT

HOW OPERATING SYSTEMS WORK

Rootkits directly manipulate the operating system, which can be likened to probing the computer's brain with a sharp needle and a pair of forceps. To understand how rootkits work, you need to understand how operating systems work.

    At the most basic level, an operating system controls all the different parts of a computer. A computer may have a hard disk, memory, a keyboard, and a mouse, but none of this equipment knows how to work with the other components without an operating system.

    Older operating systems, such as MS-DOS and CP/M-80, could run only one program at a time, but modern systems such as Linux, Windows, and Mac OS X can run multiple programs at once. So, the operating system also needs to manage which programs get loaded into memory and which programs can use the CPU, while it simultaneously checks for input from the keyboard or mouse and sends output to the computer screen.

On top of all this work recognizing and managing hardware resources, the operating system may also load additional programs called device drivers, which are simple programs that tell the operating system how to work with external equipment, such as a printer or scanner. When a program such as a word processor needs to print data, it sends this information to the operating system, which uses the device driver to send it to the printer.

Finally, an operating system runs other programs and isolates them so they can't manipulate the computer's hardware themselves. Programs, whether databases or games, send information to the operating system, which then saves this information to the hard disk. Figure 10-1 shows the different tasks of an operating system and how applications and device drivers work together.

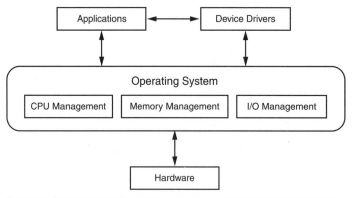

Figure 10-1: An operating system prevents applications (such as games and spreadsheet utilities) from directly accessing the computer's hardware.

THE EVOLUTION OF ROOTKITS

Rootkits have been around for years, perhaps even longer than viruses and worms. What makes rootkits particularly dangerous is how they've managed to evolve, getting stealthier and trickier to better avoid detection.

This stealth by itself is alarming, since once a hacker plants a rootkit on a computer, it's nearly impossible to clean it off the system without reformatting the hard disk and reinstalling the operating system. The biggest danger from rootkits is their use as a combined Trojan horse/worm/spyware infection tool. Ordinarily, when malware infects a computer, it's fairly easy to find and remove. But by combining rootkit technology with Trojan horses and worms, malware creators can develop programs that not only infect a computer, but also hide from any detection programs.

Even more frightening than that is the application of rootkit technology to so-called legitimate business uses. In late 2005, in an effort to copy-protect its audio CDs, Sony used digital rights management (DRM) technology created by First 4 Internet (www .first4internet.com). This copy-protection method borrows from rootkit techniques by installing itself on a computer and then hiding in memory, even when the copy-protected

CD is no longer in the computer. Removing this software can be difficult and, even if successful, it can disable the computer's CD player, making it impossible to play legally purchased CDs. Needless to say, Sony took a lot of heated criticism for this.

Both Kaspersky Lab (www.kaspersky.com) and Sophos (www.sophos.com) have classified Sony's copy-protection scheme as "spyware" since it can crash a computer and weaken its security by allowing hackers to tuck away Trojan horses, viruses, and their own rootkits in the same hidden area where Sony's rootkit resides. Following the backlash against the company, Sony quickly released a patch to make it easier to remove their rootkit. However, this patch actually made computers more prone to crashing. If so-called legitimate companies such as Sony can use rootkit technology "legally," then perhaps hackers aren't really doing anything wrong after all. They're just not doing the "wrong" things for the right people.

Modifying log files

Rootkits can delete or modify a computer's log files. To avoid detection, they try to hide their presence from the prying eyes of a system administrator. Log files keep track of who used a computer, what they did, and for how long they used the computer. This information was particularly crucial back when computers were expensive and companies sold spare time on their computer to others (known as time-sharing), but, equally important, log files could also identify what a computer was doing right before it crashed. When hackers started to invade computers, log files served another purpose: They kept track of when the hacker arrived, what the hacker did, and how long the hacker stayed on the computer—much like a surveillance camera can record a burglar breaking into a store. In many cases, the log file could also track which computer the hacker used to gain access to another computer, which could help the authorities track down the perpetrator.

Therefore, hackers look for the log files that recorded their entry as soon as they gain access to a computer. Among the information a log file might contain that may help a computer's owner track the hacker down are the following:

- The IP address of the machine that performed an action or "request" on the target computer

- The user name, which simply identifies the account being used (a perfectly valid user name could mask the presence of a hacker who has secretly hijacked that user's account)

- The date and time of a particular action

- The exact command or "request" that the user gave the target computer

- The HTTP status code (which shows what action the target computer performed in response to the user's command or "request") that the target computer returned to the user

- The number of bytes transferred to the user

Armed with this information, system administrators can often determine not only when a hacker invaded their system, but can also deduce how the hacker invaded their system.

Script kiddies (novice hackers who are often unfamiliar with different operating systems) often delete log files to prevent the administrator from seeing exactly what they did. Unfortunately, deleting the log file announces the presence of an intruder as blatantly as would using a stick of dynamite to blow away a surveillance camera. The moment an administrator notices that someone has deleted the log file, he or she immediately knows that a hacker must be on the system.

Rather than announce their presence by deleting entire log files, the smarter and more technically skilled hackers selectively remove only their own activities and leave the rest of the log files intact. At a cursory glance, a system administrator would find the log files seemingly untouched.

In many cases, just editing the log files can hide a hacker's tracks, but system administrators have their own techniques for ensuring the integrity of their log files. One of the simplest involves printing out the log files as they're generated. That way, if a hacker does delete or modify the log files at some point, the printed copy will still reveal his or her presence. If the system administrator suspects something is wrong, he or she can compare the log file on the hard disk with the log file printout.

Another technique is to study the time stamp of the log file. If a hacker modifes the log file, the computer will time stamp the modified log file with the time and date of the modification, which can pinpoint the precise time the hacker was on the computer.

Another way for administrators to preserve log files and protect themselves is to create duplicate copies. The original log file appears where hackers expect to find it, while a duplicate copy gets stored on another computer, preferably one that no one else can modify or delete, including anyone with a root or administrator account. The moment a hacker modifies the first log file, the system administrator can use log file analysis programs to detect any discrepancies.

While it's possible that hackers could stop a computer from copying its log file to another machine, the lack of a duplicate log file on the other machine would signal an obvious hacker attempt. Hackers could still try to modify both copies of the log file, but that's assuming the hacker knows the log file is being copied to another machine and that the hacker can even access this other machine.

To learn about the capabilities of various log file analysis programs, visit one or more of the following: Analog (www.analog.cx), Sawmill (www.sawmill.net), and Webalizer (www.mrunix.net/webalizer).

Trojaned binaries

Modifying the log files can hide what a hacker has done in the past, but hackers still need to hide their presence while they're active on a computer. So, after the log files, the second target that hackers go after are the programs that help system administrators notice any changes.

On Windows computers, rootkits use something called *registry DLL injection*. Rather than one massive file, the Windows operating system actually consists of multiple DLL (Dynamic Link Library) files that work together.

When you install a program on a computer running Windows, the program stores information it needs to run in a database called the registry. Each time the program runs, it checks the registry to find the location of additional DLL files it may need to use.

So registry DLL injection simply adds a Trojaned binary file of a legitimate DLL file to the computer, while leaving the original Windows DLL file alone. Then it modifies the registry so that when the program tries to use the orignal Windows DLL file, it's redirected to the Trojaned binary version instead.

Since the original DLL file was untouched, any file integrity checker will conclude that nothing is awry, hence no rootkit is present. Unless a system administrator discovers the existence of the Trojaned binary DLL files or the altered registry that points to a Trojaned DLL file, the hacker can have his way with the computer.

In the world of Unix/Linux, the most common commands that hackers try to alter include:

`find`	Looks for groups of files
`ls`	Lists the contents of the current directory
`netstat`	Shows the network status, including information about ports
`ps`	Displays the current processes that are running
`who`	Displays the names of all the users currently logged on
`w`	Prints system usage, currently logged-in users, and what each user is doing

Hackers simply substitute the computer's current programs (also called binaries) with their own hacked or Trojaned versions. Then, if an unsuspecting system administrator uses these hacked programs, the commands may appear to work normally but they secretly hide the hacker's activities from view. This buys the hacker extra time to cause damage or open additional backdoors so he can return at a later time.

Of course, when a hacker replaces the original programs or binaries with his own deceptive versions, he risks giving away his presence in another way. The problem occurs because every file contains two unique properties: a creation date and time, and a file size. If a system administrator notices that a program's creation date was yesterday, which is a sure sign that the program has been altered, she is likely to know that a hacker has infiltrated the system.

To protect their files from alterations, system administrators use file integrity programs that calculate a number, called a *checksum*, based on the file's size. The moment someone changes a file's size, even by a small amount, the checksum changes.

To avoid detection, a skilled hacker may run the file integrity checker program and recalculate new checksums for all the files, including the modified ones. If the system administrator didn't keep track of the old checksum values, the file integrity checker won't notice any differences.

With a little bit of tweaking, hackers can make their altered versions the exact same size as the files they're replacing. If they also change the date and time of this altered file to match that of the real file, checksum comparisons won't detect the substitution.

For a file integrity checker to be effective, the system administrator must run the check right after setting up a computer. The longer the system administrator waits to do this, the more opportunity a hacker has to change files.

Even more importantly, system administrators need to calculate a cryptographic checksum using an algorithm such as MD5 (Message Digest algorithm 5) or SHA-1 (Secure Hashing Algorithm). Unlike ordinary checksums, a cryptographic checksum can be difficult to fake, which means that hackers can't modify checksum values.

Hackers can, of course, crack the encryption and peek inside any files encrypted with MD5 or SHA-1. Even more revealing is a paper by security researcher Dan Kaminsky (www.doxpara.com/md5_someday.pdf) that explains how to use a tool called StripWire to create a file with identical checksums but different content, which can be used to fool file integrity checkers.

To learn more about the various file integrity programs that system administrators use, visit Samhain (www.la-samhna.de), TripWire (www.tripwiresecurity.com), GFI LANguard (www.gfi.com), or AIDE (Advanced Intrusion Detection Environment)—http://sourceforge.net/projects/aide.

Hooking program calls

Every program needs a way to communicate with the operating system in order to perform commands such as saving data or sending data to the printer. So operating systems provide a library of functions (called the *application programming interface* or *API*) that all programs can use to send commands. To help programmers create and debug their applications, special functions monitor what the operating system is doing at any given time, for example, receiving data from the keyboard or a modem.

Functions that allow another program to peek at the inner workings of an operating system are known as *hooks*. Hooks can be handy for writing diagnostic or troubleshooting utilities, but they can also be used by rootkits to subvert the operating system. This is known as *hooking*. Keystroke logging programs (see Chapter 9) work by hooking into the operating system to intercept keystrokes and record them before sending them on their way to their intended destination, as shown in Figure 10-2. Keystroke loggers also hook into the operating system to avoid being detected as running or even existing anywhere in memory or the hard disk.

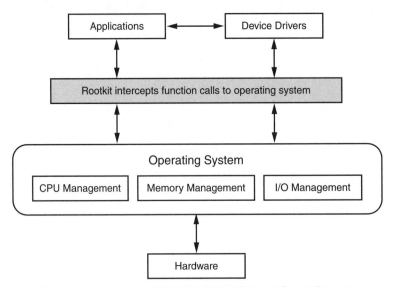

Figure 10-2: Rootkits can intercept function calls made by applications to the operating system.

Rootkits use the same principles to mask their presence on a computer. When a program tries to list all currently running applications, the rootkit hooks into the operating system, intercepts the function call, and substitutes another one that reports all currently running applications except the rootkit. This is like having the mailman deliver a substituted letter in place of what the sender put in the mailbox originally. Neither the sender nor the recipient will ever know the difference.

Rootkits can use local or global hooks. A local hook intercepts function calls from a specific program, such as an email program. Global hooks intercept function calls from any currently running program.

To guard against rootkit infection, there are programs to monitor and protect the operating system, such as Anti Hook (www.infoprocess.com.au) or Process Guard (www.diamondcs.com.au/processguard), shown in Figure 10-3. (Of course, there's always a chance a rootkit infected your computer before you could install one of these operating system monitoring programs, which means the rootkit could just feed these monitoring programs false information . . .)

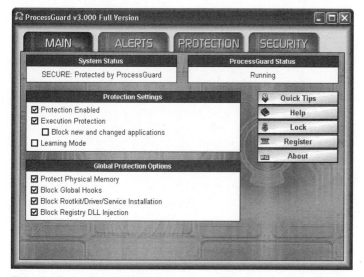

Figure 10-3: Process Guard can block RATs, spyware, rootkits, and any other unsavory malware programs that try to subvert your computer's operating system.

For even greater security, Novell offers an open-source program called AppArmor (http://en.opensuse.org/Apparmor), which lets you configure what every part of your Linux operating system can and cannot do. By forcing the operating system to behave in specific ways, administrators can prevent hackers from tricking the operating system into doing something it's not supposed to do.

Loadable kernel module (LKM) rootkits

The simplest way a system administrator can defeat an altered or Trojaned program is by storing unaltered copies of the programs that hackers commonly try to modify and recopying them back onto the computer. Using clean copies of various monitoring programs, a system administrator can hunt around the computer and find new traces of the hacker that his Trojaned versions hid from sight.

To get around this problem, hackers have started exploiting loadable kernel modules (LKMs), commonly found in Unix based systems such as Linux. In the old days, if you wanted to add a feature to Linux, you had to modify and recompile the entire source code for the operating system. LKMs eliminate this requirement by letting you attach new commands to the Linux kernel (the heart of the operating system) without recompiling the source code, which is where errors can occur. If you modify code as an LKM, the Linux kernel can still load and your entire operating system won't crash, even if the code in your LKM fails.

So rather than replace existing programs and risk detection, LKM rootkits simply load their own programs into memory so that, if a system administrator checks the file integrity of the various monitoring tools, they look untouched (because they are). But if he tries to run these seemingly untouched programs, the hacker's LKM module intercepts the command and runs its own, which masks the hacker's presence. Some popular LKM rootkits sport odd names like SuckIT, Knark, Rial, Adore, and Tuxkit.

OPENING A BACKDOOR

The most common way to open a backdoor in a computer is by opening a port, usually one of the more obscure ports that is unlikely to already be in use (unless another hacker has gotten there first). If the hacker took the time to insert Trojan versions of monitoring programs before connecting to the computer, those programs will ignore the open port (reporting it as still being closed) along with any activity coming from this backdoor.

Since a system administrator might still discover this open port during a routine scan of her system, hackers can create special "open sesame" backdoors that remain shut until the hacker transmits a certain command to the computer. When the computer receives this seemingly innocuous command, the backdoor opens a port and the hacker slides right through.

SNIFFING FOR MORE PASSWORDS

Another component of a rootkit is a sniffer, which the hacker can plant on a system to snare passwords, credit card numbers, or other valuable information transmitted across a network. A sniffer offers more flexibility than a keystroke logger, since a hacker only needs to install it on one computer and then set that computer's network interface card (NIC) to promiscuous mode. Normally, each computer on the network only peeks at traffic specifically addressed to it, but when set in promiscuous mode, the computer peeks at any data passing through.

To defeat network sniffers, some administrators create switched networks. In a non-switched network, data gets passed from one computer to another and each computer checks to see if it's supposed to receive that data. In a switched network, one computer sends data to a switch, which then routes that data to the computer that's supposed to receive it.

To defeat switched networks, hackers may also use a technique called *arp spoofing*, which tricks computers into sending their data to a hijacked computer instead of the switch. The hijacked computer, controlled by the hacker, mimics the switch, but can now peek at all data on the network.

Once the sniffer retrieves one or more valid passwords, the hacker can use them to hijack a legitimate user's account and enter the system any time he wants. As a seemingly legitimate user, a hacker can leisurely browse a computer to better understand the software being used and the configuration of the network.

If the sniffer happens to snare the password of a system administrator, the hacker will gain root access, allowing him to create additional accounts, even accounts with system administrator privileges, for accessing the computer later.

To learn more about the capabilities of sniffers, visit WinDump (www.winpcap.org/windump), Ethereal (www.ethereal.com), Sniffer (www.networkgeneral.com), EtherPeek (www.wildpackets.com), Analyzer (http://analyzer.polito.it), tcpdump (www.tcpdump.org), or Sniffit (www.tengu.be).

Sniffers do have legitimate uses for analyzing and fixing a network, but few people want a total stranger running a sniffer on their network. Rather than check to see if a computer's NIC card may be running in promiscuous mode, system administrators can run a variety of tools to help them find any rogue sniffers running on their network.

To find out if someone has installed a sniffer on your network without your knowledge, download one of the following programs: AntiSniff (http://packetstormsecurity.nl/sniffers/antisniff), PromiscDetect (http://ntsecurity.nu), PromiScan (www.securityfriday.com), or The Sentinel Project (www.packetfactory.net/Projects/sentinel).

KILLING ROOTKITS

It may be impossible to keep a computer hacker-free. A system administrator may diligently wipe out all rootkits and shut down all backdoors, but there's still no guarantee that there still isn't something the system administrator may have missed. The only sure way to remove hackers from a computer is by erasing and reinstalling everything from scratch, but this is a drastic, time-consuming, and likely only temporarily successful measure.

Despite their best efforts, system administrators can't be perfect, and hackers only need one lucky break to slip into a computer undetected. However, dedicated rootkit detectors help tilt the balance in favor of the system administrators by scanning a computer for signs that betray the existence of a rootkit. Microsoft has developed its own rootkit detector, dubbed Strider GhostBuster (http://research.microsoft.com/rootkit). F-Secure has developed a similar rootkit detector called BlackLight (www.f-secure.com/blacklight), shown in Figure 10-4. For a list of various tools to help detect rootkits, visit the home page of security researcher Joanna Rutkowska (www.invisiblethings.org), the Dutch rootkit.nl site (www.rootkit.nl), chkrootkit (www.chkrootkit.org), or SysInternals (www.sysinternals.com) to grab a copy of RootkitRevealer.

If you happen to be able to read Chinese, try downloading the highly-regarded Chinese rootkit detector called IceSword (http://xfocus.net/tools/200505/1032.html), which has gotten rave reviews even from rootkit creators.

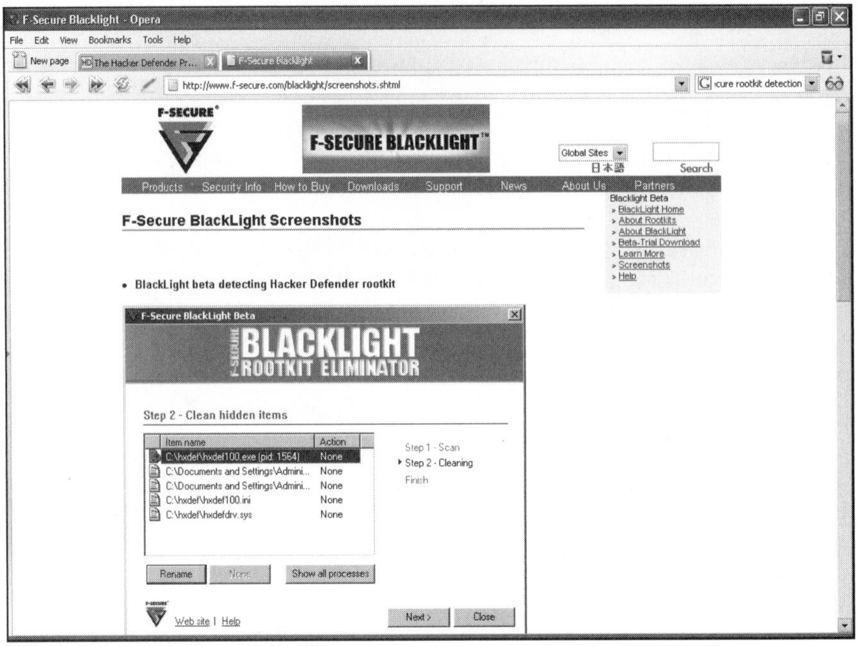

Figure 10-4: To fully protect your computer in the future, you may need a firewall, an antivirus program, and a rootkit detector such as BlackLight, shown here.

System administrators should also run a scanner to detect any open ports—a sign of sloppy administration or a backdoor left behind by a hacker.

And, when first setting up a computer, any system administrator should create cryptographic checksums of all the important files and store these checksums in a separate location, such as on a CD that can only be written to one time. System administrators should also save spare copies of crucial program utilities on the CD as well. Now if a hacker breaks into a computer, the system administrator can at least trust the integrity of the files stored on the CD.

Finally, system administrators need to keep up with the latest security flaws and vulnerabilities so they can patch them or watch out for hackers who may exploit them. To learn more about different rootkits, visit Rootkit (www.rootkit.com), as shown in Figure 10-5.

Figure 10-5: Rootkit.com provides source code for various rootkit tools, including Trojan horses and patches to hide a hacker's activity.

No matter what a system administrator does, there will always be a chance that a hacker is lurking in any given computer at any given time. Some system administrators leave hackers alone as long as the hackers leave their important data alone, but most system administrators constantly try to throw hackers off their system even while the hackers keep coming back with new techniques, new tools, and new ideas again and again and again.

11

CENSORING INFORMATION

Who gets the right to decide what you can see, read, or do? The answer is always the same—the people who have the power to punish you. Governments can punish you physically (with the death penalty) or financially (with jail time or fines). Churches can excommunicate you. Your boss can fire you, and your parents can send you to your room without dessert.

Of course, telling people what to do is one thing. Getting them to obey is an entirely different thing. As long as people have the freedom to disobey, some will. To ensure compliance, censors have to eliminate all opportunities for disobedience, and frighten their subjects into never trying to disobey them in the first place.

There are worse crimes than burning books. One of them is not reading them.

—JOSEPH BRODSKY, Russian poet

CENSORING THE INTERNET

It's impossible to censor the entire Internet, but it's not impossible to restrict or even completely block access to it. Most government censors use a variety of filtering and blocking techniques to shut out parts of the Internet they don't like, rather than cut off access entirely. The North Korean government, for example, bans Internet access to everyone but a few hand-picked individuals who can be trusted and monitored (which encourages these individuals to stay "trusted").

URL filtering

One of the simplest ways to censor the Internet is to create a list of acceptable sites that people can visit. If someone types a domain name not on the approved list, they won't see anything but an error or warning message. The problem with this approach is that it's impossible to stay ahead of new sites popping up. Adding each new acceptable website to an approved list is impractical. Instead, most Internet filtering programs accomplish their task by blocking certain Uniform Resource Locator (URL) addresses, such as http://www.playboy.com.

NOTE: *The terms* domain name *and* URL address *are often used interchangeably. Technically, a URL address is the complete text used to identify a computer, such as http://www.website.com/, and a domain name is just www.website.com.*

When a user types a URL address into a web browser, the filter compares it to a list of blacklisted addresses to which access is blocked. The filter might even alert the authorities to keep an eye on whomever tried to access the forbidden website.

Weak URL filters simply scan the URL address for incriminating words such as *Playboy* or *CNN*. Users can get around these filters by using the nslookup command to find the site's numeric Internet Protocol (IP) address. Typing the IP address rather than the site's descriptive URL can avoid matching the blacklist. Figure 11-1 shows an example of using the nslookup command through the KLOTH.NET site.

NSLOOKUP: look up IP addresses in the DNS

Query a DNS domain nameserver to look up and find IP address information of computers in the internet. Convert a host or domain name into an IP address.

This is the right place for you to check how your web hosting company or domain name registrar has set up the DNS stuff for your domain, how your dynamic DNS is going, or to search IP addresses or research any kind of e-mail abuse (UBE/UCE spam) or other internet abuse. This online service is for private non-commercial use only. Please do not abuse. No bots.

NSlookup

Domain: www.2600.com ... the name of the machine to look up.

Server: ns.kloth.net ... the DNS nameserver you want to handle your query (just start with the default server if you don't know better).

Query: A (IP address) Look it up

... here is the **nslookup** result for **www.2600.com** from server ns.kloth.net, querytype=A :

```
DNS server handling your query: ns.kloth.net
DNS server's address:  85.10.194.170#53

Non-authoritative answer:
Name:   www.2600.com
Address: 207.99.30.226
```

Figure 11-1: The nslookup command can convert a descriptive URL address into a cryptic numeric IP address.

So, instead of typing www.2600.com (the website of the underground hacker magazine *2600*) into your browser, you could type in the equivalent IP address http://207.99.30.226. If the URL filter is smart enough to block the IP address of forbidden websites too, you can go one step further and convert each part of an IP address into its equivalent binary number:

207 = 11001111

99 = 01100011

30 = 00011110

226 = 11100010

String the numbers together and create one massive binary number:

11001111011000110001111011100010

Finally, convert this massive binary number into its decimal equivalent:

11001111011000110001111011100010 = 3479379686

So instead of www.2600.com, you can just type **http://3479379686** to load the very same web page. Most Internet filters will block the descriptive URL but not any of its numeric equivalents.

Content filtering

Internet censoring software often combines URL filtering with content filtering, which scans the words or phrases stored on a web page to decide whether it should be blocked or not. Content filters often scan for obvious words like *sex* or *breasts*, but each filter uses its own algorithm for determining how many times certain words can appear on a web page before it's considered objectionable.

For example, blocking a web page just because it has the word *breast* on it may accidentally block a supermarket website that sells chicken "breasts" or a medical website that discusses "breast" cancer. As a result, content filtering alone is prone to errors, either letting questionable websites slip past or blocking legitimate ones altogether. (Beaver College in Pennsylvania actually had to change its name to Arcadia University after too many content filters blocked people from visiting its website.)

Content filtering is so unreliable that it may even block the websites of the very people who support such Internet filtering. In July 1997, a librarian named David Burt launched the now-defunct FilteringFacts.org website that advocated the use of filtering software in public libraries. Ironically, a parental control program named SurfWatch blocked his website, classifying it as an objectionable "Drugs/Alcohol" site, as shown in Figure 11-2. Apparently, in explaining the importance of using filters to block objectionable content, the FilterFacts.org website gave examples of certain trigger words. The content filters worked as designed and blocked FilterFacts when it found those words mentioned on the site.

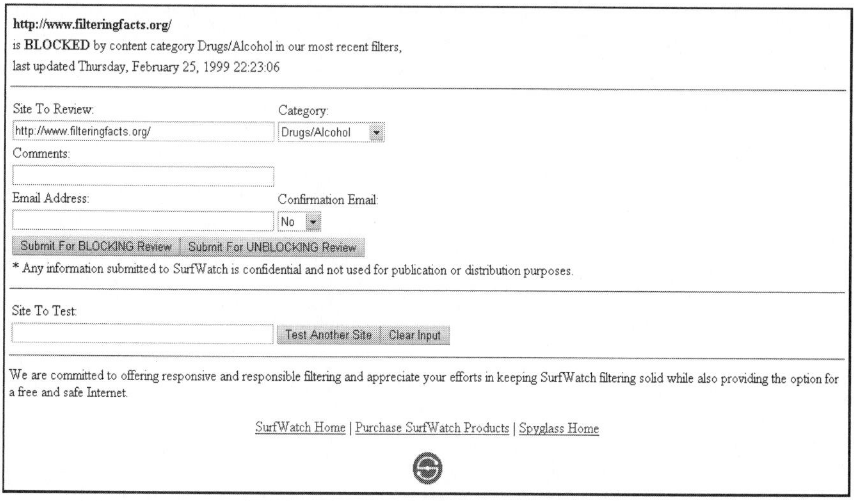

http://www.filteringfacts.org/
is **BLOCKED** by content category Drugs/Alcohol in our most recent filters,
last updated Thursday, February 25, 1999 22:23:06

Site To Review: Category:
http://www.filteringfacts.org/   Drugs/Alcohol
Comments:

Email Address: Confirmation Email:
                                   No

Submit For BLOCKING Review   Submit For UNBLOCKING Review
* Any information submitted to SurfWatch is confidential and not used for publication or distribution purposes.

Site To Test:
                          Test Another Site   Clear Input

We are committed to offering responsive and responsible filtering and appreciate your efforts in keeping SurfWatch filtering solid while also providing the option for a free and safe Internet.

SurfWatch Home | Purchase SurfWatch Products | Spyglass Home

Figure 11-2: SurfWatch blocked access to a website that supported Internet censoring.

No matter how much they are refined, content filters will never be 100 percent accurate. Here's yet another example. In July 2002, WebSense, the publisher of an Internet filtering program, boasted that competing products allowed access to several prominent pornographic websites. So, users whose web access passed through those other Internet filtering programs would simply visit the WebSense site to get a list of those pornographic websites that their filters wouldn't stop. What started out as a marketing ploy to discredit the competition turned into a regularly updated porn list that anyone who wanted to get around the filters could consult.

DNS poisoning

Perhaps the subtlest method of Internet censorship is DNS (or Domain Name System) poisoning. When you type in a domain name such as www.cnn.com, your computer sends this information to your Internet service provider (ISP), which in turn sends it to a DNS server. The DNS server matches the domain name with its numeric IP address and sends the web page to your browser.

DNS poisoning works like this. The ISP routes the user's domain name request to a DNS server that returns an entirely different IP address than that of the actual website. If someone types in www.yahoo.com, the DNS server should return the valid Yahoo! IP address as 68.142.226.32. But if the DNS server has been poisoned, it will return whatever IP address the censor has associated with the www.yahoo.com domain name. This might be a message explaining that the requested website is blocked or a bogus website designed to look like the real thing.

By substituting a bogus site for a real one, censors can fool users into thinking they're accessing forbidden sites when they're really looking at fake ones. The substituted sites could even contain subtle revisions so users will think they're reading forbidden news when they're actually reading cleverly disguised propaganda. So, the next time you're surfing the Web, keep in mind that someone could be manipulating the information you're seeing, and you may never know it.

To get around DNS poisoning, configure your Internet connection to use a DNS server other than the one your ISP automatically uses. To get a list of DNS servers, visit ftp://ftp.rs.internic.net/domain/named.root or ftp://ftp.orsn.org/orsn/orsn.hint, or use one of the following noncensoring DNS servers:

dns2.de.net	194.246.96.49	Frankfurt, Germany
ns1.de.eu.orsn.net	217.146.139.5	Hildesheim, Germany
resolver.netteam.de	193.155.207.61	Alfter-Impekoven, Germany
sunic.sunet.se	192.36.125.2	Stockholm, Sweden
master.ns.dns.be	193.109.126.140	Leuven, Belgium
ns1.lu.eu.orsn.net	195.206.104.98	Belvaux, Luxembourg
merapi.switch.ch	130.59.211.10	Zurich, Switzerland
prades.cesca.es	192.94.163.152	Barcelona, Spain
michael.vatican.va	212.77.0.2	Vatican City, Italy
dns.inria.fr	193.51.208.13	Nice, France
ns0.ja.net	128.86.1.20	London, UK
nic.aix.gr	195.130.89.210	Athens, Greece
ns.ati.tn	193.95.66.10	Tunis, Tunisia

ns1.relcom.ru	193.125.152.3	Moscow, Russia
trantor.umd.edu	128.8.10.14	College Park, MD, USA
ns1.berkeley.edu	128.32.136.9	Berkeley, CA, USA
merle.cira.ca	64.26.149.98	Ottawa, Canada
ns2.dns.br	200.19.119.99	Sao Paulo, Brazil
ns2.gisc.cl	200.10.237.14	Santiago, Chile
ns.uvg.edu.gt	168.234.68.2	Guatemala, Guatemala
ns1.retina.ar	200.10.202.3	Buenos Aires, Argentina
ns.unam.mx	132.248.253.1	Mexico City, Mexico
ns.wide.ad.jp	203.178.136.63	Osaka, Japan
ns.twnic.net	192.83.166.11	Taipei, Taiwan
ns3.dns.net.nz	203.97.8.250	Wellington, New Zealand
box2.aunic.net	203.202.150.20	Melbourne, Australia

To configure your Internet connection on Windows XP to use a different DNS server, follow these steps:

1. Click the Start button and click Control Panel.
2. Click Network and Internet Connections.
3. Click Network Connections.
4. Right-click your Internet connection icon, and when a pop-up menu appears, click Properties. A Properties window appears as shown in Figure 11-3.

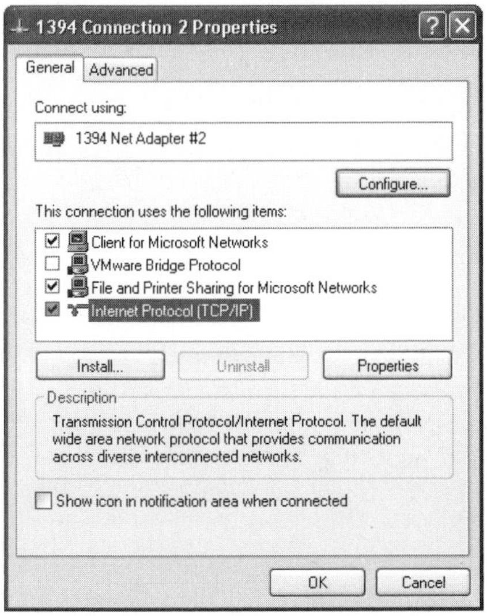

Figure 11-3: Right-click your Internet connection icon to display the Properties window.

5. Click Internet Protocol (TCP/IP) and click Properties. An Internet Protocol (TCP/IP) Properties window appears as shown in Figure 11-4.

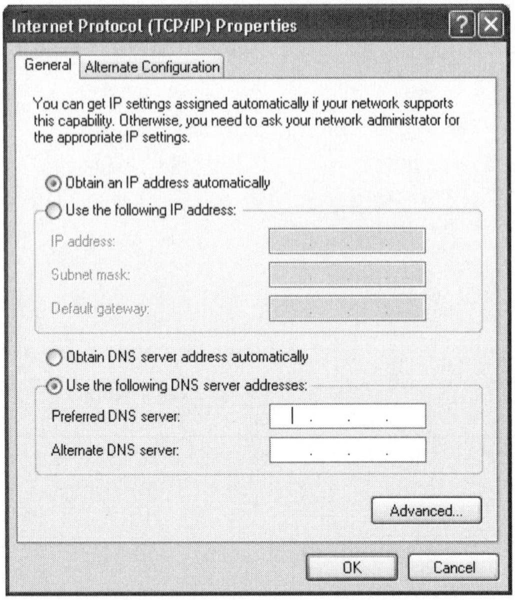

Figure 11-4: Rather than accept a DNS server automatically, you can specify a DNS server to use instead.

6. Click the Use The Following DNS Server Addresses radio button and type a DNS IP address in the Preferred DNS Server field; you can also specify an alternate DNS server in the second box.

7. Click OK.

Port blocking

Another way to censor the Internet involves port blocking. As discussed in previous chapters, every computer on the Internet uses certain ports to send and receive information. For example, port 80 is used to receive web pages, the file transfer protocol (FTP) uses port 21, and email is sent using port 25. So to block file transfers and email, governments can just block ports 21 and 25. Users can then do anything they want—except transfer files or send and receive email, which is like saying prisoners have all the freedom they want, so long as they don't want to walk beyond the prison walls. Figure 11-5 shows how port blocking can prevent a computer from accessing the Web or an IRC chat room.

To get around port blocking, you can use a technique known as tunneling. This essentially lets one port perform the functions of other ports.

Tunneling works by connecting to another computer, known as a proxy server, through whatever open port your computer can access. Figure 11-6 shows a computer tunneling through a firewall. Instead of sending FTP file transfers through port 21 or web page requests through port 80, the computer sends all this information through port 25, the only port allowed through the firewall. This information gets sent to a proxy server on the other side of the firewall, which then accesses the normal ports needed to transfer files via FTP (port 21) or access web pages (port 80). As far as the censoring firewall can tell, the computer is using only port 25.

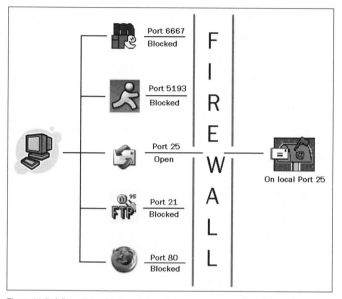

Figure 11-5: A firewall can block certain ports to prevent access to web browsing or FTP file transfers.

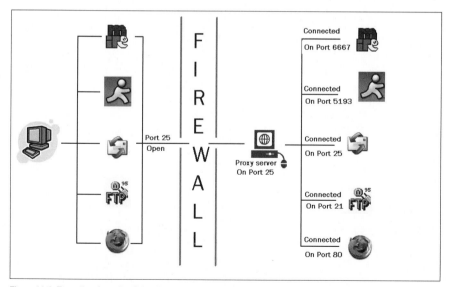

Figure 11-6: Tunneling through a firewall to a proxy server can allow access to forbidden Internet services.

To detect firewall tunneling, some firewalls will not only block ports but also analyze the data going through their open ports, a process known as protocol analysis. Encryption can mask your data, but if a firewall doesn't recognize any data flowing through its open ports, it may just block them altogether.

THE INTERNET CENSORS

The biggest Internet censors are national governments, but they couldn't censor as effectively without the help of companies that specialize in selling Internet censoring technology to parents, schools, businesses, and (of course) oppressive dictatorships. When it comes to profiting from Internet censoring technology, the price of free speech is always negotiable.

Countries that censor the Internet

A map of countries that censor the Internet to at least some extent would probably cover just about the entire world, but three of the most prominent Internet censors are China, Saudi Arabia, and Cuba. Although few Americans believe that China's communist government offers its citizens absolute freedom of speech, plenty of them (especially those in the White House) are still ignoring Saudi Arabia's equally questionable record of censorship, human rights violations, and lack of democratic reforms.

The question isn't just which countries practice censorship, or even how they do it, but why they do it. Specifically, what are governments afraid their citizens might see?

The Great Firewall of China

With one of the fastest-growing economies combined with an Internet-savvy, educated population, China has a problem. How do you let millions of people use the Internet for business while preventing them from using the same technology to protest the government? China's answer has been simple: Create a Chinese-only Internet within the larger Internet, where all objectionable websites (such as CNN and the *New York Times*) are blocked.

To clarify its Internet policies, China's Ministry of Public Security issued these guidelines, which were reprinted by Human Rights Watch (www.hrw.org):

No unit or individual may use the Internet to create, replicate, retrieve, or transmit the following kinds of information:

1. Inciting to resist or violate the Constitution or laws or the implementation of administrative regulations;

2. Inciting to overthrow the government or the socialist system;

3. Inciting division of the country, harming national unification;

4. Inciting hatred or discrimination among nationalities or harming the unity of the nationalities;

5. Making falsehoods or distorting the truth, spreading rumors, destroying the order of society;

6. Promoting feudal superstitions, sexually suggestive material, gambling, violence, murder;

7. Engaging in terrorism or inciting others to criminal activity; openly insulting other people or distorting the truth to slander people;

8. Injuring the reputation of state organs;

9. Other activities against the Constitution, laws or administrative regulations.

Notice that clauses 1, 2, 3, and 8 all refer to protecting the government (no surprise there), but clauses 5 and 7 would seem to prevent the government from issuing any form of propaganda of its own, which might distort the truth and slander governments of other countries.

Unfortunately, the above guidelines also give the Chinese government the right to loosely define acts of "terrorism" and "criminal activity" any way it chooses (just like every other government in the world), so someone could be considered a criminal for "inciting to overthrow the government or the socialist system" merely by discussing democratic reforms.

Although China's Internet censorship may seem imposing, Chinese citizens still manage to access forbidden sites regularly. A New York–based site, Human Rights in China (HRIC; www.hrichina.org), claims dozens of hits each week from people inside China. Founded by Chinese scientists and scholars in March 1989, HRIC monitors the implementation of international human rights statutes in China and provides information about human rights for Chinese people both inside China and abroad.

Although the Chinese government can restrict access to particular sites from inside their country, it can't screen the flood of email that crosses the Chinese borders every day. Exploiting this weakness, Chinese dissidents write and edit a weekly electronic magazine called *Tunnel* (www.geocities.com/SiliconValley/Bay/5598), sending their articles from inside China to a US email account from which the magazine is then distributed via email to readers in China. Using this method, the magazine hopes to prevent the Chinese government from identifying the writers and blocking the magazine's distribution.

For more news about China's censorship practices, visit VIP Reference (www.bignews.org), Epoch Times (www.epochtimes.com), or the Home for Global Internet Freedom (http://internetfreedom.org/gb).

One man, Bill Xia, founded Dynamic Internet Technology (www.dit-inc.us) to provide Internet service to users in hostile climates. Xia claims that his website (https://www.1.beijing999.com) can act as a proxy server, allowing Chinese users to access sites banned by their government through his own. (Until, of course, the Chinese government gets wise and blocks access to Xia's site.)

Figure 11-7a shows Xia's website. The middle of the page displays a text box where users can type the URL address of another site, such as www.dajiyuan.com.

Figure 11-7b shows the www.dajiyuan.com site, but notice that the browser is actually accessing this site through Xia's site, as shown by the address https://www.1.beijing999.com/dmirror/http://www.dajiyuan.com/index.htm.

Figure 11-7a: Users can launch Bill Xia's website as a browser to view other websites.

Figure 11-7b: When you visit other websites via Xia's, you will still see his URL address (https://www.1.beijing999.com) in your browser.

The Internet censors of Saudi Arabia

Saudi Arabia's Internet Services Unit (ISU)—www.isu.net.sa—tends to be most concerned about protecting the country's Islamic values. ISU claims to be "filtering the Internet content to prevent the materials that contradict with our beliefs or may influence our culture." Where China's Internet censorship is more concerned with touchy issues like democracy and freedom, Saudi Arabia's Internet censorship is more concerned about religion.

Anything that supports Judaism or Israel is banned by ISU, along with "pages related to drugs, bombs, alcohol, gambling and pages insulting the Islamic religion or the Saudi laws and regulations." A Harvard Law research study, titled "Documentation of Internet Filtering in Saudi Arabia" (http://cyber.law.harvard.edu/filtering/saudiarabia), found rather haphazard blocking. Sites with images of women in lingerie and swimsuits, sites advocating women's rights, and gay community sites were routinely blocked, but a surprisingly large number of pornography sites could still be accessed.

Naturally, the web pages of international human rights organizations were blocked, especially those criticizing Saudi Arabia, such as the Human Rights Watch website (www.hrw.org) and The Movement for Islamic Reform in Arabia (MIRA)—www.islah.tv. However, ordinary news sites, such as CNN, remained accessible. Apparently the ISU concentrates its efforts on those sites known to promote anti-Saudi views on a regular basis, but leaves many other sites alone.

Still, as the Harvard Law study showed, Saudi Arabia's Internet filters are relatively easy to circumvent. The simplest way is to dial long-distance to an ISP in another country and access the Internet from there.

Castro's censors in Cuba

Like North Korea, Cuba has a simple way to censor the Internet: ban its use altogether. Only trusted individuals, such as doctors, can obtain a permit to use the Internet. Even then, the only Internet gateway goes through Cuba's state-owned telecommunications operator Empresa de Telecomunicaciones de Cuba (ETECSA)—www.etecsa.cu—which practices censorship.

Then again, Internet access is rather useless, since Cuba also makes it illegal to possess a computer. The country's few existing cybercafés are reserved for the use of tourists, and are under strict control.

Nevertheless, thousands of Cubans manage to gain Internet access by pirating, or phone phreaking, the ETECSA telephone network. Once on the Internet, Cubans can visit the website of one of the more prominent anti-Castro groups, the Cuban American National Foundation (CANF) at www.canfnet.org. CANF provides firsthand reports of Cuban human rights violations (written by Cuban refugees), as well as reports of religious repression and debates about US foreign policy toward Cuba.

Another site, CubaNet (www.cubanet.org), posts information (in Spanish, French, and English) that it receives from Cuba's underground democracy movement and sends email back into Cuba. Once dissidents inside Cuba receive information from CubaNet, they can spread it to others through the country.

Internet censorship around the world

China, Saudi Arabia, and Cuba may be the most prominent Internet censors, but they are far from the only ones, or the most oppressive. The military government of Burma (Myanmar) limits Internet access to a handful of trusted officials. Even then, access is severely restricted to approved websites. The government filters completely block, among other things, an online magazine by Burmese citizens living in exile called *The Irrawaddy* (www.irrawaddy.org).

Tunisia blocks access to thousands of websites and ports to prevent the use of email, FTP transfers, and peer-to-peer services. The United Arab Emirates (UAE) bans access to any site deemed to harm the moral values of the UAE (although censorship apparently isn't one of them). South Korea blocks access to websites deemed sympathetic to North Korea, and even Australia passed tough censorship laws (although in Australia's case, the laws are rarely enforced), according to the OpenNet Initiative (www.opennetinitiative.net).

If you're specifically interested in Eastern Europe, visit the Radio Free Europe (www.rferl.org) website. By promoting free speech in any available form (Internet, newspapers, radio, etc.), Radio Free Europe hopes to create a well-informed citizenry that will act as a foundation for democracy in countries still struggling to shake off the lingering destructive effects of communist rule.

For more information about censorship around the world, some helpful websites include the Electronic Frontier Foundation (www.eff.org), the Electronic Privacy Information Center (www.epic.org), the Global Internet Liberty Campaign (www.gilc .org), the Internet Free Expression Alliance (www.ifea.net), Reporters Without Borders (www.rsf.org), Oppression.org (www.oppression.org), and The Index on Censorship (www.indexonline.org).

Companies that censor the Internet

Fortunately, most governments aren't smart enough to censor the Internet on their own. But that doesn't get in their way. Rather than try to develop filtering technology themselves, governments all over the world turn to American companies to develop the censoring technology they need to oppress their people.

According to the OpenNet Initiative, Saudi Arabia and Iran use filtering technology (SmartFilter) from Secure Computing, and Cisco Systems reportedly built a special $20,000 router and firewall box to help China Telecom filter the Internet. Nortel has allegedly sold voice and closed-circuit camera recognition software to China's Public Security Bureau. Users of Microsoft's China-based Internet portal can't search for words including *democracy*, *freedom*, and *human rights*, and Microsoft's Chinese blogging service, MSN Spaces, won't let anyone use words such as *Taiwan independence* or *demonstration*. WebSense's filtering technology has helped boost China's censoring abilities. Even Yahoo! and Google have altered their search engines to prevent users in any country from uncovering anything forbidden when searching the Internet.

Yahoo! even helped the Chinese government identify journalist Shi Tao, who was accused of "divulging state secrets abroad." Shi Tao had distributed the text of an internal Chinese government memo that warned Chinese journalists about the dangers of social destabilization from dissidents on the 15th anniversary of the Tiananmen Square massacre.

For the crime of leaking this memo to foreign journalists, the Chinese government sentenced Shi Tao to 10 years in prison. If anyone at Yahoo! feels guilty about it, he hasn't leaked an internal memo saying so.

The American government complains about human rights violations by other countries (except those oppressive governments currently friendly to the United States) even while American companies profit from the business of censoring and tracking dissident Internet sites and users. So, who is really doing the censoring? Is it the oppressive governments that block access to banned sites? Or is it the American companies that sell the technology that the oppressive governments use?

CENSORSHIP BEGINS AT HOME: PARENTAL CONTROL SOFTWARE

Just as national governments use filtering software to block certain websites, parents can use software to monitor and filter their children's Internet activity. Few people deny that parents have the right to decide what their children can see, so the debate in this case centers on the types of websites that parental control programs block. Most parental control programs block the obvious offenders, such as Condom Country, Playboy, or Hustler. But because new pornographic websites appear every day, the publishers of parental control software must constantly update their lists of banned sites to remain effective, which presents a problem of time versus resources. They can't afford to hire enough people to visit and check suspect websites, so most publishers use programs that automatically scan the Internet and search for keywords.

When these programs determine that a site contains too many banned keywords, they store that site's address in their updated blacklist. The result is that many innocent websites get blocked along with the offending ones. Even worse, many blocked sites have no idea they've been singled out by a particular parental control program.

Although this censorship may seem justified to protect children, there's still the question that always surrounds any form of censorship: Who decides what can and cannot be seen, and why should anyone be an exception to the rule?

Parental control software gone bad: blocking political and educational sites

Blocking pornography is to be expected from a parental control program. What isn't expected is the widespread blocking of many scientific, political, and innocuous sites due to one or two objectionable keywords. Here are some examples of what parental control programs have blocked in the past:

- SmartFilter (www.securecomputing.com) blocked the home pages of the Traditional Values Coalition (www.traditionalvalues.org), a conservative organization that wants "to take back the courts from the ACLU and the anti-God Left." SmartFilter also blocked access to web pages with mentions of the *Holy Bible*, the US Constitution, the Declaration of Independence, anti-drug information, all of Shakespeare's plays, *The Adventures of Sherlock Holmes*, and the *Koran*.

- Cyber Patrol (www.cyberpatrol.com) blocked the Ontario Center for Religious Tolerance (www.religioustolerance.org), an organization devoted to promoting religious diversity and acceptance, and Adoption Links Worldwide (www.alww.org).

- CYBERsitter (www.cybersitter.com) blocked virtually all gay and lesbian sites and even blocked Amnesty International after detecting the phrase *at least 21*, which appeared in a news story that read, "Reports of shootings in Irian Jaya bring to at least 21 the number of people in Indonesia and East Timor killed or wounded."

- Net Nanny (www.netnanny.com) blocked the Banned Books page at Carnegie Mellon (http://www.cs.cmu.edu/People/spok/banned-books.html), and also blocked House Majority Leader Richard "Dick" Armey's official website upon detecting the word *dick*.

Parental control software isn't perfect and has never claimed to be, but the comical mistakes it makes in blocking some websites illustrate the fluid nature of censorship in any form.

Parental control software gone really bad: CYBERsitter

Perhaps the most controversial parental control program is CYBERsitter (www .cybersitter.com), which has blocked the websites of both NOW (The National Organization for Women)—www.now.org—and the Human Awareness Institute (www.hai.org), which runs workshops for personal growth focusing on love, intimacy, and sexuality.

Whereas most parental control programs allow sites to appeal a block, CYBERsitter seems to have constructed a wall of self-righteousness. For example, when NOW appealed its ban by CYBERsitter, Brian Milburn, the CEO of Solid Oak Software (CYBERsitter's publisher) replied, "If NOW doesn't like it, tough . . . We have not and will not bow to any pressure from any organization that disagrees with our philosophy."

CYBERsitter on the offensive

A heated battle has been waged between CYBERsitter and Bennett Haselton, cofounder of Peacefire (www.peacefire.org), an anti-censorship site. After Haselton posted information on the Peacefire site criticizing CYBERsitter, along with instructions for disabling various parental control programs, Peacefire was promptly added to CYBERsitter's list of banned websites.

Peacefire also claimed that during installation of the trial version, CYBERsitter would scan the user's Internet Explorer cache and abort the installation with a cryptic error message if it found evidence of visits to the Peacefire site (such as the files peacefire.html or peacefire.gif).

Milburn defended his company's software to a PC World NewsRadio interviewer by saying, "We reserve the right to say who gets to install our software for free. It's our software—we own it, we publish it, we have an absolute legal right to protect our software from being hacked in any way, shape or form."

Cyber Patrol vs. cphack

In a similar dispute, Microsystems Software, the publisher of Cyber Patrol, once filed a lawsuit against two computer programmers, Eddy L.O. Jansson and Matthew Skala, for creating the cphack program, which allows children to uncover their parents' passwords and view Cyber Patrol's entire list of more than 100,000 banned websites.

"I oppose the use of Internet filtering software on philosophical grounds," Skala said. "The issue here was to see what does Cyber Patrol actually block. Parents have a right to know what they're getting and without our work they wouldn't know."

To avoid a drawn-out legal debate, Microsystems announced in 2000 that Jansson and Skala had settled with the company and granted them all rights to their cphack program for the cost of one Canadian dollar, as reported by CNN. Microsystems now claims that websites that post the cphack program are violating its copyright.

Project bait and switch: the double standard of censorship

To demonstrate the arbitrary nature of parental control software, Peacefire ran an experiment to see whether certain content hosted on a personal web page would be treated the same as identical content found on the website of a large, well-funded and well-known organization.

The Peacefire researchers collected anti-gay quotes from websites of the Family Research Council (www.frc.org), Concerned Women for America (www.cwfa.org), Focus on the Family (www.family.org), and radio personality Dr. Laura Schlessinger (www.drlaura.com). Then they posted these anti-gay quotes on free websites and submitted the pages anonymously to the publishers of SurfWatch, Cyber Patrol, Net Nanny, Bess, SmartFilter, and WebSense.

All of the companies agreed to block some or all of the bait pages (because the pages met their criteria for "denigrating people based on sexual orientation"), at which point Peacefire.org revealed the sites that were the actual sources of these quotes. Not surprisingly, none of the publishers agreed to block any of the four originating websites, yet they continued to block the bait pages, even though the homophobic quotes were identical.

Researching parental control programs

If you're going to use a parental control program, learn what type of websites they block (and why), and decide whether you want to censor your children's access using someone else's criteria. If you don't want a stranger to tell you what you can and cannot let your children see and read, would you want a parental control program to do the same thing?

For more information, visit Families Against Censorship (www.netfamilies.org) and the Censorware Project (http://censorware.net).

AVOIDING INTERNET CENSORSHIP

Even though URL filtering can be fooled and content filtering can never be 100 percent effective, these methods can still restrict access to the Internet when working in concert. Rather than trying to defeat Internet filtering programs, you can slip past them altogether using email, proxies, and encryption.

Accessing banned web pages by email

Blocking access to specific websites is easy. Scanning email to determine whether someone is sending or receiving banned information is much more time-consuming and labor-intensive. To exploit this flaw in most Internet filters, programmers have developed a way to retrieve web pages by email through something called a webmail server.

To read a website blocked by a filter, just send an email to a webmail server listing the URL address of the web page you want to see (such as http://www.cnn.com). Within a few minutes, hours, or days (depending on the server), you'll get an email containing the web page as either plain text or HTML code, bypassing the filtering.

For example, you could email the agora@dna.affrc.go.jp server with the following message:

To: agora@dna.affrc.go.jp

Subject: [none]

SEND http://www.cnn.com

In this example, the SEND field identifies the URL address of the web page you want to see. Basically, only two items are needed:

– The email address of the webmail server

– The URL address of the web page you want to view

If you type any additional information, such as a signature at the end of your email message, most webmail servers will ignore them, but it's best to strip them out just to make sure.

Here are some webmail servers and the syntax to put in the body of your message. Leave the subject line blank in all cases.

WEBMAIL ADDRESS	SYNTAX-TO USE
agora@dna.affrc.go.jp	SEND <URL>
agora@kamakura.mss.co.jp	SEND <URL>
agora@capri.mi.mss.co.jp	SEND <URL>
(If you want to receive the page as an HTML attachment, omit the GET command.)	
www4mail@access.bellanet.org	GET <URL>
www4mail@wm.ictp.trieste.it	GET <URL>
www4mail@ftp.uni-stuttgart.de	GET <URL>
www4mail@collaborium.org	GET <URL>
www4mail@kabissa.org	GET <URL>
www4mail@www4mail.org	GET <URL>

To learn more about setting up your own www4mail server to help others access the Internet using email, visit www4mail (www.www4mail.org).

NOTE: Because webmail servers tend to come and go, double-check the list of operational webmail servers at www.expita.com/servers.html.

For other services that let you retrieve web pages by email, visit one of the following:

ILIAD   http://prime.jsc.nasa.gov/iliad

PageGetter   www.pagegetter.com

Webgate   http://vancouver-webpages.com/webgate

Accessing banned web pages through proxy servers

An Internet filter may keep you from accessing a specific website, such as www.playboy .com, but it won't necessarily block you from accessing a website that appears harmless. Once you've accessed this seemingly harmless website, you can use it as a browser to access banned websites, as explained in "Port blocking" on page 142.

To find a proxy server, visit Public Proxy Servers (www.publicproxyservers.com). You'll then have to configure your browser to access that proxy server as shown in Figure 11-8.

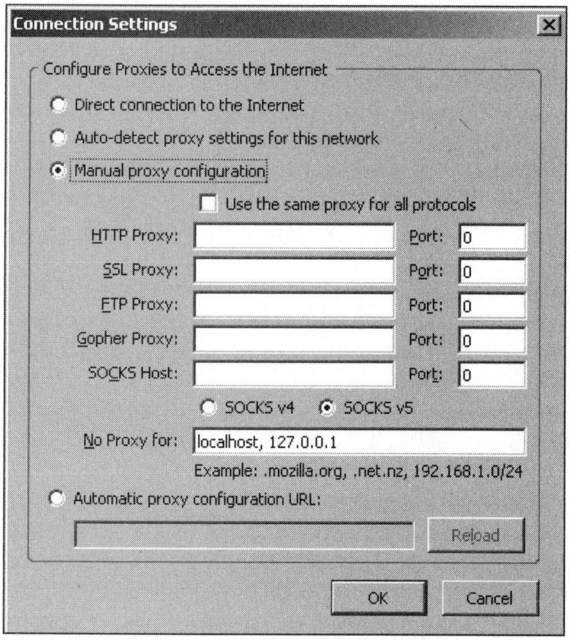

Figure 11-8: The Firefox browser lets you define a proxy server and a port number to use for accessing different services.

Accessing a proxy server can skirt Internet filters, but information you send and receive from a proxy server can still be monitored. To protect your privacy, you can use one of the following to encrypt your information:

ProxyWay Pro	www.proxyway.com
Anonymizer Total Net Shield	www.anonymizer.com
Secure-Tunnel	www.secure-tunnel.com

An Internet filter can still block the ports needed to communicate with a proxy server, however, so many will use a seldom-used port instead. To find a list of proxy servers that use uncommon ports, visit the Proxylist (www.web.freerk.com/proxylist.htm), which is updated weekly.

Internet censors may be suspicious of known proxy servers, but they are less likely to be suspicious of individual computers. Therefore, one way to help defeat Internet censorship is to turn your computer into a proxy server for others.

For example, the Peekabooty Project (www.peek-a-booty.org) lets anyone run a program to link his individual computer to the Peekabooty network, which consists of individual computers scattered all over the world.

When somebody wants to access a banned website, he can connect to the Peekabooty network, which selects a computer out of its network at random. This computer then grabs the requested web page and sends it back to the user.

Peacefire offers a similar program, dubbed Circumventer. Once you install Circumventer on your computer, you'll get a URL address that you can give to anyone trapped behind an Internet filter (someone in Saudi Arabia or Burma, or just a kid with a copy of NetNanny or CyberPatrol on his computer). That person can then browse the Internet through your computer.

For greater security, try the Six/Four program (http://sourceforge.net/projects/sixfour) or JAP Anon Proxy (http://anon.inf.tu-dresden.de/index_en.html), which is shown in Figure 11-9. JAP encrypts your information and mixes it through multiple servers so no one, not even the servers, knows which information is being sent to which computer.

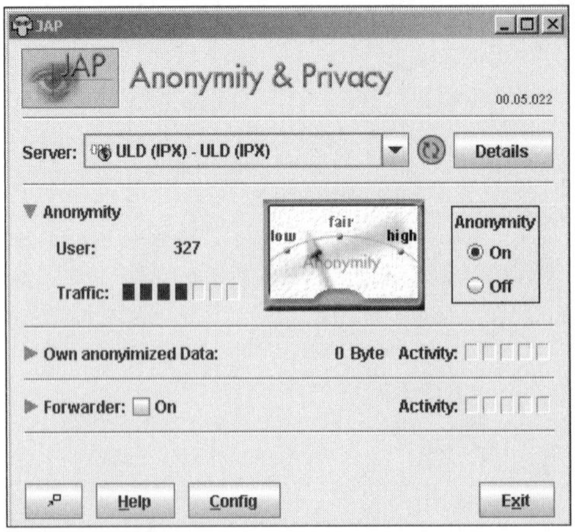

154

Figure 11-9: The JAP Anon Proxy program visually displays your anonymity level on the Internet.

Sometimes access to the Internet isn't as important as posting information there anonymously. If you want to share information with others online, but want to keep your identity secret, do it at FreeNet (http://freenet.sourceforge.net).

If someone living under an oppressive dictatorship tries to contact people through the Internet, his communication may be monitored and he may be punished. So rather than communicate in plain sight, he can hide a message inside an ordinary graphic file (known as steganography) and post this GIF image on an approved website that anyone can access.

When users access this approved website, all they'll see is an ordinary GIF image, but if they access this same site using a program called Camera/Shy (http://sourceforge .net/projects/camerashy), Camera/Shy will automatically detect and retrieve the messages buried inside the graphic image.

READING BANNED BOOKS ONLINE

In 1726, Jonathan Swift published his classic novel *Gulliver's Travels*, which satirized the foibles of mankind. Besides traveling to a land of tiny people, where Gulliver is a giant, and then to a land of giants, where Gulliver is tiny, Gulliver also travels to a floating island run by scientists who are so focused on their research that their own homes are falling apart. Afterwards, Gulliver travels to a land of intelligent horses, where human beings are called Yahoos and they spend their time fighting each other for useless gems they find scattered along the shore. Sadly, more than 200 years later, *Gulliver's Travels* remains completely relevant in exposing how people argue over trivial matters and are ruled by emotions rather than reason.

Of course, depending on where you happen to live at any given time, you might never have gotten a chance to read *Gulliver's Travels*, *To Kill a Mockingbird*, *The Catcher in the Rye*, or *Uncle Tom's Cabin* because all of these books have been banned at some time in history. The American Library Association (www.ala.org) reports that book burnings still continue on a regular basis today, as shown in Figure 11-10.

"On Sunday evening, members of the Harvest Assembly of God Church in Penn Township sing songs
as they burn books, videos and CDs that they have judged offensive to their God."

Published in the *Butler Eagle*, March 26, 2001. Courtesy of the Butler Eagle.

Figure 11-10: As the American Library Association reports, book burning is alive and well in the 21st century.

Many parents, teachers, and government authorities still insist on the right to ban books that they consider harmful to someone else's intellectual, emotional, or spiritual development. To ensure that such censorship doesn't succeed, a number of websites have devoted themselves to distributing free electronic copies of famous works, such as *The Adventures of Huckleberry Finn*, *Dracula*, and *A Tale of Two Cities*. The books are available as plain ASCII text files, which any computer can display and print. No matter how many books are burned, there will always be another copy that anyone can print or read off the Internet.

To find an online version of a banned book, visit Banned Books Online (http://digital .library.upenn.edu/books/banned-books.html) or Project Gutenberg (www.promo.net/pg).

To search for historical books, whose copyrights have expired, visit Google Print (http://print.google.com) or the Open Content Alliance (www.opencontentalliance.org), whose partners include both Yahoo! and Microsoft. Both Google Print and Open Content Alliance focus on preserving older books in general, but you can use both services to help you find banned books too.

Of course, you still need to access the Internet to download a free ebook. But once you've done so, you can share it with others. By copying and sharing ebooks, you can preserve your right to read what other people (your parents, boss, or government) don't want you to see.

Secretly reading a banned book in broad daylight

Of course, access to a banned book doesn't solve all of the problems. You can still get in trouble if someone catches you reading a banned book on your computer screen.

To disguise what you're reading, use a program such as AceReader (www.stepware .com), as shown in Figure 11-11, which displays the entire text of an ASCII document across your screen in large letters, one word at a time, at speeds up to 1,000 words per minute, so that it's virtually impossible for anyone to recognize what you're reading at a glance. With this program, you can read the ASCII text of a book that your parents, school officials, or government authorities don't want you to read, right in front of their eyes without their ever knowing it. (Just make sure they don't find the ASCII text file on your hard disk.)

Secretly browsing the Web in broad daylight

Sometimes you may want to browse the Internet, but your boss, parent, teacher, or other authority figure feels otherwise. Rather than sneak a peek at a website and risk having your browser window give you away, try running Ghostzilla (www.ghostzilla.com) instead.

Ghostzilla is a browser, based on Firefox, that can appear within the window of another program, such as Outlook Express, as shown in Figure 11-12.

With another program window open, move the mouse pointer to the left side of the screen, then to the right, then back to the left again, and up pops Ghostzilla in the currently active program window. Now you can browse the Internet all you want. The moment someone peeks over your shoulder, click the mouse outside the Ghostzilla display, and your normal program pops back into view. As long as no one's otherwise monitoring your activities, you can safely view the Internet while appearing to be doing something else.

Figure 11-11: The AceReader program flashes text on the screen so you can read an entire novel one word at a time.

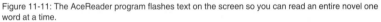

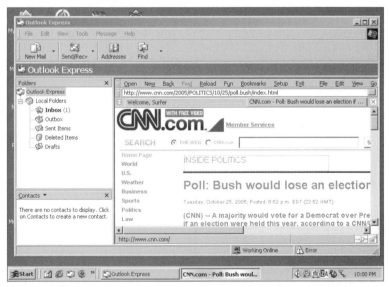

Figure 11-12: Ghostzilla lets you secretly browse the Internet within the window of another program, such as Outlook Express.

IS ANYONE CENSORING THE CENSORS?

Even today, many people continue to insist that censorship of some kind is necessary—just so long as they're the ones who get to pick and choose what others can and cannot see.

Ironically, for some foreign translations of this book, certain chapters had to be deleted before the government would allow it to be published. If certain information is deemed too harmful for the public, shouldn't it also be too harmful for the censors to see too?

Fortunately, no matter what obstacles people may use to block others' access to information, there will always be ways to defeat or avoid them. All it takes is a little bit of creativity. Perhaps the only form of censorship we have to worry about is self-censorship, when people are too frightened to speak honestly and openly. Once that happens, often under the guise of "political correctness," then censorship may finally have succeeded in stifling free speech for good.

12

THE FILESHARING NETWORKS

It all began in 1999, when an 18-year-old college dropout named Shawn Fanning got fed up with trying to find and download music files off the Internet. So he wrote a program that could search for and share music files and exchange instant messages with other people on the Internet. When Fanning released his creation, called Napster, little did he know that he would wind up changing the world.

NOTE: *For more information about filesharing, pick up a copy of* Steal This File Sharing Book, *published by No Starch Press.*

Criminal: A person with predatory instincts who has not sufficient capital to form a corporation.

—HOWARD SCOTT, Economist

A SHORT HISTORY OF INTERNET FILESHARING

Fanning didn't invent Internet filesharing with Napster, but he definitely made it more convenient. Of course, people have been sharing recorded information for years. Software pirates copied floppy disks, and later CDs, and traded them with each other (see Chapter 6 for more information about software piracy), and music lovers recorded and swapped tape cassettes of their favorite albums, long before Internet filesharing existed.

People have been sharing files over the Internet through websites, FTP sites, and Usenet newsgroups for as long as such technology has existed. Although these vehicles made sharing files easy, searching for files was difficult.

You could use a search engine such as Google to find specific files on different websites, but you'll wind up sifting through lots of irrelevant links. Or you could use a special FTP search engine to find certain types of files stored on FTP servers around the world, but you'd have to repeat the search for each file and visit and search each FTP site separately.

Usenet newsgroups are great for sharing files anonymously (because nobody knows who posted any file), but they aren't searchable; people just have to take whatever happens to be available at the time.

The beauty of Napster was that it combined the abilities to search for files and to download files conveniently within a single program. Although originally designed to share only music files, typically those stored in the MP3 file format, Napster defined the basic filesharing model: create a network of computers that can search for and share files with every other computer on that same network.

HOW FILESHARING WORKS

At the simplest level, filesharing becomes possible whenever two or more computers connect to each other. To search for files on the original Napster, people connected directly to Napster's server and submitted their requests, and then the server queried every other connected computer to determine which ones had the requested files, as shown in Figure 12-1.

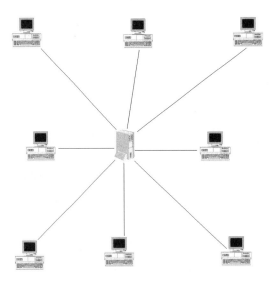

Figure 12-1: Napster's network used a centralized server.

Because all search requests went through that main server, the Recording Industry Association of America (RIAA) managed to close Napster down by getting a court order that simply required Napster to shut down its servers. Without the servers, no search requests could take place and, hence, no filesharing could occur. As far as the RIAA was concerned, it had eliminated a rampant source of copyright infringement by stopping people from trading MP3 files of their favorite songs.

The birth of Gnutella

After studying the weaknesses of Napster's centralized server network design, a programmer named Justin Frankel created a similar filesharing network dubbed Gnutella. Unlike Napster, search requests went through every computer connected to the network, not just the central server, as shown in Figure 12-2. As a result, a Gnutella network could never be shut down at a single choke point.

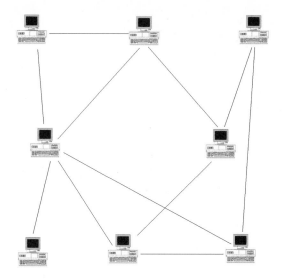

Figure 12-2: Gnutella created a decentralized network that is nearly impossible to shut down.

To publicize Gnutella's existence, Justin posted the Gnutella source code on the website of a company called NullSoft on March 14, 2000, so that others could study his creation. Within hours, America Online (the owner of NullSoft) ordered the source code removed, but not before copies had managed to spread all over the Internet and a new filesharing network had been born.

Because of its decentralized nature, nobody really controls Gnutella, which means nobody can really shut it down either. Over time, many programs, called *clients*, have been written to allow users to tap into the Gnutella network. Although there are dozens of different Gnutella clients available, two of the more popular ones are BearShare (www .bearshare.com) and LimeWire (www.limewire.com), which is shown in Figure 12-3.

WARNING: *Many filesharing client programs may come loaded with adware/spyware. When in doubt, always look for a client that specifically advertises that it is adware- and spyware-free.*

Since so many people have created clients to access the Gnutella network, it's difficult to update and improve the Gnutella network without everyone's cooperation. As a result, programmers have created a similar, but more advanced, version dubbed Gnutella2, or just G2 (www.gnutella2.com).

Although based on Gnutella, Gnutella2 is an entirely separate filesharing network designed to accelerate file searches. Despite the improvements, most Gnutella2 clients still connect to the older Gnutella network as well, allowing users to search for files on both networks simultaneously.

Two popular Gnutella and Gnutella2 clients are Gnucleus (www.gnucleus.com) and Shareaza (http://shareaza.sourceforge.net).

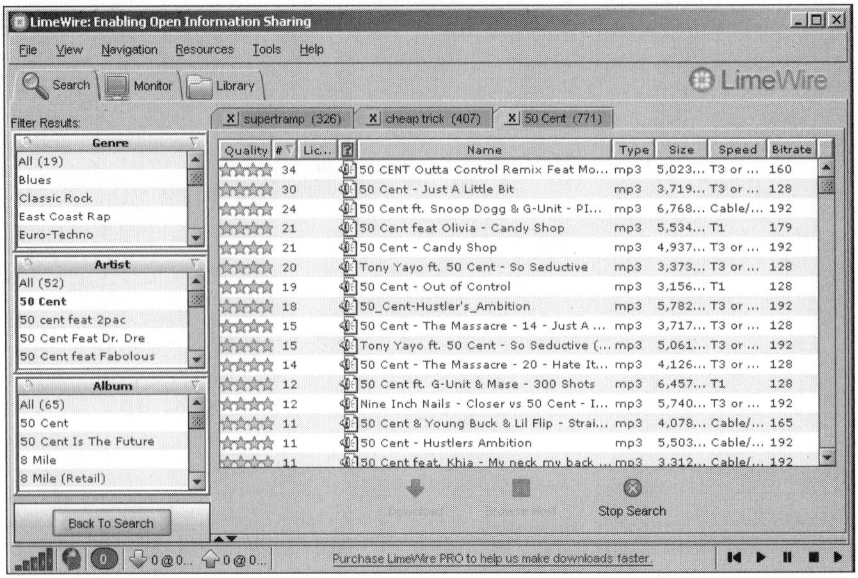

Figure 12-3: LimeWire is one of the few Gnutella network clients that can run on Windows, Macintosh, and Linux.

The Ares network

Dozens of client programs tap into the Gnutella network every day. Unfortunately, Gnutella's popularity has also limited its growth. With no one effectively controlling it, the network cannot change or improve unless all Gnutella clients change and improve at the same time, which is nearly impossible.

Moreover, even though Gnutella's greatest strength is its decentralized network, that also causes file searching to take a long time, since each file request has to go through every computer connected to the network. Given these limitations, many former Gnutella clients have broken away and started their own filesharing networks. One of the first examples of these is called Ares (http://aresgalaxy.sourceforge.net).

The Ares filesharing network primarily carries MP3 music files, but you can find a variety of other types of files as well. Figure 12-4 shows some pirated copies of Microsoft Windows XP found on the Ares network, along with Windows XP cracks and key generators.

The FastTrack network

Perhaps the most infamous filesharing network of all is FastTrack, which can only be officially accessed using the Kazaa (www.kazaa.com) client developed by the same company. Unlike Gnutella, FastTrack is a closed, proprietary network that only licensed clients are allowed to access.

Like Gnutella, FastTrack is a decentralized network, but it offers three major advantages. First, FastTrack can download files from multiple sources to speed up file transfers and ensure that you get the file you want, even if one or more computers disconnect from the network. Second, FastTrack can resume downloading an interrupted file transfer

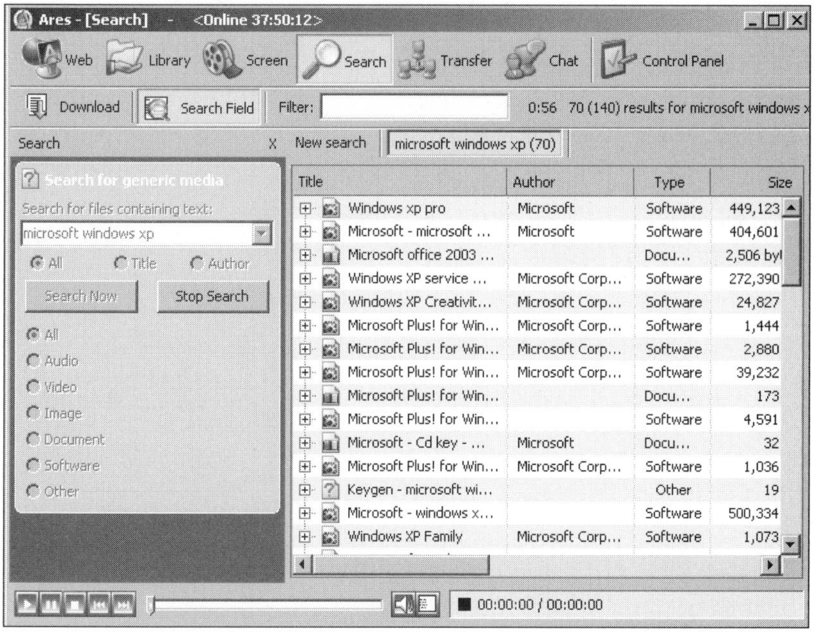

Figure 12-4: Ares is an independent filesharing network that lets you trade music, video, and software.

so you don't have to start all over again. Third, FastTrack can search for files quickly by dividing its network into sections, called *nodes*, where each node is linked to a computer designated as a Supernode.

Rather than search every computer on the network like Gnutella does, FastTrack searches only each Supernode; each Supernode searches its linked nodes for the requested file. This accelerates file searching so that, regardless of how many computers are connected to the network, file searching won't slow down, as can happen on the Gnutella network.

The biggest drawback of the FastTrack network is that the free version of Kazaa comes loaded with adware/spyware. Figure 12-5 shows a typical agreement specifying all the different adware/spyware that may get installed on your computer when you install the Grokster filesharing client program, which once connected to the FastTrack network just like Kazaa.

If you don't want adware/spyare installed on your computer but you still want to access the FastTrack network, you can either pay for the non–adware/spyware version of Kazaa, or you can use an unofficial FastTrack client called KLT K++ (www.klitetools .com). The owner of FastTrack, Sharman Networks, frowns upon any unofficial FastTrack clients, however, so they're constantly changing the network to keep rogue client programs like KLT K++ from working. But then the programmers of KLT K++ rewrite their client program and reconnect to FastTrack once more, until the next time Sharman Networks changes FastTrack again.

To make connecting to the FastTrack network even simpler, grab a copy of Kazaa along with a copy of Diet K (www.dietk.com). Diet K will remove all the adware/spyware that Kazaa installed without sacrificing any of the benefits of the official client program.

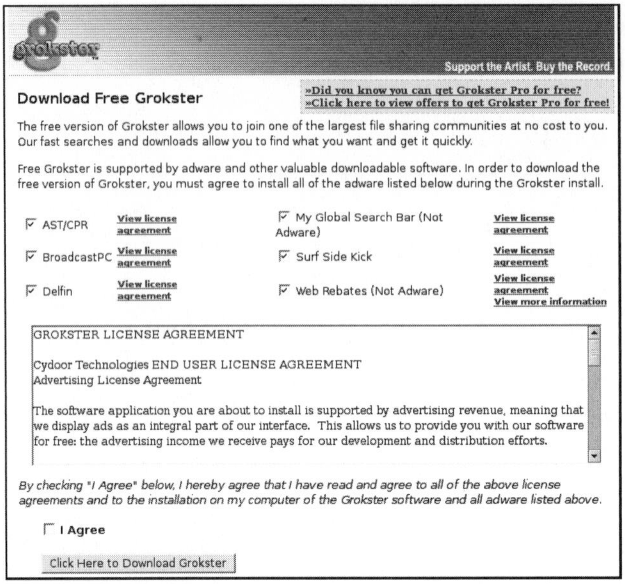

Figure 12-5: To install many free filesharing clients, you must first agree to load your computer with adware/spyware.

SHARING LARGE FILES

No matter how many filesharing networks pop up, they're all based on the original Gnutella design of a decentralized network. The minor differences among the different networks mostly concern the searching and downloading of different files.

The filesharing networks already discussed were great for music files (typically MP3 files ranging in size from 3MB to 10MB), but they weren't so great for sharing massive files of the contents of an entire CD or DVD, such popular programs as Adobe Photoshop, or an illegal video file copy of *Star Wars*. It simply took too long, as much as several hours, to share the contents of a CD (typically 650MB in size) or a DVD (typically 4.7GB in size).

For that reason, programmers soon came up with special filesharing networks dedicated to large files. The two most popular are eDonkey and BitTorrent.

With most filesharing networks, you can't start sharing any files until you've finished downloading them from another computer. With both eDonkey (www.edonkey.com) and BitTorrent (www.bittorrent.com), you can start sharing files even while you're receiving them, which means you can download and share a file simultaneously, making large file transfers faster and more reliable.

THE PROBLEM WITH FILESHARING

From a technical point of view, there's nothing wrong with filesharing. The creators and owners of many types of files want to distribute them freely as widely as possible. Many musicians release MP3 files of their songs, hoping to attract an audience. Aspiring radio broadcasters can store interviews as MP3 files and distribute them as sound files, known as *podcasts*, that anyone can download and listen to whenever they want. To find different podcasts, visit the Podcast Directory (www.podcast.net).

Amateur filmmakers may release their projects over filesharing networks to spread the word, and software publishers often release demos of their products via filesharing networks. Many Linux distributions actually depend on people using filesharing networks to spread them around the world.

So, from a technical standpoint, filesharing is great for people who want to distribute their own copyrighted material. The problem is that legal applications of filesharing are dwarfed by the widespread illegal ones.

Because both BitTorrent and eDonkey are optimized for sharing large files, you can often find the latest Hollywood movies being swapped on these networks, sometimes even before they're officially released in theaters. BitTorrent and eDonkey are also favorite networks for swapping entire music albums and CDs or popular programs such as Microsoft Office or Adobe Illustrator.

If they just want individual songs from an album, most people flock to the older filesharing networks, such as Gnutella or FastTrack. There, they can copy the best songs off an album, store them as MP3 files, and then pass the files around. Their convenience and ease of use make the filesharing networks havens for rampant software, music, and video copyright violations, as shown in Figure 12-6.

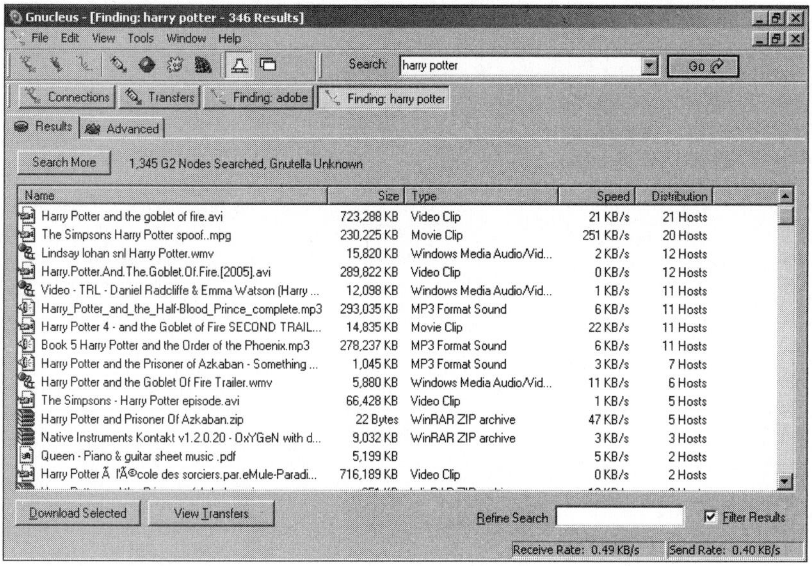

Figure 12-6: On a typical filesharing network, you can find pirated Harry Potter movies, audio books, and printed books ready to be downloaded and shared illegally.

The RIAA, the movie studios, and book publishers are trying to crack down on such blatant copyright infringement, but, with so many different filesharing networks available and nearly all controlled by nobody in particular, trying to shut down a filesharing network is nearly impossible. Tracking down individual violators is often too costly and time-consuming, except in extreme cases where individuals are sharing hundreds or thousands of movies or songs, or distributing the latest blockbuster movie or eagerly awaited pop album before it's officially released.

Although the RIAA has had limited success suing blatant copyright violators, it's having more success taking legal action against the companies that make the file-sharing programs in the first place. In 2005, US courts shut down Grokster, one of the few licensed clients allowed to access the FastTrack network. That same year they also shut down WinMX, a filesharing program that originally tapped into the OpenNap network, but later evolved to form an independent filesharing network. The RIAA will likely continue to pursue legal action against any company that makes money selling filesharing programs. (This still leaves the free filesharing programs untouched.)

Like it or not, filesharing is here to stay. The real debate isn't how to stop it but how to take advantage of it—legally. The RIAA and Hollywood movie studios claim that filesharing hurts their business. The producers of the 2004 bomb *Soul Plane* actually claimed that the movie did poorly at the box office because too many people had downloaded an advance copy off filesharing networks, rather than seeing it in theaters. For anyone who hasn't seen *Soul Plane*, the quality of the movie can be summed up in one person's comment on the Internet Movie Database site (www.imdb.com): "Glad I didn't pay to see this movie."

Even musicians are torn between the advantages and disadvantages of filesharing. Some claim that it hurts album sales, but others say it increases their potential audience and actually encourages people to buy their albums. The band Queen has even collected the best bootleg recordings of their old concerts and offers them for sale on their own website.

For more information about the latest filesharing networks popping up or getting shut down, visit ZeroPaid (www.zeropaid.com) or Slyck (www.slyck.com), shown in Figure 12-7.

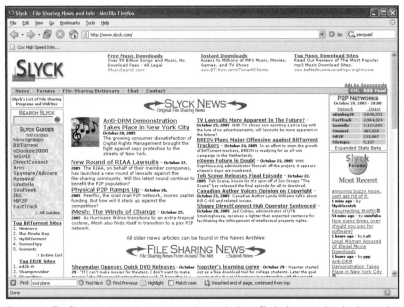

Figure 12-7: The Slyck website can keep you up to date on the latest filesharing network technology and news.

Filesharing networks represent a new opportunity for some and a threat to others. Which side of the debate you take depends entirely on how you stand to profit (or lose) from the continuing growth of filesharing technology.

PART 4

THE REAL WORLD
HACKERS

13

THE INTERNET CON ARTISTS

When most people think of Internet crime, they picture hackers stealing credit card numbers and racking up huge charges for somebody else to pay. Although this can and does occur, the biggest threat on the Internet isn't hackers, it's con artists, many of whom are no more competent at using a computer than the people they're victimizing.

Whether con artists are fleecing a victim in person, through the mail, over the telephone, or over the Internet, all follow the same basic approach:

1. Promise a fantastic reward in return for little or no effort. (Victims are usually too blinded by their own greed to question why the con artist would want to help them in the first place.)

2. Exploit the victim's trust. (Con artists encourage victims to demonstrate their trust in order to show they deserve the promised reward.)

3. Collect the victim's money. (Con artists must trick a victim into giving up money or something equally valuable.)

Not surprisingly, con artists and politicians often use identical tactics. Politicians always promise that they're serving the voters' interests without revealing their own motives (Step 1). Then they appeal to the voters' trust by implying that they'll benefit if the particular politician is elected to office (Step 2). Finally, the politician appeals for the voters' support (Step 3), which leads to power and money for the politician. In the case of usual politics, the money goes toward promoting the politician's reelection and other political maneuvers. In the case of a crooked politician, the voters get conned and left with nothing.

Because nearly everyone would love to make a lot of money without doing any work, all of us are potential victims of con games. To avoid falling prey to an Internet scam, take some time to educate yourself on the different types of cons that have been duping people for years.

CHARITY SCAMS

Every time there's a disaster anywhere in the world, con artists try to take advantage of people's generosity. These charity scams often involve fake charity websites with legitimate-sounding names that accept online payments, such as transactions made through PayPal. After Hurricane Katrina in 2005, for example, website names that were not affiliated with any legitimate charities included www.katrinareliefonline.org, www.katrinahelp.com, and www.katrinadfamilies.com.

Phony charity websites can attract people who want to donate money, but con artists often go one step further and actively solicit donations through spam. Such unsolicited email will often mention the name of a fake charity that's very similar to a legitimate one, such as the National Cancer Society (instead of the legitimate American Cancer Society) or the National Heart Institute (instead of the legitimate American Heart Institute).

These con artists can scam you in two ways. First, if you donate money, you'll be giving your cash to a con artist instead of to a charity. Second, if you give the con artist your credit card number, you'll risk having him run up huge charges.

To avoid charity scams, never donate money to any organization that sends unsolicited email, and never provide your information to a telemarketer seeking donations over the phone. Because blanket telemarketing is expensive and time-consuming, few legitimate charities rely on it to raise money. A legitimate organization will provide a website or mailing address if you ask, and making this your standard procedure will ensure that you have the time and ability to investigate the charity. Before you make any donations, check out the charity's name. Bogus websites often create logos that look similar to those of legitimate charities. A simple search using Google or on the Better Business Bureau website (www.bbb.com) will uncover well-known frauds. You can often tell a fake charity from a legitimate one by doing a WHOIS search (www.networksolutions.com/whois) on the domain name. If the WHOIS search reveals that the owner of the domain name is the charity you expected, such as the American Red Cross for the redcross.org domain name, as shown in Figure 13-1, then the website is most likely legitimate. If the WHOIS search reveals an individual or an organization other than the charity promoted by the website, you might want to investigate the charity more closely before sending any money.

Even legitimate charities themselves can fall prey to con artists. The former chief executive of the United Way once pled guilty to stealing $500,000 from the charity, channeling donations into his own pockets instead of toward the worthy causes they were meant to support. So even if you give to a legitimate charitable organization, it's possible that your money will not help someone who actually needs it.

If you really want to help others, do the research to find a reputable charity. When you give to that charity, use the methods you've researched and verified (by clicking on a secure online link, sending your check to a mail address, or by calling a phone number). Better yet, donate your time by volunteering. That way you can be sure your money isn't being wasted. For more on giving money to charities, visit the Better Business Bureau's Wise Giving Alliance at www.give.org. To research and learn about different (valid) charities, visit Charity Search (www.charitynavigator.org). If you suspect that a charity could be fraudulent or dishonest, visit Google and search for the charity name along with words like *scandal* or *scam* to find information from people who might have been conned by that particular charity.

WHOIS Record For

redcross.org

Certified Offer Service - Make an offer on this domain
Backorder - Try to get this name when it becomes available
Private Registration - Make personal information for this domain private
SSL Certificates - Make this site secure
Site Confirm Seals - Become a trusted Web Site

Registrant: Make this info private
American Red Cross
8111 Gatehouse Road
Falls Church, VA 22042
US

Domain Name: REDCROSS.ORG

Administrative Contact :
American Red Cross
admin@USA.REDCROSS.ORG
8111 GATEHOUSE RD
FALLS CHURCH, VA 22042-1203
US
Phone: 703-206-6011
Fax: 703-206-7015

Technical Contact :
American Red Cross
netops@USA.REDCROSS.ORG
8111 GATEHOUSE RD
FALLS CHURCH, VA 22042-1203
US

Figure 13-1: A WHOIS search can reveal the true owner behind charity domain names.

Even if you find a valid charity, be careful of their privacy policies. To earn additional income, some charities may sell your name, address, and email address to market research firms, which means you could donate money for a good cause and then wind up getting junk mail and spam in return for your effort.

THE AREA CODE SCAM

Some scams leverage the proliferation of newly created telephone area codes. The con artist starts by leaving a phone message or by sending an email claiming that you've won a fabulous prize in a contest, or that your credit card was incorrectly charged, or that one of your relatives is in trouble—anything to prompt you to return the call or respond to the email.

If you call the phone number provided in the message, you may be placed on hold, directed to a long-winded recorded message, or put in touch with someone who speaks broken English. In any event, the person on the other end simply tries to keep you on the phone as long as possible because (surprise!) the phone number is really a pay-per-call service (much like a 1-900 number) that charges you (the caller) astronomical rates, which can amount to as much as $25 per minute.

The area code most commonly used in this scam is 809, which is actually located in the Caribbean. Thus, the scammer can avoid American laws, such as those requiring that he warn you in advance of the charges being incurred and state the per-minute rate involved, or that there must be a provision for terminating the call within a certain time period without being charged. However, because no international code is required to reach the phone number, most people won't even realize that they're making an international call.

Area code scams are extremely hard to prosecute. The victim actually initiates the call, so neither the local phone company nor the long distance carrier is likely to be of any assistance or to cancel the charges.

To avoid this scam, be careful when returning unknown phone calls with unfamiliar area codes. As more people are learning about the 809 scam, con artists have switched to other area codes such as 242 (the Bahamas), 284 (British Virgin Islands), and 787 (Puerto Rico), as well as 500 and 700 prefixes, which are commonly used for pay-per-call adult entertainment services.

If in doubt, check an area code's location first by visiting the LincMad website (www.lincmad.com).

THE NIGERIAN SCAM

Many people in other countries hate Americans, which isn't surprising when you realize that many foreigners know the United States only through the actions of stereotypical "ugly" American tourists and American politicians (many of whom are disliked in their own country, too).

People in other countries get most of their information about Americans from American television shows. After watching shows like *Sex and the City*, lots of people in other countries believe that Americans are not only rich and beautiful, but lousy actors as well.

Regardless of the foreign perception of Americans, the fact remains that the United States is one of the wealthiest countries on the planet. Given the wide disparity between the average American's income and that of people in other countries, for many people there's not much guilt or shame in conning Americans out of their money at every available opportunity.

Not only have many scams originated in Nigeria, but the Nigerian government itself has been involved to the point that many believe that international scams are the country's third largest industry. The general view in Nigeria is that if you can cheat an American out of his money, it's the American's fault for being gullible in the first place.

Nigerian scams are often called "Advance Fee Fraud," "419 Fraud" (four-one-nine, after the relevant section of the Criminal Code of Nigeria), or "The Fax Scam." The scam works as follows: The victim receives an unsolicited email message, fax, or letter from Nigeria containing a money-laundering proposal disguised as a seemingly legitimate business plan involving crude oil or as a notice about a bequest left in a will.

The fax or letter usually asks the victim to facilitate transfer of a large sum of money to the victim's own bank and promises that he will receive a share if he pays an "advance fee," "transfer tax," "performance bond," or government bribe of some sort. If the victim pays the fee, complications mysteriously arise that require the victim to send more money until he runs out of money, patience, or both.

With the growing popularity of the Internet, Nigerian con artists have been very busy. Don't be surprised if you receive email from Nigeria asking for your help. The following is an example:

Dear Sir

I am working with the Federal Ministry of Health in Nigeria. It happens that five months ago my father who was the Chairman of the Task Force Committee created by the present Military Government to monitor the selling, distribution and revenue generation from crude oil sales before and after the gulf war crisis died in a motor accident on his way home from Lagos after attending a National conference. He was admitted in the hospital for eight (8) days before he finally died. While I was with him in the hospital, he disclosed all his confidential documents to me one of which is the business I want to introduce to you right now.

Before my father finally died in the hospital, he told me that he has $21.5M (twenty one million five hundred thousand U.S. Dollars) cash in a trunk box coded and deposited in a security company. He told me that the security company is not aware of its contents. That on producing a document which, he gave to me, that I will only pay for the demurrage after which the box will be released to me.

He further advised me that I should not collect the money without the assistance of a foreigner who will open a local account in favor of his company for onward transfer to his nominated overseas account where the money will be invested.

This is because as a civil servant I am not supposed to own such money. This will bring many questions in the bank if I go without a foreigner.

It is at this juncture that I decided to contact you for assistance but with the following conditions:

1. That this transaction is treated with Utmost confidence, cooperation and absolute secrecy which it demands.

2. That the money is being transferred to an account where the incidence of taxation would not take much toll.

3. That all financial matters for the success of this transfer will be tackled by both parties.

4. That a promissory letter signed and sealed by you stating the amount US $21.5M (twenty-one million five hundred thousand US Dollars) will be given to me by you on your account and that only 20% of the total money is for your assistance.

Please contact me on the above fax number for more details. Please quote (QS) in all your correspondence.

Yours faithfully,

DR. AN UZOAMAKA

To learn more about scams originating in Nigeria, visit the 419 Coalition website (http://home.rica.net/alphae/419coal). If you're foolish enough to send money to the con artist running this scam, you'll most likely receive a subsequent email saying that there were additional delays or problems, such as unforeseen fees, fines, or bribes that need to be paid. The goal is to keep you sending money for as long as possible. In some cases, people have sent thousands of dollars to these con artists while others have actually traveled to Nigeria to meet with the con artists in person. In 2003, a 72-year-old man in the Czech Republic lost his life savings to a Nigerian con artist and took his frustration out by shooting a Nigerian diplomat.

Since the United States sent troops to Afghanistan and Iraq in 2001, a new variation on the Nigerian scam has emerged. In this adaptation, potential victims receive an email supposedly from an American soldier who has discovered a large stash of money and needs help sneaking it back to the United States. Other than using the name of an American soldier instead of a Nigerian official, the scam is the same.

Similar to the Nigerian scam is the advance loan scam, which promises to loan you money at an extremely low interest rate. All you have to do is pay an advance fee for "processing." Once the con artist receives your money, complications mysteriously occur. You never get the loan you expected, and the con artist walks away with your advance fee.

WORK-AT-HOME BUSINESSES

Another common scam often promoted in unsolicited email promises fabulous money-making opportunities that can be achieved at home with little effort. This type of scam is not new. Con artists originally perpetrated these scams using post office boxes and letters; today's scam artists use the reach of the Internet and the simplicity of email to reach more potential victims faster than ever before. This should give you yet another reason to avoid receiving, let alone reading, any unsolicited email (see Chapter 18 for more information about spam). This section lists some typical examples of these scams.

Stuffing envelopes

The most common work-at-home business scam claims that you can earn hundreds or thousands of dollars stuffing envelopes in your spare time.

First of all, who in his right mind would want to spend his life stuffing envelopes? If this prospect actually appeals to you and you send money for more information, you need to seriously examine your aspirations in life. If you send money, you'll probably receive the following:

- A letter stating that, if you want to make money, you should just place your own ad in a magazine or newspaper offering to sell information to others about how they can make money by stuffing envelopes. There's no envelope-stuffing involved at all.

- Information about contacting mail-order companies and offering to stuff their envelopes for them. Unfortunately, you'll soon find that stuffing envelopes pays less than Third World wages.

Make-it-yourself kits

Another work-at-home business scam offers to sell you a kit (such as a greeting card kit). You're supposed to follow the kit's instructions to make custom greeting cards, Christmas wreaths, flyers, or other products and then sell the products yourself as a quick way to start your own business. The business may sound legitimate, but the kit is usually worthless, and always overpriced, and the products that it claims you can sell will rarely earn you enough to recoup the cost of your original investment.

Work as an independent contractor

Rather than start your own business making products from do-it-yourself kits, why not work as an independent contractor for a company that will take care of the hassles of marketing and selling for you? This scam claims that a company is willing to pay thousands of dollars a month to have you help it build something, like toy dolls or baby shoes. All you have to do is manufacture these items at home and sell them to the company.

If you're foolish enough to send money, you'll receive instructions and materials to build whatever product you're supposed to make. However, the materials are often cheap and easily obtainable for a fraction of the price at your local stores.

What usually happens is that the work is so boring that most people give up before they even get to the point of selling one batch of the product (often there is a high minimum purchase amount listed in the instructions). For those with greater perseverance, the company will often claim that the workmanship is of poor quality (whether it is or not) and thus refuse to pay you for your work. Either way, someone else now has your money.

Fraudulent sales

People have been fooled into buying shoddy or nonexistent products for years. The Internet just provides one more avenue for con artists to peddle their snake oil. Scammers can reach a mass audience by spamming thousands of email addresses every day. Two popular types of fraudulent sales involve "miracle" health products and investments.

Miracle health products have been around for centuries, claiming to cure everything from impotence and indigestion to AIDS and cancer. Of course, if you buy one of these products, your malady doesn't get any better—and may actually get worse. In the meantime, you're stuck with a worthless product that may consist of nothing more than corn syrup and food coloring.

Investment swindles are nothing new either. The typical stock swindler dangles the promise of large profits and low risk, but only if you act right away (so the con artist can get your money sooner and keep you from researching the "bait," only to realize its true nature as a scam). Many stock swindlers visit investment forums or chat rooms, such as those on America Online, and scout these areas for people willing to believe their promises of "ground-floor" opportunities and to hand over money to complete strangers.

Like worthless miracle health products, investment scams may sell you stock certificates or bonds that have no real value whatsoever. Typically these investments focus on gold mines, oil wells, real estate, ostrich farms, or other exotic investments that seem exciting and interesting but prove to be nonexistent or worthless.

PYRAMID SCHEMES

The idea behind a pyramid scheme is to get two or more people to give you money. In exchange, you give them nothing but the hope that they can get rich too—as long as they can convince two or more people to give them money, and so on. The most common incarnation of a pyramid scheme is a chain letter.

A typical chain letter lists five addresses and urges you to send money (one dollar or more) to each of them. It instructs you to copy the chain letter, removing the top name from the list of addresses and putting your own name and address at the bottom, and mail five copies of the chain letter to other people. The promise in the letter is that if you send the five dollars (or more), you can just sit back and wait for fabulous riches to come pouring into your mailbox within a few weeks—one dollar at a time. (Those who want to con others out of money probably realize that it's faster to simply start a new chain letter with their name at the top.)

Many chain letters require you to sign a letter agreeing that you are offering the money as a gift or that you are buying the five addresses as a mailing list. In this way, the chain letter author says, you will not be breaking any laws.

Most people receive chain letters as unsolicited email, but a unique twist on the chain letter scam, called Mega$Nets, appeared in the early '90s. Unlike a text-only chain letter, Mega$Nets was a computer program that let people type in their name and address using a specially generated code, which users could buy and then offer to sell to others.

Mega$Nets claimed that it wasn't a chain letter because people were paying for its software (which was actually just an electronic version of a chain letter). Mega$Nets was spread by people posting copies on personal websites where others could download it and join this "incredible money-making opportunity."

After receiving a copy of Mega$Nets in the mid-'90s, I spent an afternoon dissecting the program and discovered that it wouldn't run unless it included the VBRUN300.DLL file, which meant that the program had been written in Visual Basic 3.0. Next, I used a Visual Basic disassembler to convert the program from an executable file back to its original Visual Basic source code, so I could see how it stored names and addresses and generated its "secret codes." Then, I wrote another Visual Basic 3.0 program, dubbed Mega$Hack, that allowed users to edit any names and addresses stored in the Mega$Nets program and generate their own "secret codes" without paying a penny. By releasing the Mega$Hack program into the public domain and allowing skeptics to modify Mega$Nets for free, I hoped to foul up the Mega$Nets scam and highlight the foolishness of paying for a "secret code" to join a chain letter. This was my small contribution to battle against con artists, and to make the Internet a safer place for everyone.

Multilevel marketing (MLM) business opportunities are similar to chain letters. Valid MLM businesses offer two ways to make money: by selling a product or by recruiting new distributors. Most people who get rich within an MLM business do so by recruiting new distributors. Unfortunately, many scams masquerade as legitimate MLM businesses with the key difference that you can make money *only* by recruiting others; the only product being sold is a nebulous "business opportunity."

Pyramid schemes often make a few people very wealthy, but at the expense of nearly everyone else at the bottom of the pyramid. Nowadays, those running pyramid schemes can recruit new members through Usenet newsgroups or by spamming multiple email accounts (see Chapter 18). Once you realize that pyramid schemes need your money to make other people rich, you won't be taken in by the offers that come your way, no matter how tempting.

The Ponzi scheme

Among the oldest and most common investment scams is a variation on the pyramid scheme known as the *Ponzi scheme*, named after post–World War I financier Charles Ponzi, who used money from new investors to pay off early investors. Because the early investors received tremendous returns on their investments, they quickly spread the news that Charles Ponzi was an investment genius. New investors rushed forward with wads of cash, hoping to get rich too, at which point Charles Ponzi took the money and ran.

NOTE: *Social Security is basically a Ponzi scheme, because it pays current recipients out of current investors' funds. This requires more people to pay into the system all the time, which explains why it's perpetually in danger of going bankrupt.*

Con artists are now running Ponzi schemes over the Internet through email, faxes, or websites offering "Incredible investment opportunities!" In 2006, the US Securities and Exchange Commission (SEC) accused the owners of 12dailypro.com of running an Internet Ponzi scheme that bilked "investors" out of more than $50 million. These would-be investors were allegedly promised a 44 percent return on their investments in 12 days. After purchasing "units" at $6 apiece, investors would get paid to look at advertisements on the Internet. The money supposedly came from the advertisers, but the SEC claims the money really came from other so-called investors.

Any time anyone promises you unbelievably high returns in an extremely short period of time, chances are good they're offering you a Ponzi scheme, and if you take the bait, you can kiss your money good-bye.

The infallible forecaster

Any time you receive a letter or email from a stranger who says he wishes to help you for no apparent reason, watch out. Many con games start by offering a victim something for nothing, which plays to the victim's inevitable greed (proving the adage "You can't cheat an honest man").

In the "infallible forecaster" investment scam, a "broker" visits an investment chat room or forum and sends an email to everyone he finds there, offering an investment prediction at no charge whatsoever. The email says the purpose of the offer is simply to demonstrate the broker's skill at forecasting the market. The free forecast will tell you to watch a particular stock or commodity, and sure enough, the price will go up, just as he said it would.

Soon you'll get another message from the same broker, containing the prediction that a stock price or commodity is about to drop. Once again, he just wants to convince you of his infallible forecasting abilities—and once again, the price will do exactly what was predicted.

After that, you'll receive a message with a third prediction, but this time you'll have a chance to invest. Because the broker's previous two predictions seemed accurate, many people will jump at this shot at a sure thing. Then the broker takes his victims' money and disappears.

Here's what really happened. For the first mass-emailing campaign, the broker contacted 100 people. In half of those letters, he claimed a stock or commodity price would go up; in the other half, he claimed that the price would go down. No matter what the market does, 50 people will probably believe that the broker accurately predicted it.

With these 50 people, the broker repeats the process, telling 25 of these people that a price will go up and 25 of them that the price will go down. Once more, half of the scammer's potential victims will receive an accurate forecast.

So now the con artist has 25 people (out of the original 100) who've seen evidence that he can accurately predict the market. They send the broker their money—and never hear from him again.

The next time you visit an investment-related chat room, newsgroup, or website, remember that you will likely become a target for the con artists who specialize in these kinds of investment scams. So, be careful, keep your money to yourself, and warn others of investment scams. Be vigilant about applying common sense to every offer, and you should be all right.

THE LONELY HEARTS SCAM

The lonely hearts scam involves fleecing a rich victim with the promise of love and affection. In the old days, the con artist had to meet and talk with the potential victim in person, but nowadays, con artists can use the Internet to work their magic from afar.

The con artist contacts potential victims and claims to be a beautiful woman currently living in another country such as Russia or the Philippines. After sending a photograph (usually of someone else), the con artist steadily gains the trust and confidence of the victim through emails, faxes, or letters.

When the con artist believes he has gained the victim's trust, he makes a simple request for money to get a visa, so the foreign pen pal can travel to meet the victim—purportedly to live together happily ever after. If the victim sends money, complications inevitably arise requiring more money for bribes or additional fees, as in the Nigerian scam.

Sometimes the victim realizes he's been fleeced and stops sending money, but other times the victim honestly believes that the con artist is a beautiful woman trying to get out of her country. The longer the con artist can maintain this illusion, the more money he can fleece from the victim.

INTERNET-SPECIFIC CON GAMES

Many con games have been around for years, but others are brand new, created in the wake of the development of the Internet. The primary con game on the Internet involves stealing credit card numbers. Con artists have several ways of doing this: packet sniffing, web spoofing, phishing, using keystroke loggers, and using porn dialers. (Some of these methods have been covered in previous chapters.)

Packet sniffers

When you send anything over the Internet (such as your name, phone number, or credit card number), the information doesn't go directly from your computer to the website you're viewing. Instead, the Internet breaks this information into packets of information and routes it from one computer to another, like a bucket brigade, until it reaches the computer hosting the website you're sending the information to.

Packet sniffers work by intercepting these packets of information. Typically, a hacker will plant a packet sniffer on a computer hosting a shopping website. The majority of packets intercepted on that host computer will contain credit card numbers or other information a thief might find useful.

The packet sniffer copies the credit card number before sending it to its final destination. Consequently, you may not know your credit card number has been stolen until you find unusual charges on your bill.

To help protect yourself against packet sniffers, only type your credit card number into a website that uses encryption (a tiny lock icon appears on the screen, usually at the bottom right, when you're connected to an online shopping site that uses encryption).

Despite current public perception, the Internet isn't the easiest vehicle for stealing a credit card number. When you use your credit card in a restaurant, the waiter could copy down the number for his own personal use later. That's much easier than the time and trouble it takes to install a packet sniffer. A bigger threat to your credit card actually occurs when a company stores it on its (usually insecure) computer. Hackers can break into that computer and steal all the credit card information stored there, including yours, and there's nothing you can do about it.

In 2005, intruders broke into the network of CardSystems Solutions, a company that processed credit card orders for MasterCard, Visa, Discover, and American Express. The hackers copied the records of more than 200,000 credit card holders. That same year, scammers hoodwinked ChoicePoint, a company that provides consumer data to insurance companies and government agencies, and stole more than 110,000 records containing names, addresses, Social Security numbers, and credit reports. Even Stanford University fell victim to a hacker who broke into the school's computers and took more than 10,000 records containing names and Social Security numbers. No matter how safe your computer may be, your data stored elsewhere will always be at the mercy of others' computer security.

Web spoofing

Web spoofing is similar to packet sniffing, but involves setting up a website that masquerades as a legitimate site. To attract victims, con artists may rely on common misspellings of a URL address. For example, someone trying to visit Microsoft's website at www
.microsoft.com might type www.micrsoft.com by mistake and access what appears to be the legitimate site they wanted. But any credit card number sent to this site goes directly to the con artist.

To prevent yourself from falling victim to web spoofing, always verify the correct spelling of a URL address in your browser window. To play it safe, rather than type a URL address yourself, visit a search engine to find the website you want, such as Microsoft or eBay, and follow the link displayed in the search results. Bookmark commonly used pages so that they don't have to be typed often.

Phishing

Rather than wait for someone to mistype a URL address, however, most con artists actively phish for victims by sending out bogus emails claiming to be from a bank, eBay, PayPal, or other legitimate organization, as shown in Figure 13-2.

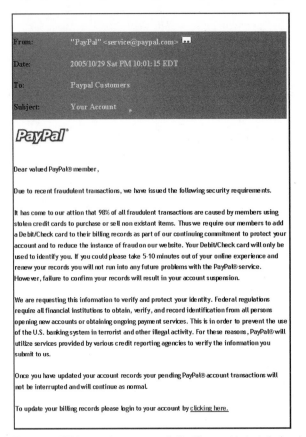

Figure 13-2: Phishers send out mass emails like this one, claiming to be from legitimate businesses and telling recipients to click a link and enter personal information.

The tone and content of phishing emails are always the same. First, they warn that users must update their account by typing in some valuable information, often a credit card number. To lend a sense of urgency, the email also threatens that the account could be suspended if action isn't taken. Finally, the email provides a convenient link that leads to a seemingly legitimate web page where the victim can type in his credit card number. Victims enter their credit card numbers and unknowingly give that information to a con artist.

To prevent yourself from falling victim to web spoofing, always verify the correct spelling of a URL address in your browser window. To play it safe, rather than type a URL address yourself, visit a search engine and find the website you want, such as Microsoft or eBay, and follow the link displayed in the search results.

Even then you can't always be sure that you're visiting a valid website. Many phishers now take advantage of the way browsers interpret international characters such as the ă or ğ characters in something known as the International Domain Name (IDN) vulnerability.

Phishers simply create a fake website that mimics a real one, such as PayPal's site. Then they give this fake website the domain name identical to the real one, except they substitute international characters, such as www.păypăl.com. When victims visit this site, the browser can't display the international characters, so the address appears with the international characters stripped away, as www.paypal.com. Ironically, the only browser immune to this type of spoofing is Internet Explorer, simply because Microsoft never bothered to update their browser to handle International Domain Names.

You can often recognize phishing emails by misspellings in the text, as seen in the words *attion* and *non existant* in the phishing email in Figure 13-2. Another way to recognize a spoofed website is by examining the link provided in the email. If you move your mouse pointer over the link, your browser will display the actual URL address to which the link points. As shown in Figure 13-3, spoofed websites typically embed the name of the company (such as PayPal) in the URL address along with words such as *signin* to create the illusion of legitimacy. However, the legitimate business's domain is not the actual domain of these phishing sites, such as http://paypal.signin0794.com.

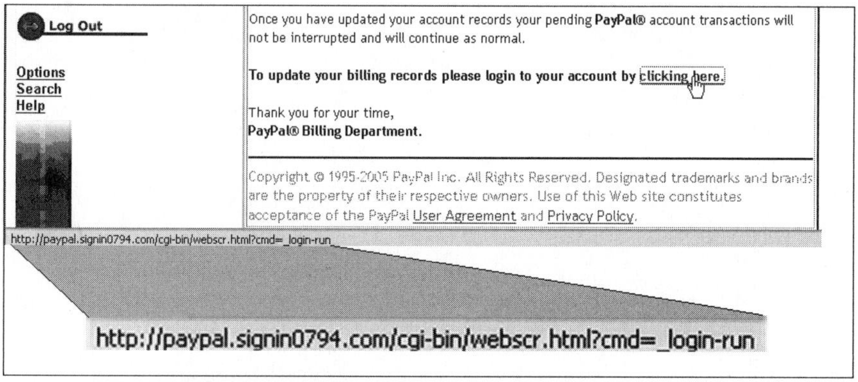

Figure 13-3: Your browser can display the actual URL address of a link for you to examine.

If a URL address contains a bunch of letters and numbers that don't seem to make any sense, chances are good it's taking you to a con artist's website.

Since most experienced computer users have received numerous phishing messages purporting to be from PayPal or eBay, it's getting harder and harder to scam people this way. So, phishers are getting more selective about whom they target, a tactic known as *spear phishing*.

Unlike ordinary phishers, who indiscriminately send out messages claiming to be from organizations such as PayPal or a national bank, spear phishers send their messages to a select group of individuals, typically those working for a large company such as General Motors or a government organization such as the Department of Agriculture. The messages appear to come from an existing group or department within that organization, asking for a user name or password to gain access to the corporate network. Because the bogus email appears to come from another company department, people are more likely to respond and get conned.

To learn more about phishing, visit the Anti-Phishing Working Group (www .antiphishing.org). To avoid falling victim to the latest phishing scam, grab a copy of PhishGuard (www.phishguard.com), which contains a database of bogus website addresses that phishers use to mimic other companies' websites, such as CitiBank or eBay. The moment PhishGuard detects that you're visiting a phishing site, it alerts you. PhishGuard stays up-to-date and effective by having users submit the latest sites to its database.

Keystroke loggers

A keystroke logger is special software or hardware that records a user's keystrokes, such as the characters a person uses to enter a password or credit card number. Software keystroke loggers run like other programs, except they hide in memory. Hardware keystroke loggers connect between the computer and the keyboard. Visit KeyGhost (www.keyghost .com) to view examples of different hardware-based keystroke loggers, including one disguised as a normal keyboard, as shown in Figure 13-4.

Figure 13-4: Your keyboard could be spying on you and recording all of your keystrokes.

If a hacker doesn't have physical access to your computer, he can still install a keystroke logger by using a remote-access Trojan horse or RAT (see Chapter 5). The con artist simply contacts potential victims through email or chat rooms and convinces them to download and run the Trojan horse, which opens a port and contacts the hacker. Then the hacker can read any files on the victim's computer or watch the keystrokes the victim types without his knowledge.

To protect yourself against keystroke loggers, buy a program such as SpyCop (www.spycop.com) or Who's Watching Me? (www.trapware.com). These programs will scan your computer for signs of keystroke loggers and root them out.

Porn dialers

Porn dialers won't steal your credit card number. Instead, they use another method to empty victims' bank accounts. Porn dialers get their name from the fact that they often claim to be free programs that grant access to pornographic websites.

Once you download this "free" program, it takes control of your telephone modem, turns off your computer's speakers, cuts off your local Internet connection, and then secretly dials a long-distance number to connect you to another Internet service provider (ISP), typically located in a faraway land, such as Africa or Eastern Europe.

As far as the victim can tell, the program does exactly what it claimed; it provides access to free pornography. What the victim doesn't know is that his Internet connection is now on a long-distance phone call to a place halfway across the world. The longer the victim views the pornographic files, the longer he stays connected to this foreign Internet service provider, which may ring up toll charges of several dollars a minute. The customers don't realize they've been scammed until they receive their phone bills. Because the calls were initiated from the victim's end, it's difficult to get the charges removed from the phone bill.

Although porn dialers won't work if the victim connects to the Internet using a cable or DSL modem, they can fool anyone still using a phone modem with a dial-up connection. If you have an external modem, watch the status lights to make sure your modem doesn't disconnect and then mysteriously reconnect all by itself. If you have an internal modem, your only defense generally is to be careful if a website lures you into downloading "free" software with pornography. (Besides, you should already be suspicious of anyone offering you something for free when you haven't even asked for it.) If the phone line is used only for the computer, you may be able to remove all long-distance and pay-per-call access by requesting this from the phone company. That option must be implemented before charges show up, however.

ONLINE AUCTION FRAUDS

One of the more recent crazes on the Internet is online auctions where people can offer junk, antiques, or collector's items for sale to anyone who wants to bid on them. Millions of people visit online auction websites (such as eBay), making them a tempting target for con artists. Sellers often have to deal with fraudulent bids from people who have no money or intention of buying. Buyers have to watch out for con artists selling fraudulent or nonexistent items.

The simplest con game is to offer an item for auction that doesn't even exist. For example, every Christmas there is a must-have toy that normally costs about $10 to purchase, but because of its scarcity in stores, it can cost up to several thousand dollars when purchased from a private seller. Many con artists will claim to offer such a product, and then disappear once they've got their victims' money.

Misrepresentation is another common online auction fraud. Con artists may sell counterfeit collector's items such as autographed baseballs or sports jerseys. To protect yourself against online auction fraud, follow these guidelines:

- Identify the seller and check the seller's rating. Online auction sites such as eBay allow buyers and sellers to leave comments about one another. By browsing through these comments, you can see if anyone else has had a bad experience with a particular seller.

- Check to see if your online auction site offers insurance. eBay will reimburse buyers up to $200, less a $25 deductible.

- Make sure you clearly understand what you're bidding on, its relative value, and all terms and conditions of the sale, such as the seller's return policies and who pays for shipping.

- Consider using an escrow service, which will hold your money until your merchandise arrives safely.

- Never buy items advertised through spam. Con artists use spam because they know that the more email offers they send out, the more likely they'll run across a gullible victim. If someone's selling a legitimate item, he's more likely to go through an online auction site.

The Scambusters website (www.scambusters.org/Scambusters31.html) offers additional sage advice:

- Don't conduct business with an anonymous user. Get the person's real name, business name (if applicable), address, and phone number. Verify this information before buying. Never send money to a post office box.

- Be more cautious if the seller uses a free email service, such as Hotmail or Yahoo!. Of course, many people who use these services are honest, but Hotmail and its ilk also make it very easy for the seller to keep his or her real identity and information hidden.

- Always use a credit card (not a debit card, cash, or money order) for online purchases. If there's any dispute, you can have the credit card company remove the charges or help you fight for your product.

- Save copies of any email correspondence and other documents involved in the transaction.

CREDIT CARD FRAUD

Credit card fraud is actually a bigger headache for merchants than it is for customers. If a thief steals someone's credit card and orders thousands of dollars worth of merchandise, the merchant pays for the loss, not the owner of the stolen credit card.

So if you're a merchant, be extra careful when accepting credit card orders. To help protect your business, follow these guidelines:

- Validate the full name, address, and phone number for every order. Be especially vigilant with orders that list different "bill to" and "ship to" addresses.

- Watch out for any orders that come from free email accounts (hotmail.com, juno.com, usa.net, etc.), which are easy to set up with phony identities. When accepting an order from a free email account, request additional information before processing the order, such as an alternate email address, the name and phone number of the bank that issued the credit card, the exact name on the credit card, and the exact billing address. Most credit card thieves will avoid such requests for additional information and look for a less vigilant merchant to con.

- Be especially careful of extremely large orders that request next-day delivery. Thieves usually want their merchandise as quickly as possible—before they're discovered—and don't mind adding a bit to the overall charge, which they aren't planning to pay anyway.

- Likewise, be careful when shipping products to an international address. Validate as much information as possible by email or, preferably, by phone.

For more information about protecting yourself from credit card fraud and other online thievery, visit the AntiFraud website at www.antifraud.com.

PROTECTING YOURSELF

To protect yourself from scams in general and online scams in particular, watch out for the following signs of a scam:

- Promises of money with little or no work.

- Requirements of a large payment in advance before you have a chance to examine a product or business.

- Guarantees that you can never lose your money.

- Assurances that "This is not a scam!" along with specific laws cited to prove the legality of an offer. When was the last time you walked into a supermarket or a restaurant and the business owner had to convince you that you weren't going to be cheated?

- Ads that have LOTS OF CAPITAL LETTERS and punctuation!!! or that shout "MIRACLE CURE!!!" or "Make BIG $$$$ MONEY FAST!!!!!" should be viewed with healthy skepticism.

- Hidden costs. Many scams offer free information, then quietly charge you an entrance or administrative fee.

- Any unsolicited investment ideas that appear in your email inbox.

To learn more about scams, visit your favorite search engine and look for the following strings: *scam*, *fraud*, *pyramid scheme*, *ponzi*, and *packet sniffer*.

For more information about protecting yourself, you can contact one of the following agencies.

Cagey Consumer

This website offers updated information about the latest promotions, offers, and con games (http://cageyconsumer.com).

Council of Better Business Bureaus

Check out a business to see if it has any past history of fraud, deception, or consumer complaints filed against it at the Better Business Bureau website (www.bbb.org). If you have been the victim of a scam, instructions for reporting it are available through this website.

Federal Bureau of Investigation (FBI)

The FBI runs its own Internet Crime Complaint Center (www.ic3.gov). By visiting the FBI's regular website, you can find the latest news about the most recently uncovered frauds (www.fbi.gov).

Federal Trade Commission (FTC)

Information about consumer protection rules and guidelines that all businesses must follow, along with news on the latest scams, are available from the Federal Trade Commission (www.ftc.gov).

Fraud Bureau

The Fraud Bureau is a free service established to alert online consumers and investors of prior complaints against online vendors, including sellers at online auctions. It also provides consumers, investors, and users with information and news on how to surf, shop, and invest safely on the Net (www.fraudbureau.com).

ScamBusters

ScamBusters provides information regarding all sorts of online threats ranging from live and hoax computer viruses to con games and credit card fraud. By visiting this website periodically, you can make sure you don't fall victim to the latest Internet scam (www.scambusters.org).

Scams on the Net

For multiple links to various scams circulating around the Internet, which you can search through to make sure any offers you receive aren't scams that have tricked others, visit this website (www.advocacy-net.com/scammks.htm).

ScamWatch

ScamWatch provides a forum where people can share and discuss the latest cons circulating around the Internet. By talking with others, you can learn how to avoid becoming the next victim (www.scamwatch.org).

Securities and Exchange Commission (SEC)

The SEC regulates securities markets and provides investing advice, information on publicly traded companies, warnings about investment scams, assistance to investors who believe they may have been conned, and links to other federal and state enforcement agencies. If you're one of those boomers flinging money into the stock market, check it out (www.sec.gov).

THE RECOVERY ROOM SCAM

"Been Ripped Off? We'll Get Your Money Back!"

After getting ripped off by con artists, many people want nothing more than to get their money back. That makes them easy prey for another kind of scam, known as a recovery room scam. Con artists get the names of people who have been conned and call or send them email, claiming to be federal attorneys or agents who can recover all or part of their lost money for a fee.

Victims are usually so eager to get their money back that they willingly pay this fee up front, not realizing that they've just been ripped off by another set of con artists (or possibly even the same one that ripped them off in the first place). Naturally, the victims never get their money back from either con. Recovery room scams can be particularly insidious because they can keep victimizing the same people over and over and over.

Just remember: You can't get something for nothing. If you want to get something for nothing, do the honest thing and become a dishonest politician. Then you can make laws for your financial benefit and claim that it's perfectly legal.

14

FINDING PEOPLE ON THE INTERNET

In real life, people have reasons to be polite. You can't shove other people out of the way to get to the front of a line or tell your boss what you really think of him because you'll have to face the consequences of your actions. On the Internet, nobody knows who you are or even where you are unless you tell them. (Or unless they track down your IP address and trace your name and street address through your ISP.)

You can discover what your enemy fears most by observing the means he uses to frighten you.

—ERIC HOFFER, writer

There's a sense of distance and anonymity that frees people to drop any social pretense and act upon whatever impulse seizes them. That's what makes the Internet so dangerous. Without the threat of exposure or fear of punishment, some people don't just cease being good, they become evil.

WHO ARE THE STALKERS?

Stalkers can be anyone—a next-door neighbor, a coworker, an ex-spouse or ex-boyfriend/girlfriend, a former or current employee, a relative, even a complete stranger. However, few stalkers have the motivation to pick a stranger at random just so they can attack and harass someone they don't even know. In the majority of cases, stalkers know their victims. Some keep up the harassment for days, weeks, months, and, sometimes, even years.

Although anyone can be a stalker (or a victim), men are typically the stalkers and women are typically the victims. Some different types of stalkers include the following:

Former intimate partners The most common stalkers are former spouses, girlfriends, or boyfriends who are hurt or angry that the relationship with the victim is over. They try to extend the relationship through harassment (following the victim, hanging around the victim's home or workplace, sending letters or emails, constantly calling, etc.). In most cases, the stalker simply wants to revive the relationship and actually believes that stalking can make that dream come true.

Vengeful stalkers   This type of stalker harasses through threats and even outright acts of violence, such as slashing tires or assaulting or killing his stalking target. Vengeful stalkers believe they are correcting some real, exaggerated, or even imaginary wrong and that the only way to rectify it is to continually harass and threaten or hurt the victim.

Delusional stalkers   These stalkers can range from dangerous to harmless, but since they base their stalking on some imagined love for or anger toward the victim, they can be unpredictable and frightening. They may alternate between being nice and exploding into a sudden fit of rage. Typically delusional stalkers target high-profile victims such as movie stars or other types of celebrities, although it's still possible for a delusional stalker to be a coworker or someone else who has a genuine connection to the victim.

NOTE: *Stalkers don't always fit neatly into one category or another. A stalker might start out as a former intimate lover, then get angrier and turn into a vengeful stalker.*

The stereotypical stalker tends to be a loner and social misfit with few friends, poor personal hygiene, and an uneven job history. He often lives alone and rarely cleans or takes care of his home, clothes, or even himself. In general, he cares so little about himself that, not surprisingly, he doesn't care about anyone else either. Rather than learn the proper way to behave around others, he chooses to stalk someone. It's not necessarily a conscious or welcome choice on nis part, but it's the only way he knows how to express his emotions, whether for good or bad.

STALKING ON THE INTERNET

Stalkers have been around since long before the Internet, but cyberspace has given stalkers a new sense of power and anonymity along with the reach to harass victims anywhere in the world. In the old days, stalkers had to rely on making obscene phone calls or leaving notes in places where a victim might find them. Today, stalkers can do this electronically by sending a barrage of email or instant messages. Typically, these messages are designed to taunt or threaten the victim and create the impression that the stalker is always nearby, even if physically in another state or country.

One stalker even taped a cell phone, with GPS (global position system) tracking turned on, to his ex-girlfriend's car. That way he could follow her movements at all times. If a stalker sends enough email or instant messages, he can flood the victim's computer with useless information and prevent her from receiving any legitimate communications. Some stalkers may try to infect a victim's computer with viruses, RATs (see Chapter 5), or spyware (see Chapter 20) to steal more information (such as credit card numbers or passwords), spy on that person's personal life and activities, or simply to foul up her computer.

Rather than contact a victim directly, a stalker may spread rumors or embarrassing information through newsgroups or chat rooms. He might impersonate the victim to send bogus email or chat room messages to other people. By insulting or angering others under the guise of the victim, stalkers can confuse a victim, who will not know why or how so many other people seem to be turning against her for no apparent reason.

Besides insulting or embarrassing a victim, stalkers may try to set up a victim for harassment from others. For example, stalkers might give a victim's email address to spammers, thereby encouraging spammers to flood the victim's email account. A stalker might also give a victim's name, address, phone number, and email address to peculiar characters such as religious cults, sadomasochists, pedophiles, or other unsavory characters, who will then contact the unwitting victim, sowing further confusion and nuisances in the victim's life.

By tricking others into harassing the victim too, stalkers hide their own complicity while still enjoying the satisfaction of making their victim's life as uncomfortable as possible.

Internet stalkers are protected by outdated laws that define "stalking" as physically threatening someone. Thus, Internet stalking falls outside the usual boundaries of the law. If someone were physically stalking a victim, she could at least call the local police. Over the Internet, however, the local police are generally helpless; the stalker may not even be in the same country as the victim and may be difficult to track down.

FINDING PERSONAL INFORMATION ON THE INTERNET

You can't become a victim if nobody can find you, so the first information every stalker needs is a way to find a chosen victim. On the Internet, that means getting the victim's email address, instant messaging ID, or even IP address. Armed with this, stalkers can usually retrieve other types of information such as telephone numbers, home and work addresses, and even Social Security numbers. Give a stalker just one bit of information and he can likely parlay it into an avalanche of personal data.

Searching personal websites

The easiest way to find information about someone is to search for his personal website. Not only will it probably offer an email address, but it will often include other information such as the person's hobbies, job history, membership in any organizations, and the proper spelling of his or her name. If the personal website has its own unique domain, such as www.JohnDoe.com, stalkers can do a WHOIS search to find the contact information registered for that site. Figure 14-1 shows a WHOIS search for Bill Gates, which reveals that he uses a separate company to protect his address from potential stalkers. And all this information was practically handed to the stalker by the victim himself.

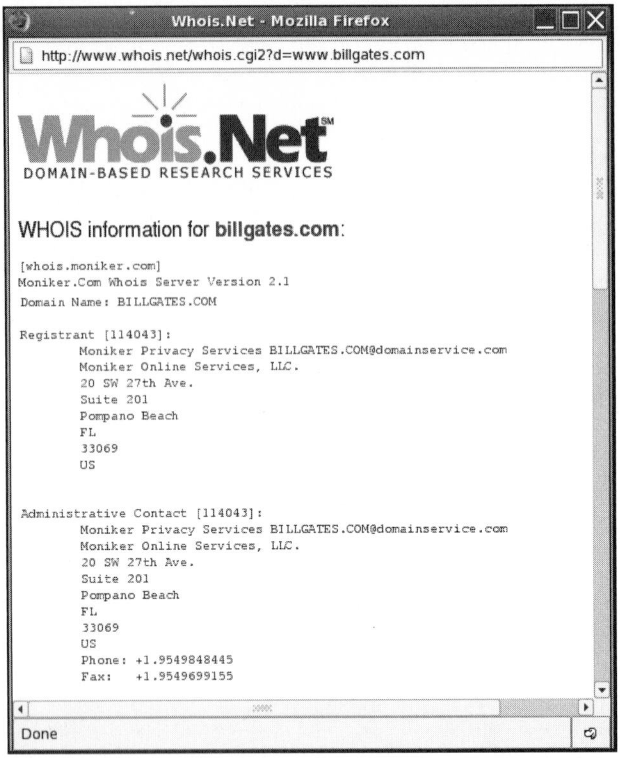

Figure 14-1: A WHOIS search on a descriptive domain name can identify the name, address, and phone number of the website's owner.

Finding names, addresses, and phone numbers

Not everyone has a personal website, but most everyone will have their private information scattered across the Internet in various forms. Anyone with telephone service will likely be listed in a phone book that can be searched online, such as AT&T's AnyWho (www.anywho.com) directory. Just type in someone's name and you'll be able to find his home address, telephone number, and even directions and a map to his house, as shown in Figure 14-2.

You could also use the people-finding sites listed below to track down someone's relatives, friends, or former neighbors. Although the person you're trying to find may be erasing his or her paper trail, chances are good that ex-colleagues or neighbors are not, and they might be able to tell you about a person or where she might have moved.

555-1212.com

Now a paid service, this website (www.555-1212.com) lets you search for companies and individuals in both the yellow and white pages to find addresses and telephone numbers. Using a reverse lookup, you enter a phone number, home address, or even an email address to find the name associated with it.

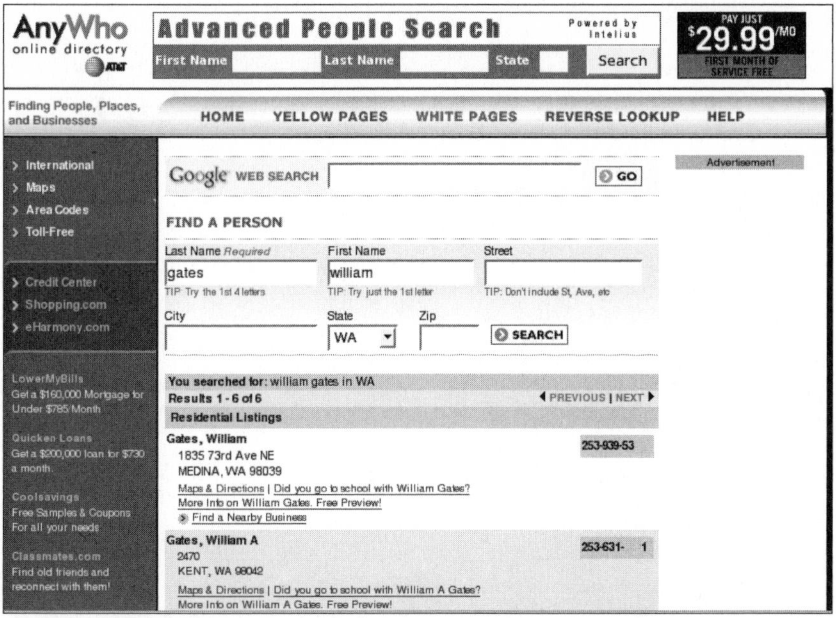

Figure 14-2: Public information about individuals can be used to find private information about them on the Internet.

Freeality

Look for individuals based on name, city, and state using a variety of the most popular people-finding search engines such as Switchboard, WorldPages, and Four11 at www.freeality.com/find.htm.

ICQ White Pages

ICQ is a popular instant-messaging service, and the ICQ White Pages helps people find their friends' ICQ number based on a name or email address (www.icq.com/whitepages).

Infobel.com

Infobel.com provides links to almost all the phone books in the world, including those covering the United States, Europe, Asia, Africa, the Middle East, and South America, just in case you need to find someone living in Uruguay (www.infobel.com/teldir).

InfoSpace

At InfoSpace, you can search for companies by name, category, or city. To search for individuals, you just need a last name and a state to find the matching home address, city, and telephone number (www.infospace.com).

Lycos People Search

Lycos allows you to search for people by name to find their email address, phone number, or any web pages that contain their name. It also offers a reverse lookup that can translate a phone number into an address (http://peoplesearch.lycos.com).

Switchboard

To search for businesses and individuals based on their name and/or place of residence, try www.switchboard.com.

USSearch.com

This fee-based search service offers a variety of results ranging from basic street address and phone numbers to property records, lists of friends and relatives, and marriage and divorce records (www.ussearch.com), as shown in Figure 14-3.

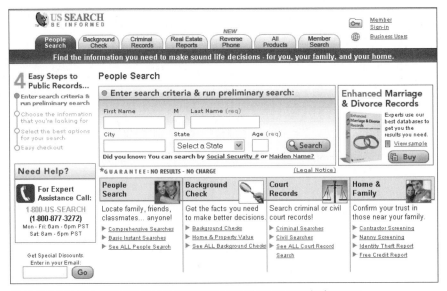

Figure 14-3: For a price, USSearch.com can unearth the court and property records of a person.

WhitePages.com

Searches for names, business listings, phone numbers, addresses, area codes, and zip codes, along with reverse lookups of both phone numbers and addresses, are available on the WhitePages website (www.whitepages.com).

Yahoo! People Search

Yahoo! People Search can provide address, phone number, and email information for individuals given a name, city, or state (http://people.yahoo.com).

ZabaSearch

Searches by phone number, Social Security number, and name are available (www.zabasearch.com).

Finding someone using a Social Security number

Because it is required by employers, the Internal Revenue Service, and banks, and is used by many other institutions such as colleges and health insurance companies, a Social Security number can be the quickest tracking device to pinpoint where someone in the United States currently lives and works.

Finding a Social Security number may be difficult, however, unless you once employed or were married to the person in question. For example, if you're trying to track down a former spouse, look for his Social Security number on an old joint tax return. You can order copies of your old returns from the IRS or your local State Tax Commission. Joint applications for credit cards, loans, and bank accounts almost always list both applicants' Social Security numbers, and you may ask the credit agency or bank for a copy of these old applications. Divorce papers may list this information, too. If you're trying to track down a former employee, you can get his or her Social Security number off employment applications or tax forms.

Once you have a person's Social Security number, you can pay a fee to websites such as Computrace (www.amerifind.com), Fast-Track (www.usatrace.com), USSearch (www.ussearch.com), or Find A Friend (http://findafriend.com) that will provide that person's last known address.

Finding people in the military

If you're looking for someone who is currently serving in the military, visit VetFriends (www.vetfriends.com). If you know which branch of the military and which unit someone served in, you can pay VetFriends a small fee to find out where he or she might currently be stationed. If you can't find the person you're trying to find, you may be able to contact others who served in that same unit, who might be able to give you additional clues to the person's whereabouts.

If you're searching for someone no longer on active duty (such as an old army buddy), try one of these websites: Department of Veterans Affairs (www.va.gov), GISearch (www.gisearch.com), or Ancestry (www.ancestry.com).

Searching public records

The public records database, offered for a fee by KnowX (www.knowx.com), provides a variety of ways to track someone down. If he or she ever ran a business, filed a DBA for a business name, earned a pilot's license, owned a boat, filed a lawsuit, bought real estate, filed for bankruptcy, or got married or divorced, the information would be stored in public records.

To check a person's driving record, credit history, voter registration information, criminal record, or birth and death certificates, visit the following website and have your credit card ready to pay a fee: National Credit Information Network (www.wdia.com).

If you're looking for someone who has committed a major crime, visit the Most Wanted Criminals website (www.mostwanted.org). Who knows? If you find a criminal before the police do, you could get yourself a reward.

Maybe you're not trying to track someone down, but you just met somebody new and want to investigate a bit before you risk dating or hiring him. To do a background check on someone, try Who Is He/She? (www.whoishe.com) or Instant Background Check (www.instant-background-check.com).

If you're adopted and would like to find your birth parents, or if you gave up your child for adoption and would like to see what became of him or her, visit one of the following websites, which seek to reunite birth parents and children: AdoptionRegistry.com (www.adoption.com), International Soundex Reunion Registry (www.plumsite.com/isrr), Reunion Registry.com (www.reunionregistry.com), or Seekers of the Lost (www.seeklost.com).

Finding email addresses

With so many people flocking to the Internet, the odds are getting better all the time that the person you want to find has an email address. To track down somebody's email address, you need his or her name and, if possible, location (city and state, or country). Start at one of the following websites.

EmailChange

If you know someone's old email address or name, EmailChange may be able to find a current email address. This generally works for the person's last known email address, so the more recent the email you know, the more likely it is to work (www.emailchange.com).

Meta Email Search Agent (MESA)

This meta search engine uses several search engines simultaneously to look for someone's email address by name (http://mesa.rrzn.uni-hannover.de).

NedSite

Search for someone's email address by name, phone or fax number, street address, college attended, ancestors, or military history at NedSite (www.nedsite.nl/search/people.htm#top).

Other options

If you don't know the person's location, or if the above search engines don't turn up anything, try Google Groups (http://groups.google.com). Maybe your target has contributed messages to a newsgroup recently. If so, searching Google Groups for his or her name will find the message and the elusive email address.

STALKING CELEBRITIES

If you're a celebrity, stalking is just the drawback of being famous. Celebrities worry about strange people approaching them at all times, and now it's even worse with the introduction of a website that lets anyone jot down sightings of famous people so others can keep track of their movements.

Known as Gawker Stalker (www.gawker.com/stalker), this site constantly lists sightings of celebrities from all over the world and even provides a map showing their last known location, as shown in Figure 14-4.

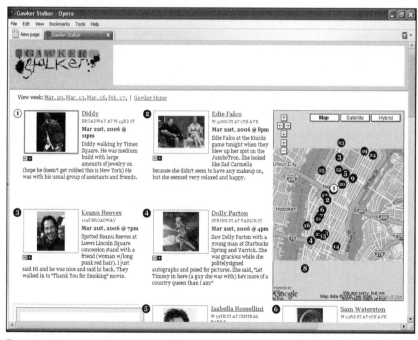

Figure 14-4: If you're a celebrity, someone will spot you in public and report your whereabouts on the Internet so others can track your movements.

PROTECTING YOURSELF

Now that you know how to track someone down, you also know how others can track you down, and you can take steps to protect your private information. If you don't want to find your name and home address splashed across the World Wide Web, try one or more of the following techniques:

- Get an unlisted phone number. This prevents most of the people-tracking websites from finding your name, address, and phone number (since it won't be in the telephone directory). Phone companies typically charge for this.

- Use a fake or misspelled name. The phone company doesn't care what name you use, just as long as you pay your phone bill on time. A fake name will throw off the majority of these people-tracking websites.

- If you are listed, avoid listing your street address. This way, even if someone finds your phone number in a directory, they won't be able to find out where you live. Plus, this service is generally free.

- Contact the people-finding website directly and request that your name be removed from its listings. Unfortunately, with so many people-finders popping up all the time, this might mean having to contact a dozen different websites—and then there's no guarantee that a new website won't turn up with your information anyway. Even worse, just because you request that your name be removed doesn't mean that the website will do so.

- If you include a signature file in every email you send out, make sure you don't give out any personal or important information in it, such as a home phone number or a website address (unless you've taken care to hide any personal information off of your website).

If you don't want to make your email address available to anyone searching for it, try one or both of the following techniques:

- Use an anonymous remailer before posting any messages to a Usenet newsgroup. This also helps keep your email address off lists used by spammers.

- Change email addresses frequently. If receiving email isn't that important to you, use multiple email accounts, and shut them down periodically.

If you really need to hide, avoid leaving a paper trail of any sort. Don't sign up for telephone service (or, if you must, use a fake name); avoid using credit cards; pay with cash for everything; and avoid magazine subscriptions that use your real name. Eliminating your paper trail can be a lot of work, but it might be worth it if you're hiding from someone dangerous (like the Internal Revenue Service).

Despite your best efforts, you may wind up becoming an online stalker's next victim. The moment someone starts sending you harassing emails or instant messages, send them exactly one message asking them to stop. In many cases, a firm and short message such as, "I'm sorry you feel that way, but I feel that you are crossing some boundaries for me and I would prefer it if we end our communication here," will be enough to stop most people. If the person continues harassing you, do not reply. Some stalkers simply enjoy provoking people; if you refuse to rise to the bait, they may get bored and look for more satisfying prey.

More frightening are the stalkers who target you specifically, either because they know you or because they hold a personal grudge against you because of something as simple as what you posted in a chat room. If you continue receiving harassing emails, examine the email header to find the harasser's ISP and then send an email informing the ISP of the harassment. Many times the ISP will send a warning to the harasser, and that will be enough.

If the harasser's ISP doesn't respond to you and the harassment continues, store copies of every form of harassment as evidence. If the stalker makes a direct threat to you or your family, such as naming what schools your children go to or what color car you drive, contact the police immediately and give them copies of all the evidence you have collected. Sometimes stalkers delight in terrifying victims from afar and have no intention of harming or getting anywhere near you, but it's better to play it safe and protect yourself.

Just as you would never wander around a dangerous neighborhood and not expect trouble, so you shouldn't roam the Internet without taking precautions. For more information about protecting yourself from cyberstalkers (and stalkers of any kind), visit the following sites:

Anti-Stalking website	www.antistalking.com
Bully Online	www.bullyonline.org
CyberAngels	www.cyberangels.org
LoveFraud.com	www.lovefraud.com
Stalking Resource Center	www.ncvc.org/src
Stalking Victim's Sanctuary	www.stalkingvictims.com
Working to Halt Online Abuse	www.haltabuse.org

Although you can't predict which acquaintance will grow into a full-on stalker, you can minimize your risk by being polite and civilized to everyone you meet. It also makes sense not to rush into intimate encounters with people you barely know; this can eliminate the largest threat of stalking. You can never stop someone from stalking you if they are determined to do so, but with a little foresight, you can often stop someone from wanting to stalk you in the first place or prevent them from being able to carry it to the next level by keeping your personal information private.

15

PROPAGANDA AS NEWS AND ENTERTAINMENT

In the winter 2004 issue of *2600*, a hacker wrote an article about how to break into the website of CBS and alter the voting process for a reality show called *Star Search*. Although the article was technically accurate and informative, it showed the true limitations of hacking and aptly demonstrated what author Thomas Pynchon once said: "If you can get people to ask the wrong questions, they'll never find the right answers."

> The public will believe anything, so long as it is not founded on truth.
>
> —EDITH SITWELL,
> British poet

After describing how easy it was for hackers to manipulate the online voting process, the hacker wondered, "Why is the CBS Star Search online voting security so lax?" Here are two possible answers:

1. Security is lax because CBS and *Star Search* don't know how to make it better because they don't even realize there's a problem.
2. Security is lax because online voting doesn't count in the first place.

Where the hacker made his mistake was in assuming the first answer to be correct—assuming that CBS had set up a valid online voting system for *Star Search* that conscientiously made an effort to accurately count votes from viewers to determine the ultimate winner of the competition.

But what if he had assumed that the second answer was the truthful one, that CBS didn't really care about the security of its online voting system because no one ever bothered to count viewers' votes anyway?

In the fine print of every reality TV show application, there's a disclaimer similar to the following, taken from an application for the CBS program *The Amazing Race*:

> *All decisions by the Producers concerning selection of participants and other matters is final and not subject to challenge or appeal.*

That sounds harmless enough, but it really means that the producers have the final and ultimate authority to decide which contestants get picked for the show and which ones get eliminated. So, regardless of whether the show has a panel of judges, telephone voting, or online voting open to the public, the producers still reserve the right to override any decisions made by anyone other than themselves.

Comedians Drew Carey and Brett Butler found this out when they served as talent judges for the now-canceled NBC reality show *Last Comic Standing*:

> *LOS ANGELES (March 8, 2004) - At least two big-name comedians, Drew Carey and Brett Butler, are fuming that the joke was on them when they served as talent judges for a new edition of the NBC reality show "The Last Comic Standing."*
>
> *The two sitcom veterans complained Monday that NBC executives and producers of the show overruled their votes for the 10 aspiring comics worthy of advancing to the televised competition set to air this summer.*
>
> *"I thought it was crooked and dishonest," Carey, star of the ABC sitcom "The Drew Carey Show," told entertainment trade paper The Hollywood Reporter.*
>
> *Separately, Butler, the former star of "Grace Under Fire," posted a message on her website saying the judges were "both surprised and disappointed at the results and . . . we had NOTHING to do with them."*
>
> *NBC said it was up to network brass and producers to decide who made the cut, weighing the opinions of the celebrity panel as just one factor. An NBC spokeswoman said a disclaimer to that effect airs as part of the show's credits.*

(Read the full Reuters article on MSNBC: http://msnbc.msn.com/id/4483013.)

Stacey Stillman, one of the contestants on CBS's *Survivor*, claimed that the reality show was rigged because Mark Burnett, the producer, coached contestants to vote her off and keep Rudy. (You can read her deposition online at http://news.findlaw.com/hdocs/docs/survivor/segstillmanbeendp525.pdf.)

Bob Jaffe, a producer for the reality show *Manhunt*, claims that executives from Paramount Network Television "felt that there wasn't enough conflict among the contestants," so they asked him "to fake entire segments of the game, create phony story lines and misstate the game rules." (Read the entire story here: www.thestingray.net/manhunt.probe.)

To learn more about claims that various reality TV shows are rigged, contestants are coached, and voting decisions are overridden, visit the Reality Blurred site at www.realityblurred.com. (In case you're wondering why more reality TV show contestants don't reveal how they were manipulated, they can't because of the contracts they signed. To appear on the TV show, contestants are barred from discussing the show without the television networks approval.)

In Hollywood, it's an open secret that reality TV shows are rigged for purely pragmatic business reasons. Throw a bunch of strangers together and what usually happens? If you've ever been to a party, you know that, almost always, the answer is "not much." But watch a reality TV show and what happens? Someone always turns out to be a villain and someone else always turns into an underdog. There's always conflict between contestants involving backstabbing, vicious gossip, and exciting dramatic events that capture our imagination and encourage us to watch the next episode.

Most reality show contestants aren't ordinary people but aspiring actors and actresses whose managers and agents got them on the TV show to gain national exposure and jump-start their careers. With actors pretending to be ordinary people and producers coaching them to behave a certain way, you're guaranteed to end up with a show full of conflict and drama. If hacking is the ultimate in manipulation and control, then reality television producers have hacked the viewing public, because nothing you see on reality TV shows is real.

If a network is going to invest millions of dollars in a reality TV show, they can't take the chance that something exciting won't happen. They have to take control and actively manipulate the results to make something exciting happen. Check out the job notices at EntertainmentCareers.net, and you can even find ads searching for reality TV show writers, such as this one:

> This is a FULL TIME JOB Location: Miami FL Date Posted: 2/14/2005 6:07:48 PM Description: New show is seeking a seasoned writer with a background in dramatic non-fiction writing. Will write the script and storyline for a new program.

> Requirements: Must be able to create dramatic stories with strong climaxes and resolutions. Experience in writing for a reality show is preferred.

Once the writers have mapped out storylines and character conflicts, the director takes over and films the contestants in such a way that viewers only see scenes that follow the writers' recommendations for creating phony plots around each contestant. What you see on TV isn't necessarily what happened. It's only one version of many possible alternatives that were filmed. The games and contests you see are just what the writers expected would generate the most conflict and drama to fit their preplanned storyline.

Some reality TV shows also invite the audience to vote for winners through a 1-900 number phone line or a website. Here's where you discover the real reason why *Star Search* and many other reality shows have such lax security for online voting: They don't care because the votes don't count.

The purpose of telephone and online voting isn't to choose a winner. The producers, with the aid of the director and a team of writers, made that decision months earlier when the reality show was filmed. Instead, the purpose of telephone and online voting is to give the audience an emotional stake in the show's outcome and encourage them to watch the next episode

If you dial the 1-900 number to vote, you're just paying money to the producer, not having an impact on the final outcome of the show. If you vote online, you can vote as many times as you want and even hack into the voting system, and nobody cares because nobody's counting the votes. Voting for a reality show contestant is like trying to vote today for the Nixon-Kennedy election of 1960. It's already happened, and nothing you can do will change the result. If you're looking to influence the results of a reality TV show through voting or hacking, you've already lost before the game's begun and you don't even know it.

Reality TV shows are a business, and business is about minimizing risks for maximum financial return. If computer hackers really want to affect the evolution of a reality show, the best way isn't to manipulate the votes; it's to stop everyone from voting in the first place and expose the deception of the reality show producers when they publicize the so-called results. If you can prevent 100 percent of online votes from even being cast, anything the producers say occurred can be revealed as the lie it really is. (But even then, the reality show producers are one step ahead of you. They grant themselves the right to ignore online voting due to "technical difficulties.")

The lesson to learn from reality TV shows is that hacking is more than mere technical skill; it's seeing beyond the obvious, questioning unspoken assumptions, and exposing lies. Hack away at all the reality TV voting sites as much as you like. It won't matter; the outcome has already been decided, and it's never going to be decided by you. (To learn how American presidential elections can be eerily similar to reality TV show voting, visit ElectionArchive.org at http://uscountvotes.org.)

Before you hack any system, make sure that someone hasn't secretly hacked you first. In the world of reality TV show programming, you've been hacked and deceived from the start, and I guarantee it. Oh, wait a minute. I don't have to guarantee that because reality TV show producers have done that for me already.

THE NEWS AS REALITY TV

There's nothing wrong with suspending belief when it comes to watching TV shows for entertainment. The problem comes when people mistake illusions for reality and accept deliberate deceptions as the truth. Whereas reality TV lies to viewers in the interest of greater entertainment value, news sources lie for a variety of reasons, none of which benefits their audience.

- On September 8, 2004, the CBS television news show *60 Minutes* failed to verify the authenticity of National Guard memos that appeared to prove that George Bush didn't serve his entire term in the National Guard.

- Between 1999 and 2003, *New York Times* reporter Jayson Blair faked facts, quotes, and entire interviews for as many as 36 stories.

- In 1994, ABC journalist Cokie Roberts wore a coat, stood in front of a fake backdrop, and claimed she was reporting live from Capitol Hill when she was really standing inside an ABC studio.

- In 2003, the White House released video showing President George Bush receiving a standing ovation from a cheering crowd after he signed a Medicare bill into law. White House officials later admitted that the people portraying the crowd and journalists were actually actors hired for the videotaping.

- On October 27, 2004, President Bush's reelection campaign released a television ad called "Whatever It Takes," which depicted a crowd of American soldiers listening while President Bush said, "I will never relent in defending America, whatever it takes." The images of American soldiers in the ad, however, were doctored so that identical soldiers turn up in multiple locations to make the favorable crowd seem larger, as shown in Figure 15-1.

- On October 13, 2005, President George Bush held a teleconference billed as "a conversation with U.S. troops." The White House later admitted that the soldiers had been coached to ask the President only those questions choreographed to match his goals for the war in Iraq and the upcoming vote on a new Iraqi constitution.

- In December 2005, the *Los Angeles Times* reported that the Pentagon had hired a Washington-based contractor, the Lincoln Group, to plant "positive news stories" in Iraqi newspapers without attributing the source as being the US military itself.

Figure 15-1: A television ad, purporting to show troops supporting George Bush, actually shows the same soldiers' faces copied and pasted in several places within the crowd.

With so many documented cases of deliberate lies and distortion of the facts by the news media, it's hard to know what to believe. The only sure fact is that the news has never been and never will be 100 percent trustworthy. (Read newspapers around the world, and you'll often get widely varying interpretations of identical "facts.") If you accept that, you're already way ahead of anyone who wants to believe otherwise.

CORPORATE INFLUENCE ON THE NEWS

Most news media outlets (newspapers, television and radio stations, and magazines) are owned by corporations that rely on advertisements to pay the bills. So what are the odds that a newspaper will run a story criticizing a major advertiser or run a story exposing malfeasance by the media's corporate owner? More important, what news outlet is going to risk raising the ire of its own government, jeopardizing its access to future press conferences that the competition will surely be allowed to attend?

NOTE: Ever wonder why news reporters never seem to ask tough questions of presidents? It's because reporters are screened for "trustworthiness" and their questions "approved" beforehand. To prevent further embarrassment, most government press conferences are taped to hide any problems that could occur during a live broadcast.

Project Censored: the news you never read about

If you want to know what bias, influence, or subtle censorship may be influencing your favorite news media, don't look at the stories they print or broadcast. Look at the stories they *won't* print or broadcast. Every year, Project Censored (www.projectcensored.org) offers its list of the top 10 stories that the news media conveniently ignored, which often turn out to be major environmental, political, or social disasters that make a prominent corporation or government look corrupt, exploitative, or criminally incompetent.

Some recent stories that Project Censored highlighted include the following:

– A report by the Institute for Policy Studies and United for a Fair Economy that discloses how CEOs in the defense industry have seen a 200 percent pay increase since September 11, 2001, compared to a 7 percent increase for CEOs in other industries.

– That the US military has been secretly dropping napalm in Iraq, despite a 1980 United Nations ban on the use of incendiary weapons. Of course, the US never signed the UN protocol and calls the weapon "firebombs" or MK-77s, which is just the military term for napalm according to the Federation of American Scientists (FAS) website (www.fas.org/man/dod-101/sys/dumb/mk77.htm), shown in Figure 15-2.

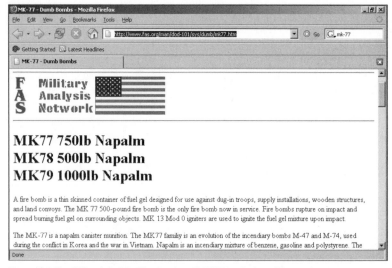

Figure 15-2: The FAS website identifies napalm with MK-77 and other military acronyms.

– News that the World Health Organization has approved genetic modification of the smallpox virus, while the Department of Homeland Security claims they are experimenting with the virus in order to develop smallpox vaccines in case of a terrorist attack. Scientists estimate that the accidental release of the smallpox virus could threaten millions of lives.

Drink milk—the chemicals are good for you

Rather than stir up trouble, many newspapers and television stations simply avoid any controversy related to their advertisers, readers, or corporate owners.

In 1997, according to SourceWatch.org, husband-and-wife journalists Steve Wilson and Jane Akre claimed that they were fired from FOX-owned WTVT Channel 13 in

Tampa, Florida, for refusing to broadcast a diluted version of their story, "Mystery in Your Milk," which warned about the Monsanto Corporation's synthetic bovine growth hormone (BGH), called rBST. Wilson described the story:

> We set out to tell Florida consumers the truth a giant chemical company and a powerful dairy lobby clearly doesn't want them to know. That used to be something investigative reporters won awards for. As we've learned the hard way, it's something you can be fired for these days whenever a news organization places more value on its bottom line than on delivering the news to its viewers honestly.

FOX forced Wilson and Akre to rewrite their story 83 times over the course of nearly a year, and not one of those 83 rewrites was to correct factual errors. Instead, they were intended to downplay the story's findings about the potential dangers of BGH contamination in the nation's milk supply. A Florida state court jury unanimously determined that FOX "acted intentionally and deliberately to falsify or distort the plaintiffs' news reporting," according to SourceWatch. To learn more about Monsanto and WTVT's efforts to hide the truth about BGH-contaminated milk, visit the BGH Bulletin site (www.foxbghsuit .com), shown in Figure 15-3.

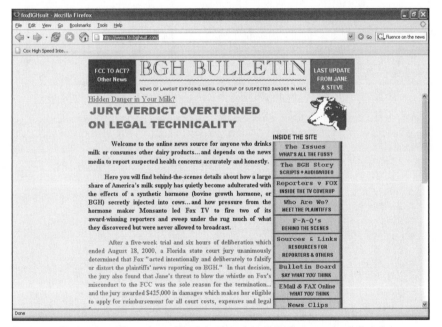

Figure 15-3: The American milk supply may already be contaminated with dangerous chemicals, and you can learn more about this problem from the BGH Bulletin—but not from watching the local Tampa news.

The objective news from ABC and Wal-Mart

The Fairness & Accuracy in Reporting site (www.fair.org) reported that Wal-Mart sponsors the "Person of the Week" segment on ABC's *World News Tonight* (which sports multiple ads for Wal-Mart, as shown in Figure 15-4) and the "Only in America" series on ABC's *Good Morning America*, and even sells a line of perfume that was featured on one of ABC's soap operas.

Figure 15-4: ABC's "Person of the Week" web page mentions Wal-Mart more often than it mentions ABC News.

Given this cozy relationship, how did ABC News report the largest class action suit in US history, in which more than 1 million workers accused Wal-Mart of sexual discrimination?

ABC News interviewed three people who criticized the case, including Lee Scott, Wal-Mart's CEO; Steve Bokat from the US Chamber of Commerce, who called the suit "fundamentally unfair"; and Tim Kane of the right-wing Heritage Foundation, who said, "It will make the management risk-averse, that adds cost to you and I."

ABC News reporter Geoff Morrell added, "Economists say that could have a chilling effect on big retailers, forcing them to raise prices and implement stricter policies for promotion."

Only plaintiff Chris Kwapnoski spoke out against Wal-Mart in the ABC segment. Even then, Morrell helped undercut her credibility by mentioning, "Ironically, Chris Kwapnoski was promoted three days after filing her suit." ABC News failed to question whether her promotion was part of Wal-Mart's strategy to buy her silence.

The mystery bulge on George Bush's back

During the 2004 presidential debates, photographs appeared showing a mysterious bulge underneath George Bush's jacket. White House officials immediately dismissed rumors that the bulge was a secret communications device that allowed Bush to receive answers from someone else. Other reports claimed that the bulge was nothing more than a strap for a bulletproof vest. The White House tailor even claimed that the bulge was nothing more than a wrinkle in the fabric.

One explanation for the bulge that nobody heard about from the mainstream media was from Dr. Robert Nelson, a senior research scientist for NASA and Caltech's Jet Propulsion Laboratory, who also happens to be an international authority on image analysis. His recent work has involved analyzing digital photos of Saturn's moon Titan to determine whether different shapes are craters or canyons.

"I am willing to stake my scientific reputation to the statement that Bush was wearing something under his jacket during the debate," Dr. Nelson stated in a Salon.com article (www.salon.com/news/feature/2004/10/29/bulge/index_np.html), shown in Figure 15-5. "This is not about a bad suit. And there's no way the bulge can be described as a wrinkled shirt."

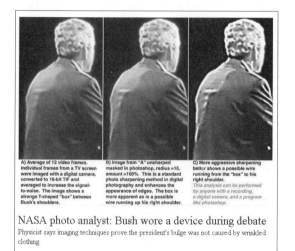

A) Average of 12 video frames. Individual frames from a TV screen were imaged with a digital camera, converted to 16-bit TIF and averaged to increase the signal-to-noise. The image shows a strange T-shaped "box" between Bush's shoulders.

B) Image from "A" unsharped masked in photoshop, radius =15, amount =100%. This is a standard photo sharpening method in digital photography and enhances the appearance of edges. The box is more apparent as is a possible wire running up his right shoulder.

C) More aggressive sharpening better shows a possible wire running from the "box" to his right shoulder.
This analysis can be performed by anyone with a recording, a digital camera, and a program like photoshop.

NASA photo analyst: Bush wore a device during debate
Physicist says imaging techniques prove the president's bulge was not caused by wrinkled clothing.

Figure 15-5: Could the mystery bulge under Bush's jacket be a hidden communication device?

Outside of Salon.com's readers, most people have never heard about Dr. Nelson's analysis. The *Pasadena Star-News* didn't print the story because senior editors killed it right before its publication. The *New York Times* almost ran the story, but also killed it at the last minute. Why would the news media kill such an interesting story based on credible analysis? Perhaps the real story isn't the bulge underneath George Bush's jacket, but who gave the orders and why for making sure the news media never reported it.

For more information about media bias and sources of alternate news, visit the websites for Chicago Media Watch (www.chicagomediawatch.org), Free Speech TV (www.freespeech.org), and WebActive (www.webactive.com).

THE NEWS ONLY REPORTS THE FACTS—AND ANYTHING ELSE ANYONE WILL TELL THEM

No matter how much you trust a particular news source, it can be wrong, whether knowingly or unwittingly. The news media gets its information from its own reporters, from wire services, and from anyone else who contacts them with an interesting story. Slip misleading information to the news media, and it's possible that the reporters won't bother to verify the facts and will simply present the information as news in the interest of higher ratings.

One self-proclaimed multimedia artist, Joey Skaggs (www.joeyskaggs.com) has turned misinformation into an art form, using the media itself as his canvas to demonstrate their frequent gullibility in broadcasting "news" without verifying the source's credibility. Joey Skaggs has appeared on *Good Morning America* and CNN, and in print in the *Philadelphia Inquirer* and the *Washington Post*, discussing such outrageous "news" as a vitamin pill made from cockroaches; a brothel for dogs; a new genetically engineered chemical, dubbed BioPEEP, that gets people addicted to eating certain foods; and a "celebrity sperm bank," where Bob Dylan and The Beatles had allegedly left deposits.

Joey Skaggs boasts that he leaves plenty of clues for news reporters to identify his pranks, yet they never find this information simply because they never bother verifying the "facts" he provides. One television station even won an Emmy for reporting on Joey Skaggs's brothel-for-dogs story ("A cat house for dogs featuring a savory selection of hot bitches"). Later, when Joey insisted that he had made up the whole thing, the news station reported his denial as further "evidence" that he was trying to avoid criminal responsibility for running his (fictional) dog brothel.

Next time you form an opinion based on something you've read, seen, or heard from your favorite trusted news source, remember that it could be the truth, it could be partial information lacking crucial facts, or it could just be another media hoax perpetrated by someone like Joey Skaggs. Whatever the case, read the news carefully and be aware that, no matter how strongly you hold an opinion, you could always be completely wrong.

THE NEWS AS HISTORY

There's no better way to learn about the past than by seeing what people were reading and watching back when historical events actually occurred. For a trip back in time, visit the Internet Archive (www.archive.org). You can get a feel for the mood surrounding a particular newsworthy event, such as the September 11 terrorist attack on the World Trade Center, by browsing through old web pages, as shown in Figure 15-6.

The Internet Archive also stores video clips of old television reports, along with a library of TV commercials and government films distributed since the 1940s. From these old government films, you can see how much (or how little) the American government has really changed.

Some classics include the infamous "Duck and Cover" film, which taught children to survive a nuclear attack by holding a jacket over their heads, and another short film explaining the hazards of biowarfare, which warns that Communist agents could attack the United States by pouring toxins into our water supply or by using crop dusters to spray an entire area with germs. Substitute the word *terrorist* for *Communist*, and you can see how relevant this particular film remains today.

FEAR, FUTURE, FUN, AND FAKES: *THE WEEKLY WORLD NEWS* AS A ROLE MODEL FOR THE NEWS MEDIA

They've skewered the news to avoid upsetting corporate sponsors, gotten fooled by media manipulators like Joey Skaggs, and buried anything that might embarrass the

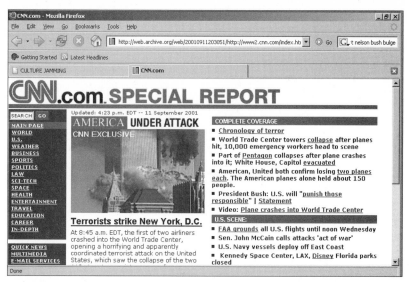

Figure 15-6: Viewing history through web pages from the past.

government, so what's left for the news media besides focusing on ratings? To understand how the news media works at a base level, check out the *Weekly World News* (www.weeklyworldnews.com), a sensationalist tabloid, as shown in Figure 15-7, which uses tactics similar to those of the more "respected" news media in order to attract an audience: Fear, Future, Fun, and Fakes.

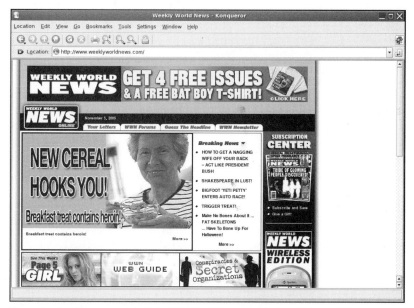

Figure 15-7: Despite appearances to the contrary, the *Weekly World News* is more similar to other newspapers than you might like to think.

Fear: attracting an audience

Whether it's the *Weekly World News* or the *New York Times*, the news media have to get people to pay attention to them, and the best way to do that is to appeal to people's fears. Fear headlines frighten but intrigue readers in much the same way that looking at a traffic accident can horrify but fascinate people at the same time. Consider these headlines from the *Weekly World News*:

"Aliens using e-mail to seduce Earth women!"

"Real reason for war in Iraq: Bush wanted to protect the Garden of Eden from Saddam"

"Dolphins are growing arms and legs" ("If they learn to walk and make weapons, they would become a formidable foe for all mankind!")

If you browse the headlines of "respected" media around the world on sites such as WorldPress.org (www.worldpress.org), World Headlines (www.worldheadlines.com), or Science Daily (www.sciencedaily.com), you can find similar fear-inducing stories, including:

"Cheney appeals for torture exemption" (*Seattle Times*)

"Bush said God told him to invade Iraq, Afghanistan" (BBC)

"Scientists show how thinking can harm brain cells" (University of Rochester Medical Center)

What makes the *Weekly World News* headlines funny is that we know they're fake. What makes the headlines from "respected" news media horrifying is that they're real (assuming you believe anything the news media report in the first place).

Future: distracting from the present

People can stand only so many threats of global warming, killer flu epidemics, or terrorist attacks, so the news media also serve up healthy doses of stories focused on an imaginary future. These headlines can take people's minds off the present, as shown in the following *Weekly World News* headlines:

"Bigfoot to join the cast of 'The Sopranos'"

"Bill Gates to buy Mars!"

"Moon will hit Earth in five years!"

The "respectable" news media also speculate about the future, but since the future changes so rapidly, predictions made today often get buried and forgotten behind newer predictions made tomorrow. The result is that the news media rarely have the time, space, or even desire to follow up on the accuracy of previous predictions, such as the following:

"Economic 'Armageddon' predicted" (*Boston Herald*)

"Experts warn of cyber terrorist attacks" (*Datamation* magazine)

"Many in India getting ready for the coming upheaval of 2012—will we survive?" (*India Daily*)

Did any of these headlines about the future come true? More importantly, did anyone even bother to check and run the follow-up story? As the *Weekly World News* knows, people will quickly forget past predictions as long as you keep bombarding them with new ones.

Fun: keeping people happy

After frightening readers and distracting them with meaningless predictions about the future, the media finally needs to give people something to feel good about. Such trivia, also called human interest stories, focuses on entertaining stories and topics that appeal to the emotions, such as the following *Weekly World News* headlines:

"How to tell if you've been abducted by aliens"

"Are demons talking to you? (Useful things you can learn from them!)"

"How to fool babes into thinking you're a doctor"

In the "respectable" news media, the fun trivia stories provide a respite from the constant barrage of negative news and keep the audience from fleeing. You probably won't learn much from such trivia news stories, but then again, that might be the point, as the following headlines demonstrate:

"Einstein Managed His Inbox Just Like You" (FOX News)

"Hunting Season Opens for Mythical Creature" (Associated Press)

"Think your house is haunted? Find out now" (CBS News)

While everyone agrees that the *Weekly World News* distorts the truth and fabricates lies just to sell papers, few people want to admit that traditional news media do the exact same thing. The *Weekly World News* is just more upfront about it.

Fakes: lies are more interesting than the truth

No one's really fooled by the poorly doctored "photographs" that appear regularly in the *Weekly World News* showing the president meeting with space aliens at the White House, a World War II B-17 bomber found on the moon, or a Titanic survivor peering through the closed porthole of the ship.

But plenty of people are fooled by photographs that have been subtly altered to distort reality and portray a vision that never existed in the first place, especially when those distorted images appear in "trusted" news outlets.

TV Guide *and Oprah Winfrey*

For its August 26, 1989, cover, *TV Guide* featured a picture of daytime talk-show host Oprah Winfrey. Unfortunately, it wasn't real. *TV Guide* later admitted that its editors had combined the head of Oprah with the body from a 1979 publicity shot of Ann-Margret.

Neither Oprah nor Ann-Margret had given *TV Guide* permission to use their pictures. The fraud was detected by Ann-Margret's fashion designer, who recognized the gauzy dress shown in Figure 15-8.

Newsweek *and Martha Stewart*

The March 7, 2005, issue of *Newsweek* had a picture of a laughing Martha Stewart for its cover story about the domestic diva's imminent release from prison. However, the picture was actually a picture of Martha Stewart's head pasted on the body of a model who had been photographed in a Los Angeles studio, as shown in Figure 15-9. *Newsweek* did mention (in fine print) that the image wasn't real.

Figure 15-8: This *TV Guide* cover depicts the head of Oprah atop the body of Ann-Margret.

Figure 15-9: *Newsweek* pasted the head of Martha Stewart on the body of a Los Angeles model.

O.J. Simpson *and* Time

On June 27, 1994, *Time* displayed an altered version of O.J. Simpson's police mug shot, darkened to make it look more sinister. This alteration might have gone unnoticed if *Newsweek* hadn't used the exact same mug shot on its cover too, as shown in Figure 15-10.

Diversity at the University of Wisconsin

In an attempt to show diversity in the student body of their school, editors at the University of Wisconsin's magazine *Wisconsin* digitally added a black man's face to a photograph of cheering students. The altered image appeared on the magazine's cover, as shown in Figure 15-11.

Figure 15-10: *Time* darkened an ordinary mug shot to create a fictional portrayal of O.J. Simpson.

Figure 15-11: To demonstrate racial diversity, the University of Wisconsin's magazine added a black man's face to this cover photograph, rather than actually finding a black man on campus.

Bobbi McCaughey, Newsweek, *and* Time

In 1997, Bobbi McCaughey gave birth to the first set of surviving septuplets. Unfortunately, Bobbi's looks were deemed not suitable for publication by *Newsweek*, so when the magazine put her on its cover, editors straightened and whitened her teeth. *Time* published a similar picture, but only whitened her teeth, as shown in Figure 15-12. Ironically, the only newspaper that showed Bobbi's teeth unaltered was the *National Enquirer*.

Figure 15-12: *Newsweek* digitally straightened Bobbi McCaughey's teeth and whitened them for presentation on its cover. *Time* whitened the teeth, but did not straighten them.

USING SATIRE TO REPORT ON REALITY

Humor is most effective when it reflects either the truth or what people believe to be the truth. As a result, humor can often expose events in ways that ordinary news stories cannot. Perhaps one of the best satirical newspapers around is *The Onion* (www.theonion .com), which prints articles with just enough facts to make its news stories credible and hilarious at the same time, as shown in Figure 15-13.

Other headlines from *The Onion* include "Iraqi Cop Moonlighting As Terrorist Just To Make Ends Meet," "Pope Condemns Three More Glands," and "Mom-And-Pop Loan Sharks Being Driven Out By Big Credit-Card Companies."

The Abrupt website (www.abrupt.org) also uses humor to satirize current events, which its writers refer to as "culture jamming." The idea is to twist corporate logos and marketing psychology to surprise and shock people into looking at the message from a fresh perspective, as shown in Figure 15-14.

BLOGS AS NEWS SOURCES

Rather than deal with the self-censorship and timidity of the established press, many people are reading eyewitness accounts posted online independently. These individual

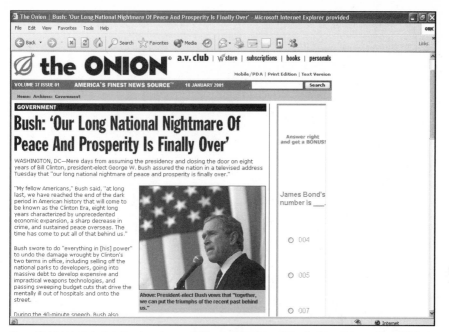

Figure 15-13: This *Onion* headline, from January 2001, was closer to predicting the future than anything published elsewhere.

diaries, known as *blogs*, as shown in Figure 15-15, provide raw, unedited stories from ordinary people who just happen to be caught in the crossfire of world events.

Blogs are uncensored and unedited so you get one person's thoughts, along with his or her misspellings and grammatical errors. By reading blogs from people on both sides of a conflict, you can get a more complete and possibly accurate idea of what's really happening in the world.

To give you an idea how truthful (and thus dangerous) blogs can be, bloggers have even been detained and arrested by governments all over the world, including Libya, Egypt, and China. To find a blog, visit Google Blog Search (http://blogsearch.google .com), Technorati (www.technorati.com), Daypop (www.daypop.com), or Bloogz (www .bloogz.com).

By definition, blogs are one-sided and opinionated, but if you read several blogs written by different people, you're sure to get a more balanced perspective. In many countries, blogs may be the only way to get news out to the rest of the world and represent one way to overcome a government's censorship.

Freedom of speech means nothing if nobody has anything to say, and freedom of the press is useless if the media gives you entertainment instead of information. Blogs combine freedom of speech with freedom of the press to form a new medium of communication, entertainment, and information. Considering how easily fooled the traditional news media are, blogs may be your best source for the unvarnished truth. Unless, of course, someone writes a blog specifically to distort the truth or lie about it.

In an effort to sway public opinion, Martha Stewart, HealthSouth's Richard Scrushy, and Enron's Kenneth Lay all started their own websites and blogs to present their side of

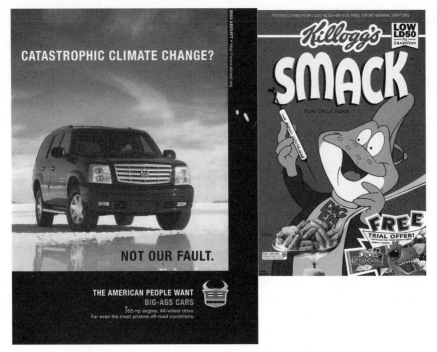

Figure 15-14: Culture jamming warps normal corporate images to subvert their intended messages.

the story before their much-publicized trials. Kenneth Lay's site even listed his community service awards, including his association with local churches, being named "Father of the Year" by a local community group, and his work as Houston's finance committee chairman for George Bush in 1988. By promoting such "wholesome" images of accused criminals, these websites and blogs hope to convince the public that they couldn't possibly be guilty. After all, would someone named Father of the Year really deceive a company like Enron for his own personal benefit?

While blogs often represent "grassroots" campaigns, corporations and public relations firms have noticed the influence such blogs can have and have started to fight back by using blogs of their own. Corporate use of blogs, to mimic grassroots campaigns, are often "astroturfing," to emphasize their fake grassroots origin.

In 2001, Microsoft was accused of astroturfing when newspapers received a flood of letters, protesting the Department of Justice's antitrust suit against Microsoft. When traced, the names and addresses of these letters eventually led to dead people and nonexistent towns.

In 2006, bloggers suddenly started attacking state legislation that would force Wal-Mart to spend more on employee health insurance. "All across the country, newspaper editorial boards—no great friends of business—are ripping the bills," pro–Wal-Mart bloggers claimed, and they used those exact same words because it was later revealed that they had been written and distributed to the bloggers by Wal-Mart's public relations company. While there's nothing wrong with bloggers reprinting someone else's words, there is something wrong when they don't reveal the source of those same words and pretend that they're original thoughts of their own.

Figure 15-15: Blogs can bring you news from the eyewitnesses themselves.

After exposing Wal-Mart's astroturfing of blogs, the *New York Times* later revealed the contents of an internal Wal-Mart memo that focused on these same health care issues. According to this memo (www.nytimes.com/packages/pdf/business/26walmart .pdf), Wal-Mart suggests that one way to discourage unhealthy job applicants is to make sure "all jobs to include some physical activity (e.g., all cashiers do some cart-gathering)."

The memo further states that "it will be far easier to attract and retain a healthier work force than it will be to change behavior in an existing one. These moves would also dissuade unhealthy people from coming to work at Wal-Mart."

Trying to sort out facts, lies, and altered perceptions on blogs will likely become a new Internet pastime. Many blogs are now as unreliable as the traditional news media when it comes to reporting the truth, and as the effectiveness of using blogs to propagate one's view becomes more widely known, they will increasingly tend toward the same weaknesses that keep the traditional media from reporting the truth. Reality is only what you choose to see, and alarmingly, what people choose to see is what someone else decides they should see.

16

HACKTIVISM: ONLINE ACTIVISM

Guess who has more political power in a democracy—an individual who can cast a single vote once every few years, or a major corporation that can shower politicians with campaign donations and other monetary favors any day of the week?

As much as the powers that be would like you to believe that your vote actually counts (when it's not being lost by a voting machine), the reality is that most individuals feel powerless and helpless in the face of lobbyist groups and corporate influence. That's why desperate people often resort to violence to force governments to deal with long-standing problems. For example, blacks protested against racial inequality during the April 1992 Los Angeles riots (sparked by the acquittal of four white police officers accused of beating Rodney King), and French immigrants rioted in October 2005 to protest high unemployment rates and police brutality in their community. Before riots brought attention to these issues, the problems were largely ignored by the governments that should have been actively looking for solutions.

Rather than waiting until situations reach such a boiling point, many individuals channel their energy into activist organizations. Before the Internet, activists had to rely on meetings, newsletters, and mass mailings to attract supporters and to keep their members organized and informed. However, the Internet has given them a medium for spreading their ideas and publicizing their goals to a worldwide audience.

To learn more about using the Internet to form or improve an activist group, read The Virtual Activist, a training course offered by NetAction (www.netaction.org). If you want to find a protest rally near you, visit Protest.Net (www.protest.net), which lists events around the world and offers an Activist Handbook to help people get involved, as shown in Figure 16-1.

Email, websites, and instant messaging let activists communicate faster and more conveniently, but the real promise (or threat) of the Internet is as a protest medium in and of itself. The Internet provides the opportunity for virtual sit-ins and blockades, email bombing, web page defacing, and the creation and spread of worms and viruses for a cause.

You need only reflect that one of the best ways to get yourself a reputation as a dangerous citizen these days is to go about repeating the very phrases which our founding fathers used in the struggle for independence.

—CHARLES AUSTIN BEARD, historian

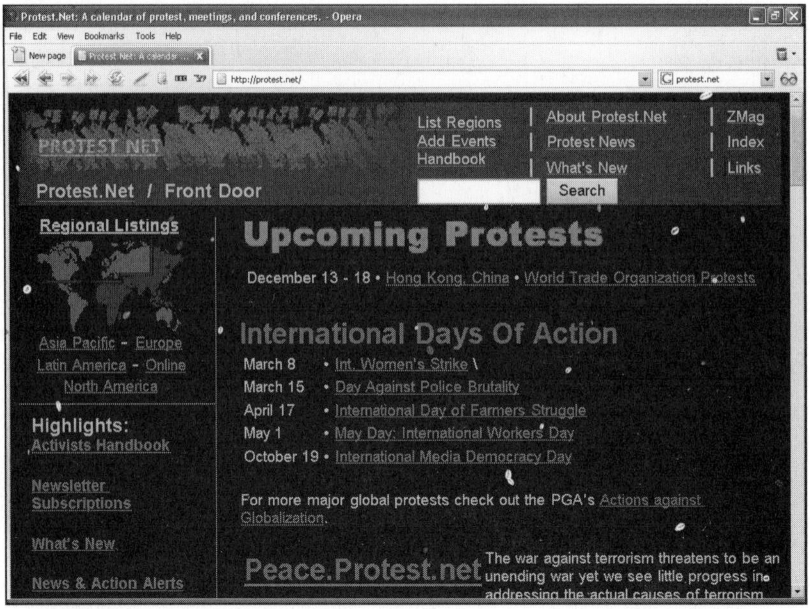

Figure 16-1: Protest.Net lists different events by geographic location, date, and topic so you can demonstrate around the world at your convenience.

VIRTUAL SIT-INS AND BLOCKADES

One common form of protest involves physically taking over or blocking access to an area or a building, such as the April 9, 1969, takeover of a Harvard University administration building by 300 students protesting the Vietnam War. Such sit-ins rarely cause any damage, but they help bring attention to the protesters' cause, especially if the protesters can occupy and shut down a high-profile target like Harvard. (Taking over and holding the men's room at a gas station in Barstow, California, wouldn't have quite the same dramatic effect, no matter how many people might be involved.)

Because physical takeovers can be difficult to organize, many activists engage in virtual sit-ins and blockades that anyone can join, no matter where they are. The goal of such virtual protests is the same as for their offline counterparts—to shut down access to a high-profile target and gain publicity.

The world's first Internet strike

On December 21, 1995, a group calling itself the Strano Network organized the world's first Internet strike with the following announcement:

> BOIKOTT THE FRENCH GOVERNMENT'S INSTITUTIONS!
>
> French Goverment has shown a total contempt for French people, for international community, for common people who just would like to grow up their sons in a better world as it:
>
> - goes on with nuclear experiments in Pacific Ocean's islands

- goes on with use of nuclear energy as mainly source of "civil" energy

- goes on with its projects of "social redrawing" without taking into account the enormous presence of people in recent demonstrations of protest against such kind of policy.

At a designated hour, the Strano Network asked that protesters visit a wide range of French government agencies' websites, including Le Ministere des Affaires Etrangeres (www.france.diplomatie.fr), Le Ministere de la Culture et de la Francophonie (http://web.culture.fr), and the OECD Nuclear Energy Agency (www.nea.fr). With such a massive flood of visitors, the Strano Network hoped to overwhelm the French government's web-servers and knock their sites offline, which, according to some reports, they succeeded in doing.

What was unique about the world's first virtual sit-in was that it not only attacked a target and prevented legitimate users from accessing it, but it did so using completely legal methods. Participants in a physical sit-in risk arrest for trespassing, among other things, but there's nothing illegal about individuals visiting a single website simultaneously. The result, however, is a denial of service attack for which one individual person cannot be held responsible.

Zapatistas on the Internet

Few people know where Chiapas is (it's on the southern tip of Mexico), and even fewer people know who the Zapatistas are (they're the indigenous people of Chiapas, named for Emiliano Zapata, an early–20th-century Mexican revolutionary leader who fought for land and freedom for his people). All that changed on January 1, 1994, when the Zapatista Army of National Liberation (EZLN) declared war against the Mexican state and demanded the liberation of the people of Chiapas and Mexico. As part of the Zapatistas' war declaration, they explained how the state of Chiapas was one of the poorest in Mexico, yet accounted for much of Mexico's oil wealth, along with exports of lumber, coffee, and beef.

The Zapatistas initially tried communicating their mission to the world through traditional news media, such as CNN and the Mexican state-controlled TV network, Televisa, but they found their letters, reports, and stories severely edited, which prevented others from understanding the true nature of their rebellion. Only the Mexican newspaper *La Jornada* published the Zapatistas' materials complete and unedited, but this newspaper rarely reached anyone outside of Mexico City. As far as the traditional news media were concerned, the Zapatistas didn't exist and most people reading the limited news coverage concluded that they were simply troublemakers who deserved to be put down.

Even when the Mexican government rushed in 15,000 troops to suppress the rebellion militarily, the media continued to downplay news about the Zapatistas, effectively muzzling their pleas for freedom and ignoring their reports of government suppression and exploitation. To circumvent the indifference of the traditional news media, Zapatista supporters started typing or scanning information from the group and distributing it over the Internet.

People translated the Spanish text into English and other languages, and soon the Zapatistas' plight began attracting attention from overseas newspapers and magazines that might never have bothered to cover the rebellion otherwise. When the Mexican

Army surrounded 12,000 guerillas, the Zapatistas reported through the Internet that they had escaped the encirclement and conquered several nearby villages, which caused confusion in world markets and brought about a sudden drop in the value of the Mexican peso. As more independent news media sources confirmed the Zapatistas' claims (to the embarrassment of the Mexican government), the Zapatista movement gained more credibility and garnered more interest. In this case, the Zapatistas didn't have to stage a virtual sit-in to publicize their plight; they simply used newsgroups, email, and websites to broadcast the Zapatista struggle to the rest of the world.

To learn more about the Zapatistas, visit the Zapatistas Network (www.zapatistas .org), shown in Figure 16-2, or Chiapas Watch (www.zmag.org/chiapas1).

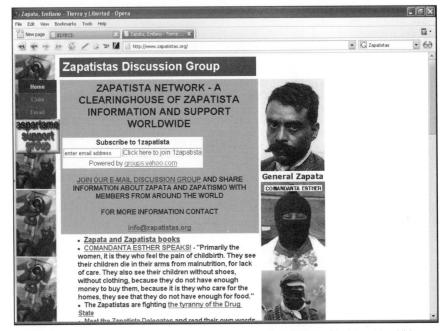

Figure 16-2: The Zapatistas were one of the first dissident groups to take advantage of the Internet to publicize their plight.

Disturbance on demand

A group calling itself the Electronic Disturbance Theater (www.thing.net/~rdom/ecd/ EDTECD.html) has taken the Zapatistas' cause to a new level by developing virtual activism software and organizing Internet strikes, as shown in Figure 16-3.

To organize its Internet strikes, the Electronic Disturbance Theater created a special Java applet dubbed FloodNet that participants could install to reload the target websites automatically every few seconds. According to the Electronic Disturbance Theater, more than 10,000 people from all over the world participated in the Internet strike on September 9, delivering 600,000 hits per minute to each targeted site using FloodNet.

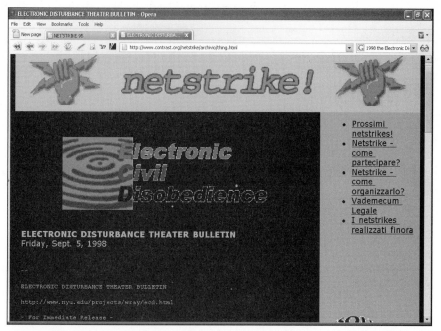

Figure 16-3: On September 5, 1998, the Electronic Disturbance Theater called for an Internet strike against the Pentagon, the Frankfurt Stock Exchange, and Mexican President Zedillo's website to support the Zapatistas.

When the Pentagon detected FloodNet's attacks, it redirected FloodNet users to another web page with a Java Applet program called HostileApplet, which would end-lessly reload a document in the participant's browser, effectively tying up his computer and preventing him from attacking the Pentagon's site.

President Zedillo's site didn't retaliate during the September 9 attack, but later, during a similar attack the following June, his site caused protesters' browsers to keep opening windows until their computers crashed. Despite these countermeasures, the Electronic Disturbance Theater declared their second Internet strike a success too, not-ing that "our interest is to help the people of Chiapas to keep receiving the international recognition that they need to keep them alive."

On January 3, 2000, Zapatista supporters wrote messages to the Mexican soldiers fighting to suppress the Zapatista rebellion, folded these messages into paper airplanes, and then launched the Zapatista "Air Force." To commemorate this event, the Electronic Disturbance Theater created the Zapatista Tribal Port Scan (ZTPS) program, which works in a similar way by scanning a random port on a target computer and sending it a text message as shown in Figure 16-4.

Besides the Zapatistas, the Electronic Disturbance Theater has supported a variety of other causes as well. To oppose US military strikes and economic sanctions against Iraq, the Electronic Disturbance Theater used its FloodNet program to attack the White House website, and in January 1999, it also helped organize animal-rights activists to protest different websites in Sweden. If you have a cause that needs worldwide publicity, consider contacting the Electronic Disturbance Theater for help.

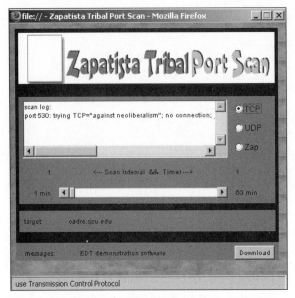

Figure 16-4: The Zapatista Tribal Port Scanner can bombard a target computer's ports with text messages.

EMAIL BOMBING

One way people can make their voices heard is by writing letters to politicians. Although one letter might not make much of a difference, hundreds or thousands of letters can cause even the most hardened politician to take notice.

NOTE: Since it's so easy for individuals or organizations to send multiple email messages, many politicians take email messages less seriously than physical letters. Handwritten letters, written in your own words, are often more effective in reaching politicians than mass-produced form letters.

In the realm of the Internet, sending email is simple and easy. Indeed, it's possible to send a barrage of messages, flooding a target's mailbox and preventing the recipient from reading or receiving legitimate messages. Known as email flooding or bombing, the end result is one form of a denial of service attack. Figure 16-5 shows a typical mass emailing program that can be used to send multiple messages to a single target (mail bombing) or a single message to multiple targets (spamming).

The first known use of email bombing for political means occurred in 1998 when the Tamil guerillas of Sri Lanka reportedly swamped Sri Lankan embassies with thousands of email messages that read: "We are the Internet Black Tigers and we're doing this to disrupt your communications." Perhaps because of the uniqueness of the attack, this one email bombing attack generated more publicity for the Tamil guerillas than the multitude of suicide bombings they had carried out in all the years before.

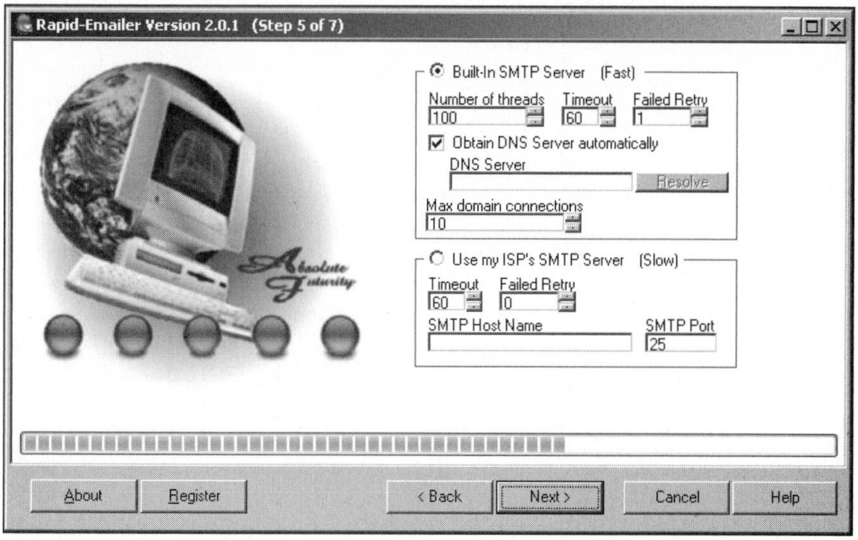

Figure 16-5: An email bomber can flood the Internet with custom messages directed to the target specified by the user.

In March 1998, a single hacker sent more than 2,000 messages a day to NATO's website to protest the organization's role in the Kosovo conflict (a friendly euphemism for war). When one California resident, Richard Clark, heard of this hacker attack against NATO, he reportedly co-opted the technique to retaliate, deluging the Yugoslavian government's website with more than 500,000 messages a day until its site went down. (Richard Clark's ISP, Pacific Bell, later canceled his service for violating its antispam policy.)

The Institute for Global Communications (IGC), a San Francisco–based Internet service provider, was hit by an email bombing attack in 1997 for hosting the website of the *Euskal Herria Journal*, an online publication supporting the Basque separatist movement in Spain and France. Protesters claimed that IGC supported terrorism because part of the *Euskal Herria Journal* site contained information from the terrorist group Euskadi Ta Askatasuna (ETA), which killed more than 800 people during its 30-year struggle for Basque independence.

In an effort to convince IGC to stop hosting the *Euskal Herria Journal* website, protesters bombarded the company with thousands of messages, which were routed through a multitude of different computers so ICG wouldn't be able to block mail from a single source. To add further pressure, protesters also email-bombed IGC employees as well as any other company with a website hosted by IGC, and clogged up the online ordering forms of commercial websites hosted by the target with bogus credit card orders.

IGC finally took down the *Euskal Herria Journal* site, but not before archiving its web pages. Within days, several other sites had posted copies of the *Euskal Herria Journal* site on three different continents. Although the protesters succeeded in censoring IGC, they failed in their ultimate objective to shut out the *Euskal Herria Journal* from the rest of the world. In fact, they gave the journal international publicity.

WEB HACKING AND COMPUTER BREAK-INS

Email bombing and virtual sit-ins can disrupt a target, but unless people know why you're doing what you're doing, it could come across as simply an act of electronic vandalism rather than a political protest. To deliver their message another way, hacktivists often deface the home pages of prominent websites such as NASA, the FBI, and even the White House. By defacing high-profile websites, hacktivists can ensure that a large group of people will read their message. Here are a few examples.

One of the earliest politically motivated web page defacements occurred in 1998, when Portuguese hackers broke into several Indonesian government websites to protest Indonesia's treatment of East Timor, a former Portuguese colony, as shown in Figure 16-6.

Figure 16-6: A defaced website, such as this hijacked version of the Indonesian Department of Foreign Affairs, can publicize a cause while embarrassing the hacked website at the same time.

In June 1998, a group of hackers calling themselves Milw0rm hacked into the website of India's Bhabha Atomic Research Center (BARC)—www.barc.ernet.in—and defaced it to show the distinctive mushroom cloud explosion of an atomic bomb along with the text, "If a nuclear war does start, you will be the first to scream. . . . "

In 1999, Pakistani and Indian military forces were engaged in combat along the Kargil region. Pakistani hackers targeted various Indian government websites including www.armyinkashmir.com, which provided factual information about Indian military forces in the Kashmir Valley. Pakistani hackers defaced the site and posted photographs showing Indian military forces allegedly killing Kashmiri militants with captions that read "Massacre," "Torture," and "The agony of crackdown." Pakistani hackers also targeted India's Department of Information Technology (www.mit.gov.in) site and replaced it with Flash movie images as shown in Figure 16-7.

Figure 16-7: Pakistani hackers have posted political messages on various Indian government websites.

Hackers on both sides of the 1998 Kosovo conflict targeted their opponents' websites. An American hacking group called Team Spl0it claims to have defaced web pages of the Yugoslavian government with messages saying, "Tell your governments to stop the war." The Serb Black Hand hackers group claims it retaliated by deleting all the data on a US Navy computer.

Perhaps more frightening is that hackers have targeted many sensitive US government websites and claim to have gotten in. In May 2001, the official White House site (www.whitehouse.gov) even shut down for three days due to a nonstop denial of service attack by unknown hackers. Another hacker group, Hong Kong Danger Duo, later claimed to have broken into the White House site and left the message, "Stop all war. Consintrate on your problems. Nothing was damaged, but we are not telling how we got in."

After NATO accidentally bombed the Chinese embassy in 1999, Chinese hackers entered the fray, targeting official US government websites. The Department of the Interior's website was defaced with pictures of the three Chinese journalists who had been killed in the bombing, while the Department of Energy's website contained a message that read:

> Protest U.S.A.'s Nazi action! Protest NATO's brutal action! We are Chinese hackers who take no cares about politics. But we can not stand by seeing our Chinese reporters been killed which you might have know. Whatever the purpose is, NATO led by U.S.A. must take absolute responsibility. You have owed Chinese people a bloody debt which you must pay for. We won't stop attacking until the war stops!

Of course, the Chinese government has come under its own share of hacker attacks by hacktivists protesting the country's lack of democracy and human rights. One hacker group, the Hong Kong Blondes, allegedly infiltrated police and security networks to monitor China's intelligence activities and warn political dissidents of imminent arrests. Two hackers, called Bronc Buster and Zyklon, claimed they disabled five Chinese firewalls, allowing Chinese citizens uncensored Internet access.

After Taiwan's President Lee Teng-hui declared on July 9, 1999, that China had to deal with Taiwan on a "state-to-state" basis, a cyberwar quickly erupted between each country's respective hackers. The Taiwanese hackers planted a red and blue Taiwanese national flag and an anti-Communist slogan: "Reconquer, Reconquer, Reconquer the Mainland," on Chinese Internet company websites. In turn, the Chinese hackers defaced the website of Taiwan's Democratic Progressive Party (www.dpp.org.tw) and displayed digitally altered images of the President and Vice President, as shown in Figure 16-8.

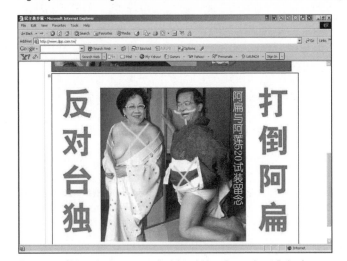

Figure 16-8: Chinese hackers reportedly defaced this web page in retaliation for Taiwan's demands for independence.

Back in the US, on January 18, 2005, a hacker group called "the Internet Liberation Front (ILF)" defaced six Republican Party websites and left the following message:

> *In solidarity with the billions around the world who are being oppressed under the Bush agenda, The Internet Liberation Front has hacked and defaced six Republican websites who push forward the sick and violent ideology of warfare, capitalism, and profit over people.*

Following the publication of a cartoon, in a Danish newspaper, depicting the prophet Mohammed carrying a bomb on his head, Muslims rioted around the world to protest. One hacktivist group, calling themselves the Red Devils Crew, took their protests to the Internet and on February 27, 2006, defaced the website of a company called Plasq.com, which sells a comic book–making program called Comic Life. In place of the original home page, the Red Devils Crew hacktivists posted the following message.

We were deeply shocked seeing a Danish newspaper (Jyllands Posten) offending almost 1.5 billion Muslims around the world by publishing a cartoon of the Prophet Mohammed seen as a terrorist carrying bombs on his head!

I just wonder, would your government reaction have been the same if the cartoon displayed Prophets Jesus or Moses!? I don't think so ...

Defacing web pages to promote a cause only works if people get a chance to see your message before the affected website administrator takes it down. The window of opportunity can be anywhere from a few hours to a few days.

Wherever there's war, conflict, disagreements, and power, you'll find web page defacements following closely behind physical force. Although it may be illegal, and breaking into a computer may be considered trespassing, it's certainly a less destructive alternative to shooting, bombing, and slaughtering. In that regard, hacking could actually be considered more ethical than any traditional show of military force.

COMPUTER VIRUSES AND WORMS

Another alternative for hacktivists has been to disseminate their messages via (sometimes benevolent) worms and viruses that can spread across the world and reach thousands of people for years to come.

One of the earliest hackivist viruses was the 1988 MS-DOS Fu Manchu virus, which buried itself in a computer's memory and waited for the user to type in the name of Ronald Reagan, Margaret Thatcher, or former South African President P.K. Botha. When one of these names was typed, the Fu Manchu virus would change it to an obscene word. Another early hacktivist worm appeared when anti-nuclear protesters tried to stop NASA from launching the Galileo probe toward Jupiter, because the probe's booster contained radioactive plutonium as fuel. On October 16, 1989, hackers infected NASA's network with the WANK worm, which NASA officials estimate cost a half a million dollars' worth of time and resources to clean up. When run, the WANK worm displayed the following message:

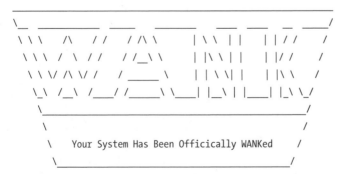

```
W O R M S     A G A I N S T     N U C L E A R     K I L L E R S
```

```
You talk of times of peace for all, and then prepare for war.
```

HACKTIVISM: ONLINE ACTIVISM

In a hacktivist action to protest French nuclear testing, someone wrote the 1996 Nuclear macro virus to infect Microsoft Word and insert the text, "STOP ALL FRENCH NUCLEAR TESTING IN THE PACIFIC!" at the end of every document.

Computer viruses can spread from one computer to another, but they rarely match the distribution speed of an email worm. Two hacktivist worms include the Mari@mm worm and the Injustice worm. These worms work like many others; each can send a copy of itself to every email address stored in a target's Microsoft Outlook address book. When the Mari@mm worm infects a computer, it puts a marijuana icon on the screen. If the user clicks on this marijuana icon, a dialog box appears, as shown in Figure 16-9, promoting the legalization of marijuana.

IMPORTANT: PLEASE READ

I think i speak for every pot smoker in North America when i say: "Legalize Marijuana"...I mean if people with AIDS, Cancer and other deaises can use it then why cant the rest of us (pot smokers) use it?, I dont think that's very fair (Do you?). If it's legal to grow and use in places like: Australia (for personal use) then why not in North America? If doctors are useing it as a treatment for illness then it must not be *THAT* harmful (So why can't other people use it?). I really do think the federal goverment should consider legalization of marijuana. Well that's really all i have to say on the matter, but i do hope somebody, somewhere listens to what i have to say and does not just regard this as just another *virus* because it's more then that, it's a message, a message for freedom, the freedom to smoke up and have the chose to do so *WITHOUT* fear of punishment from the law and the goverment. Thank you for your time.

[OK]

Figure 16-9: The Mari@mm worm promotes the legalization of marijuana.

The Injustice worm emails itself to the first 50 email addresses stored in a Microsoft Outlook address book and displays the following message:

PLEASE ACCEPT MY APOLOGIES FOR DISTURBING YOU.
Remember that one day YOU may be in this situation.
We need every possible help.
Israeli soldiers killed in cold blood 12 year old Palestinian child
Mohammad Al-Durra, as his father tried to protect him in vain with
his own body. As a result of the indiscriminate and excessive use of
machine gun fire by Israeli soldiers, journalists and bystanders
watched helplessly as the child was savagely murdered.
Palestinian Red Crescent Society medic Bassam Balbeisi
attempted to intervene and spare the child's life but live
ammunition to his chest by Israeli fire took his life in the process.
The child and the medic were grotesquely murdered in cold blood.
Mohammad's father, Jamal, was critically injured and permanently
paralyzed. Similarly, approximately 40 children were slain, without
the media taking notice or covering these tragedies.
THESE CRIMINAL ACTS CANNOT BE FORGIVEN OR FORGOTTEN!!!!
HELP US TO STOP THE BLOOD SHED!!

Some other examples of hacktivist viruses and worms include the 2002 Yaha-e worm, written by Indian hackers, which attempted a denial of service attack on a Pakistani government website (www.pak.gov.pk); and the 2001 Mawanella virus, which protests the burning down of two mosques and 100 Muslim-owned shops in Mawanella, Sri Lanka, as part of the ongoing conflict between Muslims and Buddhists there, as shown in Figure 16-10.

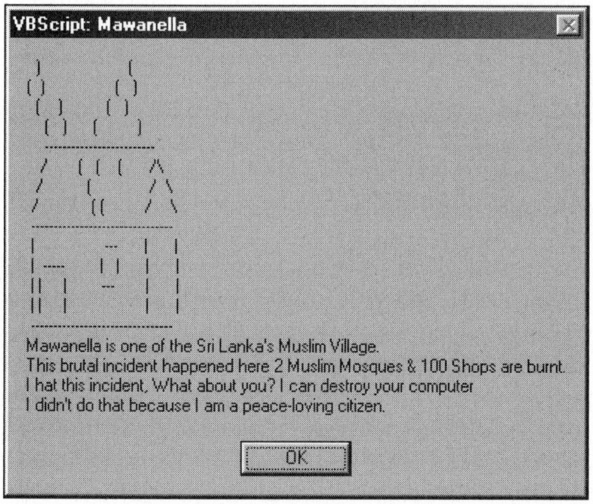

Figure 16-10: The Mawanella virus seeks to publicize the conflict in Sri Lanka.

Unlike regular viruses or worms, hacktivist creations rarely destroy data deliberately; their intent is to spread a message, not harm users. That wasn't the case in February 1999, however, when 14-year-old Israeli Nir Zigdon told the London *Sunday Telegraph* that he had single-handedly wiped out an Iraqi government website that, he said, "contained lies about the United States, Britain and Israel, and many horrible statements against Jews." Nir Zigdon said, "I figured that if Israel is afraid of assassinating Saddam Hussein, at least I can try to destroy his site."

Nir Zigdon reportedly sent an email attachment to the site and "claimed I was a Palestinian admirer of Saddam who had produced a virus capable of wiping out Israeli websites. That persuaded them to open the message and click the designated file. Within hours the site had been destroyed. Shortly afterwards I received an email from the site manager, Fayiz, that told me to 'go to hell'."

ACTIVIST VIDEO GAMES

Since web page defacements, viruses, and worms can be destructive or, at minimum, annoying, some activists have turned to making political statements by creating video games. Molleindustria (www.molleindustria.it) offers a game called Tamatipico, wherein players control a factory worker to make him more productive. Watch out though. Work him too hard and let his happiness level drop, and he'll actually become less productive (which is a lesson that too many managers seem to forget).

Newsgaming (www.newsgaming.com) offers two unique political video games called Madrid and September 12th. In Madrid, you must click candles held by people in a crowd to keep them lit, as shown in Figure 16-11. Click too slowly and the candles will burn out one by one.

Figure 16-11: The Madrid game asks you to keep hope alive by keeping everyone's candle lit for as long as possible.

The September 12th game depicts the hopeless struggle to kill terrorists without hurting innocent civilians. In this game, players aim missiles at known terrorists stalking the streets. If you accidentally kill an innocent bystander, you wind up creating more terrorists until, eventually, you end up with more terrorists than you started with, as shown in Figure 16-12.

Figure 16-12: The September 12th video game challenges you to kill terrorists without inadvertently killing civilians and creating more terrorists.

During the 2004 Presidential elections, the Republican Party even released a political video game called Tax Invaders. The goal of the game was to shoot at an ever-increasing barrage of John Kerry tax plans using the face of President Bush, as shown in Figure 16-13. Failure to win meant John Kerry had succeeded in raising your taxes.

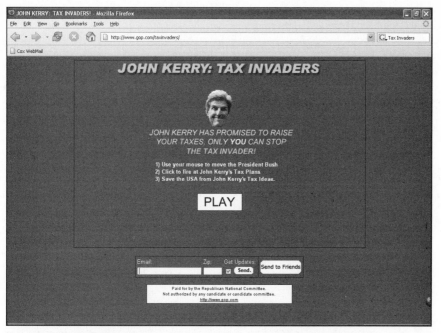

Figure 16-13: Play the Tax Invader game and help keep John Kerry from raising your income taxes.

Perhaps one of the oddest activist video games appeared November 22, 2004, when a Scottish company called Traffic Management released JFK: Reloaded. The idea behind this game was to prove that Lee Harvey Oswald could have been a lone gunman who killed John F. Kennedy with his sniper rifle. The player assumes the role of Oswald and gets a chance to re-create history by trying to assassinate the president. The closer your shots mimic what Oswald did, the higher your score. Initially, Traffic Management even offered a $100,000 reward to the first person that could re-create Oswald's shots most accurately.

By playing a video game like JFK: Reloaded, you can rewrite history and aim for Jackie Kennedy or even go for the driver, instead of JFK himself. If you kill the driver, the motorcade might stop and then you can pick off the stranded occupants one by one. Alternately, if you shoot the driver, the game might have the driver slump forward and crash the limousine into a lamppost.

Although the publisher claimed it had developed the game to debunk conspiracy theories about shots coming from other places, such as the grassy knoll, it caused a storm of controversy that eventually drove the company out of business. While derided as tasteless by many, JFK: Reloaded does raise an interesting question. If shooting an animated figure of a president is so despicable, why is it considered "entertainment" to shoot nameless animated figures in other video games?

GOOGLE BOMBING

As the most popular search engine (at the time of this writing), Google controls which websites people find when they hunt for specific words or phrases. Search for *Dell* and

Google responds with hundreds of results, although the top websites listed relate directly to Dell Computers. These results are determined by measuring the websites' perceived popularity, which is partly based on the number of sites that link back to them. Google bombing entails artificially inflating a website's Google ranking by fabricating links to that site and scattering them all over the Internet.

While it's nearly impossible for one individual to create enough links to affect a website's ranking, it's pretty easy once you have lots of other people posting links on their websites, in newsgroups, in chat rooms, on blogs, in email messages, and so on, until the Internet is inundated.

In 1999, people found that if they typed the phrase *more evil than Satan* into Google, Microsoft's home page came up in the top rankings. In 2005, Google bombing linked the words *miserable failure* to both George W. Bush's and Michael Moore's websites. Searching for the phrase *worst President* also returned George W. Bush's website, so Bush supporters Google-bombed the Internet in retaliation so that *great President* would also point to George W. Bush's website.

In another example, a search for *Jew* in Google ranks the top website as JewWatch, an anti-Semitic site run by white power nationalist Frank Weltner. (See Chapter 17 for more information about hate groups.) As a result, the editor of the blog Jew School (www.jewschool.com) is now soliciting websites to help him Google bomb the JewWatch site off its top ranking.

So the next time you search Google, check the list of results carefully. Some of the websites may be legitimate, but some may be benefactors of artificially inflated rankings. How can you tell the difference? You can't, which is why you may have to examine every website to figure out its real political agenda.

BECOMING A HACKTIVIST

If you want to use the Internet to promote your beliefs, you, too, can become a hacktivist. At the most basic level, you can petition your representative in Congress or debate current events at http://e-thepeople.com. In addition to email addresses for government representatives, this website lists various petitions you can support and even gives you a chance to create and post your own petition online.

Another site, Progressive Secretary (www.progressivesecretary.org), allows anyone to start or join a letter-writing campaign to petition various American government officials on topics ranging from the environment and arms proliferation to the death penalty and the Cuban embargo. By combining forces with thousands of other individuals, you can make your voice heard much faster than if you wrote a single letter on your own.

Of course, email is simply a faster version of the mass mailings and faxing that activists relied on before the growth of the Internet. However, cyberactivists have greater visibility due to websites that promote a particular group, its goals, and its philosophy to a worldwide audience. For greater influence, many activists have formed alliances with similar organizations. To learn more about networking with other activist groups over the Internet, visit the Coalition for Networked Information (www.cni.org), the Global Internet Liberty Campaign (www.gilc.org), the Digital Freedom Network (www.dfn.org), the Internet Free Expression Alliance (www.ifea.net), or, as shown in Figure 16-14, the People's Global Action (www.nadir.org/nadir/initiativ/agp).

Figure 16-14: The People's Global Action website lets you learn about the latest global issues in the language of your choice.

If you want to join a particular activist group, visit Action Without Borders (www .idealist.org), GuideStar (www.guidestar.org), or Activism.net (www.activism.net) for more information. Activism.net also provides more technical data about using a computer to promote your cause, including discussions about anonymous remailers and cryptography.

Of course, even activists need help once in a while, so Cause Communications (www.causecommunications.com) and Grassroots Enterprise (www.grassroots.com) provide consulting services to help activists achieve their goals. If you need facts to support your cause, try Political Research Associates (www.publiceye.org), which offers its research on various antidemocratic, authoritarian, and oppressive movements, institutions, and trends.

In case you have information that your government doesn't want anyone to see, you can contact Cryptome (http://cryptome.org), which will post any secretive or banned information on its website.

To help learn specific tactics involving hacktivism, you can even attend a training camp offered by the Ruckus Society (www.ruckus.org), which has previously trained protesters for disrupting the 1999 World Trade Organization (WTO) summit in Seattle. The Ruckus Society tends to attract all types of hacktivists, from those opposing Microsoft's monopoly on the operating system market to those fighting to allow free speech on the Internet by all citizens, regardless of nationality.

Other sources of information and inspiration about hacktivism include Anarchist Resistance (http://anarchistresistance.org), Counter Inaugural (http://counter-inaugural .org), CrimethInc.com (www.crimethinc.com), Infoshop.org (http://infoshop.org), the Independent Media Center (www.indymedia.org), The Hacktivist (www.thehacktivist .com), and Hack This Site (www.hackthissite.org).

Of course, activists aren't always right and their actions can be destructive regardless of the nobility of their intentions. Some activists have no qualms about breaking the law or aligning themselves with questionable organizations in order to further their agenda, which doesn't make them morally or ethically superior to the politicians, governments, or corporations they're attacking.

For another look at different activist groups, visit the ActivistCash.com site (www .activistcash.com), which provides "in-depth profiles of anti-consumer activist groups, along with information about the sources of their exorbitant funding." Among its findings, ActivistCash.com claims that environmental group Earth First! formed in 1979 when its founder, Dave Foreman, was approached by the Sierra Club and the Wilderness Society, who wanted to fund a new extremist group that would make them look moderate by comparison. Foreman reportedly accepted a 10-year deal to act as the unofficial radical wing of the environmental movement. In this role, he was free to pursue controversial activities that neither the Sierra Club nor the Wilderness Society could publicly support, such as the torching of a housing development in San Diego and the burning of Hummer and SUV dealerships in Los Angeles. In his book *Confessions of an Eco-Warrior*, Dave Foreman even bragged that that "ecotage [economic sabotage] in the National Forests alone in the United States is costing industry and government $20–25 million annually."

People for the Ethical Treatment of Animals (PETA) has also come under the scrutiny of ActivistCash.com, which claims PETA paid $27,000 for the legal defense of Roger Troen, who was arrested for taking part in an October 1986 burglary and arson at the University of Oregon. Elsewhere, $7,500 went to Fran Stephanie Trutt, who tried to murder the president of a medical laboratory, and $5,000 went to Josh Harper, who attacked Native Americans on a whale hunt by throwing smoke bombs, shooting flares, and spraying their faces with chemical fire extinguishers.

Even Mothers against Drunk Drivers (MADD) is not free from criticism by ActivistCash.com, which claims that the group has unnecessarily expanded its mission to prohibit alcohol use entirely. MADD founder Candy Lightner even broke ties with the group, saying, "I didn't start MADD to deal with alcohol. I started MADD to deal with the issue of drunk driving."

By examining ActivistCash.com's claims, you can see different sides of the issues and pick which side you want to support. Then again, you might want to research the people behind ActivistCash.com to see what agenda they might be hiding, too.

No matter what causes you decide to champion, you ultimately need to take action to back up your point of view. Defacing web pages or writing computer viruses and worms will publicize a problem but never solve it. Take action now. You may be surprised at how much power you, as an individual, can wield if you only give it a try.

17

HATE GROUPS AND TERRORISTS ON THE INTERNET

In the course of filming of the 1968 movie *Planet of the Apes*, actor Roddy McDowall (who played the character Cornelius) noticed something unusual. The actors in ape costume always sat together during lunch, while the actors dressed up as orangutans sat in another area. It might seem amusing that actors would only feel comfortable socializing with those in similar costumes, but it does highlight a general trait among humans. People naturally gravitate toward others who look like them and unconsciously avoid anyone who doesn't.

Historically, the human race has always divided itself based on various characteristics such as skin color, religious beliefs, ideology, or artificial national boundaries. Such distinctions wouldn't be problematic if so many people didn't use them as excuses to hate, discriminate, and kill.

It is inaccurate to say that I hate everything. I am strongly in favor of common sense, common honesty, and common decency. This makes me forever ineligible for public office.

—H.L. MENCKEN

HATE GROUPS ON THE INTERNET

In the old days, hate groups usually operated regionally, setting up secret meetings, passing out mimeographed pamphlets, and mailing photocopied newsletters. That all changed with the spread of the Internet. The mass communication medium of the Internet allows hate groups to use websites, email, and newsgroups to establish an international presence to recruit new members and share ideas with similar groups anywhere on the planet.

In a March 13, 1995, *New York Times* article, Don Black, an ex–Grand Dragon of the Ku Klux Klan and owner of the white supremacist homepage Stormfront (www.stormfront.org), was quoted as saying that the "Internet has had a pretty profound influence on the [white supremacist] movement whose resources are limited. The access is anonymous and there is unlimited ability to communicate with others of a like mind."

Of course, hate groups aren't limited to just white supremacists, skinheads, and neo-Nazis. There are also anti-Semitic Holocaust deniers, black radicals, Christian nationalists, anti-gay activists, anti-Christian groups, and anti-Arab groups. For virtually any group of people, you can be sure there's someone else with a reason to hate them.

To fight back against intolerance in any form, several organizations have dedicated themselves to tracking hate groups and monitoring their online activities. To learn more about hate groups and ways to combat their influence, you should visit the websites for Tolerance.org (www.tolerance.org), The Hate Directory (www.bcpl.net/~rfrankli/hatedir .htm), and the Southern Poverty Law Center (www.splcenter.org).

Tolerance.org even tracks hate groups by state, so you find the ones near you, as shown in Figure 17-1.

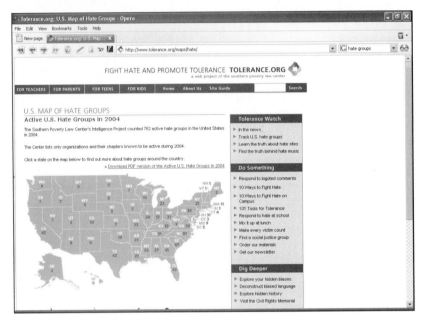

Figure 17-1: Tolerance.org tracks hate groups by state.

Perhaps the most well known white supremacy group is the Ku Klux Klan (www .kkk.com), whose homepage proudly boasts that it is "Bringing a Message of Hope and Deliverance to White Christian America! A Message of Love NOT Hate!" Unlike earlier incarnations of the Klan, today's organization has toned down the hateful rhetoric and emphasizes the positive aspects of white pride by claiming to be "America's Largest, Oldest, and Most Professional White Rights Organization—We Love You!"

Hate groups also create separate websites to attack their enemies, often without revealing their own involvement. One of the more devious tricks of white supremacy groups is to snatch up domain names that appear to belong to legitimate organizations. For example, MartinLutherKing.org and MLKing.org are owned by the two white supremacy groups Stormfront and National Alliance, respectively. Both domain names point to the same website, which derides Martin Luther King as "Just a sexual degenerate, an America-hating Communist, and a criminal betrayer of even the interests of his own people." Ironically, much of the negative information posted about Martin Luther King on these sites comes from declassified government documents from the 1960s, when the FBI organized a smear campaign against King. Although the FBI's propaganda has been largely discredited, it does show how the agency (with the support of the US government) discriminated against blacks at one time and, by today's standards, would be considered a white supremacy hate group too.

Some hate groups might filter the content on their own websites to appear moderate but provide links to other sites that espouse their point of view in more extreme terms. Using this method, the Jewish Defense League (JDL)—www.jdl.org.il—directs visitors to websites that attack Islam, such as the AnsweringIslam site (http://answering-islam.org.uk), which claims:

> The truth is that Islam is a man-made religion, full of hatred and venom and the followers of this horrible cult are being led away from God and salvation at an astonishing pace.

Another self-serving tactic that hate groups use to mislead visitors is to display a moderate homepage and bury their more radical rhetoric deeper within the site. An example of this is the Holocaust-denying Institute for Historical Review (www.ihr.org), whose homepage states:

> Founded in 1978, the Institute for Historical Review is a public interest educational, research and publishing center dedicated to promoting greater public awareness of history, and especially socially-politically relevant aspects of twentieth century history. The IHR particularly strives to increase understanding of the causes, nature and consequences of war and conflict.

Such sober-minded, scholarly language gives the organization credibility and makes it seem balanced, but when you get to the Leaflet section, you'll find yourself bombarded with anti-Jewish articles that dispel any illusion of scholarly research and debate. Some titles of such articles include "Iraq: A War for Israel," "Auschwitz: Myths and Facts," and "The Holocaust: Let's Hear Both Sides."

RACIST VIDEO GAMES

Besides creating websites that promote their agenda, hate groups are also spreading their rhetoric through racist video games. If you visit Resistance Records (www.resistance.com), you can buy a video game called Ethnic Cleansing, a first-person shooter game in which players wander through urban streets and subway tunnels in search of African American, Hispanic, and Jewish characters to gun down.

Neo-Nazi Gary Lauck, of Lincoln, Nebraska, known as the "Farmbelt Führer," also offers several racist video games on his website (www.auschwitz.biz), including one in which players manage a concentration camp. Another white supremacist, Tom Metzger, runs The Insurgent (www.resist.com), which offers online Flash games including Border Patrol (in which the object is to shoot people sneaking across the Mexican border), Drive By (in which players drive through a neighborhood and shoot at joggers, bicyclists, and hookers), and Kaboom! (in which players control a Palestinian suicide bomber and try to kill as many Jewish people as possible), as shown in Figure 17-2.

Figure 17-2: Racist video games let you try to kill people of different ethnic and religious backgrounds.

Racist video games provide yet another way for hate groups to influence people and spread their messages of intolerance. Racist groups gear these games primarily to young men and boys, the exact demographic group from which they need to recruit future members. Just like any good business, hate groups understand the effectiveness of targeted marketing.

So the next time your children are playing a video game, peek over their shoulders. They could be playing a commercially acceptable game like Grand Theft Auto, in which the goal is to steal cars, sell drugs, and escape from the police, or they could be playing a racist game like Border Patrol, in which they attempt to shoot people they don't like. In either case, you have to ask yourself, are these the values you want your children to grow up embracing?

TERRORISM: THE COMMUNIST THREAT OF THE TWENTY-FIRST CENTURY

Hate groups rarely do more than threaten, intimidate, and taunt their targets. In general, they avoid military-style confrontations.

Terrorists, on the other hand, want to kill anyone who doesn't share their way of thinking.

Although terrorism isn't new, the way terrorists communicate and coordinate their attacks has changed with the introduction of the Internet, which offers terrorists the same advantages it offers other users:

- Anonymity

- Instantaneous global communication

- Ease of use

The myth of cyberterrorism

One of the most pervasive threats to national security has been the fear of *cyberterrorism* or a "digital Pearl Harbor," where terrorists destroy a nation's infrastructure using nothing more than a computer, well-crafted viruses or Trojan horses, and hacking skills. Examples of what cyberterrorism could accomplish range from the frightening to the bizarre, as outlined in the 1997 paper "The Future of Cyberterrorism" (http://afgen.com/terrorism1.html) by Barry C. Collin of the Institute for Security and Intelligence.

One possible cyberterrorist scenario, envisioned by Collin, involves hacking into an air traffic control system and redirecting civilian aircraft to collide. A more unusual scenario warned that hackers could break into the processing control system of a cereal manufacturer and raise the level of iron supplement in cereal, causing children to overdose on iron, get sick, and possibly die.

Another scenario has cyberterrorists disrupting the computers that control international financial transactions, causing banks to fail and stock markets to crash (which means that corrupt politicians and CEOs of major corporations could be classified as cyberterrorists, if they only used a computer).

Although the idea of cyberterrorism sounds frightening, the reality is much less exciting. It's not that cyberterrorism isn't possible, but that it isn't probable. Just as it's possible for a rogue nation-state to launch an intercontinental ballistic missile at the United States, it's also possible that such large, coordinated attacks on computer systems could be carried out. However, just as an actual attack from a country like North Korea or Iran is much less likely than a terrorist attack involving conventional explosives, the threat of nightmare cyberterrorism scenarios is actually relatively small.

Cryptography expert Bruce Schneier has even written a book, *Beyond Fear* (www.schneier.com/book-beyondfear.html), that dispels much of the threat of cyberterrorism. Some of his amusing quotes include: "Did you ever wonder why tweezers were confiscated at security checkpoints, but matches and cigarette lighters—actual combustible materials—were not? . . . If the tweezers lobby had more power, I'm sure they would have been allowed on board as well," and "When the U.S. Government says that security against terrorism is worth curtailing individual civil liberties, it's because the cost of that decision is not borne by those making it."

Most terrorists have a vested interest in keeping the Internet running, because it's what they use to communicate with each other, too. Hacking into an air traffic control computer could cause a plane crash, but it's much simpler to shoot the plane down with a shoulder-launched anti-aircraft missile or sneak a bomb on board instead. Moreover, it's hard for the authorities to deny a terrorist attack when a bomb blows up. Terrorists want to frighten people with the certainty of an imminent attack and the fear of future attacks. Cyberterrorism is too difficult to conduct and less dramatic and certain in its results.

Terrorists on the Internet

Nobody doubts that terrorists would engage in cyberterrorism if they could and if it were as effective as blowing something up. Instead, they're more likely to use the Internet simply as a communication medium.

At the simplest level, terrorist groups can post information about themselves on websites to promote their cause, recruit new members, and provide the latest news about their enemies. As an example, the Hizbullah of Lebanon site (www.moqawama.net) is shown in Figure 17-3.

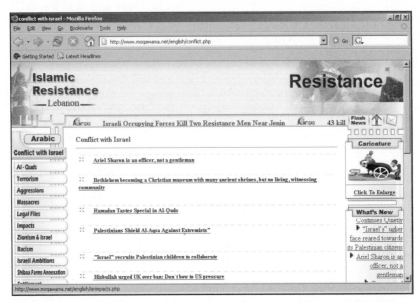

Figure 17-3: The Hizbullah of Lebanon website describes Israeli aggression and its own attacks against Israeli targets.

Some other terrorist groups that have established websites include Hamas (Islamic Resistance Movement)—www.palestine-info.info, Hizbullah (Party of God) of Iraq (www.nasrollah.org), Palestine Islamic Jihad (PIJ)—www.qudsway.com, and the Liberation Tigers of Tamil Eelam (www.eelam.com).

Like those of hate groups, terrorist websites often use moderate language to explain their mission and gain sympathy from the public, and cleverly omit references to such harsh facts as the group's tendency to kill innocent people in pursuit of its long-range goals.

To learn about terrorist groups around the world, visit TerroristFiles.org (www.terrorismfiles.org), Global Terror Alert (www.globalterroralert.com), or the Interdisciplinary Center Herzliya (www.ict.org.il).

Besides websites, terrorists use all the other ordinary tools of the Internet to communicate with one another, such as email, IRC chat rooms, and instant messaging. Some government officials believe that terrorists could even be using steganography, which involves hiding messages in pictures posted on websites that other terrorist members can download and read.

Although terrorists could use encryption and steganography to mask their messages, it's probably easier for them to communicate in plain language, using code words that nobody else will understand. Paradoxically, encryption can highlight the fact that a person is trying to hide something.

Ramzi bin al-Shibh, one of the planners of the 9-11 terrorist attacks, reportedly received a phone call from Mohamed Atta, the leader of the hijackers, who told him,

"Two sticks, a dash and a cake with a stick down," which meant that they were ready to execute their planned attack. Anyone intercepting this type of information would probably dismiss it as useless, making encryption completely unnecessary.

A message using plain English code words might be ignored, but an encrypted message raises questions—who sent it, who's receiving it, and what does it really mean? In some ways, using encryption can actually bring unwanted attention to terrorists.

From an economic point of view, large-scale terrorism is expensive to fund. It involves training people, buying equipment, and housing terrorist cells all over the world. Drug smuggling has long been a favorite source of funding, but now terrorists may be delving into Internet fraud as well.

Online scams (see Chapter 13) can be the perfect source for funds because they're easy to run, difficult to trace, and nearly impossible to prosecute across national boundaries, especially in developing countries where terrorists are most likely to congregate and where cyberlaws are weak or nonexistent.

Imam Samudra, the convicted mastermind behind the 2002 bombing in Bali, Indonesia, even wrote a chapter in his autobiography (written while on death row) titled, "Hacking, Why Not?" In this chapter, Samudra urges fellow Muslim radicals to fund their activities through online credit card fraud and money laundering. Evidence found on Samudra's laptop revealed that he even tried to finance the Bali bombing through phishing attacks to swipe credit card numbers from unsuspecting victims.

If terrorists start profiting from Internet scams, they could actually be the primary victims if a cyberterrorist attack succeeds in shutting down the Internet. Then maybe we'll see cyberterrorists terrorizing the old-fashioned, bomb-carrying terrorists.

THE FUTURE OF TERRORISM

To learn more about different terrorist groups, visit the Terrorism Research Center (www.terrorism.com), Special Operations (www.specialoperations.com/Terrorism), or Terrorism: Questions & Answers (http://cfrterrorism.org/home). From these sites you can learn about different terrorist groups around the world, how they organize, what their goals may be, and how they typically launch an attack.

Most interesting is that none of these terrorist information sites mention how terrorist groups often evolve from hate groups to terrorists to political parties to ruling governments, as witnessed by the Palestine Liberation Organization (PLO) and later, Hamas.

Perhaps the real threat of terrorism is that any terrorist group could get themselves elected as a "legitimate" government and further their objectives using military soldiers, instead of terrorists, to attack and kill innocent civilians. When this happens, anyone who supports the violence perpetrated by their government will be no better than the terrorists they so loudly condemn.

PART 5

THE FUTURE—
HACKING FOR PROFIT

18

IDENTITY THEFT AND SPAM

Not everyone who can manipulate a computer is a hacker, and not every hacker is a computer expert. Hacking is an attitude of exploration. However, real hackers can often use their computer skills and knowledge to take advantage of other people. When hackers want to use their computer skills to steal from other people, they usually engage in some form of identity theft. When hackers want to use their computer skills to bombard people with advertisements for legitimate (and not-so-legitimate) products, they use spam.

Whatever the motivation may be, the end result of identity theft and spam is the same: Someone is hacking your life without your consent.

The rise of computer crime and armed robbery has not eliminated the lure of caged cash.

—JAMES CHILES, technology writer

UNDERSTANDING IDENTITY THEFT

Computers aren't required to conduct identity theft, but they do make it easier and more convenient. In simple terms, identity theft involves masquerading as someone else so they get stuck paying your bills. This can be as easy as a waiter copying down your credit card number when you pay your dinner bill and then using it to order expensive merchandise by mail or over the Internet.

On a more extreme level, identity theft could occur when someone uses your name, Social Security number, current address, and date of birth to access your bank accounts, take out loans, and even to commit crimes that will be traced back to you.

How identity theft works

Relatively few people know you personally, so most people you do business with or otherwise meet in the course of your daily life rely on unique information to identify you, such as your full name, date of birth, Social Security number, mother's maiden name, zip code, and credit card number.

For all intents and purposes, however, anyone who possesses this information can trick others into thinking that he or she is you. The identity thief needn't have the skills to physically mimic your behavior, appearance, or manner of speaking to assume your identity.

Minimizing the threat of identity theft

Anyone can become a victim of identity theft. Just ask Oprah Winfrey, Steven Spielberg, and Tiger Woods. But when identity thieves target ordinary people, it's almost always because they have the opportunity, not because they took the time to target you specifically.

Identity thieves usually get your personal information one of three ways:

- Hacking into corporate computers that store your personal information, such as the databases kept by banks and credit card companies. Hackers can also target any large company that stores its employee records on a computer.
- Dumpster diving in your trash or the trash of a company where you work or do business.
- Phishing and other social engineering tricks to get your personal data.

If a hacker breaks into a bank's computer and steals your account numbers and Social Security number along with your mother's maiden name, there's not a thing you can do about it. Your personal information is only as secure as the computers it's stored on, so it's important to share such data only with trusted institutions. And then pray that they protect it as best they can.

Dumpster diving just means digging through someone's trash looking for something valuable. Identity thieves look for documents with personal information printed on them, such as unopened credit card offers that already have a name and address on them. The identity thief can then fill out the application and have a credit card sent to you. Next, unless you have a locking mailbox, he watches your mail until the new card arrives. At this point, the identity thief can start racking up charges on a credit card that you don't even know exists (but that has your name printed on it, as will the bills that start pouring in a month later). Military bases are popular places for identity thieves to work because these locations often give them access to mail for a large number of people, which they can then intercept even without being a postal employee.

Another objective of dumpster diving is finding useful items such as bank account numbers on deposit slips, credit card bills (with credit card numbers printed on them), or tax return information (which can include Social Security numbers).

To protect yourself against dumpster divers, shred anything that contains personal information, and destroy credit card applications to prevent someone from filling them out without your knowledge. For further protection, get a mailbox with a lock.

If you're truly paranoid, get a post office box and have all financial information, such as credit card and bank statements, sent there. Of course, you still have to trust the people sorting the mail at your post office.

Finally, identity thieves can get your personal information through phishing, either by sending you email or calling you on the phone and pretending to be a legitimate company. To reach as many potential victims as possible, identity thieves may send a bogus email to thousands of people at once (a more malicious form of spam) and wait for a certain percentage of the recipients to fall for the scam and enter their personal information on their website.

Another strategy of phishers is to call potential victims directly, typically targeting senior citizens. Phone call phishing takes more time and effort, but can still yield the desired personal information.

In rare cases, identity thieves may set up sidewalk polls and ask respondents to provide their name, address, and phone number in the process. Since people aren't giving away anything that can't be found in a telephone book, they often see nothing wrong with doing this. What they don't realize is that they've made the identity thief's job a lot easier. He can use this information to find that person's Social Security and credit card numbers later.

The key to minimizing your risk of becoming an identity theft victim is to give out your personal information only sparingly, shred any papers with information that someone could exploit or use to find additional information about you, and never respond to unsolicited phone calls or emails.

Also be careful when giving out information to "trusted" organizations like banks or businesses. While they may request sensitive information like Social Security numbers for "marketing" purposes, you can always refuse to give them this information if it isn't legally required. By restricting who has access to your personal data, you limit the chances that someone can steal your personal information from someone else.

Protecting your credit rating

Despite taking every precaution, you could still fall victim to an identity thief. To help you monitor and protect your credit rating, start by getting a free copy of your credit report, which you can request once every 12 months in one of the following ways:

- Visit www.annualcreditreport.com.

- Call 877.322.8228 (toll free).

- Fill out an Annual Credit Report Request Form and mail it to Annual Credit Report Request Service, P.O. Box 105281, Atlanta, GA 30348-5281. You can print this form from the www.ftc.gov/credit website.

Under federal law, you can also receive a free copy of your credit report if a company takes adverse action against you, such as denying your application for credit, insurance, or employment. If this happens, you can request a free copy of your credit report within 60 days of receiving notice of the action. Reviewing your credit report can help you determine whether an identity thief has ruined your credit rating.

If you want to buy a copy of your credit report, contact one of the following:

Equifax	800.685.1111; www.equifax.com
Experian	888.EXPERIAN (888.397.3742); www.experian.com
TransUnion	800.916.8800; www.transunion.com

To avoid receiving credit card offers in the mail (and having to shred them to protect yourself), you can have credit card companies stop sending you their applications in the first place. To opt out of credit card offers by mail, call 1.888.5.OPTOUT (1.888.567.8688). Finally, create a document with all the bank and credit card phone numbers to call in case you need to close an account in a hurry.

Protecting your identity is much easier than trying to clean up your life after an identity thief has struck, so it makes sense to take the time to prepare now. For more information about identity theft, visit the following websites:

Identity Theft Resource Center	www.idtheftcenter.org
Federal Trade Commission	www.consumer.gov/idtheft
Privacy Rights Clearinghouse	www.privacyrights.org/identity.htm
Identity Theft Prevention and Survival	www.identitytheft.org
Fight Identity Theft	www.fightidentitytheft.com

SPAM: JUNK MAIL ON THE INTERNET

Even if you use the Internet infrequently, you've probably been spammed by a long list of junk email from companies advertising products from the totally useless (bogus vitamins) to the illegal (child pornography), offering "free" vacation giveaways, or promoting money-making schemes. Unlike newspaper or magazine advertisements that you can ignore without losing a moment's thought, spam just doesn't seem to leave you alone.

Spamming means sending unsolicited messages to multiple email accounts or Usenet newsgroups. Victims of spamming must then take time to delete the unwanted messages so they can make room in their inboxes for useful email. Spam can include anything from legitimate advertisements to scams and bogus messages from identity thieves trying to phish for personal information. One of the more common types of spam involves chain letters or other suspicious "business opportunities" like this one:

$$$$$$$$ FAST CASH!!!! $$$$$$$$

Hello there, Read this it works! Fellow Debtor: This is going to sound like a con, but in fact IT WORKS! The person who is now #4 on the list was #5 when I got it, which was only a few days ago. Five dollars is a small investment in your future. Forget the lottery for a week, and give this a try. It can work for ALL of us. You can edit this list with a word processor or text editor and then convert it to a text file. Good Luck!!

Dear Friend,

My name is Dave Rhodes. In September 1988 my car was repossessed and the bill collectors were hounding me like you wouldn't believe. I was laid off and my unemployment checks had run out. The only escape I had from the pressure of failure was my computer and my modem. I longed to turn my avocation into my vocation.

This January 1989 my family and I went on a ten day cruise to the tropics. I bought a Lincoln Town Car for CASH in February 1989. I am currently building a home on the West Coast of Florida, with a private pool, boat slip, and a beautiful view of the bay from my breakfast room table and patio.

I will never have to work again. Today I am rich! I have earned over $400,000.00 (Four Hundred Thousand Dollars) to date and will become a millionaire within 4 or 5 months. Anyone can do the same. This money making program works perfectly every time, 100 percent of the time. I have NEVER failed to earn $50,000.00 or more whenever I wanted. Best of all you never have to leave home except to go to your mailbox or post office.

I realized that with the power of the computer I could expand and enhance this money making formula into the most unbelievable cash flow generator that has ever been created. I substituted the computer bulletin boards in place of the post office and electronically did by computer what others were doing 100 percent by mail. Now only a few letters are mailed manually. Most of the hard work is speedily downloaded to other bulletin boards throughout the world.

If you believe that someday you deserve that lucky break that you have waited for all your life, simply follow the easy instructions below. Your dreams will come true.

To further entice people, many spam chain letters include headings such as "As seen on Oprah" to lend them credibility. No matter how they disguise themselves, however, chain letter spam just another form of pyramid scheme (see Chapter 13) in which a few people benefit at the expense of everyone else.

WHY COMPANIES SPAM AND HOW THEY DO IT

Nobody likes to receive spam because it wastes time and clogs email inboxes, yet many companies continue to send it anyway because, unlike direct mail and other forms of advertising, spamming is essentially free. For the cost of a single Internet account, anyone can reach a worldwide audience potentially numbering in the millions. In the eyes of spammers, even if they upset 99 percent of the people on the Internet, having 1 percent buy their product makes it all worth the trouble.

When sending spam, there's no need to type multiple email messages either; just as bulk mailers never lick their stamps, bulk emailing software automates the process for spammers. Click a button and you, too, can scatter unwanted email messages across the Internet.

Spammers are often stereotyped as scammers and con artists, but many are legitimate businesses that see spam as a low-cost, low-risk method for reaching potential customers. Of course, they realize that most people don't like receiving spam so they substitute euphemisms like "bulk email marketing." So the next time hordes of unwanted messages clog your email account, relax. You're not receiving spam; you're receiving bulk email marketing messages. Now don't you feel better?

To learn more about spam from the spammer's point of view, visit the websites of companies that sell bulk emailing programs, such as ClickZ Network (www.clickz.com), Internet Marketing Technologies (www.marketing-2000.net), Email Marketing Software (www.massmailsoftware.com), MailWorkz (www.mailworkz.com), or MTI Software (http://desktopserver.com).

Collecting email addresses

Spammers often flood Usenet newsgroups, where they can target their products to people with specific interests. For example, a spammer selling vitamin supplements will likely find a receptive audience in the misc.health.alternative newsgroup.

Of course, newsgroups represent only a fraction of potential customers on the Internet. Before spammers can flood the Internet with their messages, they need a list of email addresses. Although email lists can be bought, they are not always accurate or up to date. So spammers use email address extracting programs to build their own lists. These programs harvest addresses from three sources: newsgroups, websites, and database directories.

Newsgroup extractors

When you post a message to a Usenet newsgroup, your message appears with your email address. Newsgroup extractors simply download messages stored in a Usenet newsgroup, strip away the text, and store the return email addresses, as shown in Figure 18-1.

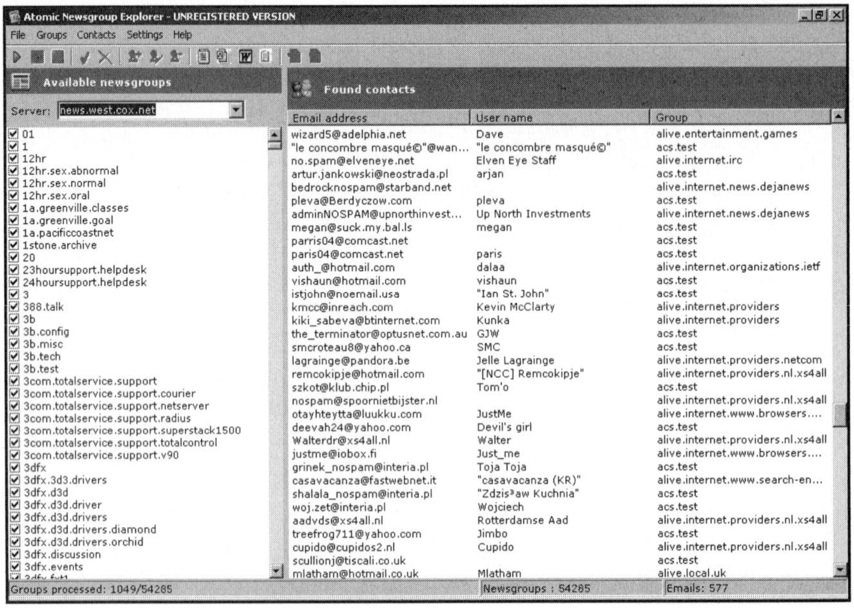

Figure 18-1: A newsgroup extractor can scan newsgroup postings and retrieve a list of email addresses within seconds.

To prevent your email address from getting sucked up by a newsgroup extractor, use a phony address or an anonymous remailer when posting messages to a newsgroup. Although this will prevent other newsgroup users from contacting you directly, it also prevents spammers from flooding your account with garbage.

Because newsgroup extractors harvest thousands of email addresses at once, some people substitute the @ symbol in their address with the word *AT*, such as swapping joesmith@yahoo.com with joesmithATyahoo.com. Initially, email extractors wouldn't recognize the word *AT* in the middle of an email address, but newer versions are smart enough to replace the word with the @ symbol, so even this technique is slowly losing its effectiveness.

Website extractors

Website extractors work just like newsgroup extractors except that they pull their email addresses from websites. When people create personal websites, they often provide a link where visitors can reach them. For a business website, they often list a number of company contacts, such as salespeople, technical support people, and even the CEO and president. Spammers prowl the Internet, with the guidance of search engines, to find web pages and pluck email addresses to store for future use.

To trick website extractors, many people replace characters in their email address with the ASCII code equivalents. So, rather than type the @ symbol, web page designers can substitute the ASCII code equivalent of the @ symbol, which is &#64, as shown below.

```
<html>
<body bgcolor="#FFFFFF" text="#000000">
E-mail: joesmith&#64yahoo.com
</body>
</html>
```

The website extractor will probably strip away the invalid joesmith&#64yahoo.com, even though this email address appears correctly as joesmith@yahoo.com when viewed in a browser window.

Unfortunately, the latest email extractors can even snare email addresses masked by ASCII codes and convert them into valid ones, so many websites now display their email addresses as a graphic image. People will know how to type it in correctly but email extractors won't, which can stop them for now.

SMTP server extractors

An SMTP (Simple Mail Transfer Protocol) server is a computer that sends and receives email. An SMTP server extractor is a program that retrieves valid email addresses from an SMTP server, as shown in Figure 18-2.

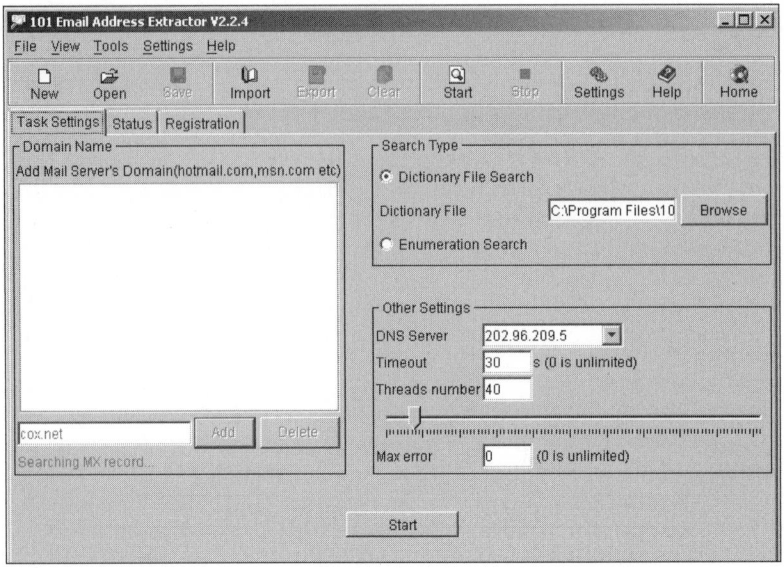

Figure 18-2: An SMTP server extractor can dig out valid email addresses from any SMTP server.

This is how it works. First, the extractor makes up an email address and asks the SMTP server if it's valid. It repeats this process indefinitely with fabricated addresses until it stumbles across a valid one that it can store for future spamming. To snare as many valid email addresses as possible, SMTP extractors typically target the servers of Internet service providers (ISPs), which can have thousands of customer email addresses waiting to be discovered.

P2P network harvesters

When people join a filesharing network to swap music, movies, or programs, they often type in their email address, which anyone else on that filesharing network can view. This is yet more fertile territory for spammers in search of email addresses. To protect yourself, never type your email address anyplace where others might be able to view it without your knowledge. To make matters worse, many people, when they configure a filesharing program, inadvertently share all the files on their computer, allowing spammers to peek inside and copy address books from their email program, such as Microsoft Outlook. With that information, the spammers can start spamming you and all the people you know.

Phishing for email addresses

Responding to pressure from people annoyed by telemarketers, the government created a Do Not Call list (www.donotcall.gov) where people could register their phone numbers. Telemarketers then had to scrub their phone lists to remove any numbers stored on this Do Not Call list.

So back in 2004, one spammer mimicked the Federal Trade Commission's site with his own bogus Do Not Spam site. The idea was that you could type in your email address here and spammers would be barred from sending you email. Unfortunately, this site was actually run by a spammer in the first place, so anyone who registered there wound up getting *more* spam. The Federal Trade Commission quickly shut down that bogus website, but the spammer had already succeeded in harvesting a huge list of valid email addresses.

In 2005, another phisher used spam to send out a Trojan horse. Anyone foolish enough to run the attached file installed the Trojan horse, which sat quietly on the infected computer until it detected the user visiting an online banking website. Then the Trojan horse would wake up, capture all keystrokes to snare passwords and account numbers, and then send this information back to the hacker, who could then access the victim's account as his leisure.

Masking the spammer's identity

Spammers may incur the wrath of several hundred (or several million) irate victims. Some spam recipients respond with angry messages; others launch their own email bomb attacks, sending multiple messages to the spammer's own address, clogging it and rendering it useless.

Unfortunately, crashing or clogging the spammer's ISP can also punish innocent customers who happen to use the same service provider. To avoid such counterattacks, many spammers create temporary Internet accounts (on services such as Hotmail or Juno), send their spam, and then cancel the account before anyone can attack them. Getting kicked off an ISP and opening new accounts is just part of the game bulk emailers play. If someone actually wants to buy the spammer's product, he can click a link in the spam message that will take him to the spammer's website.

Of course, for those spammers who can't be bothered to open and close email accounts, there's an easier way. Many bulk emailing programs simply omit or forge the sender's email address to avoid counterattacks.

Most ISPs limit the amount of email a single individual can send to avoid bandwidth hogs from impeding other customers' Internet access. If an ISP catches someone sending out an inordinate amount of email, it can cancel the account. So, spammers may sign up for bulk emailing accounts, which are special mail servers that allow anyone to send massive amounts of email—for a price, of course.

Another alternative is the less expensive (and less ethical) method of sending spam through "zombie" computers, which have been previously hijacked by a worm or Trojan horse (see Chapter 5).

After infecting a network of computers with worms or Trojan horses, the hacker can control the infected or zombie computers with a program, called a bot, which may be stored on an IRC chat room. The hacker then rents out his network of infected computers to spammers, who send their spam to the controlling bot, which in turn distributes it through the zombie network. This has several advantages over other spamming methods for the unscrupulous bulk emailer.

First, since the spam appears to be coming from the email account of each individual zombie computer, or through each infected computer's ISP's mail server, tracing the spam to its source leads to an innocent person, not to the spammer himself. Second, by sending spam through a network controlled by a bot, known as a botnet, the spammer isn't directly violating his ISP's ban on bulk mailing. Third, and most importantly, many spam filters work by blocking messages from known bulk email accounts. When the spam comes from computers connected through different ISPs such as Earthlink, spam can often circumvent any filters people have installed. (If a filter detects massive amounts of email coming from a single ISP, the spam filter will block it. But if the email is coming from multiple ISPs, the filter often wrongly assumes the email is valid.)

Spammers can also hijack legitimate email accounts and use that account to flood the Internet with spam. Now if anyone traces the spam back to its source, they'll find an innocent (and likely confused) person, while the real spammer has long since disappeared to hijack other email accounts to send spam through over and over again.

PROTECTING YOURSELF FROM SPAMMERS

Now that you know how spammers find email addresses and send out spam, how can you fight back? Depending on your mood and temperament, your response may range from politeness to hostility. And you may never get any satisfactory response or resolution. But maybe you can vent some steam, at least.

Complain to the spammer

When you receive spam, the message may include an email address where you can request to have your address removed from the spammer's list. Sometimes this works, but it's more likely that this email address itself is phony, or that your reply simply alerts the spammer to the fact that yours is a valid email address, which might encourage him to sell your address to other spammers.

Complain to the spammer's ISP

Even if you can't find a valid return address in to the spammer's message, you may still be able to uncover one elsewhere. To do so, search the spam's header for the ISP's address, such as earthlink.net, buried in the From field or Message-ID heading. Once you identify the ISP, you can complain directly to it.

For example, consider the following email:

Received: from flpvm07.prodigy.net by yipvme with SMTP; Mon, 28 Nov 2005 11:24:25 -0500

X-Originating-IP: [198.31.62.48]

Received: from mta.offer.omahasteaks.com (mta.offer.omahasteaks.com [198.31.62.48])

by flpvm07.prodigy.net (8.12.10 083104/8.12.10) with ESMTP id jAS-GNxvH018752

for <bothecat@prodigy.net>; Mon, 28 Nov 2005 08:24:07 -0800

X-MID: <Kilauea87671-36598-218255-1-1010@flonetwork.com>

Date: Mon, 28 Nov 2005 11:24:24 -0500 (EST)

Message-Id: <Kilauea87671-36598-218255-1-1010@flonetwork.com>

From: "Omaha Steaks" <OmahaSteaks@offer.omahasteaks.com>

The "From" heading identifies the message as coming from OmahaSteaks@offer
.omahasteaks.com, and the "X-Originating-IP" heading identifies the IP address of the
sender as 198.31.62.48.

To verify that the IP address (omahasteaks.com) matches the numeric IP address
shown in the X-Originating-IP heading, you need to do a reverse DNS lookup, using the
tools on a site such as through ZoneEdit (www.zoneedit.com/lookup.html), as shown in
Figure 18-3.

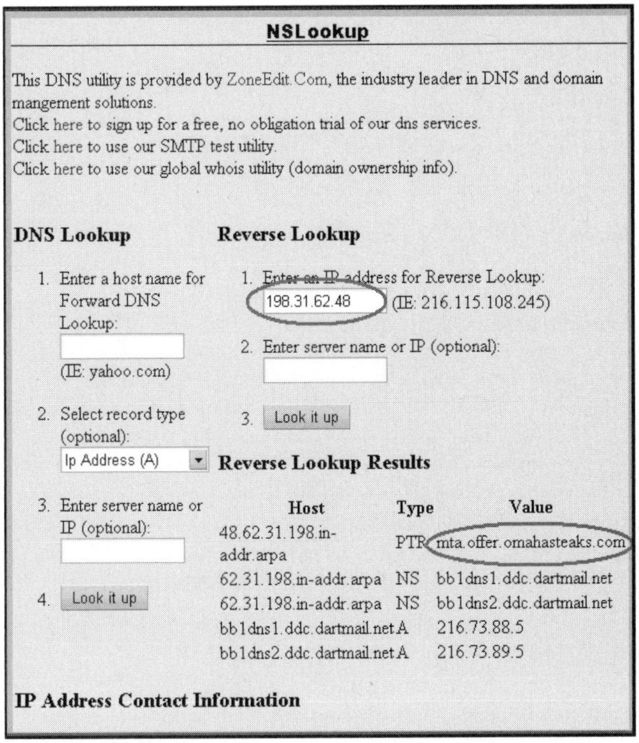

Figure 18-3: A reverse DNS lookup can verify that an IP address belongs to a certain
domain name, such as omahasteaks.com.

In this case, the numeric IP address matches the domain name, so the email
probably hasn't been forged. This means you should be able to contact the sender
(OmahaSteaks@offer.omahasteaks.com) directly and request to be removed from its
list for future mailings. You could also try contacting the ISP used by the sender, which in
Figure 18-3 is identified as DartMail.net. However, if you visit the DartMail.net site, you'll
find that it's a service that specializes in mass emailing, so complaining to them about
unwanted spam won't get you very far.

In this next message example, the email address (James.Horne@unex.es), which
looks like it's from a site in Spain, appears to be forged. A reverse DNS lookup of the IP
address identified by the X-Originating-IP heading reveals that 69.61.230.16 belongs to
Fuse.Net, which is a Cincinnati-based ISP. Since the email address is phony, you can't
complain directly to the spammer but you can complain to what appears to be his ISP,
Fuse.Net.

Received: from flpvm21.prodigy.net by mailapps2 with SMTP; Tue, 22 Nov 2005 11:47:22 -0500

X-Originating-IP: [69.61.230.16]

Received: from cn-esr1-69-61-230-16.fuse.net (CN-ESR1-69-61-230-16.fuse.net [69.61.230.16])

by flpvm21.prodigy.net (8.12.10 083104/8.12.10) with SMTP id jAMGi3lr025787;

Tue, 22 Nov 2005 08:44:04 -0800

Received: (from tomcat@localhost)

by 82.51.63.111 (8.12.8/8.12.8/Submit) id j0CHmn4V425775

for cruise41@prodigy.net; Tue, 22 Nov 2005 08:46:29 -0800

Message-ID: <464n236e.2447002@207.115.57.16>

Date: Tue, 22 Nov 2005 08:46:29 -0800

From: "sileas Workman" <James.Horne@unex.es>

ISPs can't monitor all of their users, but if they receive a flood of complaints about one particular customer, they can take action against the spammer and stop future abuses (maybe).

To notify an ISP of a spammer, email your complaint to postmaster@spammer.site, root@spammer.site, admin@spammer.site, or abuse@spammer.site, where *spammer.site* is the site from which the spammer sent the junk email.

Not all spammers use bulk emailing services or botnets to mask their identity, so complaining to the spammer's ISP might actually get the spammer kicked off.

Complain to the Internal Revenue Service

Because many spammers promote get-rich-quick schemes, there's a good chance they don't keep proper tax records of their earnings. So one way to take revenge on these spammers is to contact the Internal Revenue Service (or your own government's tax agency) to investigate. American citizens can forward spam either to net-abuse@nocs.insp.irs.gov to report fraudulent make-money-fast (MMF) schemes or to hotline@nocs.insp.irs.gov to report tax evaders. Reports of tax fraud should be sent directly to your regional IRS Service Center, for which there is currently no Internet email address for reporting suspected offenses.

To avoid getting caught by their government's tax agency, many spammers make their physical location hard to find. They may live in one country but host their website in another. And it's hard to tell for sure who actually owns the website, especially if the spammer uses a free web hosting service such as Geocities or Tripod. With electronic payment transfers, spammers can live anywhere in the world and collect money from their websites, regardless of where they're hosted. This can make tracking them down to pay income taxes nearly impossible. But hey, you've gotten it off your chest anyway, right?

Locating the spammer's postal address

Once you know the IP address or domain name of a spammer's website, you can do a WHOIS lookup using a service such as DNS Stuff (www.dnsstuff.com). This will tell you the name of the company or person who registered the IP address or domain name, as shown in Figure 18-4.

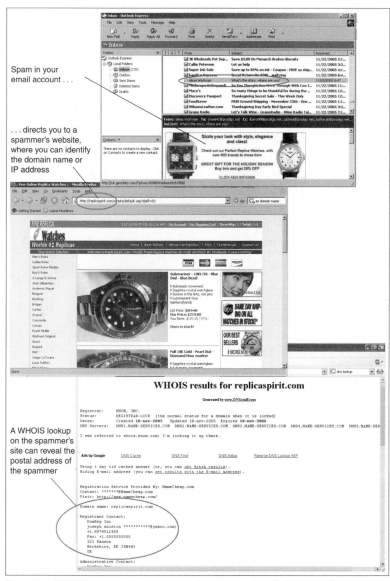

Spam in your
email account . . .

. . . directs you to a
spammer's website,
where you can identify
the domain name or
IP address

A WHOIS lookup
on the spammer's
site can reveal the
postal address of
the spammer

Figure 18-4: A WHOIS lookup on a domain name or IP address can identify the person who owns a particular website.

Unfortunately, spammers know that their websites will become targets so they often disguise their real site address through a third-party server, such as a specialized bulk email ISP. One such ISP even advertises the following:

IP Tunneling is a method where the recipient of your email message accesses your website through a (non traceable) binary encrypted link similar in appearance to the following:

(.....unique.site.net .co.fr |https.am2002.opt.com:8096)

Once the recipient clicks the email message, their browser references our servers through the binary encoding within the link. Our servers (behind the scenes) then call upon your web site's IP which resides either on your server or a 3rd party's server. This technology provides its users with COMPLETE protection and anonymity.

As a result, it's possible to browse a spammer's website without ever knowing the exact domain address that you can use to look up the spammer's real address and telephone number.

HOW SPAM FILTERS WORK

Spam filters can reduce, but not eliminate, spam. Many ISPs now run spam filters to weed out the most obvious offenders, but you may still want your own filter to catch any additional spam that slips through. Common techniques that spam filters use include content filtering (also called Bayesian filtering), blacklists and whitelists, DNS lookups, and attachment filtering.

Content (Bayesian) filtering

Content filtering is the most common type of spam filtering. It works by analyzing the text in each message using probability theory developed by the mathematician Thomas Bayes. Most spam can be readily identified by subject and text headings like "!!!MAKE MONEY FAST!!!" However, other types of spam can be more subtle.

If you identify any spam messages that slip past the filter, the program can gradually "learn" and get better at sifting through similar spam in the future, as shown in Figure 18-5. Because spammers constantly change their tactics, you're always going to get some spam, but content filtering can gradually reduce a potential flood to a mere trickle.

Blacklists and whitelists

Another filtering technique involves blacklists or whitelists, or both. A blacklist is simply a list of known spammer email addresses or domains, including domains of entire countries (because many spammers route spam through mail servers located in Russia or Romania), as shown in Figure 18-6. The moment the filter recognizes that a message has come in from a known spammer, it blocks the message.

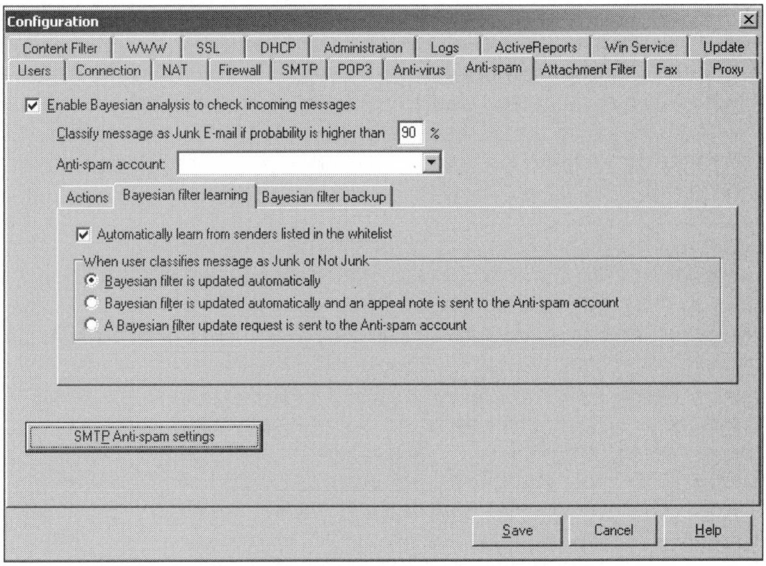

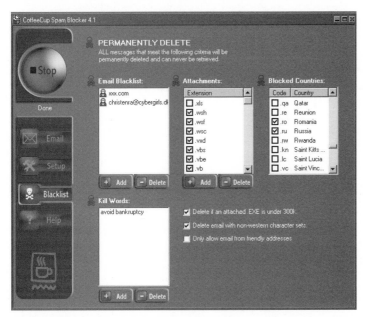

Figure 18-5: You can configure a Bayesian filter to "learn" how to recognize spam.

Blacklists can supplement content filtering, but are easily fooled by themselves because spammers change email addresses so often. As a result, some filters also use whitelists.

Figure 18-6: Blacklists and whitelists define banned and approved email addresses.

A whitelist defines acceptable email addresses. If the filter receives email from any-one on its whitelist, the email may pass freely. All others will be rejected. In many cases, the filter will respond to any rejected email address, requesting that the user resend the message to a specific address or using a specific code. Any person sending legitimate email will have no trouble with this, but a spammer isn't likely to take the time to read and follow these additional instructions.

DNS lookup lists

Several organizations, such as SpamCop (www.spamcop.net) and ORDB (Open Relay DataBase)—www.ordb.org, maintain lists of known spam sources. To get their information, the maintainers of these lists deliberately solicit spam for analysis. To supplement its list of known spam sources, SpamCop creates lists of bogus email addresses that nobody uses, which they post on web pages. When spammers harvest these bogus email addresses and try to use them, SpamCop immediately recognizes them as spam.

Many mail servers on the Internet don't accurately record where email comes from, either through negligence or deliberate intent (such as special bulk mailing ser-vices). These types of mail servers are known as Open Relays, and because spammers tend to use these to mask their own email addresses, DNS lookup lists record known open relay servers and either reject any messages sent from them outright or scrutinize messages from these servers extra carefully to weed out spam, as shown in Figure 18-7.

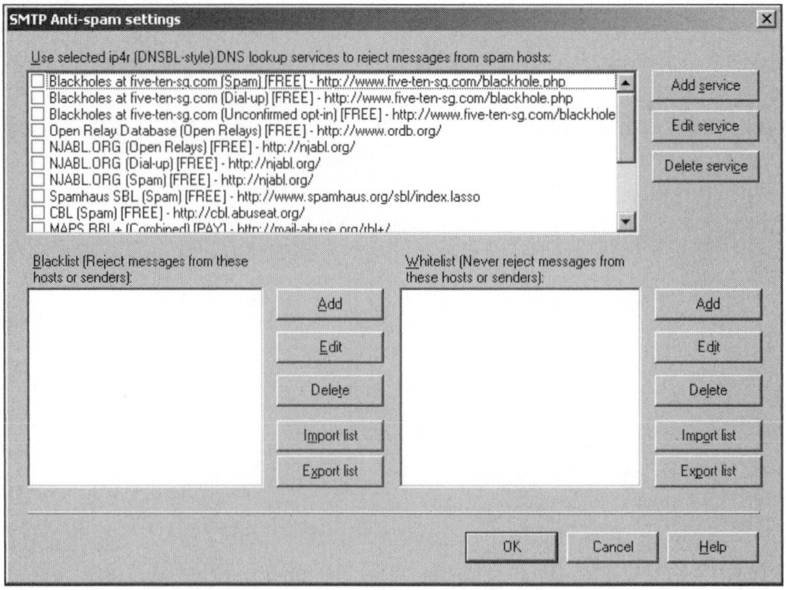

Figure 18-7: You can tell your spam filter to reject all email from known spam mail servers.

Attachment filtering

Many spammers send their entire message as a graphic image that can't be read by content filters. In response, some spam filters include attachment filters that look for email messages containing nothing but graphic images. Of course, these attachment filters can't identify the visual content of a graphic image, but, when combined with other filtering techniques, they can flag suspicious messages.

Attachment filtering can also help prevent infection by screening out .exe (executable), .wsh (Windows Script Host), or .vbs (Visual Basic Script) files that could contain viruses, worms, or Trojan horses.

STOPPING SPAM

You can never completely stop spam, but you can eliminate much of it. First, find out whether your ISP offers a spam filter, and if so, then turn it on. If your ISP's spam filters don't seem terribly effective, consider switching your email account to a special filtering service such as SpamCop (www.spamcop.net) or Aristotle Internet Access (www.aristotle .net/business-services/email-filtering). These services screen your email for spam and route suspicious messages to a designated location where you can review them before downloading.

For a second layer of defense, turn on filtering in your email client program, such as Microsoft Outlook or Mozilla Thunderbird, as shown in Figure 18-8. Email programs often allow you to automatically route suspected spam into a designated junk or spam folder where you can more safely review it before deleting it.

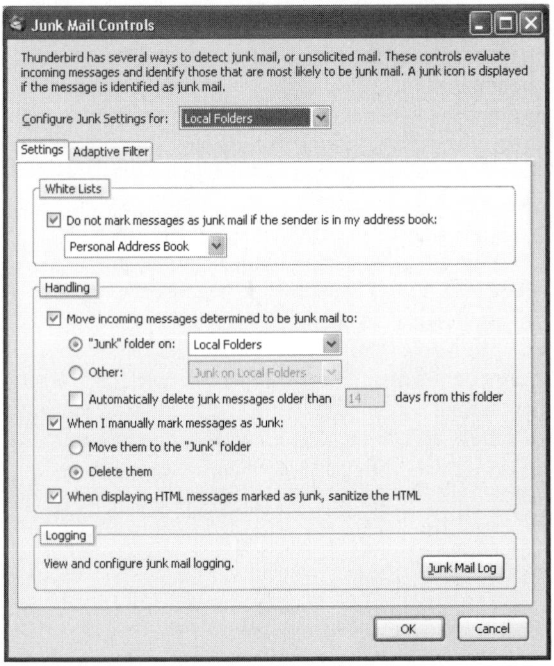

Figure 18-8: Most email programs can automatically route suspicious email into a junk folder.

Finally, consider getting a separate spam-filtering program such as SpamBuster (www.contactplus.com), SpamButcher (www.spambutcher.com), CoffeeCup Spam Blocker (www.coffeecup.com), or SpamKiller (www.mcafee.com). These programs can also flag potential spam so your email program routes it to a special junk folder or just deletes it altogether.

To reduce the chances of receiving spam in the first place, give out your email address only sparingly. Create a separate account with a free service such as Hotmail to use for posting messages in Usenet newsgroups, registering at websites, or making online purchases (many companies sell your email address when you sign up with them). By creating a decoy email account, you can redirect spam to accounts that you rarely use and keep your everyday email account free of the most annoying spam.

NOTE: *When using multiple spam filters, make sure you always have a way to retrieve any messages that the spam filters weed out since there's always a chance that a legitimate message might get caught in a spam filter by mistake.*

POSSIBLE FUTURE SOLUTIONS TO SPAM

Many people are engaged in developing ways to stop spam entirely. One idea proposed by Bill Gates is to force everyone to buy "postage" to send email. This postage wouldn't cost money in the traditional sense. Instead, it would require the sending computer to calculate a mathematical problem, temporarily tying up its resources. It would cost the sending computer a trivial amount of time and resources for regular emailing, but it could cripple the spammer who wants to send 10,000 email messages at once.

Some Internet service providers are proposing to stamp outgoing messages with a digital signature of the customer's domain name, using strong encryption so no one could alter or forge it. One of the first implementations of this idea has come from Yahoo! (http://antispam.yahoo.com/domainkeys) and its open-source program DomainKeys, which verifies the domain of email senders. If someone tries to forge an email address, DomainKeys will automatically flag the message as spam.

Forcing computers to pay "postage" or reveal their true email address through encryption might work, but only if the entire structure of the Internet changes to adapt these practices en masse. Until then, spammers will continue flooding the Internet with advertisements while everyone tries to agree on a solution.

Microsoft is currently testing a unique email filter called SNARF (Social Network and Relationship Finder). SNARF doesn't analyze content. It works by analyzing to whom you send email and from whom you receive it. The idea is that you're more likely to want email from people you've contacted before, and that email from unknown addresses is more likely to be spam. To grab a copy of SNARF, visit Microsoft Research (http://research.microsoft.com/community/snarf).

Going on the offensive

Filtering will never stop spam, so some people prefer to go on the offensive and attack spammers directly. In 2004, Lycos Europe distributed a special screensaver called Make Love Not Spam, as shown in Figure 18-9.

Figure 18-9: The Make Love Not Spam screensaver would launch an email bombing attack against sites known to advertise through spam.

When a computer was idle, the Make Love Not Spam screensaver would kick in and request to view a known spammer's website. If enough screensavers sent their requests at the same time, the spam website would become slow and overloaded, either making it inconvenient for legitimate users to purchase the spammer's products or denying them access altogether.

Shortly after the Make Love Not Spam screensaver appeared, however, Lycos Europe killed the project. Public outcry over a commercial organization using a denial of service attack created too much controversy. Still, it shows that corporations are not above using hacker techniques and that the real future of hacking might lie within the payroll of a corporation.

IBM has developed a similar tactic for its FairUCE (www.alphaworks.ibm.com/tech/fairuce) spam filter. Unlike traditional filters that examine a message's content to identify spam, FairUCE analyzes email to determine where the message might have been sent from, despite forged email addresses and spoofed headers that mask its true source. Instead of trying to identify the spammer's email address, FairUCE tries to identify the domain that sent the spam in the first place. Then, it bounces the spam back to the sending domain in an attempt to slow it down and prevent it from sending more spam.

Another tool in the fight against spam, the OptOutByDomain (www.OptOutByDomain .com) site, lets you tell spammers which domains you don't want them to spam, rather than listing one email address at a time. Under the CAN-SPAM Act of 2003, spammers must legally comply with such a request or they can get sued, which is what OptOutDomain's companion site, SueASpammer (www.sueaspammer.com) is all about, as shown in Figure 18-10.

Figure 18-10: The SueaSpammer site hits spammers in the pocketbook by threatening and taking legal action.

Antispam organizations

Despite laws, threats, and physical action against it, spamming is so cost-effective that it's probably here to stay. If spam really irritates you, consider joining and supporting the Coalition Against Unsolicited Commercial Email (CAUCE)—www.cauce.org—an organization consisting of Internet users who have banded together to lobby for new laws to regulate unsolicited email.

To show you how influential one person can be in the fight against spam, visit Netizens Against Gratuitous Spamming (www.nags.org). This website shares tips for identifying and dealing with spam and offers an example of chaff, which is garbage data designed to fool spammers who retrieve email addresses from websites.

To keep up with the latest news regarding spam and to learn more about how to defeat spam, visit Death to Spam (www.mindworkshop.com/alchemy/nospam.html), Spam News (www.spamnews.com), Junk Busters (www.junkbusters.com), Fight Spam (http://spam.abuse.net/spam), and The Spamhaus Project (www.spamhaus.org).

No matter how assiduously you protect your email address or run filters, you're going to get spammed, so it's nice to know that at least you have allies on the Internet who want to help you trace, identify, and stop spam as much as humanly possible.

A POSTSCRIPT: SPAM AS PROPAGANDA

Spam is hard to stop, which makes it a useful tool for spreading messages across the Internet. In December 2005, a neo-Nazi sympathizer reportedly created a variant of the Sober worm modified to send spam containing phrases like "Multicultural = multicriminal." The messages also included links to racist German websites and news articles that support anti-immigrant views.

One Chinese dissident group that publishes a newsletter called VIP Reference (www.bignews.org) has found another use for spam. Because Chinese citizens can't access certain websites without fear of government retribution, VIP Reference floods Chinese computers with spam containing its pro-democracy newsletter. Now Chinese citizens can read censored information without being guilty of soliciting it themselves. So the next time you're cursing the spam flooding your email account, it might comfort you to think about how spam is helping Chinese citizens read censored information. Maybe spam could become less of a dirty word if it were used to promote ideas like democracy and freedom, instead of Viagra and pornography.

19

BANNER ADS, POP-UP ADS, AND SEARCH ENGINE SPAMMING

Nothing is really free. When you listen to the radio or watch TV, advertising covers the expenses and pays for the sponsors' right to broadcast their messages during your viewing time. Most people tolerate radio and television advertising and have grown accustomed to its constant interruptions.

However, in the world of the Internet, people don't have so much patience for advertising. While advertisements underwrite many websites and hosting services, there's a fine line between product promotion and invasion of privacy. Ideally, an Internet ad would pop up once and give you the option of making it go away. Instead, not only do online ads pop up (and keep popping up repeatedly), but they may also track which web pages you visit. That would be like having a TV that could peek into your living room to see which brand of potato chips you're eating and then could target you for commercials for a competitor's chips.

To attract your attention, Internet advertisers use a variety of formats, including banner ads and pop-up/pop-under ads. Any of these ads, however, can be an opportunity for abuse.

BANNER ADS AND CLICK FRAUD

The simplest online ads are banner ads, which can appear in different places on a web page and typically display some sort of animation to catch your attention. Clicking on the banner ad will take you to the advertiser's website. Figure 19-1 shows a web page with three different banner ads.

Advertisers place their banner ad on a web page and then pay a fee to the website operator each time someone clicks on it, an arrangement known as *pay-per-click (PPC)*. For greater flexibility, many website operators partner with Google (www.google.com/ads), Yahoo!, and other search engines to provide different advertisements targeted to their specific audience. Every time someone clicks on an ad, the advertiser pays both the website operator and the search engine. Each click can cost the advertiser anywhere from a nickel to $50.

Theoretically, the more times a banner ad gets clicked, the more effective it is at reaching potential customers. The problem for the advertiser is that the pay-per-click method can only confirm that someone clicked on the ad, not whether

Figure 19-1: Can you spot all the banner ads on this web page?

he or she is really interested in the ad. Even worse, the advertiser has to pay the website operator (and any search engine partner) for every click, regardless of the outcome.

This loophole has attracted dishonest website operators interested in making easy money at the advertisers' expense. One such company, called Auctions Expert International LLC, launched a website and signed up with Google AdWords in 2003. According to a lawsuit filed by Google, Auctions Expert hired approximately 50 people to sit at computers and click ads, artificially inflating the click-through rate and driving up the bills sent to advertisers. By engaging in such click fraud, Google's lawsuit claims, Auction Experts International generated $50,000 in revenue for itself, which Google then had to refund to the scammed advertisers.

An article in the May 3, 2004, edition of *The Times of India* reported that click fraud is even driving one of the fast-growing areas for outsourcing. According to the newspaper, many companies are hiring Indian housewives, urban professionals, and college students to sit around and click ads, earning 18 to 25 cents per click, which can add up to $200 a month.

Rather than hire hordes of people to click banner ads, some website operators run automated programs known as *autoclick software*. According to a US Department of Justice press release, in March 2005, the Secret Service arrested Michael Anthony Bradley, a 32-year-old programmer from California, who threatened to release an automated clicking program dubbed Google Clique, unless Google paid him $100,000 (www .usdoj.gov/usao/can/press/html/2004_03_19_bradley.html).

If you look to buy autoclick software, however, you'll find it's marketed as a tool to test your website to see how many users it can support, not as something to artificially boost your site's click rate. Some popular autoclick programs include Internet Macros (www.iopus.com) and CT AutoClick (http://camtech2000.net). One such program, I-Faker (www.i-faker.com), shown in Figure 19-2, even claims the following on its website:

DOES THE SCRIPT GIVE IMPRESSIONS TO MY BANNERS?

To put it simply, YES. Although not a practice we condone, our software can help you gain profits from your advertisers banner impressions. Although we are not aware of any advertising companies that can enforce a rule on this they may in the future come up with a method to prevent it.

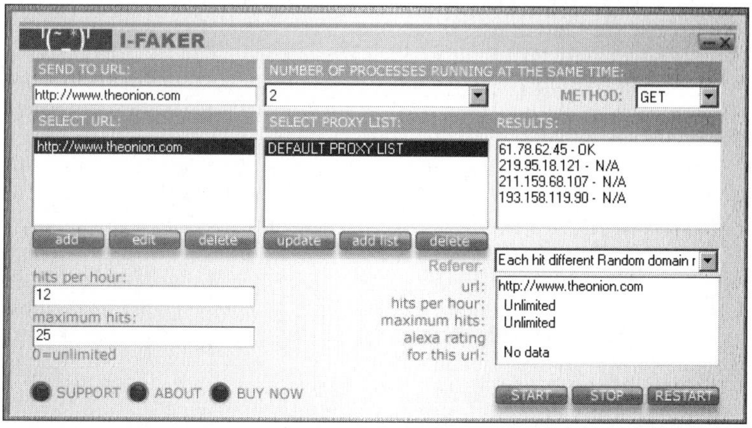

Figure 19-2: I-Faker is one of many programs that enables a computer to click banner ads on a website automatically.

The maker of another program, called FakeZilla (www.fakezilla.com), makes the following claim:

Web page requests are routed through a massive list of anonymous proxy servers which can be defined by you. Counters and banners "see" these fake hits just as if a real user was browsing your site. When used with the Web Server Log extractor the fake hits and traffic appear 100% realistic—you can't tell the difference between FakeZilla traffic and real traffic! The most powerful and sophisticated software of its kind, FakeZilla is not only a "fake" or "virtual" hit generator, but in conjunction with your web and marketing resources it can improve your site profits.

One way advertisers can spot bogus traffic is by identifying the IP address of each click and how long that IP address remains on the website. If 1,000 clicks come from the same IP address, which only stays at the advertiser's website for two seconds at a time, chances are good that those clicks were faked. That's why FakeZilla boasts that it can route your clicks through "a massive list of anonymous proxy servers."

There's even a plug-in for the Mozilla Firefox browser called SwitchProxy (www.roundtwo.com/product/switchproxy), which lets you switch rapidly to different proxy servers so that each activity you perform on the Internet will appear to come from a different IP address.

Besides worrying about unscrupulous website operators, advertisers also have to worry about unscrupulous competitors. Some companies will hire people to click their competitor's ads on different websites or run autoclick software, forcing their rivals to waste money on phony clicks.

To prevent click fraud, many advertisers would like to change the current "pay-per-click" model to a "cost-per-action" arrangement, meaning they'd only pay for clicks that turn into actual sales.

Until websites can verify the legitimacy of all clicks, advertisers can try enlisting one of the various click auditing services. To learn more about click fraud services, such as the one shown in Figure 19-3, visit Click Auditor (www.keywordmax.com), Who's Clicking Who (www.whosclickingwho.com), or Click Defense (www.clickfraudservices.com).

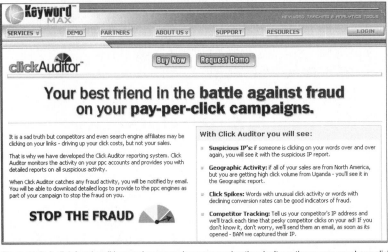

Figure 19-3: A click fraud auditing service can make sure an advertiser isn't wasting money on phony clicks.

POP-UP/POP-UNDER ADS

Banner ads are easy to see, which also means they're easy to ignore. Advertisers designed pop-up ads to get right in your face. Since a pop-up ad opens a new window that covers the web page you really want to see, you can't ignore it. This is like having an advertiser rush into your house, grab your head, and shove your face in front of the TV when a commercial plays.

Many websites, especially those offering pornography, pirated music and software, or hacker tools, may bombard you with multiple pop-up ads, as shown in Figure 19-4. Sometimes, if you shut down one pop-up ad, three more appear in its place, so that the only way you can disable all the pop-up ads is to shut down your browser completely. If you don't shut down all these pop-up ads, they can often flood your browser and freeze or crash your computer.

Pop-under ads are a bit more subtle. They also appear in little windows all over your screen, but they hide under—not on top of—your currently displayed web page. The moment you close your browser, those pop-under ads seem to appear magically, cluttering up your screen, and you probably won't have any idea which website opened them. Since pop-under ads don't intrude upon your browsing activities, advertisers believe they're more effective than pop-ups, which people swat away like pesky mosquitoes every time one appears.

Figure 19-4: Pop-up ads force you to look at them whether you want to or not.

Either way, the intrusive nature of both pop-up and pop-under ads can annoy people who might have been customers otherwise.

How to create a pop-up/pop-under ad

Advertisers create pop-up and pop-under ads using JavaScript, Dynamic HyperText Markup Language (DHTML), or Flash. To see how to create a simple pop-up ad in JavaScript, use an ordinary text editor (such as Windows Notepad), type the following in a new file, and save it under the name "home.htm":

```
<html>
<head>
  <title>A pop-up and pop-under example</title>
</head>
<body>
<script language = "JavaScript">
<!--
  PopUp = window.open('ad.htm','ADVERTISEMENT','height=400,width=325,toolbar=no,direc
tories=no,status=no,menubar=no,scrollbars=no,resizable=no');

//-->
</script>
<P>
This is an example of a pop-up ad created using JavaScript. This is the HTML code
that created this web page.
```

```
</P>
<IMG SRC = "HTML.gif">
</body>
</html>
```

The above HTML code uses the `window.open()` JavaScript command to load a second HTML file called ad.htm as a pop-up window, which appears as soon as someone loads the home.htm file in a browser. (You may have to turn off your browser's built-in pop-up blocker to view the sample ad.)

This HTML code also displays a graphic image called HTML.gif, which opens the NotePad window with the HTML source code, as shown in Figure 19-5.

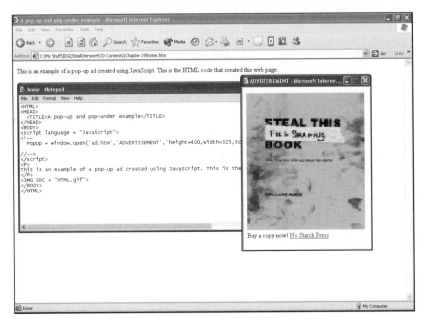

Figure 19-5: When you load the home.htm file, the pop-up ad appears automatically.

The HTML code to create the ad.htm pop-up ad appears below:

```
<html>
<head>
  <title>ADVERTISEMENT</title>
</head>

<body bgcolor="#FFFFFF" text="#000000">
<img src="fileshare.jpg" width="301" height="337">
<text>
Buy a copy now!
</text>
<a href="http://www.nostarch.com"> No Starch Press</a>
</body>
</html>
```

This HTML code displays a graphic file called fileshare.jpg in the pop-up window with the title *ADVERTISEMENT*, along with the text *No Starch Press* as a hyperlink that points to the www.nostarch.com domain.

This JavaScript example will get stopped by most pop-up blockers. For another example of creating pop-up ads with JavaScript, visit http://icant.co.uk/articles/how-to-create-popunders or www.hypergurl.com/generators/popupads.html.

If you want to create a pop-up ad that can slip past pop-up blockers, but you don't want to bother writing JavaScript code yourself, you can try the JavaScript Coder (www.javascript-coder.com) program or the Pop-Up Maker (www.jvwinc.com/popupmaker.html) program, shown in Figure 19-6. The publisher of Pop-Up Maker, Jimmy's Value World, even claims that its program "was one of the first popup [sic] makers that could create popups which will bypass XP service pack 2 Internet explorer popup blocking utility."

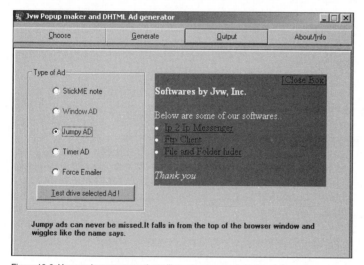

Figure 19-6: You can buy programs that will create pop-up ads that can slip past many pop-up ad blockers.

How to stop banner and pop-up/pop-under ads

Almost every browser can be set to block all pop-up/pop-under ads by default, although you may want to configure your browser to allow them on certain trusted sites. Figure 19-7 shows the dialog box options for blocking pop-up ads in Internet Explorer 6.

To avoid seeing banner ads, you can buy a program that will automatically refuse to load graphic images that link to other websites. Not only do these special ad-cleaning programs keep you from seeing annoying ads, but they can also speed up your browsing by eliminating the time it would take to load the graphic images associated with banners. Some popular banner ad-stripping and pop-up blocking programs include AdsCleaner (www.adscleaner.com), SuperAdBlocker (www.superadblocker.com), Ad Annihilator (http://adannihilator.com), Privoxy (www.privoxy.org), and Norton Internet Security (www.symantec.com).

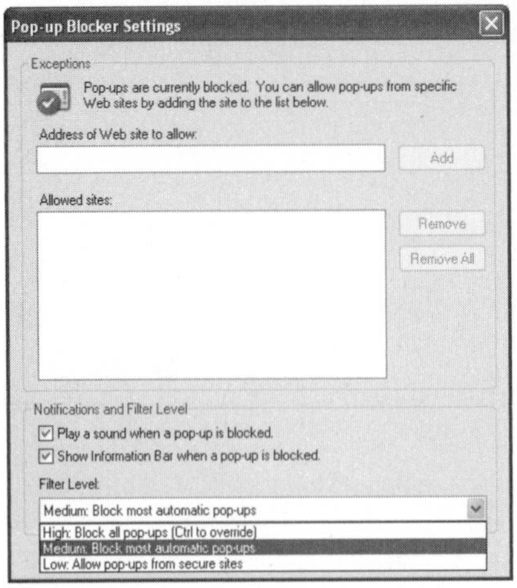

Figure 19-7: Internet Explorer 6 gives you different options for blocking pop-up ads.

WATCHING OUT FOR WEB BUGS

Advertisers always want to measure the effectiveness of their marketing campaigns. Since the Internet spans the world, it's very difficult to track how many people look at a particular ad and who they are. To meet these two needs, advertisers created a special tracking device called a *web bug*.

Tracking the websites you visit

When you visit a website, your browser asks it to send all the text and graphic images contained on that page. Thus, a webserver needs to know the IP address of the visitor's computer in order to send the reply to his or her browser.

When a webserver sends a web page to your browser, it is encoded as HyperText Markup Language (HTML) instructions that tell your browser how to display and position text and graphics, the name of the different graphic files in the page, and other data about the page, such as the name of the server that sent it to your computer. In the following example of an HTML graphics statement, the graphic file is called dotclear.gif, its width and height are both one pixel, and the server that sent it is located at http://ad.doubleclick.net (it's this server that uses the web bug to retrieve information about your computer).

```
<IMG SRC=http://ad.doubleclick.net/dotclear.gif width=1" height="1">
```

The example above is actually a web bug, so tiny in size that it's essentially invisible. When the server sends the web bug to a browser, the DoubleClick.net server can immediately identify the following:

- The IP address of the computer

- The specific web page that contains that web bug

- The time and date the web bug was retrieved

- The type of browser in use

Web bugs typically appear on web pages, but they can also appear inside banner ads, pop-up/pop-under ads, or HTML files send through email or posted in newsgroups. In their simplest usage, web bugs help advertisers determine how many people have visited a particular website and viewed a particular web page. On a more insidious level, web bugs can be used with browser cookies to track which websites a particular person visits and tailor advertisements specific to that individual's interests.

Cookies are small text files that contain unique information about you and your last visit to a specific website. For example, a cookie from Amazon.com can store a user ID to match your computer to its database that lists the last 20 items you browsed, along with any recent purchases.

Normally, cookies can only be used by the website that created and placed them on your computer. So a cookie placed on your computer by Amazon.com can't be read or used by any other websites, such as Barnes & Noble or Borders bookstores.

Unfortunately, circumventing this restriction is what webservers like DoubleClick do when they place web bugs (and cookies) on your computer. Only DoubleClick's servers can read its own cookies, but since DoubleClick's web bugs appear on so many websites, they can effectively track what you do across multiple websites. Visit sites like Amazon.com, Best Buy, and CompUSA and DoubleClick's web bug/cookie combination can track what you've done on each site and thus create a more detailed profile of your browsing habits than any single website could do on its own. Armed with this information, DoubleClick can create unique customer profiles linked to specific IP addresses, essentially spying on your buying habits without your approval (or knowledge).

To learn more about what type of information web bugs can retrieve off your computer, visit the Analyze Your Internet Privacy site (http://network-tools.com/analyze) and Cookie Central (www.cookiecentral.com).

Using web bugs in spam

The next time you receive spam, there's a good chance that it will contain HTML code (where a web bug can hide). The reason is simple. As soon as you view spam (such as in the Preview pane of an email program like Thunderbird or Outlook Express), your computer retrieves the text and graphic images defined by that HTML code. As soon as your computer requests the web bug, the web bug's server can identify not only your IP address and operating system, but also when you viewed the spam. This information can be particularly important because it tells the spammer that someone actually viewed the spam so the email address is valid (and can be sold to other spammers too).

Many email programs let you block graphics from being viewed, but you may want to test your email program by taking the web bug test at www.nthelp.com/OEtest/oe.htm. This test will send you an email and after you open it in your email program, you can return to the website to see if the server managed to determine if you opened the "spam" or not.

Even if you're using a supposedly "secure" email program like Thunderbird, you may find yourself being victimized by web bug spam if you rely on the program's default settings. Thunderbird will only strip away HTML graphics or web bugs if it properly identifies the message as spam. Since Thunderbird won't identify the web bug test message from the nthelp.com site as spam, it will let the test message's web bug slip through, which also means that any spam that can slip past Thunderbird's spam filters will also be able to verify your email address, too. (In my limited testing with different email programs, both Outlook Express and Thunderbird failed to block the nthelp.com's test message, but Microsoft Entourage on Mac OS X did block the test message web bug.)

If a recipient doesn't view the web bug in his email, it could mean that the email address isn't valid or that this particular person didn't bother to read it. In either case, the advertiser will likely remove that person's email address from its distribution list and avoid sending advertisements that will be ignored.

Some companies accused of planting web bugs in email marketing messages include Experian (www.experian.com), Digital Impact (www.digitalimpact.com), and Responsys (www.responsys.com). By browsing their websites, you can get a better idea how email marketing firms work and how spam (better known by businesses by its euphemism of "email marketing") has now become a profitable and legitimate business model that includes clients such as Victoria's Secret, Microsoft, Marriott, and New York Life. Like it or not, spam, in one form or another, has become just another marketing strategy.

Bugging newsgroups

Newsgroups are another area where web bugs have started to appear. If you leave a message on a newsgroup as plain text, anybody can read the message anonymously. But if your newsgroup message contains HTML code, viewing that HTML newsgroup message causes the viewer's computer to request the HTML text and graphics from a server; this server must then identify the computer's IP address to send the requested HTML text and graphics.

By itself, HTML code can be harmless—except it allows a server to identify the IP address of the person reading the message and the time and date they read it. The extremely paranoid believe that HTML code (and web bugs) can identify people who subscribe to politically incorrect newsgroups, while others believe that governments might use web bugs to track down anyone trading child pornography or illegal MP3 files. By reading HTML code in newsgroup messages, you are no longer anonymous in a newsgroup, which is one major advantage of newsgroups in the first place.

Protecting yourself against web bugs

Since web bugs often work with cookies to track your browsing habits, your first line of defense is to make sure your browser refuses all cookies. Since this won't always be practical, especially when you visit online shopping sites which need the user to have cookies enabled, you should download the free Bugnosis tool (www.bugnosis.org).

As you browse different websites, Bugnosis scans each page, gives an audible warning, and highlights suspicious web bugs. By using Bugnosis with Internet Explorer, you can see how prevalent web bugs are, especially if Bugnosis finds suspicious GIF images on favorite websites such as the *New York Times* (www.nytimes.com), the *Detroit News* (www.detnews.com), or the *Direct Marketing News* site (www.dmnews.com) as shown in Figure 19-8. Despite Bugnosis's help, there's still no fool-proof way to determine if you're browsing a web page with a web bug hidden on it.

One of the largest email and Internet marketing companies is DoubleClick (www.doubleclick.com), which offers Internet users a way to store a special cookie on their browser that prevents your computer from receiving any advertisements from DoubleClick.

Figure 19-8: Bugnosis can identify when websites are using web bugs to track your activity.

Just visit the DoubleClick site, click the link for "Privacy at this Website," and scroll down to find the directions to opt out from DoubleClick's advertising. To opt out of other Internet marketing companies, visit the Network Advertising Initiative (NAI) site (www .networkadvertising.org/optout_nonppii.asp).

Even if you decide to opt out from DoubleClick's ads, you may still find yourself bombarded by pop-up and pop-under advertisements from other marketers. So to learn how to stop pop-up and pop-under ads from wrecking your Internet experience, visit the Web Ad Blocking site (www.ecst.csuchico.edu/~atman/spam/adblock.shtml).

If you only visit a handful of sites on a regular basis, you can configure your browser to let you choose to accept or reject all cookies from every site you visit. If you visit different sites on a regular basis, this can be a nuisance, but if you only visit a few sites, this might be one acceptable way to block cookies and keep others from spying on your browsing habits.

SPAMDEXING: SEARCH ENGINE SPAMMING

When most people use a search engine like Google or Yahoo!, they often click the first results listed at the top of the page. For example, type **Apple** in a search engine like Google and the top result will be for the Apple Computer website. Two pages of search results later, you'll find a travel agency called Apple Vacations. Google, like most search engines, assumes that more people are likely to want to visit Apple Computer than Apple Vacations and ranks its results accordingly. Companies actually vie with one another to be at the top of the results returned by search engines.

To determine which companies appear as the top results, search engines use algorithms to estimate which sites are most relevant to any given search term. Companies can also pay to get their websites ranked higher up in the results by using Yahoo!'s sponsored search marketing (http://searchmarketing.yahoo.com), Google's AdWords (https://adwords.google.com/select), or MSN's Keywords (http://advertising.msn.com.sg).

Paying for additional exposure is nothing new or unethical. The problem comes when companies try to scam their way to the top of the search engine results. This is known as *spamdexing* (spamming and indexing). Spamdexing involves the use of several techniques to fool search engine algorithms and improve search result rankings.

Keyword stuffing

The simplest way that search engines rank websites is by the number of times keywords appear on each page. A website that uses the word *computer* multiple times on many pages is more likely to be relevant to someone searching for information about computers than a website that discusses computer-controlled sewage disposal and has only a single use of the word *computer* on its pages.

So in its simplest form, *keyword stuffing* simply fills a web page with the words that people are most likely to search for. For example, if you're in the pool cleaning business, you could fill your web page with words like *pool*, *pool cleaning*, *pool chemistry*, and *pool safety*. Of course, this could clutter up the appearance of your web page and ruin its readability. Instead, the keywords are hidden using tiny fonts in text that appears as the same color as the page background. In this way, the text isn't visible to ordinary users, but search engines still find multiple instances of the embedded keywords and will rank the website higher than a competitor's website with the same keywords mentioned only three or four times.

To limit the success of keyword stuffers, most search engines now analyze *how* the website uses keywords and not just how often.

Keyword content creators

Since search engines examine the content (text) of your web pages, another way to trick search engines is like keyword stuffing but involves copying text and rewriting it slightly so that it appears differently to the search engine. This tricks the search engine into thinking the website has twice as much relevant content as it really does. While you could rewrite a single chunk of text to make it appear as two or more different chunks, it's much easier to let the computer do it for you. Strike Saturday Inc. sells a program called ArticleBot (www.articlebot.com), shown in Figure 19-9, that can rewrite text automatically.

The more rewritten text you post on your website, the more keywords a search engine will find and the higher your website's ranking will be. Two other content creator programs include Webspinner (www.webspinnersoftware.com), Article Equalizer (www.articleequalizer.com), and Traffic Equalizer (www.trafficequalizer.com), which boasts:

Traffic Equalizer will do all the work FOR you!

In a nutshell.

1. You import a list of keywords

2. You fill in a few form fields

3. The program automatically creates optimized pages

Figure 19-9: A content creator program, like ArticleBot, can rewrite a single chunk of text to make it appear different and fool search engines.

Another company called Hot Nacho (http://hotnacho.com) sells a program called ArticleWriter, a "custom word processor" that guides a human writer through the process of using the keywords most likely to get noticed by search engines. (To discourage people from crafting text solely to boost their rankings in a search engine, Google refuses to list Hot Nacho's website at all, essentially making the site invisible to anyone looking for it using Google. According to the owner of HotNacho.com, Google has punished him further by refusing to list any of his other websites, a dispute you can read about at http://hotnacho.com/wordpress-fracas.)

Link farming

Many search engines assume that if other websites link to a certain domain, that domain must be popular enough to merit a higher ranking. As a result, many websites artificially boost the number of sites linking back to them by creating bogus websites called *link farms*, which contain nothing but links to the site whose rankings they want to improve.

Another trick is to post website links on the many blogs scattered all over the Internet, known as *blog comment spamming*. As far as search engines are concerned, blogs are websites and links on blogs are as valid as any other.

To combat link farms and blog comment spamming, many search engines now rank links based on their source, so a link to your website from a major site, such as www.cnn.com or www.microsoft.com, is weighted more heavily than a link from a blog or site on a free web hosting service like Geocities or AngelFire.

Cloaking and code swapping

When search engines examine websites, they scan the HTML code to analyze the content. However, some sites rely exclusively on displaying information through Flash animation. A search engine can detect a Flash movie on a website, but it can't determine its content, so Flash-heavy websites send a description to the search engine. Of course, nothing prevents a dishonest website operator from sending anything to the search engine in his quest for inflated search rankings. This is known as *cloaking*. Search engines often threaten to ban websites that use cloaking.

Another technique is to create a temporary web page full of keywords and then, once it achieves a high ranking, to replace it with the original web page, a process known as *code swapping*. Code swapping is harder to prevent because a dishonest website operator can claim that he legitimately updated the site after the search engine examined the original web page.

Doorway pages

Sometimes websites use an opening web page called a *doorway* that displays animation or graphics before asking visitors to click a link to access the rest of the site. On legitimate websites, doorway pages offer a fancy way to grab a viewer's attention. On pornographic websites, doorway pages often also contain keywords that people are likely to type when searching for something else. So when people search for something like *warez* or *hacker tools*, the search engine lists the doorway page, and when people click the link in the search results, they find themselves on a porn site.

Spamdexing for hire

If these different spamdexing practices sound too complicated for you to learn, relax. You can hire someone else to do it for you. Such consultants call their work search engine optimization (SEO), and a quick search for *SEO* will reveal hundreds of companies offering to help boost your website's rankings for a fee.

Some of these companies use legitimate techniques, but others use shadier tactics that could actually get your site banned by Google and other search engines. If you're curious to see these banned websites for yourself but don't know how to find them, you can visit Search Engine Watch (http://searchenginewatch.com), which suggests alternate search engines to use. Search Engine Watch also explains how the various search engines rank sites for their results.

The more advertising you see on the Internet, the more money somebody's making off the content there. Somebody's paying to place their ads, someone else is getting paid to distribute those ads, and other people are getting paid to defraud the advertisers with fake clicks or phony search engine rankings (while still more people are getting paid to stop and catch the people defrauding the advertisers).

With all this going on, you should always keep in mind that search engines do nothing more than filter what you can and can't see on the Internet. Considering how much money is put into advertising and advertiser fraud, it's possible that advertisers are costing honest people more money than hackers ever could.

20

ADWARE AND SPYWARE

In the early days of computers, people often wrote and released programs as shareware. Unlike commercial software that you have to buy before trying, shareware lets you take a test drive first. Some shareware programs were fully functional, while others had features crippled or omitted or incorporated a time delay that made the program stop working after a fixed length of time, such as 30 days. This was done intentionally to entice people to pay for the full version of the program.

If people didn't pay for the upgrade, the shareware programmer didn't make any money, which provided strong incentive for them to create useful programs that people would actually want to buy. However, as more people started connecting to the Internet, shareware programmers found another way to make money. They started selling space in their programs to display advertisements.

Dubbed *adware*, these types of programs simply displayed a stream of banner ads in a part of the application window. Users could still use the program as they normally would, and the ads would change continuously, as shown in Figure 20-1. Under this arrangement, shareware programmers always got paid by an advertiser, so they could lower their shareware fees or even eliminate them altogether.

Most people tolerated adware since the ads were mostly unobtrusive and helped lower shareware prices. Microsoft has even toyed with the idea of giving away free copies of various programs, such as Microsoft Works and even Windows itself, by selling advertising space. Microsoft estimates that the revenue it could generate this way could potentially exceed what it earns in software sales.

However, if you uninstall an adware-supported program, you'll no longer see the ads, and so advertisers eventually developed spyware, a malicious version of adware. Unlike adware, which may be annoying but tolerable, spyware is considered to be completely despicable.

Like adware, spyware also displays ads on a user's screen, but typically as pop-up windows. Unlike adware, spyware can't be removed simply by uninstalling the program. In fact, spyware often can't be removed without intricate knowledge of how the operating system works. Spyware will keep bombarding the average user with a constant barrage of pop-up ads or peeking at what the user's doing (and possibly stealing their passwords) and there's nothing he can do to stop it.

If advertising had a little more respect for the public, the public would have a lot more respect for advertising.

—JAMES RANDOLPH ADAMS, advertising pioneer

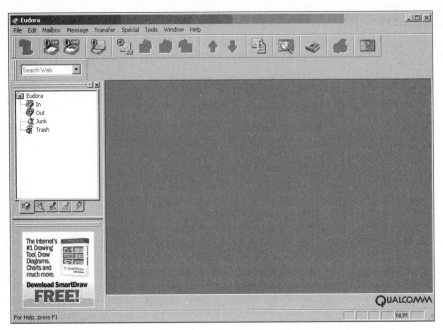

Figure 20-1: Eudora is advertiser-supported; it displays banner ads as you use the program.

NOTE: *Most spyware is designed to infect computers running Microsoft Windows. If you're running a different operating system, such as Mac OS X or Linux, most spyware can't infect your computer. (Until, of course, someone eventually writes a spyware program for your operating system.)*

WHAT SPYWARE CAN DO

Unlike computer viruses and worms, spyware doesn't intentionally try to damage your computer; that happens as a byproduct of its activities. When spyware first burrows into your computer, it often clumsily alters critical parts of the system in its attempt to hide itself. When spyware runs, it often grabs resources, such as memory, from other programs, causing them to run slowly, act erratically, or even crash. As a result, a spyware-infected computer can run sluggishly or fail to work at all—and this is even before the spyware program has done anything other than bury itself in your computer.

Once spyware has infected your computer, it waits until you connect to the Internet before taking further action. If you never connect to the Internet, the spyware won't function, but it can still hog memory and crash your computer through its mere presence.

Displaying pop-up ads

The most common function of spyware is to display pop-up ads. As soon as you connect to the Internet, the spyware program contacts a server, which feeds it a constant stream of pop-up ads.

By themselves, these ads are merely annoying. Since advertisers want to target their ads to the type of people most likely to buy their products, however, most spyware will also monitor or spy on the user's activities to determine which web pages he has visited. The spyware then displays mortgage advertisements if the user has visited home financing websites, or Viagra advertisements if the user has visited pornographic sites.

Some spyware can get trickier, popping up an ad for a company when you visit the website of one of its competitors. So, when you go to Dell Computer's site, a pop-up ad for Gateway Computers might appear. If you have multiple spyware programs infecting your computer, or one that's particularly aggressive, it's posible that you'll be so inundated with pop-ups that you may have trouble getting any work done.

Home page hijacking

To get advertisements in front of users another way, some spyware will hijack your browser's home page. Each time you launch the browser, the first thing you'll see will be the spyware website, which typically displays more banner ads. If you try to switch the setting of your browser's home page, the spyware program will prevent you from doing so.

Some sneaky spyware programs also monitor which websites you try to visit and then load an entirely different site instead, typically a competitor's site, but sometimes just random websites offering online gambling, mortgage refinancing, or Internet dating services. By replacing your home page or hijacking your browser completely, spyware can force you to look at ads whether you want to or not.

The craftiest spyware programs may let you visit any website you want, but the moment you go to a search engine, the spyware program hijacks the search engine results and displays its own list, which, naturally, consists of advertisers affiliated with the spyware manufacturer. Novice Internet users may not notice the difference and assume that the results they see were retrieved by the search engine, rather than being the work of a spyware program.

Spyware may also add to your browser long lists of bookmarked web pages that typically contain pornography. While most people will take the time to remove these unwanted bookmarks, a handful will always investigate the sites out of curiosity, especially since they may have innocent-sounding names. The moment you visit one of these planted bookmarks, you'll find yourself at a website which is likely to infect your computer with even more spyware.

Stealing information

Since spyware can track which websites you've visited, some go one step further and transfer this information back to the spyware company. Armed with information from thousands of different users, the company can then analyze browsing habits and identify patterns to help it craft more targeted advertising. None of this is different from what marketing research companies do, except that when spyware retrieves this information, it's often done without the user's knowledge.

More malicious spyware, created by criminals, may even record your keystrokes to steal passwords, bank account numbers, and Social Security numbers. Less malicious, but equally devious, spyware may scan your hard disk to determine which programs you have installed, which other companies might be interested in knowing for market research purposes.

This kind of spyware most likely won't annoy you with pop-up ads because its *raison d'être* is to steal sensitive information without your knowledge. The last thing it wants to do is alert you to its presence. But even if it's not bugging you with ads, it can still degrade the performance of your computer.

WHY COMPANIES ADVERTISE THROUGH SPYWARE

Spyware is so prevalent because it works. Throw enough advertisements in front of enough people and, statistically, a certain percentage will always buy something in response. So, it's in the advertiser's best interests to flood the market with as many advertisements as possible. (Advertising.com estimates that pop-up ads are up to ten times more effective than banner ads, partially due to the "annoyance" factor of having them obscure the user's screen.)

The five main spyware culprits are:

- Any company that wants to advertise online. These companies include pornography sites, Viagra resellers, Internet dating services, or even brand name companies like Motorola, Yahoo, Dell, Verizon, Citibank, Air France, Toshiba, American Express, Circuit City, Apple, and NetFlix.

- Internet advertising brokers. These middlemen place a company's banner and pop-up ads on popular websites via adware programs like Eudora and networks of spyware-infected computers.

- Spyware companies. These companies create the actual spyware programs that embed themselves in a computer and make themselves difficult to remove. Some infamous spyware companies and the software they distribute include 180solutions (Zango, n-Case), Direct Revenue (ABetterInternet and OfferOptimizer), Claria (ScreenScenes and eWallet), WhenU (SaveNow) and eXact Advertising (BargainBuddy, BullsEye).

- Software bundlers. These companies sell or distribute software, such as file-sharing programs or browser toolbars, and earn extra money by agreeing to include spyware with their own programs.

- Affiliates. These are website operators who agree to offer spyware-infested programs on their website. For example, the eXact Advertising spyware company runs Yubilee (www.yubilee.com), a spyware-infested site shown in Figure 20-2.

The big companies benefit from spyware because they get their advertisements distributed all over the Internet; the Internet advertising brokers get paid because they can distribute their clients' ads to as many people as possible; the spyware companies get paid by the Internet advertising brokers; the software bundlers get paid by the spyware companies; and any website operator who signs up as an affiliate with the spyware company gets paid every time someone installs the spyware on his computer.

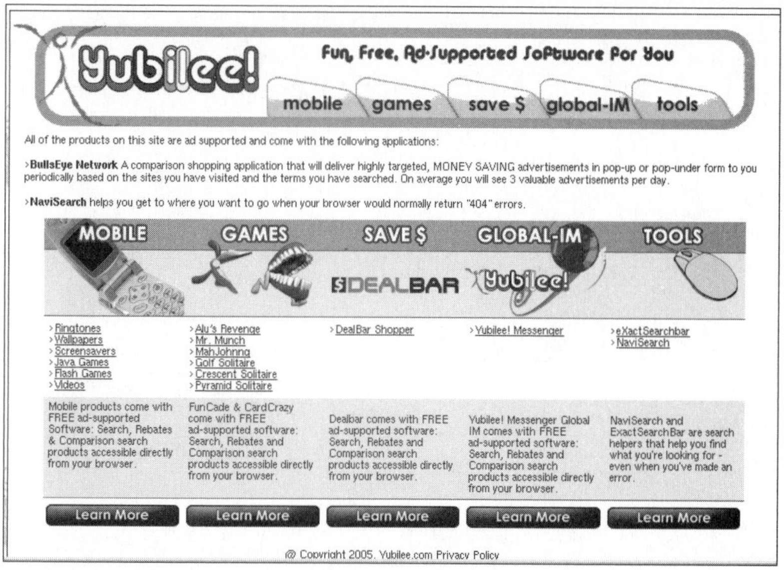

Figure 20-2: Spyware companies often run separate websites offering free software loaded with spyware.

Spyware not only works for the advertisers, but for everyone else making money along the way. Figure 20-3 shows a spyware company's website, promoting spyware programs to website operators as a way to make money (25 cents per install) and to companies that wish to advertise over the Internet.

Figure 20-3: Many "marketing" companies offer spyware programs for advertisers and website operators.

To learn more, visit the Affiliate Marketing Directory (http://affiliatemarketingworld .com/directory); read Revenue, a magazine focused exclusively on affiliate marketing (www.revenuetoday.com); browse through Klixxx Network (www.klixxx.com) to learn how the pornography industry uses affiliate marketing; read reviews of affiliate marketing software at Affiliate Software Comparison (www.affiliate-software-review.com); or read AVN Online (www.avnonline.com), shown in Figure 20-4, a magazine for helping adult entertainment websites market themselves over the Internet.

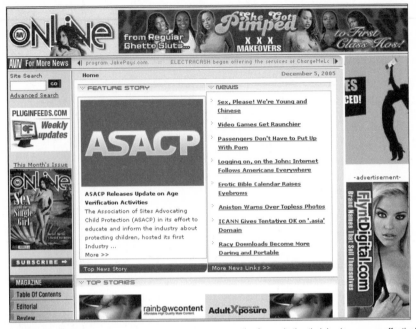

Figure 20-4: AVN Online offers pornography website operators tips for marketing their business more effectively through spyware and spam.

Spyware is especially popular with companies hawking erectile dysfunction pills, pornography, and online gambling. These companies may be perfectly legitimate, but they aren't likely to run banner ads on mainstream websites due to the sensitive nature of their products or services. As a result, spyware might be considered the best and only way for them to reach a mass online audience.

Not only is spyware a major nuisance for innocent computer users, but it can also cause more serious headaches for advertisers through something known as affiliate fraud. Affiliate fraud takes advantage of the way that many websites accept advertising. Large websites, such as CNN and Yahoo!, can demand money up front to place ads, but smaller websites don't have that clout. Instead, small websites often post the ads and receive a referral fee later if someone clicks on that ad and buys something from that merchant. Agreements that allow websites to display ads and get paid by advertisers are called affiliate networks.

To learn more about how affiliate marketing programs work, you can visit ClixGalore (www.clixgalore.com), Commission Junction (www.cj.com), LinkShare (www.linkshare.com), Performics (www.performics.com), or TradeDoubler (www.tradedoubler.com).

Figure 20-5 lists some of the different advertisers you can promote through your website along with how much each pays. (The ClixGalore website keeps the most recent list. You may recognize some of these advertisers as the same ones appearing in spyware pop-up ads.)

If a website joins an advertiser's affiliate program, the website owner can display ads and get paid every time someone clicks on that ad. Unfortunately, this only works if the website owner can attract enough visitors to his website in the first place.

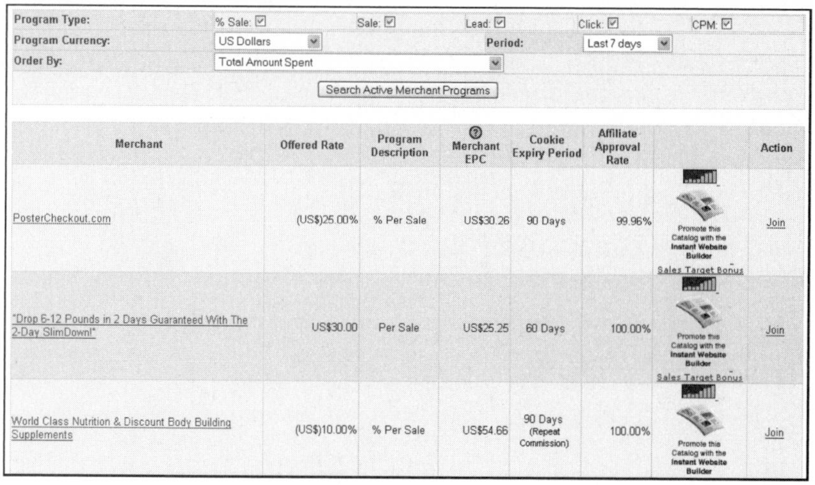

Figure 20-5: An affiliate marketing program lets you sign up to promote different advertisers.

Rather than take the time and energy to build an audience, some dishonest website owners chose a shortcut. They'll sign up as an affiliate with an advertising network and then create spyware to display advertisements. Once this spyware spreads, people will get bombarded with pop-up ads. If they click these pop-up ads, the credit (and cash) for each click goes to the affiliated website, without the user's ever having visited that affiliated website. If a company only advertises with banner and pop-up ads, there's a good chance that someone will write a program to display those ads through a spyware network without the company's knowledge.

Spyware companies can hurt legitimate affiliate websites too. Some spyware programs will wait until a visitor clicks on a banner ad before displaying a pop-up ad. When the user closes the pop-up, the spyware program tricks the merchant into thinking the visitor came from the spyware company's website (not the site with the banner ad). If the visitor buys anything, the merchant pays the commission to the spyware company instead of the honest website affiliate.

HOW SPYWARE INFECTS A COMPUTER

Like computer viruses and worms, nobody chooses to install spyware. Therefore, spyware must sneak onto a computer using tactics employed successfully by Trojan horses and viruses that either trick a user into installing it or that exploit a flaw allowing the spyware to pass undetected.

Installing infected files

The simplest way to infect a computer is to get an unsuspecting victim to download and install it. Since nobody will load spyware intentionally, spyware often hides itself within other programs such as filesharing programs (Kazaa), browser add-ins (Xupiter), games (Bonzi Buddy), or utilities (PCFriendly). When you install a spyware-infected program, you'll often see a license agreement that informs you (in fine print) that the program is advertiser-sponsored, as shown in Figure 20-6.

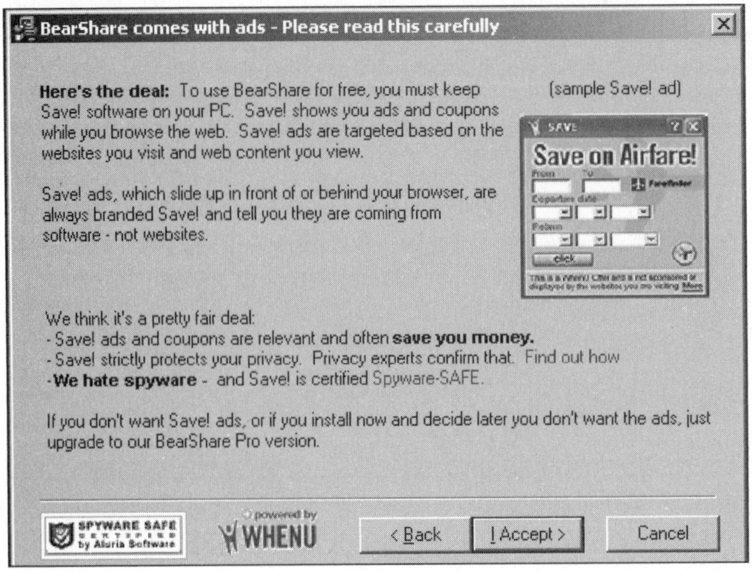

Figure 20-6: An installation program will typically warn you that it's going to install advertiser-sponsored programs (which could actually be spyware) on your computer.

The license agreement for installing the WhenU advertiser software even includes this disclaimer (which most people are likely to ignore):

> WhenU.com's Save! software shows you relevant coupon offers, contextual information and services as you surf the Web. Save! attempts to display offers at the moment when they are most relevant to you. Offers and information are displayed in the form of interstitials ("pop-up ads") and various other ad formats.

> The Save! software selects which ads and offers to display to individual users based on several factors, including: which Web pages you visit, search terms you use while searching online, content of the Web pages you view and your local zip code (if you have supplied it). Use of Save! is required to continue using these applications for free. As a result, Save! cannot be uninstalled from your computer's Control Panel independently. In order to completely remove Save! from your computer, you must uninstall all of the Save!-supported software from your computer. Once you do so, your Save! software will automatically be uninstalled as well.

By reading the above disclaimer, you learn that the WhenU software will display ads and monitor your Internet browsing activities. In some cases, viewing ads might seem like a fair trade-off to get useful software for free, but in many cases, the barrage of pop-up ads can be more troublesome than it's worth.

Examine license agreements like this one carefully. Some advertiser-supported programs are harmless, but many more are spyware. If you avoid any type of advertiser-supported program, you'll reduce the threat of being infected by spyware immensely.

Since End User License Agreements (EULAs) are often difficult to read and (purposely) confusing to understand, don't install any software until you run the text from its EULA through a free program called EULAlyzer (www.javacoolsoftware.com/eulalyzer .html), which analyzes EULAs for suspicious wording that could indicate the presence of spyware. By using EULAlyzer, you can catch spyware before it has a chance to install on your computer. Now you'll just have to worry about the spyware that doesn't display a EULA before trying to install itself.

Installing infected anti-spyware programs

While many people may not realize how or when spyware could have infected their computer, everyone can see the effects: disruptive pop-up ads, sluggish computer performance, and frequent computer crashes. Once people discover spyware on their computer, they usually want to remove it right away.

Unfortunately, spyware rarely comes with an uninstall program, so helpless victims often turn to anti-spyware programs to remove and clean their computers. Knowing this, many spyware programs now disguise themselves as anti-spyware programs. The moment you download and install one of these anti-spyware programs off the Internet, you actually install a (possibly bogus) anti-spyware program along with additional spyware. Moreover, the anti-spyware program won't detect and remove the spyware it installed on your computer, and frequently won't detect or remove any other spyware either. So, these anti-spyware programs might actually make your spyware problem even worse.

Check out the Rogue Anti-Spyware list on the SpyWareWarrior site (www .spywarewarrior.com/rogue_anti-spyware.htm). This list includes legitimate spyware programs that don't work very well and bogus anti-spyware programs that may actually come bundled with additional spyware. SpyWareWarrior also has a list of suspicious anti-spyware websites (www.spywarewarrior.com/rogue_anti-spyware.htm#sites).

One of the most infamous bogus anti-spyware programs is one called SpySheriff, also distributed under the names SpyDemolisher, SpyTrooper, or SpywareNo!. The domains www.spywareno.com and www.spytrooper.com both lead visitors to the www .spysheriff.com site. SpyDemolisher has its own website, www.spydemolisher.com, that looks similar to the others. The SpySheriff website (www.spysheriff.com) appears valid at first glance, as shown in Figure 20-7, but watch out for these telltale signs:

- No online ordering form. If this were a valid anti-spyware program from a reputable company, you'd find an online form for making a purchase. The SpySheriff website doesn't offer customers any way to buy it.

- No listed email addresses. Reputable companies offer email addresses for customers to contact for technical support or sales questions, and often an email address to reach a public relations representative. The SpySheriff site doesn't list a single email address.

- Mention of an affiliate program. The SpySheriff site offers an affiliate program link that claims you'll "earn huge money ensuring PC Protection." Affiliate programs are often the sign of an advertiser, or spyware, network.

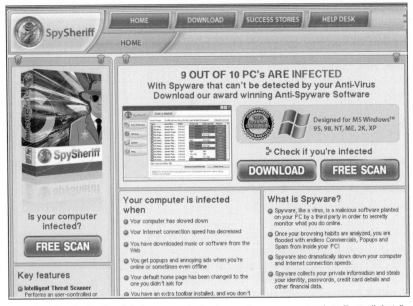

Figure 20-7: The SpySheriff website is an example of a phony anti-spyware program that will actually install more spyware on your computer.

- Misspellings and awkward grammar. Scan the SpySheriff site and you'll find such clumsy grammatical structures as, "I bought the SpySheriff because was just interested why it is so popular. But when it saved my bank account I blessed its invetors!"

- Misleading contact information. The SpySheriff website lists its company name and address as "SS Development, Tooley 73a, London EC1Y 1BL, United Kingdom" with no phone number. However, a WHOIS search, as shown in Figure 20-8, on the www.spysheriff.com domain name reveals that the real owner is a company in Greece (GR) called Popandopulos Ltd., run by someone named Alison Popandopulos, whose email address is crystaljones@list.ru, which is a Russian domain (RU).

Doing a WHOIS search on www.spytrooper.com reveals the same Alison Popandopulos in charge. A WHOIS search on www.spywareno.com reveals the owner to be the London SS Development company (listed as the publisher of the SpySheriff program), while a WHOIS search on www.spydemolisher.com reveals the owner to be:

Alexandre Ivanov spydemolisher@spydemolisher.com +3.298476322

Ikramet Ltd

Leninsky pr 95 12

Nigma, Nigeme, ECUADOR 198254

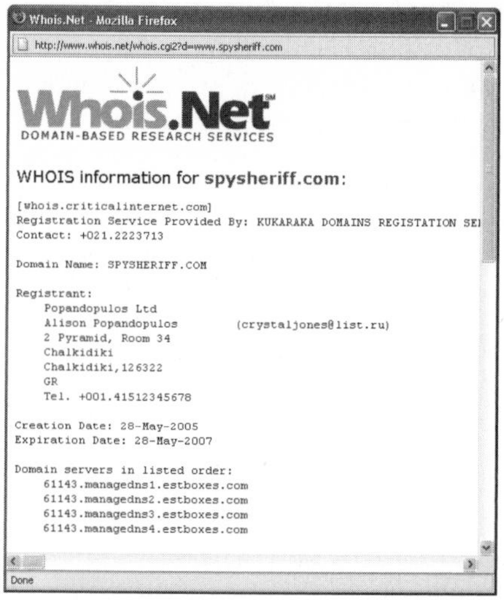

Figure 20-8: A WHOIS search on the www.spysheriff.com domain reveals the name of someone in Greece with a Russian email address.

Even though SpyDemolisher has its own website, both the SpySheriff and SpyDemolisher sites have the same testimonial quotes from satisfied customers with identical misspellings and poor grammar. The SpyDemolisher site even displays screenshots of the SpywareNo! program instead of SpyDemolisher.

For maximum safety, only buy anti-spyware programs sold in a store. If you're going to download an anti-spyware program off the Internet, make sure it's a name-brand program from a company that you trust. (Ad-Aware and Spybot are currently the two most popular anti-spyware programs that people download off the Internet.)

Drive-by downloads

Tricking people into installing spyware with another program might work, but an even more effective method is to install spyware on a user's computer without his or her knowledge or permission.

This tactic, known as *drive-by downloading*, occurs when a website lures an unsuspecting user to visit it, typically with pirated music, stolen software serial numbers, or pornography as the bait. As soon as the victim visits this website, it uses an ActiveX control to secretly install spyware.

ActiveX controls are small, self-contained programs that programmers originally used as building blocks to create their own programs in languages like Visual Basic. When the Internet grew in popularity, Microsoft developed ActiveX to be an easy shortcut for making web pages interactive. A web designer can have a page display games, stock market graphs, or animation without doing anything more complicated than adding an ActiveX control that somebody else has already written.

But ActiveX controls can do more than just display information. Many antivirus vendors, such as Trend Micro and McAfee, use ActiveX controls to scan your computer for viruses and other threats. Microsoft even uses ActiveX controls to determine which updates you might need for Windows or Microsoft Office.

Since ActiveX controls are really just miniature programs, they have the ability to copy files on to your computer. Legitimate ActiveX controls, such as online virus scanners, will ask for your permission before copying anything, but malicious ones may trick you by displaying a dialog box that asks if you'd like a free gift or software. Clicking the Yes button gives the website permission to run the ActiveX control to download spyware.

Sometimes an ActiveX control won't even bother asking for your permission. If you use Internet Explorer to visit a web page with a malicious ActiveX control embedded in it, the ActiveX control will just go ahead and load the spyware without any further ado. (Other browsers, such as Firefox or Opera, protect you from drive-by downloading of spyware by not running ActiveX controls.)

Once the spyware programs are installed, you'll suddenly start seeing pop-up ads and you may have no idea where the spyware even came from.

Spyware-infected spyware

What makes computer viruses particularly dangerous is their ability to replicate themselves. Fortunately, spyware can't copy itself (yet), but once it infects a computer, it's vulnerable to removal by an anti-spyware program. So the latest spyware tactic is to use spyware to constantly download more spyware from the Internet, in addition to retrieving pop-up advertisements. Such spyware-infested spyware programs keep adding more and more junk to your computer until either you remove it (good luck) or your computer crashes under its collective weight.

WHERE SPYWARE HIDES

Well-behaved Windows application programs install themselves in a separate folder and store program setting information in a special system database known as the Windows registry. A well-behaved program runs only when the user loads it and stops when the user exits the program. To remove a well-behaved program, a user needs only to run the uninstall program that deletes the program folder and also deletes the information stored in the Windows registry.

Theoretically, that's how installing and uninstalling a program should work, but even well-behaved progams can leave files scattered around a hard disk, or chunks of information abandoned in the Windows registry, consuming disk space and making the registry larger and more cumbersome for your computer to use (which slows down its performance).

When spyware programs install themselves, they also bury information in the Windows registry and copy files onto the hard disk, but instead of doing this out in the open, spyware creates hidden files and folders. To view hidden files and folders in Windows Explorer, follow these steps:

1. Open the Windows Explorer program.
2. Choose Tools ▶ Folder options. A Folders Options dialog box appears.
3. Click the View tab and click the Show Hidden Files And Folders radio button, as shown in Figure 20-9.

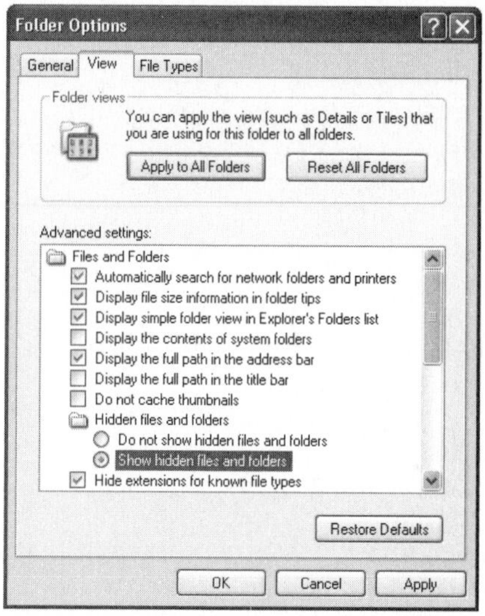

Figure 20-9: The Windows Explorer program can show you all the hidden files and folders buried on your computer.

Spyware is only effective if it's running, so spyware programs manipulate the Windows registry in order to launch themselves every time you turn on your computer. Spyware may take extra steps to hide itself in memory so that the Windows Task Manager program won't detect its presence.

After burying itself in the Windows registry, spyware scatters its hidden files and folders in multiple places on your hard disk to make itself nearly impossible to find and remove. Some may also hide a dropper program, a tiny program meant to slip past a computer's defenses and hide on the hard disk. The moment the dropper program detects that you've removed the spyware program, it accesses the Internet again and puts all the spyware right back on your computer.

ELIMINATING SPYWARE

Spam and spyware have one thing in common: neither will go away as long as people can make money off it. Since spyware only runs on Windows computers, the safest way to protect yourself is to avoid browsing the Internet using Windows or Internet Explorer. (Until spyware companies start targeting Linux and Mac OS X computers, using either of those operating systems is a safer alternative.)

Avoiding Windows isn't an option for many people, but you can use the following countermeasures to protect your computer running under Windows:

- Raise the security level of Internet Explorer

- Stop using Internet Explorer and switch to a safer browser

- Install a firewall

- Monitor your start programs

- Use a minimum of two anti-spyware programs

Securing Internet Explorer

Internet Explorer's biggest flaw is its ability to run ActiveX programs. To protect yourself from malicious ActiveX controls, you need to change the default settings that define how Internet Explorer reacts when faced with an ActiveX control on a web page.

To modify Internet Explorer's ActiveX settings, follow these steps:

1. Choose Tools ▸ Internet Options. An Internet Options dialog box appears.

2. Click the Security tab.

3. Click the Internet icon (a globe) and click the Custom Level button. The Security Settings dialog box appears, as shown in Figure 20-10.

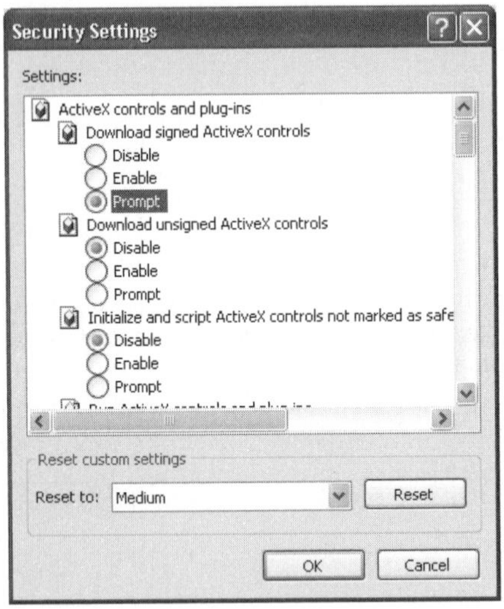

Figure 20-10: The Security Settings dialog box lets you make Internet Explorer harder for spyware to exploit.

4. Under the Download Signed Activex Controls heading, click the Prompt radio button.

5. Under the Download Unsigned Activex Controls heading, click the Disable radio button.

6. Under the Initialize And Script Activex Controls Not Marked As Safe heading, click the Disable radio button.

7. Under the Run Activex Controls And Plug-ins heading, click the Prompt radio button.

8. Under the Script Activex Controls Marked Safe For Scripting heading, click the Prompt radio button.

9. Click OK. A dialog box may appear, asking if you're sure you want to change your security settings.

10. Click Yes. The Security Settings dialog box appears again.

11. Click OK.

Switching to a safer browser

By switching to a different browser, you can eliminate the threat of drive-by spyware downloads from ActiveX controls. The two most popular Internet Explorer alternatives are Firefox (www.mozilla.com/firefox) and Opera (www.opera.com). Firefox and Opera are free and will resist drive-by download attacks that exploit ActiveX or Internet Explorer flaws. However, neither of these browsers can protect you if you deliberately download and install spyware-infested programs.

For an even safer browser alternative, download the free VMWare Player (www.vmware.com/products/player) along with a free file called the Browser Appliance. The VMWare Player creates a virtual computer in your computer's memory, and the Browser Appliance runs a modified version of Ubuntu Linux running the Firefox browser. By using Firefox within Ubuntu Linux (within the VMWare Player), you effectively isolate any Internet dangers that could infect your computer and the Windows operating system on it. Not only can't spyware affect Ubuntu Linux, but any damage it could possibly do remains cloistered within the memory confines of the VMWare Player.

Installing a firewall

A firewall can block both inbound and outbound connections to the Internet. Blocking inbound connections can stop spyware from trying to sneak on to your computer. Blocking outbound connections can stop any existing spyware from connecting to the Internet and retrieving more ads or spyware, or sending your personal information to another computer. Some popular (and free) firewalls include ZoneAlarm (www.zonelabs.com) and Jetico Personal Firewall (www.jetico.com). Some popular commercial firewalls include Look 'n' Stop (www.looknstop.com) and Norton Personal Firewall (www.symantec.com).

Monitoring your startup programs

One way to detect the presence of spyware is to monitor which programs your computer launches automatically when you boot up. Programs such as System Mechanic (www.iolo.com), Process Guard (www.diamondcs.com.au), MalWhere (www.malwhere.com), and Advanced Startup Manager (www.rayslab.com) display a list of startup programs, which you can use to study and then disable or delete any suspicious programs.

NOTE: Spyware deliberately disguises itself under cryptic names, so unless you know what to look for, it's possible that you could accidentally disable or remove a legitimate program by mistake.

Running anti-spyware programs

Spyware companies are always modifying their programs to slip past the defenses of anti-spyware programs and avoid detection and removal, so you can never rely on a single anti-spyware program to protect your computer completely.

Just as with viruses and antivirus software, one piece of spyware may slip past a handful of anti-spyware programs, but it won't get by all of them. For that reason, it's best to run at least two anti-spyware programs. The good news is that there are plenty of free anti-spyware programs to choose from, such as Spybot (www.safer-networking .org), Ad-Aware (www.lavasoftusa.com), Bazooka (www.kephyr.com), SpywareBlaster (www.javacoolsoftware.com), or Microsoft Windows AntiSpyware (www.microsoft.com). Although there currently isn't any spyware infecting the Mac OS X operating system, you may want to protect yourself with MacScan (http://macscan.securemac.com) anyway.

You should also consider buying a commercial anti-spyware program. Commercial anti-spyware programs usually offer more features for preventing spyware infection and give you added assurance that your computer is spyware-free. Some popular commercial anti-spyware programs include Spy Sweeper (www.webroot.com), PestPatrol (www .pestpatrol.com), and McAfee AntiSpyware (www.mcafee.com).

For additional help detecting and removing spyware, use the Trend Micro Anti-Spyware (www.trendmicro.com/spyware-scan) or Panda ActiveScan (www .pandasoftware.com/products/activescan.htm) online scanners. Both of these run an ActiveX control and require that you use Internet Explorer, but both Trend Micro and Panda Software are well-known companies that you can trust.

Then again, maybe not. Some spyware companies are now cutting deals with anti-spyware companies. For example, Aluria Software (www.aluriasoftware.com), the makers of Aluria Anti-Spyware, made an agreement with the adware/spyware company WhenU, whereby Aluria agreed not to classify any of WhenU's programs as spyware. WhenU later sealed similar agreements with the makers of PestPatrol and Ad-Aware.

When Microsoft was rumored to be interested in purchasing the spyware company Claria (formerly known as Gator), the Microsoft Windows AntiSpyware tool still detected Claria's spyware programs but no longer recommended that users remove them. With spyware companies jumping in bed with anti-spyware companies, there's a good chance that your computer could be infected with spyware and your anti-spyware programs won't find it, not because of technical reasons, but because of business reasons, and you'll be the one left to suffer.

PART 6

PROTECTING YOUR COMPUTER AND YOURSELF

21

COMPUTING ON A SHOESTRING: GETTING STUFF FOR (ALMOST) FREE

The Internet may be changing the way people shop, learn, and communicate, but for those who don't have a computer, it might as well be science fiction. With a little research and creativity, however, even the most cash-strapped would-be Internet surfer can get a computer and load it with software for nothing, or next to nothing.

> I always say shopping is cheaper than a psychiatrist.
>
> —TAMMY FAYE BAKKER, televangelist

INTERNET COMPARISON SHOPPING

Whether you want a new camera, computer, printer, scanner, or whatever, you should never pay full retail price for any high-tech or electronics product you find online. Before buying, shop around.

In the old days, shopping around meant driving countless hours to different stores to compare prices. Nowadays, by visiting the right shopping search engines, you can comparison shop among retailers all over the country without doing anything more exhausting than typing on a keyboard.

Shopping search engines, as shown in Figure 21-1, help you find the best price for a particular item and often include reviews of the product itself, evaluations of the retailer's customer service, and a list of similar products you might want to consider instead. A low price might seem attractive, but if it's coming from a retailer with a poor record for shipping products on time or responding to complaints of defective merchandise, you might want to take your business to a more confidence-inspiring merchant and pay a slightly higher price.

Some popular shopping search engines include Froogle (www.froogle.com), Kelkoo (www.kelkoo.co.uk), MSN Shopping (http://shopping.msn.com), and Yahoo Shopping (http://shopping.yahoo.com).

These shopping search engines compare prices for different products, but the order in which they list the retailers that match a query can be critical. The first five retailers listed in search results often get the most business, regardless of price. Knowing this, many retailers pay an additional fee to get listed at the top of the search results in the hopes of increasing potential sales. As an alternative, consider using PriceScan (www.pricescan.com), which refuses to accept fees to increase a retailer's standing on its list of results.

Apple iPod 5G (30GB, video)

📄 Add to my list   🖶 Printer-friendly version

Manufacturer: Apple
Part number: MA002LL/A
Specs: 4.8 oz, 4.8 oz, White, White, None, 1 year warranty, 1
year warranty, Digital player, Stereo, Stereo, LCD, LCD,
AAC, MP3, WAV, AIFF, Audible, Apple Lossless, 30 GB,
Lithium ion Rechargeable Player batteryIntegrated.
Apple iPod 5G (30GB, video) Specs

See more images

Sort listings by ☑ Go   Tax and shipping for 92104   Update Zip Code   Stores: 1-11

Store	mySimon Certified	Price	Tax	Shipping	Total price	State	Avail.	
circuit city Store Profile	★★★★★ Write a store review	$299.99 24/24 Pickup Guarantee	$23.25	See Site	See site	VA	Yes as of 12/15/2005	Buy it at › Circuit City or call 1-800...
eCOST Your Online Discount SuperStore Store Profile	★★★★★ Write a store review	$294.00	$22.79	Free	$316.79	CA	No as of 12/15/2005	Buy it at › eCOST.com or call 1-877...
BEST BUY Store Profile	★★★★★ Write a store review	$299.99	$23.25	$5.99	$329.23	MN	Yes as of 12/15/2005	Buy it at › Best Buy
Crutchfield Store Profile	★★★★★ Write a store review	$299.99 Money-back Guarantee!	$0.00	Free	$299.99	VA	Pre-Order as of 12/15/2005	Buy it at › Crutchfield or call 1-888...
Datavision Computer Video Store Profile	★★★★★ Write a store review	$294.00	$0.00	$11.83	$305.83	NY	Yes as of 12/15/2005	Buy it at › Datavision Computer Video or call 1-888...

Figure 21-1: A shopping search engine, such as mySimon, can compare prices from different retailers and even calculate the total cost of an order, including sales tax and shipping.

To save even more money, visit Woot! (www.woot.com) or Specialoffers.com (www.specialoffers.com), which has updated information on the latest discounts and promotions currently being offered by various merchants.

When buying anything online, try to find other people's comments about the seller. Sites like Amazon.com let buyers rate different merchants for speed, reliability, and dependability. If a merchant offers a low price but has a spotty record with other buyers, you may want to avoid that merchant and pay more from a more reliable merchant instead.

BUYING A REFURBISHED COMPUTER

Any of the shopping search engines listed in the Internet Comparison Shopping section will help you find the best prices for new computer equipment, but to save even more, consider buying a refurbished computer instead.

Refurbished computers are machines that someone returned either because of a defect or because they didn't want it any longer even though it may have been working perfectly well. Once a manufacturer receives a returned computer, it's torn apart, the components are tested, and then it's reassembled to be just like new. There's just one problem. Legally, manufacturers can't sell a returned computer as new.

Since the manufacturer has already lost money accepting a returned computer for resale, they'll reduce the price significantly just to get rid of it. If the computer were to fail a second time and force another customer to return it, the manufacturer would lose still more money fixing it again, so refurbished computers are often examined even more carefully than new ones are.

If you don't mind getting a computer that someone else may have used already, a refurbished computer can be a great way to get a top-of-the-line machine without paying top-of-the-line prices. Refurbished computers come with the same technical support and warranty as their identical brand-new models, but with one major drawback. When you buy a refurbished computer, you can only buy what the manufacturer has in stock that day. If you want to customize your computer, you'll probably have to splurge on something new or be prepared to buy the accessories you want and install them yourself.

You won't find refurbished computers for sale at your favorite store, however. Most computer manufacturers only sell them on retail sites such as Amazon.com (www .amazon.com), Dell Computers (www.dell.com/factoryoutlet), Gateway (www.gateway .com), Overstock.com (www.overstock.com), PC Factory Outlet (www.pcfactoryoutlet .com), PC Nomad (www.pcnomad.com) and SonyStyle (www.sonystyle.com).

NOTE: *Some people may use a computer and then return it later, which means a refurbished computer might still have someone else's data on the hard disk that you can undelete and peek at. See Chapter 22 for more information about recovering deleted data.*

SAVE ON PRINTER SUPPLIES

Almost everyone needs a printer, but watch out. Many printer manufacturers seduce you with low prices on their inkjet models only to gouge you on replacement ink cartridges. The cost of two or three ink cartridges can be as much as the original price of the printer itself, and inkjet printers tend to suck up ink rapidly.

A program dubbed Ink Saver (www.inksaver.com), shown in Figure 21-2, claims to reduce the amount of ink your printer uses without any noticeable difference in print quality. Ink Saver is compatible with most Epson, Canon, and Hewlett-Packard printers, but you can download a trial version to see if it works with your particular inkjet printer.

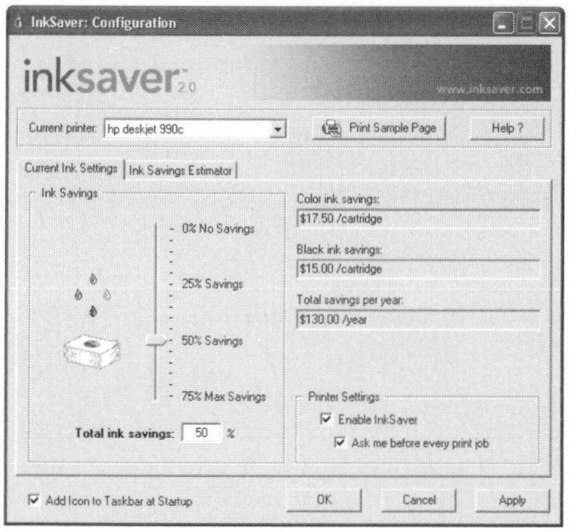

Figure 21-2: InkSaver keeps track of how much ink you're saving every time you adjust the flow.

No matter how much ink a program like Ink Saver can help you conserve, you'll eventually need to buy replacement inkjet cartridges. Instead of getting them from the printer manufacturer, buy refill kits or alternate inkjet cartridges from Amazon Imaging (www.amazonimaging.com) or RhinoTek (www.buyrhinotek.com). To find more online retailers that sell replacement inkjet, visit Buy Ink Cartridges.com (www.buyinkcartridges .com). These third-party inkjet companies sell refill kits and replacement cartridges for most printers at up to half of what the original manufacturers would charge for the exact same thing.

If you're shopping for an inkjet printer, compare the prices of replacement cartridges first. The printer that looks so appealing today might wind up costing you several hundred dollars in the future for replacement inkjet cartridges alone. Look for the cheapest cartridges and then find the printers that work with them.

To foil the companies that offer cheap replacement cartridges, printer manufacturers have come up with several tactics to force consumers to buy inkjet cartridges only from them. Hewlett-Packard puts computer chips in inkjet cartridges to prevent them from being refilled. The moment a cartridge runs out of ink, the chip prevents it from ever being used again, no matter how much you refill it with replacement ink, although you can buy new chips from SmartChipSolutions (www.smartchipsolutions.com) to trick your printer into accepting a third-party replacement ink cartridge. However, Lexmark and Hewlett-Packard have also even patented the print heads on certain inkjet cartridges, thereby preventing anyone from making a compatible replacement cartridge. If you can't find a replacement inkjet cartridge for your printer from a third party, now you know why.

If you have a laser printer, don't throw away your old toner cartridges. Check your local Yellow Pages under computer supplies and look for stores (or contact Amazon Imaging) that refill or sell used cartridges for your particular model.

FREE (AND ALMOST-FREE) SOFTWARE

The two main types of software available are commercial and open source. Commercial software costs money, although in the case of shareware or adware-sponsored programs, that cost may be minimal. Open-source software is free. You can copy open-source programs as many times as you wish and even modify them, if you know what you're doing. In many cases, open-source programs rival the features of their commercial counterparts, but don't overlook commercial programs completely. There are ways of getting commercial software much cheaper than you might think.

Getting commercial software cheaply (and legally)

It's easy to pirate software (see Chapter 6), but it's not a practical (or legal) option for most people. Before you buy anything, try one of the following methods to get that same program for free or at a lower cost.

Bundled software

Many hardware manufacturers bundle "free" software with their products to entice customers. Most computers come with a preloaded operating system (such as Windows XP) but many companies include additional software too. For example, Sony computers often include digital video software, while other computer manufacturers offer WordPerfect or Microsoft Works with their systems.

Similarly, scanner companies typically bundle graphics editing programs or optical character recognition software, external hard disk manufacturers offer free backup software, and rewritable CD/DVD drives often include disk-burning programs. Bundled software is often a scaled-down or older version of a current application program, but if it's got the features you need, a bundling deal could convince you to buy one manufacturer's equipment over another.

Buying obsolete software, upgrades, and OEM versions

Bundled software can be valuable because it gives you the legal right to purchase an upgrade, which means that, for a minimal cost, you can buy the full version of a program without paying the full cost of a new version. If you don't have any older software bundled with your computer equipment, you can often buy it at deeply discounted prices through online retailers such as Oldsoftware.com (www.oldsoftware.com), Software & Stuff (www.softwareandstuff.com), DirectDeals (www.directdeals.com), and Software Outlet (www.softwareoutlet.com).

Older software can work perfectly well while saving you up to 90 percent off the retail cost of the latest version. If you still want the newest version, buy an older one and then pay for the upgrade. The total cost for the older version, plus the upgrade, will almost always be less than you would've paid to get the full version right off the bat.

Another way to get the latest version of a program is to buy the original equipment manufacturer (OEM) version. Many software publishers bundle their latest programs with a variety of hardware, but you can find online retailers selling these OEM versions separately. An OEM program is identical to the retail package but without the fancy box and sometimes without the (nearly useless) printed manual. Figure 21-3 shows the price savings you can enjoy on OEM versions of some popular programs.

Figure 21-3: OEM programs are the same as the full retail versions but without the fancy packaging.

Buying software at academic discounts

School bookstores usually sell academic versions of nearly all major software at a substantial discount because software publishers want to get students hooked on using their products instead of a competitor's. So a program that normally costs $495 might be sold at a university bookstore for $100.

Of course, the catch is that you must have a valid student ID to take advantage of offers from a university bookstore. If you know someone currently in college, ask him to buy the software for you (and in exchange, you can buy him beer). As another alternative, just sign up for one class, get your student ID, and use your student ID to buy all the software you want at academic discounts.

Shareware and freeware

Shareware programs let you freely copy and use a program for a trial period, usually 30 days, after which it may stop working unless you pay up. Surprisingly, shareware programs are often just as good (or even better) than their higher-priced, brand-name counterparts, and no matter what type of a program you need (virus scanner, word processor, paint program, and so on), you can almost always find a good shareware version.

Freeware programs are given away—you can legally use and own them without ever paying. Some freeware is software that has been abandoned by its manufacturer or is a scaled-down version of a program that's intended to help market the commercial version. The idea is that if you like the freeware version, you might want to upgrade to the commercial version later to get more features. To find great collections of freeware and shareware, visit Simtel (www.simtel.net), Shareware.com (www.shareware.com), Tucows (www.tucows.com), SnapFiles (www.snapfiles.com), ZDNet Downloads (http://downloads-zdnet.com.com), SoftwareArchives (www.softwarearchives.com), or Jumbo (www.jumbo.com).

Name-brand alternatives

Commercial software often has the backing of a big company that can afford to support and upgrade its products on a regular basis. For that reason, many customers, especially businesses, prefer the security of having someone they can call for help (or someone they can blame).

When evaluating commercial software, it's often cheaper to avoid the most popular programs and use a lesser-known but equally competent rival program instead. For example, the retail price for the standard edition of Microsoft Office is $399, but consider any of the following less expensive alternatives: WordPerfect Suite ($299)—www.corel.com, StarOffice ($69.95)—www.sun.com, or ThinkFree Office ($49.95)—www.thinkfree.com.

Or how about this. The full retail price for Photoshop is $649, but look at these less expensive alternatives: Photoshop Elements ($99.95)—www.adobe.com—or Corel Paint Shop Pro ($129)—www.corel.com.

Lower-cost name-brand alternatives may not offer all the features of a more established program, but they do offer almost perfect compatibility with those expensive programs' file formats. If you don't absolutely need Microsoft Word, for example, why waste your money paying for it?

Finding an open-source program

Open-source programs are not only free to use and copy; they're also free to modify however you wish. Perhaps the best-known open-source program is the Linux operating system, which rivals the features of Microsoft Windows but with better reliability and security. Since anyone can modify an open-source program, many companies offer slightly different versions of Linux, known as Linux *distributions*. You can either buy a Linux distribution or download a copy for free off the Internet. Some popular Linux distributions include Red Hat Software (www.redhat.com), Mandriva Linux (wwwnew.mandriva.com/en/community), Debian (www.debian.org), Ubuntu Linux (www.ubuntulinux.org), and SUSE Linux (www.opensuse.org). There are literally hundreds of different Linux distributions available, in addition to the handful listed above, so if you want to explore more options, visit DistroWatch (http://distrowatch.com).

If you don't have the time or patience to download a copy of Linux, and you don't want to buy the full-price, boxed retail version from a store, you can order Linux CDs from Cheapbytes.com (www.cheapbytes.com). Cheapbytes just sells the discs, without the fancy retail box or any manuals, but you'll save up to 90 percent off retail while still getting the latest Linux distribution.

For true computer renegades, skip both Microsoft Windows and Linux and go for a pure Unix environment in the form of FreeBSD (www.freebsd.org) or OpenBSD (www.openbsd.org). Linux, FreeBSD, and OpenBSD are more suitable for people unafraid of digging into the guts of their operating system and typing cryptic commands. If this doesn't describe you, you may want to stick with friendlier operating systems, like Windows or Mac OS X.

Besides Linux, another popular open-source program is the OpenOffice.org office suite (www.openoffice.org). OpenOffice.org essentially duplicates the applications and features of the Microsoft Office suite, but it's absolutely free to copy, give away, and use. (OpenOffice.org is actually the free version of StarOffice, so using OpenOffice.org is like using a commercial program but without the cost.)

Two popular open-source programs that rival Photoshop include GIMP (GNU Image Manipulation Program)—www.gimp.org—and Paint.NET (www.eecs.wsu.edu/paint.net), which is shown in Figure 21-4.

To find more open-source programs, visit SourceForge (http://sourceforge.net). Not only can you download additional open-source programs, but you can also contribute to existing open-source projects or launch your own open-source program.

FREE INTERNET ACCESS

Network television is free because advertisers cover the costs of producing the shows in return for the opportunity to market their products to a vast audience. Similarly, many Internet providers now offer free accounts if you'll agree to allow them to place advertisements on your computer screen or to track your online usage for marketing purposes. Many of these services have limitations or restrictions that change over time, so read their descriptions carefully.

For example, two popular Internet service providers, Juno (http://www.juno.com) and NetZero (http://www.netzero.net), both restrict customers' free usage to a maximum of ten hours per month. To find the latest free Internet service providers, visit the Internet 4 Free website (www.internet4free.net).

If you don't have your own computer or Internet connection, most public libraries have computers connected to the Internet. You probably won't have to pay for online access, but there could be a time limit for using the terminal and a fee if you need to print anything.

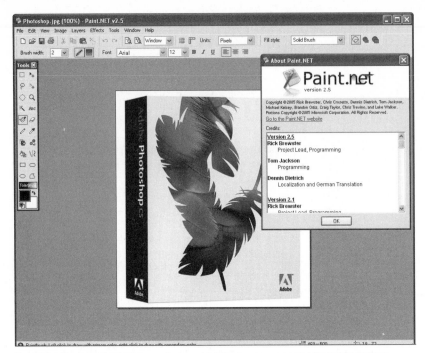

Figure 21-4: The free Paint.NET program looks and acts like the more expensive Photoshop program.

FREE EMAIL ACCOUNTS

Free email accounts are perfect if you need to send messages that you don't want traced back to you personally. They're also handy for creating temporary email addresses that you can use when registering at different websites, knowing that this registration will inevitably attract spam, thus keeping your personal or work email account spam-free.

Many free email accounts offer special features including encryption (to protect your email from prying eyes), a self-destruct capability (to wipe out your email after a specified period of time), support for multiple languages, and anonymity (to hide your true identity from the rest of the world). Some popular free email account providers include Hotmail (www.hotmail.com), Yahoo! Mail (http://mail.yahoo.com), anonMail (www.anonmail.de), Hushmail (www.hushmail.com), and myTrashMail (www.mytrashmail.com).

FREE WEB AND BLOG SPACE

Many online services and Internet providers give you several megabytes of storage space so that you can start your own website. Unfortunately, the amount of space available may be too small for you to get as creative as you want, or the Internet provider may censor the information you post. For example, America Online tends to frown on anyone using its service to post anti–America Online comments.

If the rules or storage space of your current Internet provider aren't satisfactory, try one of the many companies that offer free websites. These companies usually don't care what type of information you post—all they really care about is attracting people to their own website so they can sell ads. Some popular free web hosting services include Geocities (http://geocities.yahoo.com), Tripod (www.tripod.lycos.com), AngelFire (www.angelfire.lycos.com), and Zero Catch (www.0catch.com).

If you want to experiment for free with blogging, try Blogthing (www.blogthing.com), Blogfuse (www.blogfuse.com), or Blogger (www.blogger.com), as shown in Figure 21-5.

Figure 21-5: With free web and blog space available, anyone can publish her thoughts for the rest of the world.

THE BEST THINGS IN LIFE ARE FREE

For more free stuff, visit The Free Site (www.thefreesite.com), the Free Stuff Center (www.freestuffcenter.com), or Totally Free Stuff (www.totallyfreestuff.com) and get everything from free ring tones to free postcards, and even free condoms, to go along with the free software, free printer supplies, and free email accounts that you want.

Although the cost of computers can widen the gap between the haves and the have-nots, it doesn't have to be this way. With a little creativity and a lot of persistence, anyone can access the Internet. And who knows? With access to the Internet, you might one day help change political policy, meet new friends, or just broaden your mind by exploring the whole world from the comfort of your home—all without going bankrupt buying lots of expensive computer equipment, software, and services that you don't really need.

22

COMPUTER FORENSICS: THE ART OF DELETING AND RETRIEVING DATA

Like most criminals, hackers often bring about their own downfall by failing to remove all traces of their crime. Not only do many hackers leave incriminating notes and printouts of their latest exploits scattered around, but they also can't resist bragging about their exploits in public chat rooms. Yet even this blatant indiscretion wouldn't be so damaging if these same hackers didn't unwittingly leave incriminating evidence stored all over their own computers too.

> I believe that people would be alive today if there were a death penalty.
>
> —NANCY REAGAN

RECOVERING DELETED DATA

The biggest difference between electronic data and traditional data is that once you store electronic data on any form of magnetic media, it can stay there much longer than you expect. To understand how it's possible to recover a file that's been deleted, you need to understand how computers store and organize files on a disk.

When a computer stores information on a disk, it can't just toss it anywhere, because that would make it difficult to find it again—it would be like throwing your socks on your bedroom floor and then wondering why you can never find a matching pair when you need one. To help organize data, computers divide disks into multiple *tracks*, which you can think of as circular storage bins on the surface of a disk.

Each track is divided into smaller parts called *sectors*. A group of sectors is called a *cluster*. When you save data to your disk, your computer stores your file in multiple sectors. When you add or delete data from a file, the total number of sectors used to store your file grows or shrinks accordingly. Basically, a sector is a tiny box that contains part of a single file.

Ideally, your computer tries to store files as one continuous track, which allows it to retrieve data quickly. However, the more you save, edit, and delete files, the more likely it is that the computer will have to store one part of a file in one sector and another part of that same file in another sector, on a completely different part of the disk. When you defragment your hard disk, you're essentially rearranging all your files so the data from each file gets stored in adjacent sectors once more.

To keep track of which sectors contain which files, every disk contains a special directory, sometimes called a File Allocation Table (FAT) or a Master File

Table (MFT). The FAT or MFT (or whatever name your particular computer uses) lists all the files stored on the disk along with pointers that identify the exact tracks and sectors that contain each file.

When you delete a file, your computer takes a shortcut. Instead of physically destroying the data, the computer simply erases its existence from the disk's directory, which pretends that the file no longer exists, although the contents of the file are still intact. Only when the computer needs the space taken up by the deleted file will it actually overwrite the old information with new data. This is like taking your name off your apartment building's directory when you move out, but leaving your unwanted belongings behind in your old apartment. Only when someone else moves in do the old contents of the apartment get thrown out.

If your disk has plenty of extra space available, you could go weeks, months, or even years before the data in those deleted sectors is overwritten. (You can accomplish almost the same thing as overwriting the data, however, by defragmenting your hard drive regularly.)

You can usually retrieve a trashed file by running an undelete utility program right away. An undelete utility simply changes the disk directory to identify any "deleted" files, so that the computer will recognize the files again. Of course, the longer you wait to run the utility, the more likely your computer will have overwritten some, or possibly all, of a particular deleted file's contents with new data, making it difficult, if not impossible, to recover the original contents.

Some utility programs, such as the Norton Utilities, come with a file-deletion protection feature that saves any deleted files in a special folder so that you can quickly and accurately recover them any time in the future. Obviously, this feature can be a lifesaver if you accidentally delete something important, but it can also work against you by preserving sensitive files you thought you got rid of months ago.

To find an undelete program, try Norton Utilities (www.symantec.com), Active@DELETE (www.active-undelete.com), Restorer 2000 (www.bitmart.net), or Undelete (www.execsoft.com). Executive Software, the maker of Undelete, also offers a free Deleted File Analysis Utility (see Figure 22-1), which examines your hard disk to see how many deleted files may still be recoverable. The results may surprise you.

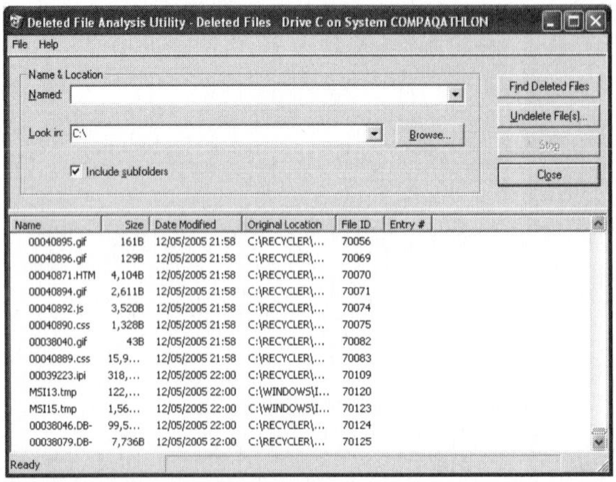

Figure 22-1: The Deleted File Analysis Utility from Executive Software can reveal all the files you deleted in the past that someone may still be able to recover and read.

FILE SHREDDERS

If you delete a file, wait a day or two, and then try to run an undelete program, there's a good chance that the operating system will have overwritten all or part of that file's contents.

If you want to intentionally overwrite old data belonging to deleted files, you can use a special file-shredding program. File shredders overwrite the storage formerly used by deleted files with random characters, one or more times. As a result, even if an undelete program manages to recover the old disk directory entry pointing to a previously deleted file, it will only find random data stored there.

Not all file shredders are equal, however. For example, to defeat an ordinary undelete program and get the job done more quickly, a file shredder may make just one pass at filling your deleted file's old data area with random data. While this quick wipeout defeats most undelete programs, it will not defeat specialized computer forensics tools. A really good file shredder offers several ways to shred your files that balance speed and security, as shown in Figure 22-2.

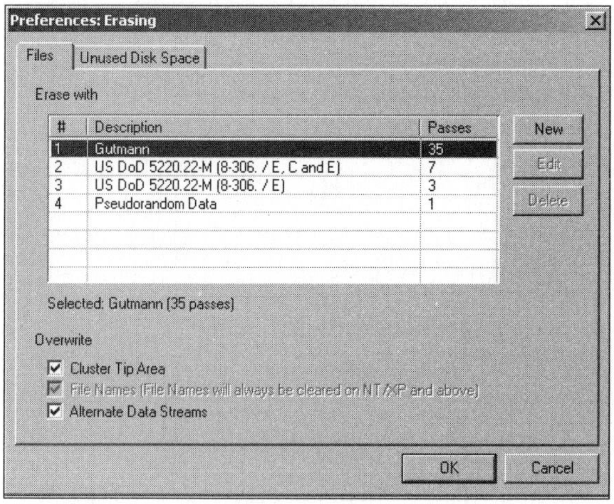

Figure 22-2: A file shredder can offer you different ways to shred your files, giving you a choice between speed and security.

Most file shredders make multiple passes over a deleted file for additional security; the more passes, the longer the deletion takes, but the more likely you'll eliminate all hope of recovery.

The Department of Defense (DoD) even has its own shredding standard, dubbed DoD 5220.22-M (www.dss.mil/isec/nispom.htm), which defines acceptable government standards for deleting computer files. The DoD technique wipes a file seven times, each pass replacing the deleted data with a different set of random data that further obscures the original. Seven passes can destroy virtually all traces of the original file, although theoretically it may be possible to recover some or all of the information later using a magnetic sensor or electron microscope to scan the storage media on an atomic scale.

The Gutmann algorithm is even safer than the DoD data deletion standard, requiring 35 passes over a file's disk storage areas to wipe away every possible trace of the original contents. For more information about securely destroying data, visit Peter Gutmann's web page (www.cs.auckland.ac.nz/~pgut001) and read his paper, "Secure Deletion of Data from Magnetic and Solid-State Memory."

STORING DELETED DATA

No matter how many times you've deleted a file or what deletion methods you may have used, there will almost always be a way to retrieve it again. The most direct approach is to recover bits and pieces of an overwritten file's data by analyzing its magnetic traces on the hard disk, as mentioned above. A more practical and much simpler approach is to look for undeleted traces of that file scattered in other places on the computer.

NOTE: *If you're trying to get rid of data, simply encrypting or deleting a file will never be enough. Encryption and file deletion hide a specific file's contents, but do nothing to hide or erase information copied from the file into temporary files on your hard disk. For example, Microsoft Word typically creates a temporary copy of your document as an emergency backup, just in case your computer crashes or the power goes out. Then you can recover your work by loading this temporary file. However, if you create a sensitive document and encrypt it, all of your sensitive data still remains inside Word's emergency backup copy of your file, which anyone can open and read.*

Finding data stored in slack space

Under Microsoft Windows, the computer divides magnetic media (hard disks, floppy disks, rewritable CDs, etc.) into chunks of a fixed size known as clusters. When you store a file, the entire file rarely fits in a single cluster, so Windows stores it in multiple clusters. Almost inevitably, the last part of a file won't completely fill up its cluster, and it's this extra space that's known as *slack space*.

Computers often use the slack space to store information about that particular file. For example, when you open a file (say, for editing) and type anything from the keyboard, the operating system may temporarily store your keystrokes in a portion of memory called the keyboard buffer. Without the keyboard buffer, you could type too fast for the computer to react, and it could lose keystrokes. When you close the file, the computer may then clear the keyboard buffer by dumping its contents into that file's slack space.

If you delete parts of a file, that file's slack space grows and traces of the previous file version are left behind there. If you delete or encrypt a file, the slack space remains untouched because it is not actually part of the file. Until you overwrite the slack space with random data, any information dumped there can still be recovered.

For maximum security, don't just encrypt your files but encrypt your entire hard disk. Not only will this protect your files, but it will also encrypt any traces of your data scattered elsewhere on your computer.

Finding data stored in swap files

One particularly vulnerable area of your computer is the swap file. A *swap file* allocates part of your hard disk for temporarily storing data from its working memory, known as *random-access memory (RAM)*, so that the computer can free up some of this space to use for running programs as needed. Without swap files, your computer would have to store both a running program and any open files it is using in RAM. So, if you opened an extremely large file, that could be enough to gobble up all of your memory and prevent other programs from running. By selectively swapping data back and forth between the hard disk and the RAM, an operating system can run more than one program at a time, even if their total memory requirement theoretically exceeds what's actually available. (This trick used by the computer to manage running programs is where the name "swap file" comes from.)

So, when you run a program such as a word processor or a spreadsheet, your operating system from time to time temporarily stores some of the associated data, such as the contents of a report or a budget that you're working on, in the swap file—typically when the program is momentarily idle. When you save or delete the data file, much of the file's data may still remain in the swap file.

Your history stored in a web browser cache

When you search the Internet, your browser stores (or *caches*) the graphic images from the pages you visit in what's called the *cache directory*. That way, if you visit the same website later, your computer can retrieve these graphics from its cache rather than directly off the Internet, which can speed up the time it takes the page to load.

By browsing the cache directory of someone's browser, you can see which websites they've visited along with the graphic images they saw, as shown in Figure 22-3.

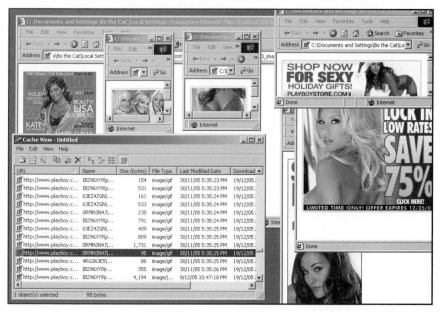

Figure 22-3: Viewing the contents of a browser's cache reveals the websites and graphic images recently viewed.

To view the cache for Internet Explorer, grab a copy of BCIView (www.debryansk .ru/~kamkov) or Cache Auditor (www.webknacks.com). For other browsers, such as Opera and Firefox, grab a copy of Cache View (www.progsoc.uts.edu.au).

If you don't want anyone knowing what you've been looking at while online, just remember that purging the cache simply deletes the files it contains and won't physically remove them—anyone can undelete your erased cache directory later. For more security, use a file shredder such as Shred XP (www.gale-force.com), 12Ghosts Wash (www.12ghosts.com), Window Washer (www.webroot.com), or BCWipe (www.jetico .com), which can also wipe the slack space of specified files and delete web cache files as well. For a Macintosh and Windows file shredder, grab a copy of ShredIt (www.mireth .com).

For added protection, use a special cache-cleaning program such as IEClean/ NSClean (www.nsclean.com), which works with both Internet Explorer and Mozilla/ Firefox, and Cache Cleaner (www.northernsoftworks.com), which can clean the browser cache of the Mac OS X Safari browser.

If you think purging your cache and wiping out temporary files is too much trouble, guess what? That's exactly what computer forensics experts are counting on when they examine a suspect's computer.

Hackers can also take advantage of computer forensics by sneaking into a computer and looking for previously deleted files containing firewall or security program logs that can identify what type of firewall or security program is running and possibly how it might work. If you're a system administrator, just remember that your computer's log files might be hidden or encrypted, but there's always a way for a hacker to use computer forensics to find it anyway.

COMPUTER FORENSICS TOOLS

Depending on the seriousness of the crime and the importance of recovering the data stored on a disk, computer forensics experts generally rely on four basic tools when retrieving deleted data: file-undeleting programs, hex editors, and magnetic sensors and electron microscopes.

File-undeleting programs

As discussed earlier in this chapter, file-undeleting programs, readily available with programs like Norton Utilities, are often sufficient to catch novices who attempt to get rid of incriminating files, such as pictures of child pornography. But they are only effective if the file contents have not already been overwritten on your hard disk, so undeleting programs are a relatively weak forensics tool.

Hex editors

Hex editors are special programs that let you peek at the physical contents stored on a disk. Programmers often use hex editors to modify or examine files, while hackers often use hex editors to peek inside copy-protected games so they can peel away the security or so they can modify the video game to find and turn on hidden features.

Hex editors can probe the contents of any disk. Instead of forcing you to view a disk's contents as organized into partitions, directories, and files, as usually shown to the user by an operating system, a hex editor lets you examine the contents of a disk in terms of its physical layout, such as scanning the surface of the storage media from the outer edges of the disk down to its inner edges.

By using a hex editor, computer forensic specialists can identify and retrieve information that can't normally be accessed by the operating system. As shown in Figure 22-4, hex editors don't rely on operating system services to open and access "files." Instead, they display the physical disk area holding the contents of a file, using hexadecimal codes to represent the actual bytes of data.

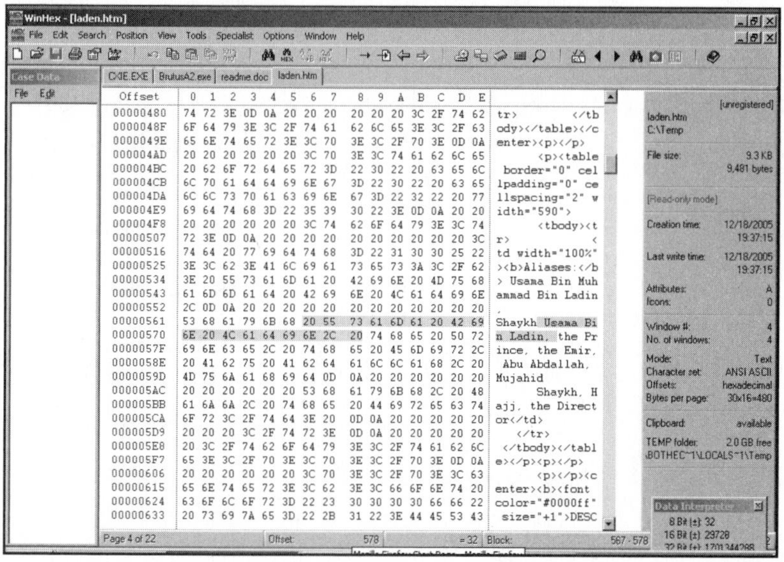

Figure 22-4: A hex editor can display the hidden contents of any disk sector or file.

Using a hex editor to examine an entire hard disk would be like scouring the inside of a skyscraper for fingerprints, so they're best used for searching only the specific parts of a drive where desired information may reside. Still, hex editors can often recover some or all of the data from a deleted file that you might not otherwise be able to access, such as in the slack space of a file. To see what a hex editor can find on your hard disk, download and try Hex Workshop (www.bpsoft.com), UltraEdit (www.idmcomp.com), WinHex (www.x-ways.net), or VEDIT (www.vedit.com).

Magnetic sensors and electron microscopes

No matter how many times you overwrite a file or format and partition a hard disk, traces of the original data may still remain. File shredders make it progressively more expensive and difficult to retrieve, but not impossible.

Every file you delete leaves residual magnetic traces of itself. Each time the computer overwrites a file's contents, the disk heads may be aligned slightly differently with respect to the surface of the media, and fragments of the deleted file may remain afterwards. Forensics experts can use sensors to measure the changes in magnetic fields on a disk's surface and then reconstruct part or all of the bytes in a deleted file, or they can use an electron microscope to do the same thing. Electron microscopes—extremely expensive but available to many governmental organizations—can also measure tiny changes in magnetic fields, left over from the original data, that not even overwriting can completely obliterate.

People may burn their floppy or hard disks, crush and mangle them, cut them into pieces, pour acid on them, and physically manhandle them in a myriad of ways, thinking there will be no possible way of using them on another computer again. However, even the physical destruction of a floppy or hard disk can't guarantee that the data has been safely destroyed, because government agencies such as the FBI and CIA are able to practice a specialized technique known as disk splicing. Disk splicing entails physically rearranging the pieces of a floppy or hard disk as nearly as possible back to its original condition. Then magnetic sensors or electron microscopes scan for traces of information still stored on the disk surface.

Obviously, disk splicing is a time-consuming and expensive procedure, so don't expect your local police force to have that kind of knowledge, skill, or equipment. But if you've destroyed evidence that might interest the NSA, CIA, or FBI, don't expect a mangled disk to hide your secrets from the prying electronic eyes of rich and powerful government agencies. In fact, the American government even has a special laboratory called The Defense Computer Forensics Lab (www.dcfl.gov), located in Linthicum, Maryland, which specializes in retrieving information from computers, no matter what condition of the hardware or disks.

The ultimate lesson to learn is that if you don't want to risk having information retrieved off your hard or floppy disk, your only absolutely foolproof option is to avoid storing it on any computer in the first place.

COMMERCIAL FORENSICS TOOLS

Identity theft, online stalking, Internet sex predators, cybercrime, and terrorism—these are all activities that promise to fuel the development of new computer forensics techniques compatible with Windows, Linux, and Mac OS X. To learn about some of the tools that law enforcement agencies have at their disposal, visit Digital Intelligence (www.digitalintelligence.com), which sells a unique forensics tool called DriveSpy for accessing physical drives using pure BIOS (Int13 or Int13x) calls, which bypass the operating system. Not only does this allow DriveSpy to access disk partitions created by any type of operating system, but it also ensures that the operating system won't modify or erase data (e.g., by changing the swap file) during normal use of DriveSpy.

DriveSpy lets you do the following:

- Examine hard disk partitions

- Copy files to a designated work area without altering file access/modification dates

- Undelete files and put them in a designated work area without altering file access/modification dates

- Search drives, partitions, and files for text strings or data sequences

- Store the slack space from an entire partition in a single file for examination

- Save and restore one or more contiguous sectors (the physical area on a disk) to/from a file

For those who need more power than DriveSpy offers, Digital Intelligence also sells dedicated computer forensics workstations, Forensic Recovery Evidence Devices (whimsically dubbed FREDs), and portable versions called Forensic Recovery Evidence Device Diminutive Interrogation Equipment (FREDDIEs). If you see the police hauling a FRED or FREDDIE into your computer room, brace yourself. They'll be able to copy data from any hard disk or other removable storage device, such as rewritable DVDs; create images of your entire hard disk; connect directly to your computer and monitor any communications that your friends are trying to send to you; examine any visible and hidden partitions for data; and capture video images of the appearance and location of equipment at the scene.

For another peek into the forensic tools that law enforcement uses, visit Guidance Software (www.guidancesoftware.com) to learn about its EnCase program. EnCase can examine MS-DOS/Windows, Macintosh, and Linux computers. EnCase can hook up to a target computer through a parallel cable, scan the hard disk for graphics files (useful for hunting down child pornographers), copy them to another computer, and then display or print the contents of these graphic files.

EnCase can also search text and other files—regardless of what application or operating system created them—to find evidence against criminals or terrorists. Once EnCase finds a file containing a specific word or phrase, it can list or copy those files for further examination.

To learn more about how governments track down criminals using computer forensics, visit the United States–based Electronic Crimes Task Force (www.ectaskforce.org) and the Scotland-based National Hi-Tech Crime Unit (www.sdea.police.uk/nhtcus.htm).

To experiment with some forensic tools on your own computer, grab a copy of Sleuth Kit (www.sleuthkit.org) or F.I.R.E. (http://fire.dmzs.com). Links to more forensic tools are available from Computer Security, Cybercrime, and Steganography Resources (www.forensics.nl), the Talisker Security Wizardry Portal (www.networkintrusion.co.uk), or the Alexander Geschonneck security website (www.geschonneck.com/security/forensic.html).

The next time you get a used computer, use one of these forensic tools to peek into the contents of the hard disk. Many people sell used computers without bothering to wipe out their personal data, which means there's a good chance you could still find someone else's financial records, personal information, and even credit card numbers, too. If you're going to give away a computer, make sure you wipe the hard disk as clean as possible, and then hope that someone won't get lucky and find some useful information still hidden on your erased hard disk anyway.

PROTECTING YOURSELF

Even if you shred files religiously, law enforcement officials, and possibly others, have a variety of computer forensics tools at their disposal to pry out any secrets your deleted files may be hiding. So how can you protect your computer from their prying eyes? Basically, you can't. While you can make recovering data harder by periodically purging your cache directory and only storing files on removable disks (such as rewritable DVDs) and physically destroying them afterwards, just remember that everything you do on your computer can potentially be recovered and examined later.

To destroy the contents of a hard disk quickly, grab a copy of DiskZapper (http://diskzapper.com), available as a bootable floppy or CD. If you boot up from a DiskZapper disk, the program starts erasing your hard disk right away. It can be a handy tool to have around when you want to destroy data quickly.

If you're a programmer and want to understand exactly how a file shredder works, download the source code for Eraser (www.tolvanen.com/eraser), written by Sami Tolvanen. Not only is this file shredder absolutely free for anyone to use, but it is also distributed with Microsoft Visual C++ source code, so you can see how it works and even customize it for your own particular needs.

Linux users can download a file-deleting program called Wipe (http://gsu.linux.org.tr/wipe). Like Eraser, Wipe is free and includes C source code so you can look under the hood and maybe even improve the program on your own to wipe out data even more securely.

But don't assume you can rest easy even if you've gone ahead and scoured your hard disk until it's squeaky clean. Just as every bullet fired can potentially be traced to a specific gun, so everything created by a computer can be traced to a specific machine given the right circumstances and a determined enough searcher.

Edward Delp (http://dynamo.ecn.purdue.edu/~ace), a professor of electrical and computer engineering at Purdue University, has developed a technique to identify the unique "signatures" of printers based on their subtle variations. The United States Secret Service is particularly interested in this technology for tracing documents and counterfeit bills back to specific printers.

Tadayoshi Kohno, a University of California Ph.D. student, has even found a way to identify individual computers over the Internet, as documented in the research paper "Remote physical device fingerprinting" (www.caida.org/outreach/papers/2005/fingerprinting). The technique works by "exploiting small, microscopic deviations in device hardware: clock skews." Essentially, Kohno's technique analyzes how a particular computer's clock timestamps the information it sends over the Internet, which can be used to uniquely identify that specific computer even if it's behind a firewall or connecting to the Internet through multiple proxy servers.

So, if your hard disk data can be retrieved despite your best attempts to destroy it, and if your printer and your computer hardware can give away your activities, can you ever keep any of your stuff private? The answer is no—unless, of course, you only use someone else's computer. Will you ever really need to go this far? That answer depends on you.

23

LOCKING DOWN YOUR COMPUTER

Perhaps the best way to protect a computer from physical theft is to keep it in a locked room, bolted firmly in one place.

Most laptops have a security slot that can hold a cable, but desktop models often require a special plate that attaches with glue to the side of the computer, monitor, or desk. Security cables, like bicycle locks, can deter novices and slow down opportunistic thieves, but they can't stop a determined thief. Given enough time, ordinary nail polish remover can dissolve the adhesives used to glue the cable attachments to the computer, and laptop security locks can be broken with a few well-placed blows of a hammer. More impatient thieves may just snap the restraining cable in half with a pair of wire cutters.

Before you fall victim to theft, make sure you record your computer's model number, make, and serial number in a safe place. Then, if someone does steal it, you can enter the information into the Stolen Computer Registry (www.stolencomputers.org), a free service that maintains a database of pilfered items. As the site explains, "Buyers, resellers, insurers, law enforcement, and security professionals check suspicious computers against this list. When stolen equipment is located, the Registry supplies information and assists in recovery and return of property to the rightful owners."

For additional protection, use an etching pen to scratch your driver's license number or other identification on the inside of the computer case (where thieves won't likely find it) or on the outside (to reduce the resale value of the equipment because the thieves must remove that identification before they can unload it).

> The power of hiding ourselves from one another is mercifully given, for men are wild beasts, and would devour one another but for this protection.
>
> —HENRY WARD BEECHER, orator

PROTECTING YOUR COMPUTER (AND ITS PARTS)

Sometimes stealing an entire computer is too obvious or difficult, but taking the components inside presents less of a challenge. After all, anyone can see when a computer suddenly disappears from a desk, but who will notice when a computer suddenly loses a hard drive (along with all the data stored on it)?

To prevent someone from opening up your computer, buy a protective cover, which is a metal case that fits over the ordinary computer case and locks it to a desk or table. Such protective metal cases not only deter thieves from stealing the computer, but also from opening it to get at anything inside.

Although many people worry about outside hackers breaking into their computers and wiping out their data, the truth is that many hacker attacks come from people who already have legitimate access, such as coworkers, consultants, or technicians. To guard against these folks, buy protective disk drive locks, which cover the front of the drive and stop anyone from inserting a floppy or CD/DVD carrying a virus or Trojan horse. Of course, you should probably check with the IT department before you start locking down your work computer, which your employer owns.

To learn more about physical security devices, such as cables, locks, and protective covers, you can browse the merchandise from CompuCage (www.compucage.com), Computer Security Products (www.computersecurity.com), FMJ/Pad.Lock (www.fmjpadlock.com), Kensington (www.kensington.com), PC Guardian (www.pcguardian.com), or Secure-It (www.secure-it.com).

USB blockers

Many companies now sell USB drives that act like a portable hard drive for carrying data or programs with you wherever you go. People use them for swapping data between computers at work and home, but thieves can use those same USB drives to steal and transport information.

While Windows Vista can block USB drives, other versions of Windows cannot. To prevent anyone from plugging a USB drive into your computer and copying your data, use a program such as Sanctuary Device Control (www.securewave.com), USB Port Protector (www.portprotector.com), or DeviceWall (http://devicewall.centennial-software.com). With one of these tools installed, your computer won't recognize an unauthorized USB drive and thieves won't be able to copy any data off your computer using one, even if they have physical access to your computer.

Alarms

An alarm can act as a deterrent because the last thing a thief wants is anything that draws attention to his activity. Many companies make motion detection alarms that plug into a computer's ordinary expansion slot and run off their own power so they can work whether the computer is on or off. When the alarm detects abnormal motion that suggests someone is moving the computer, the alarm lets out a high-pitched wail.

Barracuda Security Devices (www.barracudasecurity.com) sells another motion detector that arms itself when it senses changes in internal ambient light, indicating that the case has been opened. If a valid PIN isn't entered, the device sounds an ear-piercing alarm and dials a pager or digital cell phone number to alert the user of the theft attempt. An optional exploding dye capsule will also spray ink all over the computer (and the thief), making the parts easy to identify (and harder to sell).

Laptop computers are even more vulnerable to theft. Laptop alarms, such as those sold by Trust (www.trust.com), consist of two parts: a sensor attached to the laptop and another one carried by the user (attached to a keychain or kept in a pocket). The moment your laptop gets separated from you by a fixed distance (such as 15 feet), an alarm goes off. If this doesn't cause the thief to drop the laptop right away, you can follow the piercing whine and, hopefully, retrieve it yourself.

If the thief does get away with your laptop, the motion detection alarm can password-protect and encrypt your hard disk, essentially preventing him from copying any data.

Remote tracking services

Another protective mechanism is a tracing or monitoring program that buries itself on your laptop's hard drive. Every time you connect to the Internet, the tracking program contacts a special server and sends the IP address of the laptop's current location. If you report your laptop stolen, the server waits for your laptop to contact it again and update its new location. Then, the tracking-software company contacts the authorities to help track down the missing computer.

For this the tracking program to work, you must make sure you configure your firewall to allow the tracking program to access the Internet. Otherwise your own firewall could defeat the tracking program and wind up helping out a thief.

For added security, the server can also command the remote tracking software to encrypt your hard disk to prevent the thief from accessing your data.

For more information about various remote tracking programs available for laptop computers, visit Advatrack (www.absolute-protect.com), CompuTrace (www.computrace .com), CyberAngel (www.sentryinc.com), or zTrace (www.ztrace.com).

PROTECTING YOUR DATA

Locks, alarms, and tracking services are utterly powerless against viruses, worms, or accidents. So, after physically protecting your computer, take time to protect the data stored on it too.

Backing up your data

If your hard disk crashes, your office catches on fire, or a thief steals your computer, you'll want a second copy of the valuable data you no longer have access to. Perhaps the simplest way to back up your data regularly is with an external hard disk, which typically plugs into a USB port. Just run a program such as Retrospect Backup (www.dantz.com) and schedule it to copy your files to your external hard disk automatically.

Of course, if a fire, flood, or other accident wipes out your entire home or office, chances are good you'll lose data stored on an external hard disk too. For more security, store your data offline with a subscription service, such as @Backup (www.backup.com), which copies your data to the company's computers. Now, if anything happens to your machine, you can conveniently retrieve all your data from @Backup via the Internet.

Streamload (www.streamload.com) offers 25GB of storage for free, which makes it another option for copying your files securely to an off-site server. Unlimited storage costs extra and varies by subscription plan, and there are limits on how much data that you, or other authorized users, can download from your account each month.

Update and patch your operating system

The most secure operating system available is OpenBSD (www.openbsd.org), but unless you're willing to switch to it, your best choice is to keep your current operating system updated with the latest security patches. (Keep in mind that no operating system is completely secure and that, sometimes, installing a security patch will actually make your computer less secure, due to bugs in the patch itself.)

The latest version of Microsoft Windows can download and install updates automatically, but you should also keep abreast of the latest news about operating system flaws and holes that hackers might exploit. You can read more from NTBugTraq (http://ntbugtraq.ntadvice.com), Security Focus newsletters (www.securityfocus.com/newsletters), Symantec Security Response (http://securityresponse.symantec.com), and The Security News Portal (www.securitynewsportal.com).

Identifying and closing default weaknesses

No matter how secure your computer and operating system may be, you must still defend yourself against hackers trying to break in or install malicious software.

Many operating systems are inherently insecure. Patches and updates eliminate most flaws but do nothing to close ports that have been deliberately left open for valid purposes. For example, the default installation of Windows 2000/XP opens a port to run the Windows Messenger Service, which was originally designed to let network administrators send messages to users. However, this open port also provides a doorway straight into your computer for less welcome visitors.

To take advantage of this gaping hole, many unethical vendors scan ranges of IP addresses to find Windows 2000/XP computers with the Messenger Service port left open. Then they send pop-up ads through this open port advertising anti–pop-up software that will prevent additional pop-up ads from coming through this very same hole, essentially using extortion to convince you to buy their product.

Rather than waste your money on anti–pop-up ad programs, you can just turn off the Messenger Service for free.

To turn off Messenger Service in Windows 2000, follow these steps:

1. Click the Start button, choose Settings, and then click Control Panel. The Control Panel window appears.

2. Double-click Administrative Tools. The Administrative Tools window appears.

3. Double-click Messenger. A Messenger dialog box appears.

4. Click in the Startup type list box and choose Disabled.

5. Click Apply and close the Services window and the Administrative Tools window.

To turn off Messenger Service in Windows XP, follow these steps:

1. Click the Start button and then click Control Panel. The Control Panel window appears.

2. Click Performance and Maintenance. A Performance and Maintenance window appears.

3. Click Administrative Tools. The Administrative Tools window appears.

4. Double-click Services. The Services window appears.

5. Double-click Messenger. A Messenger dialog box appears.

6. Click in the Startup type list box and choose Disabled, as shown in Figure 23-1.

7. Click Apply and close the Services window and the Administrative Tools window.

Figure 23-1: You can turn off the Messenger Service in Microsoft Windows by choosing the Disabled option in the Startup type list box.

Manually shutting down open ports isn't difficult, but you have to know which ports to close. As an alternative, consider using something like the Computer Security Tool (www.computersecuritytool.com), which can scan a Windows computer for insecure default settings and fix them for you, as shown in Figure 23-2. Linux and Mac OS X users can secure their operating systems using Bastille (www.bastille-linux.org).

Figure 23-2: A computer security program can identify weaknesses in your operating system's default settings and correct them automatically.

Just remember that when you close a port, either manually or through a security program, you could accidentally prevent legitimate programs from working.

Choosing a firewall

With your operating system patched and unnecessary holes shut down, your computer is as safe as can be—until you connect to the Internet. Before you even consider going online, you absolutely must get a firewall. Different firewalls have different features, but you can only use one firewall at a time, so it's important to choose one that provides the most protection while requiring minimal configuration by you.

What distinguishes a good firewall from a poor one is the firewall's technical capabilities, along with its default settings. Just because you've installed a firewall doesn't mean you're protected against all types of attacks. To test your firewall's capabilities and see how many open ports it neglects to close, visit LeakTest (http://grc.com/lt/leaktest.htm), HackerWatch (www.hackerwatch.org/probe), AuditMyPC (www.auditmypc.com/freescan/scanoptions.asp), OutBound (www.hackbusters.net/ob.html), or Firewall Leak Tester (www.firewallleaktester.com).

Although most firewalls offer comparable technical capabilities, they fall apart when it comes to default settings. Few people bother to configure a firewall once they've installed it, so it's important that your firewall's default settings provide maximum protection with no extra effort.

Firewalls can't tell the difference between legitimate programs trying to access the Internet and spyware or Trojan horse programs trying to do the same thing. So every time a program tries to connect to the Internet, the firewall may ask if you want to grant it permission, as shown in Figure 23-3.

Figure 23-3: Some firewalls ask (annoy) you every time an unfamiliar program tries to access the Internet.

Unfortunately, lots of people can't tell the difference between a legitimate program and spyware, rendering such firewall notifications virtually useless. To avoid confronting users with choices they may not understand, some firewalls compile a list of acceptable programs and only annoy you with an alert when an unknown program tries to access the Internet. This still leaves room for ignorance, however. Firewalls offer a technical solution for protecting your computer, but you, the user, must furnish the intelligence to train what the firewall allows and what it blocks.

Switch to a safer browser

Internet Explorer is the most popular browser because it comes with every copy of Microsoft Windows. As a result, its popularity makes it the biggest target for spyware. To prevent rogue websites from automatically installing spyware on your computer, either modify Internet Explorer's settings for using Active X controls (see Chapter 20) or switch to a browser that doesn't use ActiveX controls, such as Opera (www.opera.com) or Firefox (www.mozilla.com). These alternatives also have built-in pop-up ad blockers and privacy controls for cleaning out your browser's cache and history, which reveal the websites you've visited recently, as shown in Figure 23-4.

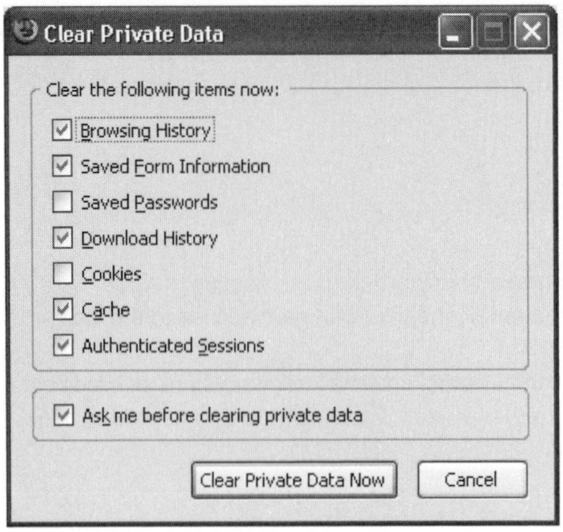

Figure 23-4: Firefox offers a feature for clearing out your browsing history at the click of a mouse.

Apple customers tend to be smug about security; the vast majority of reported flaws have been on Windows systems. But Macs may not be as safe as their owners think. In 2006, a hacker released a proof-of-concept worm that exploited a flaw in the Safari browser. So if you want to keep your Macintosh secure, stop using Safari (which most hackers will attack because it's used by default on every Macintosh computer), and start using an alternate browser such as Firefox, Opera, or Camino (www.caminobrowser.org). Just remember that every program has flaws that can be exploited. As alternate browsers like Firefox become more popular, expect hackers to start exploiting Firefox flaws as often as they target Internet Explorer flaws.

If your browser doesn't offer a cache-cleaning feature, try a separate (and free) program such as CoffeeCup Privacy Cleaner (www.coffeecup.com) or Crap Cleaner (www.ccleaner.com)

Protecting your email account from spam

Most Internet service providers (ISPs) now offer free antivirus scanning and spam filtering, but you'll want to make sure you turn those features on. (If your ISP doesn't offer these services, consider switching to a different vendor.) No matter how wonderful your ISP may claim its spam filters are, chances are they still won't be enough, so consider using a separate spam filter as well.

For a free spam-filtering program, try CoffeeCup Spam Blocker (www.coffeecup .com) or Ella for Spam Control (www.openfieldsoftware.com). Both can block spam that your ISPs filters might miss.

Even then, spam is still likely to slip past, so make sure you turn on the spam-filtering features of your email client too. Microsoft Outlook comes with a spam filter, but many worms know how to exploit Outlook to email copies of themselves to everyone in your address book. Instead, consider switching to the free Thunderbird email program (www.mozilla.com/thunderbird), developed by the same people who brought you the Firefox browser. Not only can Thunderbird foil mass-emailing worms, it can also filter out spam at the same time. By running spam through your ISP's spam filter, a separate spam filter, and finally your email program's spam filter, even though you still won't eliminate all unwanted mail, you'll reduce the flood to a mere trickle.

Protecting against phishing

Phishing occurs when online con artists use unsolicited email (spam) to direct victims to a bogus website masquerading as a legitimate one (see Chapter 13). As soon as a phishing victim types her credit card number, password, or bank account number on the website accessed by clicking a link in the email, the thief can gain access to the victim's personal accounts and money.

To foil phishing attempts, never trust unsolicited email from any bank or credit card company. (If you still can't determine whether an email is legitimate or not, call the bank or credit card company directly and ask them to verify the message's authenticity.)

For additional help identifying phishing attacks, download a copy of SpoofGuard (http://crypto.stanford.edu/SpoofGuard) for Internet Explorer. SpoofGuard examines a website's address and uses a variety of criteria, such as unusual letters or numbers mixed into the website address, to assess a site's validity, as shown in Figure 23-5.

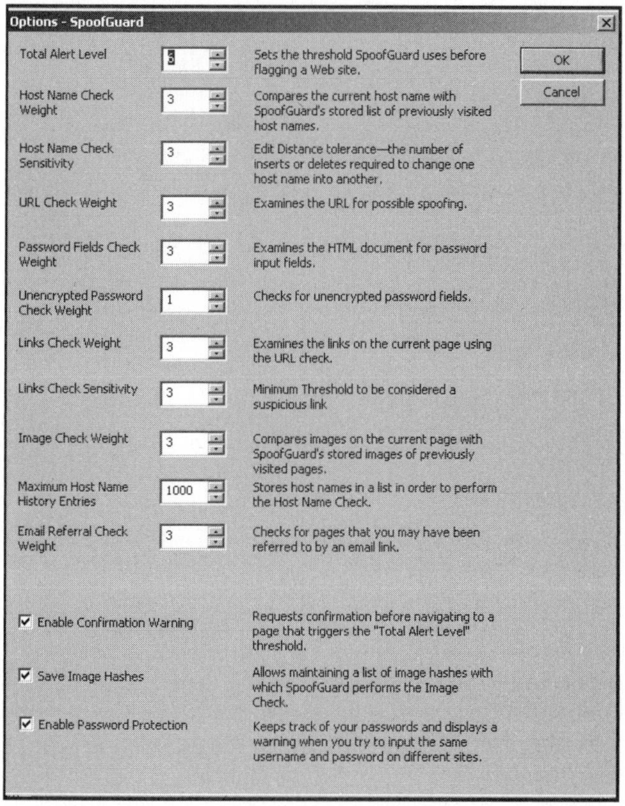

Figure 23-5: SpoofGuard uses different criteria to identify bogus websites.

For another way to identify bogus websites, download the Earthlink ToolBar (www
.earthlink.net/software/free/toolbar) or the Netcraft Toolbar (http://toolbar.netcraft.com).
Both compare website addresses against a list of known phisher sites, warning you when
it finds a match.

Because phishers create new bogus sites all the time, both the Earthlink and
Netcraft toolbars allow users to submit addresses to a central database, which helps
keep it up-to-date and comprehensive.

Other sites that offer anti-phishing tools are PhishGuard (www.phishguard.com),
SiteAdvisor (www.siteadvisor.com), and PhishFighting (www.phishfighting.com). Both
programs rely on user contributions to stay effective. When someone finds a phishing
website, she can forward the URL address to everyone else using the program to warn
them about the bogus site, proving the old theory that there's safety in numbers.

WHAT'S NEXT?

If you physically lock your computer, update and patch your operating system, switch to
a safer browser, and install firewalls, antivirus programs, anti-spyware programs, spam
filters, and anti-phishing tools, you'll have a safer computer—for a fraction of a second.
The final step to locking down your computer requires that you stay informed about
the latest online scams, malware threats, phishing techniques, and other dangers lurking on the Internet. The more you know about past, current, and future threats, the more
likely you'll be able to identify and avoid them before it's too late. For more help securing
your computer, check out CastleCops (http://castlecops.com), LabMice.net (http://
labmice.techtarget.com), TweakHound (www.tweakhound.com), and SecureMac
(www.securemac.com).

No matter how many technical solutions you throw at a problem, the only sure
protection will always be your own knowledge and education—and that applies to much
more than just computer hacking, too.

EPILOGUE

Hacking applies to more than just computers. Hacking is the practice of thinking beyond boundaries to see what lies on the other side. There is nothing inherently good or bad about hacking. It just is.

You can hack a computer, a locked door, an abandoned building, or even another person. If you're the type who's constantly learning, experimenting, and testing the world around you, you're a hacker, and you may not even know it.

Hackers appear under many different names and disguises. They've been called computer experts, phone phreakers, crackers, white/black hat hackers, social engineers, urban explorers, con artists, stalkers, liars, activists, terrorists, hate groups, spammers, troublemakers, thieves, and criminals. But in reality, hackers should also be called police officers, reporters, broadcasters, scientists, students, teachers, writers, philosophers, accountants, lawyers, judges, salespeople, chauvinists, feminists, engineers, doctors, and politicians. Everyone's a hacker and everyone knows someone who's a hacker whether they realize it or not.

Hackers are adept at managing information in any form, whether it's stored as a computer program, a written word, a physical object (such as a lock), a set of procedures, or thoughts inside somebody's head. Hacking is never a computer issue; it's always a people issue.

If you get nothing else from this book, please remember this: You are being hacked every day of your life—far beyond the simple threats of computer viruses or identity theft. Advertisers (on billboards and in TV commercials, magazine ads, and the notorious spam and spyware) are trying to rearrange your thinking. Politicians and governments have already shaped your thoughts with the "history" that's taught in schools, the "news" they disseminate, and the "laws" they pass to restrict your actions. In truth, history is nothing but a set of beliefs, news is nothing but a point of view, and laws are nothing but tools to legitimize the government's behavior.

The real threat doesn't come from faceless hordes of hackers intent on making your life miserable. The real threat comes from faceless hordes of criminals intent on making your life miserable, whether they're part of a ring of identity thieves in Eastern Europe, a bored teenager in Southern California stealing credit card numbers in Internet chat rooms, organized crime syndicates breaking into banks electronically, public relations firms planting phony stories in "reputable" newspapers and magazines, politicians holding press conferences that provide nothing but empty generalities, or religious leaders saying that the only way to get into heaven is by following their instructions.

The real threat will never come from any single, identifiable group of people. The real threat will always come from any individual motivated by dishonesty and greed.

Ultimately, hacking teaches you that nobody has your best interests at heart except you. Anyone who tells you otherwise is nothing but a hacker.

WHAT'S ON THE *STEAL THIS COMPUTER BOOK 4.0* CD

This CD contains 648MB of freeware programs that you can copy, give away, and use to protect yourself against the latest threats on the Internet, including viruses, worms, Trojan horses, and spyware.

While the programmers who wrote these programs tried to do the best job possible, there's still a chance that bugs could cause various problems with your computer. If in doubt, test these programs on a computer that you can afford to mess up before installing them on a machine that contains valuable data. Neither the author nor No Starch Press takes any responsibility for the way these programs may work or behave.

NOTE: *All files on this CD are designed to run under Windows unless specifically labeled otherwise, such as (Mac OS X) or (Linux).*

UNCOMPRESSING, UNZIPPING, UNSTUFFING, AND SO ON

Many of these programs are compressed, as indicated by their extensions. You must expand or uncompress these programs before you can run them.

- .zip files are Windows files which may be "unzipped" with StuffIt Expander or WinZip.

- .exe files are program files; double-click them from within Windows to extract them and run the application.

- .sit and .sitx files are Macintosh StuffIt files which may be "unstuffed" with StuffIt Expander.

- .dmg files are Mac OS X disk image files that you can double-click to access their contents.

- .gz and .tar are gzipped or tarred Linux files, which may be uncompressed with LinZip or tar.

CHAPTER 1—THE HACKER MENTALITY

Beginner   Text file containing "The Beginner's Guide to Hacking and Phreaking."

Cracker   White paper from Network Security Solutions entitled "Techniques Adopted By 'System Crackers' When Attempting To Break Into Corporate or Sensitive Private Networks."

Hacknov   Text file containing "A Novice's Guide to Hacking."

CHAPTER 2—THE FIRST HACKERS: THE PHONE PHREAKERS

Att_ccg.zip   AT&T credit card calling number generator.

CA_setup   Cain & Abel password recovery program that can sniff a network for data and listen in on voice over Internet protocol (VoIP) phone calls.

Ccnum.zip   Credit card number generator, includes source code written in Pascal.

Cphreak.zip   Phone boxing program for Windows.

Hackvmb   Text file explaining how to hack voice mail systems.

Phonetag.zip   War dialer.

Phreakmaster.zip   Blue box program.

Pgpfone10b2.zip   Turns your computer into a secure, encrypted telephone.

Redpalm++.zip   Red box program for the Canadian telephone network, designed to run on Palm OS 3.0 handheld computer.

Shittalker.zip   Gag program that lets your computer make crank calls.

Switchboard.zip   Mimics different telephone color boxes.

Vmbhackr.zip   Program for hacking voice mail systems.

Vmbhaq   Text file explaining how to hack a voice mail system.

(Linux) Vomit-0.2c.tar   Converts an intercepted VoIP phone call into a WAV audio file.

Winphreak.zip   Telephone boxing program.

CHAPTER 3—HACKING PEOPLE, PLACES, AND THINGS

Artoflockpick   Text file explaining the basics of lock picking.

Basictrashing   Text file explaining the fine art of Dumpster diving to retrieve useful items or information.

Carlocks   Text file explaining how car locks work and how to pick them.

Combolocks	Text file explaining how to pick and open combination locks.
Hemp_for_victory_1942	Department of Agriculture documentary encouraging farmers to grow hemp to support the war effort.
jPodder-Setup	jPodder program for retrieving podcasts.
Juice22setup	Juice program for capturing and listening to iPod podcasts.
(Mac OS X) Juice_2.2_install.dmg.gz	Juice program for capturing and listening to iPod podcasts on a Macintosh.
Lockpicking	Another text file that explains how to pick combination locks.
Podifier_v2.1_setup	Program for creating your own podcasts.
(Mac OS X) Podifier_v2.1.hqx	Program for creating podcasts on a Macintosh.
Social	Text file explaining how to use social engineering.
Socialfaq	Text file that answers the most common questions regarding social engineering.
Sparks	BlogMatrix Sparks! Program for creating your own podcasts.
Trash	Another text file explaining how to dumpster dive.
Trashing	One more text file explaining how to dumpster dive.
Trashingguide	Yet another text file explaining dumpster diving. (By reading a variety of dumpster diving tutorials, you can learn which techniques work best for different problems.)

CHAPTER 4—ANSI BOMBS AND VIRUSES

Ansibomb	Text file explaining how ANSI bombs work.
Bombansi	Text file containing the source code to a sample ANSI bomb that will format your hard drive.
Chaos07	Text file explaining how to make ANSI bombs.
Clamwin-0.87.1-setup	Open-source Clam antivirus program.
(Mac OS X) ClamXav_1.0.1.dmg	Open-source Clam antivirus program for the Macintosh.
Darkangel	Text file explaining how to write viruses.
Removeit_pro	RemoveIT-Pro program for detecting and removing viruses.
Sdefendi	Script Defender protects against all forms of malicious code (such as macro viruses) that run scripting languages such as VBScript or JavaScript.
Strap	ScripTrap program for stopping viruses from running scripts.

CHAPTER 5—TROJAN HORSES AND WORMS

Asviewer.zip	Monitors all the programs that start and run automatically whenever you boot up Windows. Can be used to detect Trojan horses or spyware running in the background without your knowledge.
Comp_trojans	Text file explaining the different types of Trojan horses and how they can infect your computer.
Errsource.zip	Delphi source code for a simple Trojan horse that displays a Fatal Network Error message on the screen and then prompts the user to type a user name and password.
Fake_freeav.zip	Trojan horse that displays a fake AltaVista login screen that tricks people into typing their a valid user name and password.
HoneyPotv1.0-Download2.zip	HoneyPot program that watches out for hacker activity accessing ports on your computer.
Irclean	Stops worms from spreading through IRC chat rooms.
Jammer17f	Defensive program for guarding against the Back Orifice and NetBus remote access Trojans.
LameBus	Delphi source code for the LameBus program designed to stop the NetBus remote access Trojan.
Morris Internet worms source code.zip	C source code to the famous Internet worm that took down the Internet in 1988.
Netbuster 1.31.zip	NetBuster program for detecting and stopping the NetBus remote access Trojan.
Nps16.zip	NetBus Protection System to protect your computer from the NetBus remote access Trojan.
Remover	Detects and removes worms and Trojan horses.
Slap	Allows you to send messages back to any hackers trying to sneak through a port on your computer.
StartUpMonitor.zip	Monitors all programs that start up automatically. Useful for catching Trojan horses or spyware running without your knowledge.
(Mac OS X) Zebrascanner3.0.2.zip	Zebra Scanner for detecting Trojan horses.

CHAPTER 6—WAREZ (SOFTWARE PIRACY)

Kf141.zip	Key Finder program for recovering the Microsoft product keys from the Windows registry.
RockXP3	Retrieves product keys from all installed Microsoft products and saves the Windows XP product activation file.

CHAPTER 7—WHERE THE HACKERS ARE

Hacker Sites   Web page listing different computer security and hacker websites.
Netirc   NetIRC program for participating in IRC chat rooms.
Virc200   Visual IRC program for communicating in IRC chat rooms.

CHAPTER 8—STALKING A COMPUTER

(Mac OS X) CrackAirport01.dmg   Cracks WEP encryption to wireless networks.

(Linux) Cst1_41.tar   CUM Security Toolkit that includes a port scanner and a script scanner for foiling Intrusion Detection Systems (IDS).

eMmyIP20   Email My IP program that identifies a computer's IP address and emails it to you.

Honeyd-0.5a-win32.zip   Honeyd program for creating "honeypots" on ports to detect and track hacker activity.

Iploc17.zip   Atelier Web IP Locator program for tracking down the physical location of an IP address.

(Mac OS X) IPLocator.wdgt.zip   Dashboard widget that can provide the physical location associated with an IP address or URL domain.

Ipscan   Angry IP scanner that can scan a range of IP addresses.

(Mac OS X) KisMACR65.zip   KisMAC program for sniffing data from wireless networks.

Lanspy.zip   Lets you remotely examine another computer on a local area network.

NBrute10   NetBrute program for scanning and detecting open ports and testing websites for password security.

Netscan   NetScan program to scan for open ports on another computer.

Netstumblerinstaller_0_4_0   NetStumbler program for detecting WiFi networks.

PCscanner   Scans a computer for open ports.

SimpleScan.zip   Visual Basic 5 source code to a simple port scanner.

Spade114   Sam Spade Internet tool that offers ping, nslookup, WHOIS, IP block, dig, traceroute, and finger commands.

Tjping.zip   Ping, traceroute, and lookup utility.

(Mac OS X) WAP_Map.dmg.gz	Wireless network mapping tool that locates access points in a wireless network.
(Mac OS X) whatPorts.dmg.sit	whatPorts program for scanning ports.
Wups	UDP port scanner for Windows.

CHAPTER 9—CRACKING PASSWORDS

Actualkeylogger	Actual Keylogger program for capturing keystrokes.
Creating a VB Keylogger	Text file explaining how to capture keystrokes using Visual Basic.
Freekgbkeylogger-193	Unique keystroke logger that can also capture foreign characters.
Freelogger	Free Key Logger program for capturing keystrokes.
Homekeylogger.zip	Home Keylogger for capturing keystrokes.
John-16w.zip	John the Ripper password cracker.
Kbhook.zip	Explains how to capture keystrokes using Visual C++ source code.
Keylogger.zip	Keystroke logging program.
Keylogger-king-free-13	Keylogger King program for capturing keystrokes.
Kreview.zip	Compares and lists information about different keystroke logging programs.
Logger.zip	Adiscon Logger keystroke capturer.
(Mac OS X) Logkext.dmg	Keylogger program for capturing keystrokes.
(Mac OS X) Mkrack.dmg	MacKrack password cracking program.
PeekaBoo	Retrieves a password hidden behind asterisks.
PWReveal10setup	Password Revealer that can "peek" behind passwords, masked by asterisks, and reveal the actual password hidden underneath.
RevelationV2.zip	Displays passwords hidden behind asterisks.
Screenlog.zip	ScreenLog Version 1 program that takes snapshots of the computer screen periodically to record what appeared there.
SnoopyPro-0.22.zip	Snoopy Pro program for sniffing data over a USB connection.
(Linux) Snort-2.4.3.tar.gz	Snort network intrusion detection system, capable of performing real-time traffic analysis and packet logging on IP networks.
Tkey-setup.zip	Tiny Keylogger program. (Requires Microsoft .NET framework 1.1.)

Unmaskit.zip	Reveals any password hidden on-screen by asterisks.
Wssetup	Super WinSpy program for monitoring activity on your computer.

CHAPTER 10—DIGGING INTO A COMPUTER WITH ROOTKITS

AriesRemoverInst	ARIES Rootkit Remover that gets rid of the rootkit developed by First4Internet and used on certain Sony CDs to hide its Digital Rights Management (DRM) software.
Fmbb_404	FileMap program for detecting when unknown files suddenly appear on your hard disk.
RootkitRevealer.zip	Scans the Windows registry for signs of kernel-mode rootkits lurking on your computer.

CHAPTER 11—CENSORING INFORMATION

Anonymous Proxy Servers	Web page that lists several free sites that allow you to surf the Internet anonymously.
Bmppacker.zip	Hides data in BMP graphic files.
CameraShy.0.2.23.1	Camera/Shy tool for downloading steganography images off web pages automatically.
Cameleon.zip	French steganography program for hiding data in GIF files using AES encryption.
(Mac OS X) Ciphire-mail-01.1.015-osx-ppc.dmg	Ciphire Mail program for encrypting your email.
Dpt32	Data Privacy Tools encryption program that can hide data in graphic files.
GhostzillaCD-1.0.1-free-v1.zip	GhostZilla program that allows you to browse the Internet from within another program.
Handbook_bloggers_cyberdissidents-GB	PDF file of a blogging handbook with guidelines for sharing information without getting caught by government authorities.
How to bypass Internet censorship	Web page that explains different techniques for overcoming Internet censorship.
ImageHide.zip	ImageHide program for hiding data in graphic images.
Infostego3	Info Stego Personal 3.0 program for hiding data in BMP graphic files.

Kidlogger	KidLogger program for recording keystrokes, capturing websites visited, and storing chat room conversations. Includes Visual C++ source code.
MP3Stego_1_1_17.zip	MP3Stego program for hiding data in MP3 audio files, includes Visual C++ source code.
Netdogv1.1.10	NetDog Internet filter for blocking access to porn sites.
(Mac OS X) PictureSpy.sit	PictureSpy program for hiding data in graphic images.
(Mac OS X) Proxify.wdgt.zip	Dashboard widget for surfing anonymously using the Proxify proxy server.
S-tools4.zip	S-Tools steganography program for hiding data in graphic and audio files.
Setup_en	Naomi filtering program for blocking sites unfit for children.
Setupex	Gif-It-Up program for hiding data in GIF graphic files.
Stegdetect-0.4.zip	StegDetect for detecting hidden messages in graphic files.
Verdict_Shi_Tao	PDF file containing the criminal verdict of a journalist sentenced to 10 years in prison after Yahoo! revealed his email address to Chinese authorities.

CHAPTER 12—THE FILESHARING NETWORKS

Binjet-107	BinJet program for retrieving large files (music, movies, software, etc.) off Usenet newsgroups.
Einstein10	Filesharing program designed for students to share homework, term papers, and tests.
File Sharing	Flash movie describing how a typical filesharing program works.
Grabit153b	GrabIt program for finding and retrieving audio, video, and program files off Usenet newsgroups.
IRC example	Flash movie that shows how to download files from an IRC chat room.
Ksr.zip	Deletes all spyware installed by the Kazaa filesharing program.
Newsgroups	Flash movie that shows how to download files from newsgroups.

(Mac OS X) PeerGuardian_1.2.zip	Macintosh Peer Guardian program for blocking IP addresses of the police and music labels who might try to see what type of files you're sharing.
Pg2-050918-nt	Windows Peer Guardian program for blocking IP addresses of the police and music labels who might try to see what type of files you're sharing.
Tribalweb_setup	TribalWeb program for creating your own private file-sharing network with friends.
Web site example	Flash movie that shows how websites share files that people can download.

CHAPTER 13—THE INTERNET CON ARTISTS

CallingID	Uses up to 52 different verification tests to identify bogus phishing websites.
Megahack.zip	Program designed to subvert the online chain letter scam Mega$Nets. Includes Visual Basic 3.0 source code.
PhishGuard-1-2-186	Detects bogus phishing websites designed to trick you out of passwords, account numbers, or credit card numbers.
TrustToolbar	Internet Explorer add-in that can alert you when you're visiting a suspected phishing website.

CHAPTER 14—FINDING PEOPLE ON THE INTERNET

Stalking Fact Sheet	PDF file of stalking facts and information produced by the Stalking Resource Center.
Stalking Investigation Guide	PDF file of a British guide that helps police investigate stalking crimes.

CHAPTER 15—PROPAGANDA AS NEWS AND ENTERTAINMENT

Newspk21.zip	Newspeak program for translating ordinary text into politically correct language.
NewsraiderP.zip	NewsRaider program that yanks news articles from different newspapers and magazines and collects them for your viewing convenience.
NewzieSetup	Retrieves news from multiple sources.
Online News Sources	Web page listing worldwide news sources, including newspapers, magazines, and news services.

| Search Engine List | Web page listing different search engines, including specialty and international search engines. |

CHAPTER 16—HACKTIVISM: ONLINE ACTIVISM

Pakistan Zindabad hack	Flash movie that shows a politically motivated website defacement.
September 12th	Flash movie that shows how the September 12th political activist video game works.
Ztps.zip	Zapatista Port Scanner.

CHAPTER 17—HATE GROUPS AND TERRORISTS ON THE INTERNET

(Mac OS X) CostOfWar.wdgt.zip	Dashboard widget that estimates the current cost of the war in Iraq.
Fallout Meter	PDF file explaining how to create your own fallout meter for measuring radiation.
FBI Law Enforcement Bulletin	PDF file that describes the seven-stage model that characterizes hate groups.
Terrorism News Links	Web page containing links to different sites offering news about terrorism and hate crimes.
Threat-1.0.4.zip	Displays the color of the current terrorist threat level.

CHAPTER 18—IDENTITY THEFT AND SPAM

CoffeeSpamBlocker41R	Spam filter.
Ellafree_full	Ella for Spam Control program for filtering spam with Microsoft Outlook.
EmC817	EmC spam filter.
Extractor.zip	Email extractor program for ripping out email addresses stored in text files.
(Mac OS X) isafe.zip	The iSafe program for storing passwords, credit card contact information, and other valuable information in one convenient location.
MailWasherFree	Spam filter that can bounce spam back to the sender with an "address unknown" message.
Mbdisp2	Mail Box Dispatcher program for filtering spam.
Spamhilator_0_9_9_9	Spam filter.

SpamAware-Setup	Spam filter for Microsoft Outlook and Outlook Express.
SpamExperts Home Installer	SpamExperts spam filter.
(Mac OS X) Spam_UCE_ 1.0_scpt.zip	Works with the Mac OS X Mail program to forward spam automatically to the Federal Trade Commission and bounce it back to the sender.
SpoofMail v1-1-7.zip	SpoofMail program that shows how to forge email headers.
(Mac OS X) TheObfuscator. wdgt.zip	Dashboard widget that converts the text of an email address into its equivalent ASCII code representation.
Vengine	Verification Engine that examines websites and alerts you to fraudulent ones that may be phishing for your password or credit card number.

CHAPTER 19—BANNER ADS, POP-UP ADS, AND SEARCH ENGINE SPAMMING

Ad.htm, Fileshare.jpg, Home.htm, and HTML.gif	Sample JavaScript code that shows how websites create pop-up ads.
PopUpStopperFree	Pop-Up Stopper program for blocking pop-up ads.
Seosurfsetup	SEOSurf program for helping you to optimize your website for the highest possible rankings on different search engines.
Sfg800c	SafeGuard Popup Blocker.
SmartPopupBlocker101	Smart Popup Blocker program that kills pop-up ads and protects your home page from being changed by spyware.

CHAPTER 20—ADWARE AND SPYWARE

A2freesetup	Scans and removes worms, Trojan horses, and spyware.
A2hijackfree	Removes browser helpers (spyware) and monitors active programs to help detect spyware.
Aawsepersonal	Ad-Aware Standard Edition Personal spyware remover program.
Ashield_1_setup_314	Arovax Shield program that detects spyware that tries to change the Windows registry or install itself as a browser toolbar.
ASRSetup—Advanced Spyware Remover	Scans and removes spyware.

Assassin.zip	Wipes out spyware without having to reboot Windows into Safe Mode.
BHODemon20setup_2022	Browser Helper Object (BHO) Demon program for removing browser toolbars installed by spyware programs.
BHR4.1	Browser Hijack Retaliator program that warns you when spyware tries to change the home page setting of your browser.
Cwshredder	CoolWebShredder program for removing CoolWeb, one of the most insidious and difficult-to-remove spyware programs currently infecting computers.
D3tr	Runs the Internet traceroute command but displays the results in a colorful 3D graph.
DisspySetupLITE	Spyware removal program.
Enough	Enough is Enough! program for locking down Internet Explorer to prevent it from allowing spyware. Note: may also block IE from browsing valid sites.
Eulalyzersetup	EULAlyzer analyzes the end user license agreements (EULA) that come with programs for signs of spyware or adware.
HijackThis	Prevents spyware from redirecting your browser and taking over your home page.
Iespyad2	Locks down Internet Explorer to prevent spyware from sneaking onto your computer.
Regprot.zip	Monitors the Windows registry and notifies you when programs (such as Trojan horses or spyware) try to change it without your knowledge.
Spybotsd14	Spybot spyware remover.
Spywareblastersetup351	SpywareBlaster program that tries to prevent spyware from being installed on your computer in the first place.
Spywareguardsetup	Spyware Guard program that scans files for spyware.
StartupList	Lists all the programs that start automatically when Windows boots up. Useful for catching traces of spyware and Trojan horses.
Winmaid.zip	WinMaid program that detects spyware.
Wpsetup	WinPatrol program that detects suspicious programs (such as spyware) running without your knowledge.

CHAPTER 21—COMPUTING ON A SHOESTRING: GETTING STUFF FOR (ALMOST) FREE

(Mac OS X) Backup_Files.zip   Macintosh Backup & Restore program for backing up your data.

Computing on a Shoestring   Web page listing links to popular freeware programs, including Microsoft Office look-alikes and antivirus programs.

Framxpro.zip   Free RAM Pro program for optimizing and managing memory to make your computer run more efficiently.

Ntregopt-setup   Optimizes the Windows Registry to make your computer work faster.

SpeeDefrag.zip   Program for defragmenting your hard disk.

CHAPTER 22—COMPUTER FORENSICS: THE ART OF DELETING AND RETRIEVING DATA

Bciview.zip   Browser Cache Index Viewer program that reads the contents of the Internet Explorer URL cache and tracks websites you've visited.

Ccsetup126   Crap Cleaner program that clears out your browser cache and Windows registry.

CoffeePrivacyCleaner20R   Wipes out all traces of what you've been looking at on the Internet.

Cryle   Cryptainer LE program that creates "vaults" where you can store files and folders that will get encrypted automatically.

Cshred110   CyberShredder program for overwriting and deleting data securely.

(Mac OS X) DashShredder.wdgt.zip   Dashboard widget for shredding files securely.

(Mac OS X) DashCrypt.wdgt.zip   Dashboard widget for encrypting files using the AES government standard.

Dban-1.0.6_i386.iso   Disk image of Darik's Boot and Nuke program for wiping out data stored on a hard disk.

Dclean157_all.zip   Disk Cleaner program for securely deleting temporary files.

(Mac OS X) DestroyerX.dmg   DestroyerX program for securely deleting data.

(Mac OS X) DisApPeAr.zip   DisApPeAr program for selectively hiding files and folders.

Diskzapr.flp	Floppy disk image of the Disk Zapper program, which can wipe out and overwrite your hard disk with random data.
Diskzapr.iso	CD disk image of the Disk Zapper program, which can wipe out and overwrite your hard disk with random data.
Dskinv	Disk Investigator program for viewing and recovering previously deleted data.
Eraser57setup	File shredder program.
Free-hex-editor	Hex editor program for examining sectors on a disk.
Krlite	Kryptel Lite file encryption program.
Pci_filerecovery.exe	PC Inspector's File Recovery program.
PrivateSurf	Clears out your browser cache so nobody can see which sites you've visited.
RawCopy.zip	Raw Copy program for copying disks by sector rather than by file.
Security-toolkit	Encrypts and securely deletes data from your hard disk and other removable media.
Sfs.zip	Simple File Shredder for securely deleting your files.
TracesViewer	Displays the contents of the Internet Explorer cache.
Unlocker1.7.6	Program that unlocks files and folders so you can access them.
Unstopcp.zip	Unstoppable Copier program for recovering data from scratched CDs or defective floppy disks.
Xcleaner_free	Free version of the X-Cleaner program that cleans your Internet cache.
Xvi32.zip	XVI32 hex editor.

CHAPTER 23—LOCKING DOWN YOUR COMPUTER

NOTE: *Although this CD includes several different firewalls, you only need to run one at a time. Installing two or more firewalls won't make your computer any more secure, and multiple firewalls can confuse and conflict with each other.*

AntiHookProSetup25.msi	AntiHook program that can prevent keystroke loggers, spyware, Trojan horses, and rootkits from intercepting operating system function calls.

Autopatcher_xp_dec_2005_ lite_english	Automatically patches Windows XP based on Microsoft's latest recommendations.
Dlpnpauditor.zip	Device Lock Plug and Play Auditor keeps track of any devices connected to your computer through USB ports.
(Mac OS X) Dtd-200.dmg	Deny Thumb Drivers program that prevents anyone from accessing your computer through a USB portable storage device.
English_Free_CompuSec.zip	CompuSec program that encrypts your hard disk and prevents others from logging on without your authorization.
Firewall	Firewall 2004 program.
Firewall_setup	SoftPerfect firewall program.
FileShield Encryption	Encrypts individual files or entire folders.
Ghostwall_setup	Ghost Wall firewall program.
Hardenit	Examines your network and shuts down vulnerabilities automatically.
(Mac OS X) Hide-Out! v2.1.sitx	Hide-Out program that conceals folders on your Mac OS X computer.
Ipig-setup	iPIG security program for protecting your computer on a Wi-Fi wireless network.
Jpfwall	Jetico firewall.
Patchwrk	PatchWork program checks for vulnerabilities identified by the FBI and, if any are found, points you to the Microsoft patches that can fix them.
Pcsecuritytest.zip	PC Security Test program that tests your computer's defenses to determine how safe (or insecure) your computer may be against common types of hacker attacks.
Preview-setup	Preview program that analyzes and rates how secure your computer may be against hacker and malware threats.
Pshld100.zip	SnoopFree Privacy Shield detects keystroke loggers and other activity monitoring programs that may be spying on your computer.
Qpassgen	Quicky Password Generator that helps you create unique and difficult-to-guess passwords (which may also be difficult to remember).
Secretmakersetup	Secret Maker program for blocking pop-up ads, filtering spam, cleaning your Internet cache, and blocking banner ads.

Secure-It	Examines your Windows computer and shuts down vulnerabilities automatically.
Securepoint_pcfirewall_ setup_3.6	SecurePoint firewall.
(Mac OS X) sunShield1.02.sit	SunShield program for configuring the built-in Mac OS X firewall.
Xp-AntiSpy_setup-english	Locks down Windows XP to prevent it from sending suspicious information back to Microsoft.
Xpy-0.9.4-bin.zip	Shuts down known vulnerabilities in Windows XP.

INDEX

VMB Hacker software, 27, 28
Vmyths.com website, 58
Voice Firewall software, 25
voice mail, 27–28
Voice of America, 38
voice over Internet Protocol (VoIP),
    28–30, 90
    regulation of, 30
Voice over IP Security Alliance
    website, 30
Voice Over Misconfigured Internet
    Telephones (Vomit) software, 29
voice recognition devices, 123, 124
Voice Security Systems website, 123
VoIP (voice over Internet Protocol),
    28–30, 90
Vomit (Voice Over Misconfigured Internet
    Telephones) software, 29
Vonage, 30

W

Wallace, Bob, 63
WANK worm, 231
war chalking, 105–106
war dialing, 23–25, 98–99
war driving, 102–106. *See also* WiFi
    networks
WarDriving.com website, 104
warez, 74, 79–82. *See also* piracy,
    software
WarezFiles, 79
Warez List website, 79
WarLinux software, 104
WebActive website, 209
Webalizer log file analysis software, 128
web browser cache, 317–318
web browsers, 329–330
web bugs, 278–281
WebGate webmail service, 153
webmail servers, 152–153
web pages, malicious, 71
WebPodStudio software, 39
WebSense, 139–140
website email address extractors, 255
website storage, free, 310–311
website vandalism, 228–231
WEP (Wireless Equivalent Privacy),
    103–104, 106
whitelists, 262–264

WhitePages.com directory, 194
Who Is He/She? website, 196
Who's Watching Me? software, 183
WiFiMaps.com website, 105
WiFi networks, 103–106
    accessing, 104–106
    protecting, 106
WiFi Protected Access, 104, 106
WiFi Seeker, 103
WindowsSearch website, 90
WinDump website, 133
Wireless Equivalent Privacy (WEP),
    103–104, 106
Wireless Geographic Logging Engine, 105
Wiretapped website, 90
Wise Giving Alliance website, 170
Wordlist Project, 121
Word (Microsoft), copy protection for,
    75–76
work-at-home scams, 174–175
Working to Halt Online Abuse
    website, 199
World of Cracktros website, 75
World War II, 40
worms, 54, 69–71. *See also* malware;
    Trojan horses; viruses
    email, 70
    hacktivist uses of, 231–233
    IRC/IM, 70
Wozniak, Steve, 14

X

X-Chat, 72
Xia, Bill, 145
XiRCON, 72

Y

Yahoo! People Search, 195
Youngsters Against McAfee (YAM), 56
Yusufali Trojan horse, 65

Z

ZabaSearch directory, 195
Zapatistas, 223, 225
    website, 223–224
ZeroPaid website, 166

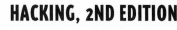

HACKING, 2ND EDITION

The Art of Exploitation

by JON ERICKSON

While many security books merely show how to run existing exploits, *Hacking: The Art of Exploitation* was the first book to explain how exploits actually work—and how readers can develop and implement their own. In this all new second edition, author Jon Erickson uses practical examples to illustrate the fundamentals of serious hacking. You'll learn about key concepts underlying common exploits, such as programming errors, assembly language, networking, shellcode, cryptography, and more. And the bundled Linux LiveCD provides an easy-to-use, hands-on learning environment. This edition has been extensively updated and expanded, including a new introduction to the complex, low-level workings of computers.

FEBRUARY 2008, 488 PP. W/CD, $49.95
ISBN 978-1-59327-144-2

THE MANGA GUIDE TO STATISTICS

by SHIN TAKAHASHI

This unique guide to learning statistics combines the Japanese-style comics called manga with serious educational content, making the challenging discipline of statistics entertaining and less daunting. *The Manga Guide to Statistics* uses real-world examples like teen magazine quizzes, bowling games, test scores, and ramen noodle prices to teach statistics. Reluctant statistics students will enjoy learning along with the book's charming heroine Rui, who wants to learn statistics in order to impress the dreamy Mr. Igarashi. With the help of her tutor, Mr. Yamamoto, Rui learns statistics—but is it enough to impress Mr. Igarashi?

NOVEMBER 2008, 224 PP., $19.95
ISBN 978-1-59327-189-3

SILENCE ON THE WIRE

A Field Guide to Passive Reconnaissance and Indirect Attacks

by MICHAL ZALEWSKI

Zalewski shares his expertise and experience to explain how computers and networks work, how information is processed and delivered, and what security threats lurk in the shadows. No humdrum technical white paper or how-to manual for protecting one's network, this book is a fascinating narrative that explores a variety of unique and often quite elegant security challenges that defy classification and eschew the traditional attacker-victim model.

APRIL 2005, 312 PP., $39.95
ISBN 978-1-59327-046-9

MY NEW MAC

52 Simple Projects to Get You Started

by WALLACE WANG

Mac OS is a beautiful and reliable operating system, but it can be confusing to brand-new Mac owners—especially if they come from Windows. Using 52 essential step-by-step projects every Mac owner should know, *My New Mac* encourages readers to treat their new computer as an opportunity for fun and exploration, not something serious and overwhelming. Rather than focus each chapter on a specific program or feature of Mac OS (as most beginner books do), Wallace Wang takes a project-oriented approach that mirrors the sorts of things people want to do with their Mac, such as surf the Internet, send email, listen to CDs, take notes, or play with digital photos.

APRIL 2008, 480 PP., $29.95
ISBN 978-1-59327-164-0

FORBIDDEN LEGO

Build the Models Your Parents Warned You Against!

by ULRIK PILEGAARD *and* MIKE DOOLEY

Written by a former master LEGO designer and a former LEGO project manager, this full-color book showcases projects that break the LEGO Group's rules for building with LEGO bricks—rules against building projects that fire projectiles, require cutting or gluing bricks, or use nonstandard parts. Many of these are back-room projects that LEGO's master designers build under the LEGO radar, just to have fun. Learn how to build a catapult that shoots M&Ms, a gun that fires LEGO beams, a continuous-fire ping-pong ball launcher, and more! Tips and tricks will give you ideas for inventing your own creative model designs.

AUGUST 2007, 480 PP. *full color*, $24.95
ISBN 978-1-59327-137-4

PHONE:

800.420.7240 OR
415.863.9900
MONDAY THROUGH FRIDAY,
9 A.M. TO 5 P.M. (PST)

FAX:

415.863.9950
24 HOURS A DAY,
7 DAYS A WEEK

EMAIL:

SALES@NOSTARCH.COM

WEB:

WWW.NOSTARCH.COM

MAIL:

NO STARCH PRESS
555 DE HARO STREET, SUITE 250
SAN FRANCISCO, CA 94107
USA

Electronic Frontier Foundation
Defending Freedom in the Digital World

Free Speech. Privacy. Innovation. Fair Use. Reverse Engineering. **If you care about these rights in the digital world, then you should join the Electronic Frontier Foundation (EFF). EFF was founded in 1990 to protect the rights of users and developers of technology. EFF is the first to identify threats to basic rights online and to advocate on behalf of free expression in the digital age.**

The Electronic Frontier Foundation Defends Your Rights!
Become a Member Today!
http://www.eff.org/support/

Current EFF projects include:

Protecting your fundamental right to vote. Widely publicized security flaws in computerized voting machines show that, though filled with potential, this technology is far from perfect. EFF is defending the open discussion of e-voting problems and is coordinating a national litigation strategy addressing issues arising from use of poorly developed and tested computerized voting machines.

Ensuring that you are not traceable through your things. Libraries, schools, the government and private sector businesses are adopting radio frequency identification tags, or RFIDs – a technology capable of pinpointing the physical location of whatever item the tags are embedded in. While this may seem like a convenient way to track items, it's also a convenient way to do something less benign: track people and their activities through their belongings. EFF is working to ensure that embrace of this technology does not erode your right to privacy.

Stopping the FBI from creating surveillance backdoors on the Internet. EFF is part of a coalition opposing the FBI's expansion of the Communications Assistance for Law Enforcement Act (CALEA), which would require that the wiretap capabilities built into the phone system be extended to the Internet, forcing ISPs to build backdoors for law enforcement.

Providing you with a means by which you can contact key decision-makers on cyber-liberties issues. EFF maintains an action center that provides alerts on technology, civil liberties issues and pending legislation to more than 50,000 subscribers. EFF also generates a weekly online newsletter, EFFector, and a blog that provides up-to-the-minute information and commentary.

Defending your right to listen to and copy digital music and movies. The entertainment industry has been overzealous in trying to protect its copyrights, often decimating fair use rights in the process. EFF is standing up to the movie and music industries on several fronts.

Check out all of the things we're working on at http://www.eff.org and join today or make a donation to support the fight to defend freedom online.

ELECTRONIC FRONTIER FOUNDATION · 454 SHOTWELL STREET · SAN FRANCISCO, CA 94110 · 415.436.9333

ABOUT THE AUTHOR

Wallace Wang is the author of several best-selling computer books, including *Steal This Computer Book*, *Steal This File Sharing Book*, *My New Mac*, *The Book of Nero*, and *Visual Basic 2005 Express: Now Playing* (all No Starch Press). He is also a successful stand-up comic who has appeared on A&E's *Evening at the Improv* and appears regularly at the Riviera Comedy Club in Las Vegas.

UPDATES

Visit **www.nostarch.com/stcb4.htm** for updates, errata, and other information.

CD LICENSE AGREEMENT

The CD-ROM bundled with *Steal This Computer Book 4.0* (ISBN 1-59327-105-0), "the Software," contains a collection of relevant free software. (See the appendix on page 335 for a complete listing and description of the CD-ROM's contents. See the specific license for each software package when you install it.)

NO WARRANTY

The Software is distributed on an "AS IS" BASIS, WITHOUT WARRANTIES OR CONDITIONS OF ANY KIND, either express or implied. The user assumes all risk regarding the quality and performance of the Software; if any part of the Software proves to be defective or insecure or to cause damage of any kind, the user bears sole responsibility for all risk and cost of repair.